Market-Augmenting Government

Economics, Cognition, and Society

This series provides a forum for theoretical and empirical investigations of social phenomena. It promotes works that focus on the interactions among cognitive processes, individual behavior, and social outcomes. It is especially open to interdisciplinary books that are genuinely integrative.

Editor: Timur Kuran

Editorial Board: Tyler Cowen Advisory Board: James M. Buchanan
Diego Gambetta Albert O. Hirschman
Avner Greif Thomas C. Schelling
Viktor Vanberg

Titles in the Series

Market-Augmenting Government

The Institutional Foundations for Prosperity

Omar Azfar and Charles A. Cadwell, Editors

The University of Michigan Press

Ann Arbor

Copyright © 2003 by the IRIS Center, University Research Corporation,
International, College Park, Maryland
All rights reserved
Published in the United States of America by
The University of Michigan Press
Manufactured in the United States of America
∞ Printed on acid-free paper

2006   2005   2004   2003   4   3   2   1

A CIP catalog record for this book is available from the British Library.

Library of Congress Cataloging-in-Publication Data

Market-augmenting government : the institutional foundations for
  prosperity / Omar Azfar and Charles Cadwell, editors.
      p.   cm. — (Economics, cognition, and society)
  Includes bibliographical references and index.
  ISBN 0-472-09817-9 (cloth : alk. paper) —
  ISBN 0-472-06817-2 (pbk. : alk. paper)
  1. Economic development.   2. Economic policy.   3. Free enterprise.
  4. Macroeconomics.   I. Azfar, Omar.   II. Cadwell, Charles 1952–
  III. Series.

HD75 .M27   2002
338.9'2 — dc21   2002075014

For Mancur Olson

Acknowledgments

Grateful acknowledgment is made to the following authors and publishers for permission to reprint previously published materials.

National Bureau of Economic Research for Table 5 from *Business Incorporations in the United States, 1800–1943* by George Heberton Evans (Washington, DC: National Bureau of Economic Research, 1948), 11. Copyright © 1948 by the National Bureau of Economic Research.

Ohio State University for material from "The Free Banking Era: A Reexamination" by Hugh Rockoff, *Journal of Money, Credit, and Banking* 6, no. 2 (May 1974). Copyright © 1974 by the Ohio State University Press. All rights reserved.

Every effort has been made to trace the ownership of all copyrighted material in this book and to obtain permission for its use.

Contents

Market-Augmenting Government: How, Why, and When States Support Markets

Omar Azfar and Charles A. Cadwell

"Market-augmenting government" is the answer Mancur Olson developed in response to the question of what type of government is needed for economic growth. The idea that markets are the best mechanism for facilitating economic growth now dominates prescriptions for economic development, but the circumstances in which markets develop are not fully understood. Despite our ability to share information nearly instantaneously between rich and poor places, in some countries markets develop while in others they do not. Where markets are undeveloped, people remain mired in poverty and attendant human ills. Why is it that in some places markets operate to permit millions to be better off while in others markets remain primitive and people poor? And what activities of the state are required for markets to function well?

Mancur Olson (1932–98) was, of course, a major figure in the evolution of thinking on these questions. When he coined the phrase "market-augmenting government" in 1997, it reflected a lifetime of scholarship and observation. Olson's famous books,[1] so familiar to graduate students and others, address some fundamental aspects of the design of good government, describing why it is difficult to organize groups, why groups may organize in ways that are inimical to economic growth, and why different types of regimes have different incentives to promote or inhibit markets. Market-augmenting government is an attempt to distill ideas that are bound up in Olson's *Power and Prosperity* (2000), the last chapter of which is entitled "The Kind of Markets Needed for Prosperity." In *Power and Prosperity,* Olson concludes that prosperity can be achieved in societies with rights-respecting governments that provide for both secure property and contract enforcement while avoiding predation of various sorts (most harmfully that benefiting narrow lobbies). In his last months, Olson was testing his new phrase, "market-augmenting government," on a variety of interlocutors, seeking to determine whether it achieved the right balance between simplicity and capturing a complex problem. Had he survived to see *Power and Prosperity* to publication, the title for its final chapter might well have been "Market-Augmenting Government." The study of how *governments* (the primary focus of political science) augment *markets* (the primary focus of economics) falls squarely into interdisciplinary political economy. It is fitting that this book is appearing in the Economics, Cognition, and Society series of the University of Michigan Press. From the inception of this series of 1990 until his untimely death, Mancur Olson served on its advisory board. In that capacity, he urged consideration of books that integrate economics with political science and sociology. *Market-Augmenting Government* is just such a book.

"Market-augmenting government" was not, for Olson, a lightly considered articulation of an ideological middle between advocates of state or market.[2] Instead, in developing this phrase, Olson turns on its head the question of how to get government out of the way of markets. Olson here suggests a key challenge for government: how to augment the markets that exist everywhere, supporting the complex transactions characteristic of successful economies. His formulation serves several useful purposes. It focuses us, first, on how it is that markets actually work and on the details of the particular institutions that contribute to that functioning. Second, he leads us beyond the question of which institutions constitute a market-augmenting government to the question of how such institutions emerge.

Sadly, Olson's sudden death in 1998 at the age of sixty-five truncated his work on this last question. In this book, nine scholars supplement the rich body of work that constitutes Olson's own output on the question. In this introductory essay we have two tasks: to provide a framework for these individual contributions, and to place them into a context that recognizes our collective debt to the scholarship of Mancur Olson. To accomplish this task we will pose three questions. What is it that governments do to augment markets? Why do governments augment markets? And how could we design government to better augment markets? Most contributions here concern themselves with all three questions to some degree, but we have organized the essay in an order that builds logically from the "what is it?" to the "how do we get more of it?"

I. The Questions to Be Answered

Let us begin by stating the issue in economic terms. Recall the two fundamental theorems of welfare economics: market allocations produce Pareto-efficient allocations, and any Pareto-efficient allocation can be produced by means of exchange (following an appropriate distribution of initial wealth). These are strong theoretical results, and taken together with the observed inefficiencies of state-led production and exchange they suggest a powerful rationale for expanding the dominion of markets (at least for private goods without externalities) and, correspondingly, constraining the role of the state. It is less well understood, however, that these theorems in fact provide a rationale for the role of the state. It is, after all, the voluntariness and regularity of exchange that leads to the efficiency of markets. *However, the rules that assure voluntariness and regularity are not found in nature.* As Hernando de Soto points out, "Westerners take this mechanism so completely for granted that they have lost all awareness of its existence. . . . It is an implicit legal structure hidden deep within their property systems" (2000, 8). Participants in any system of trade or exchange will engage in collective action to develop and enforce rules of all kinds. Market-augmenting governments are those that expand the dominion of markets *by providing rules that facilitate voluntary and reliable trade.*

In recent years, at the Center for Institutional Reform and the Informal Sector (IRIS) and elsewhere, economists have begun to remedy this neglect of the fundamental role of the state in augmenting markets. In this book, we further advance this research agenda. While both economic history and the comparative performance of modern states have been used to shed light on the importance of good government for economic performance, many questions remain. Among them are several that are addressed by the authors collected here.

1. What particular legal institutions actually augment markets? What about them produces this outcome?
2. How do dictatorships and democracies differ in augmenting markets? What forms of democracy best augment markets?
3. What explains historical cases of political and economic policy reforms that increased market augmentation?
4. How do the particular institutions within a democracy (such

as a free press) augment particular markets (such as financial markets) and thereby (for example) prevent financial crises?
5. What forms of governance can augment markets at a supranational level, where force cannot easily be used to police economic activity?
6. Can government facilitate the development of markets to address externalities such as environmental impacts?

While the gaps in our knowledge are vastly greater than this list suggests, answering these questions would be an important advance in understanding how governments augment markets. The rest of this introduction addresses three broad questions. What is it that governments do to augment markets? Why do governments augment markets? And how could we design government and its institutions to better augment markets?

II. What Is It That Governments Do to Augment Markets?

The large differences in per capita income across countries cannot be explained by differences in access to the world's stock of productive knowledge or to its capital markets, by differences in the ratio of population to land or natural resources, or by differences in the quality of marketable human capital or personal culture. The only remaining plausible explanation is that the great differences in the wealth of nations are mainly due to differences in the quality of their institutions and economic policies. (Olson 1996)

In "Big Bills on the Sidewalk: Why Some Nations Are Rich, and Others Poor," Mancur Olson (1996) addresses the logic of familiar growth theories and reviews the evidence supporting the idea that differences in endowments—of land, financial capital, human capital, or technology—account for differences in growth. Finding these lacking, Olson concludes that the quality of policies and institutions best explains why some countries achieve more of their potential than others. Differences in policies and institutions are largely marked by national boundaries, which just as clearly demarcate differences in prosperity.

So what institutions lead some societies to prosper? The particular institutions needed for growth, those that in fact augment markets, are principally a system of predictable and secure property rights and enforcement of agreements. In "Contract-Intensive Money" (1999) Olson and his coauthors outline a theory and propose an empirical measure to support the assertion that the quality of these institutions in particular explains country differences in income levels, investment, and growth rates. In "Contract-Intensive Money," a measure of the quality of these institutions is established by the authors, examined in some case studies, and then tested empirically. *Contract-intensive money* (CIM) is defined as the ratio of noncurrency money to total money supply.[3] This ratio compares financial assets that depend on functioning contract enforcement to financial assets that do not depend on contract enforcement. Then CIM is measured against several of the subjective measures of governance and institutional quality created by various commercial country-risk services and found to be positively correlated with them. Finally, the authors test the hypothesis that this measure explains investment and growth.

Of course, establishing that contract enforcement and property rights are essential sources of economic growth is to stop short of describing what it is that actually constitutes such institutions. The first essays in this volume supply some detail in this regard. Several emphasize a particular set of markets, those for capital and credit. There are two reasons for this: first, the role that finance plays in the operation of all other markets and, second, the observation that both credit and capital markets are especially sensitive to institutional quality. But the idea of market augmentation obviously has broader applicability, and not every essay is so targeted; the papers by Heal and Sandler are examples. In the remainder of this section, we will review the contributions of Summers, Levine, Lanyi and Lee, and Heal.

Augmenting Credit Markets: The Complexity of the Required Institutions

Robert S. Summers details several requirements for the augmentation of the market for loans, examining in particular the institutional elements of a system of secured credit. The analysis in the first part of his essay shows the complexity of the requirements for market-augmenting government, which makes it a little less surprising that governments everywhere do not effectively augment the market for loans. While Summers implicitly accepts the received wisdom of the day—that the central role of government is to allow private parties to interact as they will—his essay demonstrates the complex practical requirements for establishing this seemingly elementary freedom. Thus, when private parties cannot take advantage of this freedom it may be because of a government's sins of omission rather than the more familiar sins of commission.

The legal basis for augmenting the market for loans consists, first, of eight requirements for laws regarding the relationship between the creditor and debtor and, second, of good legal institutions to define, interpret, and enforce these laws. In general, these and supporting institutions provide security of contract and ease of contract. The ideas that formal requirements should be light, that the government should provide gap fillers, that security interest should be publicly announced, and that the system should be unified all promote ease of contract. The rest of the requirements—that contracts should be in writing, secured lenders be paid first, the law prescribe clear rules about how security interests are enforced, and so on—establish its security.

Second, the market for loans requires that there be institutions that design, interpret, and enforce these laws. There needs to be a legislature that formulates the laws and an executive to enforce them.[4] There should be a well-functioning court system to interpret contracts, find facts and form opinions, and do so in a predictable and systematic fashion. Finally, Summers argues, there must be well-trained lawyers to help form opinions, advise on contracts, and represent creditors and debtors in court. These requirements of competent law interpretation and enforcement are empirically more important determinants of the size of credit relative to the economy (typically measured by the M2/GDP ratio) than the statutory laws themselves (see Azfar and Matheson 2003; also see La Porta et al. 1997; Levine 1997).

In the second half of his essay, Summers concentrates on this more general set of institutions, no less important to markets than the specifics of those supporting secured lending. Indeed, it seems that they are more important in that they benefit a range of market-augmenting institutions in addition to those related to credit markets. Summers identifies eighteen aspects of "second-order" rules—rules about how specific laws are made and sustained. Examples relate to the regularity of lawmaking and law-implementing processes: that laws always be enacted prospectively, that laws be within the capacity of addressees to comply, that state-made law be in writing, the power to deviate from written law by itself circumscribed, and so on. These functional characteristics grow from the work of Summers

(1973) and others[5] to formalize a theory of law that does not presume a particular political regime or economic system, but permits comparison across systems. It is worth noting that these functional attributes are useful additions to the concepts of market-augmenting government and offer economists abundant opportunities for attention to thinking about measurement and causal relationships. In subsequent applied work, we have in fact proposed to measure the quality of governance by using the ideas developed in this essay.

Summers does not, in this essay, address the question of how you get a system that produces these functions. This is intentional on his part, as (he suggests) he is neither a legal historian nor one to set out the devices by which these functions are implemented. Other essays in this volume relate to the evolution of market-augmenting institutions (Wallis), the constraints that lead governments to provide more market-augmenting institutions (Lanyi and Lee), and the incentives of regimes to do so (McGuire). Summers's contribution is twofold: to suggest the detailed and intertwined nature of families of institutions that in fact result in market augmentation, in this case markets for secured credit; and to suggest a set of second-order principles of the rule of law that also are important parts of augmenting markets.

Measures of Market Augmentation

Is there evidence that the institutional characteristics we have described as market augmenting are pivotal? In "Contract-Intensive Money," Olson and his coauthors argue that their general measure of governance (CIM) has a causal relationship with income, investment, and growth rates. Ross Levine examines a narrower issue: the relationship between capital and credit markets and economic growth. In particular, he looks at whether steps taken to augment equity markets in Latin America have had the predicted effects.[6]

Levine begins by asking what constitutes market-augmenting government with respect to equity markets. Equity markets exist in a world where ownership is often separated from control. As suggested by Lanyi and Lee (discussed subsequently), good governance involves reducing informational asymmetries between principals and agents and empowering principals to punish and reward agents. With respect to governance of corporations, two institutions suggest themselves: good accounting standards that keep owners informed of the performance of firms and good corporate law that empowers all shareholders. In his analysis, Levine uses measures of corporate laws, including whether all shareholders can vote, whether they can vote by proxy, whether cumulative voting for directors is allowed, whether shares are blocked before general meetings, whether more than 10 percent of shares are required to call a general meeting, and whether minority shareholders can challenge management in court.[7] These measures are critical components of company law. They focus us on the mechanism of control between principals and agents, and they suggest that here, as in the area of secured credit, successful augmentation is not simply a matter of passing a law that meets an abstract standard but also of successfully arranging for its implementation.

Levine shows empirical links between two measures of market-augmenting government: an aggregate measure of corporate law and accounting standards and equity market development. Levine next demonstrates the links between financial market development—which includes measures of the size and efficiency of equity markets—and economic growth. Finally, he uses instrumental variable analysis to trace the sources of growth from corporate law and accounting standards through equity markets to economic growth.

The results are both statistically and economically significant, and Levine attempts to mitigate our doubts about causality by the use of instrumental variables and with the finding that the instruments themselves have colonial origins. The instrumental variable estimates suggest that improving Argentina's accounting standards to those set by the Organization for Economic Cooperation and Development (OECD) would increase its growth rate by 0.6 percentage points. Over a ten-year period, this represents a foregone income of approximately 50 billion dollars.[8] Institutional reform, it seems, is well worth the money.

Governance and the East Asian Financial Crisis

In 1997, after decades of rapid growth in East Asia, a banking crisis in Thailand spread to Indonesia, Malaysia, and South Korea. The crisis reverberated in Russia and Brazil, and for a brief moment there were even fears of its spread to Japan and ultimately to New York and London. Conventional explanations of the crash have concentrated on overborrowing via short-term loans, and, while there is probably some truth in financial adventurism as the immediate cause of the crisis, the deeper questions remain: why were so many short-term loans created, and what was it about the environment that led to the loans causing a financial crash? There was certainly dramatic growth in the pre-1997 period, but which institutions permitted that growth and failed when pressed by a financial crisis (and, in Indonesia, by a political succession crisis)?

In their essay, Anthony Lanyi and Young Lee analyze the political-economic roots of the East Asian financial crisis. Their central argument is that the roots of the crisis lay in poor governance of different (but related) sorts. Poor political governance, which influenced and was compounded by poor corporate and financial governance, created the crisis, which was further compounded by inadequate international financial governance. Each of these forms of governance is discussed in detail, and the authors describe possible reforms that could be directed at these various types of governance to make them more market augmenting. They also briefly discuss proposals to improve international monetary arrangements in light of these governance considerations.[9]

With a precision more useful than much of the usual rhetoric, Lanyi and Lee define *governance* as "the rules that govern relationships between principals and agents": voter–prime minister, shareholder-CEO, creditor-debtor. The vast literature on the principal-agent problem suggests that limited and asymmetric information makes for worse outcomes, and incentives, if properly designed, can improve outcomes. A free press is important to provide information on a government's actions and perhaps also on private misdeeds by chief executive officers (CEOs) and debtors. In each case, we also need incentives in terms of rewards and punishments, and voters and shareholders must therefore be empowered to remove management, whether of firms or states, in cases of fraud or incompetence.

There is an existing literature in economics on the links between democracy, governance, and economic performance that suggests that democracies have better property rights (Olson et al. 1996) and property rights affect growth (Knack and Keefer 1995; Sala-i-Martin 1999) but that after controlling for property rights democracy has no clear empirical association with economic growth (Barro 1998). In other words, the cross-country regression literature appears to show that democracy probably has a beneficial indirect effect on growth through better property rights but no direct effect on economic performance. Cross-country regressions are seldom persuasive on their own, and in this particular instance small sample sizes and questions of exogeneity compound our usual skepticism. The Lanyi and Lee essay gives reasons why the lack of democratic institutions (including a free press) may indeed negatively affect long-run economic growth.

Markets for Externalities and Institutional Needs That Exceed the Bounds of Nations

Some market transactions have environmental externalities not borne by the transacting parties and often the management of those externalities is beyond the reach of a single political jurisdiction. Indeed, research on global warming suggests that human activities are beginning to affect the basic bio- and geochemical cycles that support our very lives. The debate is about the appropriate institutional response. Are there markets that can be created, and if so how?

The essay by Geoffrey Heal discusses a number of markets that could protect or even restore the environment. Given that the quality of our lives depends on a well-functioning biosphere, the services it provides are clearly valuable. The fact that our environment is being eroded probably suggests there is some market failure in its provision. Heal suggests several ways in which governments can augment these markets to mitigate this market failure.

Consider first the market for CO_2 and SO_2 emissions. The amount of these pollutants can sometimes be controlled most efficiently by issuing emissions permits, which are bought by those users who most need to pollute. This market, however, would not exist without a government that established and clearly allocated property rights (to citizens for cleaner air and to some would-be polluters to pollute). While there may be no property rights without government,[10] some are more "natural" than others. Governments need to protect all property rights, but some—like those over a store-bought private good—can be assigned quite intuitively without government intervention. This is not true for externalities and public goods: governments need to define *who has the rights* before they can be traded. Thus, markets for externalities and public goods need willful augmentation by government beyond the ubiquitous requirement of maintaining social peace.

Assigning property rights to clean air or pollution improves outcomes but does not approach efficiency because it neglects the possibility of providing services that reduce atmospheric pollution. Carbon dioxide, which can have potentially disastrous effects on the global ecosystem, can be effectively sequestered by growing forests. Current estimates of the value of sequestering carbon and the volume sequestered by growing forests in Costa Rica suggest that there may be large gains to be had from establishing markets for "growing carbon." It appears, though, that more precise estimates are needed of both the value and the volume of sequestered carbon before we can be sure this is a cost-effective land use. This underscores, yet again, the importance of research in solving these problems.

Forests, of course, provide other services, too. Areas with intense interspecies competition encourage the evolution of plants and animals that produce pharmacologically active substances. These substances can be of great medical value. To augment these markets, governments must allocate property rights in such a way as to preserve incentives for both developing countries and indigenous communities to preserve their environments and for pharmaceutical companies to develop drugs. The assignment of intellectual property rights is another important form of market-augmenting government.

Heal also discusses other examples of how governments can augment markets for ecosystem services. New York City, for instance, could "purchase clean water" from a company that preserves the Catskills at a fraction of the cost of a water purification plant. Conscorp in South Africa has found it profitable to restore low-grade farmland to its original ecosystem and charge sport hunters thousands of dollars to hunt leopards (which were poisoned when the area was farmland).

In all these cases, we need governments to willfully augment markets. Governments must assign property rights in the form of emission permits, affirm intellectual property rights in pharmacologically active substances, and on wild animals on private property. Governments must offer to purchase environmental services on behalf of their populations because, in the presence of even trivial transaction costs, the probability of millions of citizens agreeing to purchase a clean environment without a government role is astronomically low (see Olson's 2000 paper coauthored with Dixit). In this case, the government "replaces" one side of the market to augment the other.[11] To suggest that government could, with appropriate institutional innovation, not only augment but create these markets is a different question than explaining the incentives of governments to do so and is separate from thinking about the effects of differing political institutions on these incentives. These questions define the task begun in the remaining essays in this volume.

III. Why Do Governments Augment Markets?

The question of why some societies suffer more or less than others from the distortions and deadweight costs of special interest policies occupied the core of Olson's scholarly interest and output. In his 1982 *Rise and Decline of Nations,* Olson advanced the ideas laid out in his earlier *Logic of Collective Action* (1965) to consider how groups influence narrow or broadly beneficial policies. In *Logic,* Olson explained why it is wrong to think of organizations as unitary interests. In *Rise and Decline,* he explained the inverse relationship between the breadth of an interest group and the likelihood that its interests will mirror those of the public at large. An "encompassing" interest will bear a greater share of the costs of market distortions and thus engage in fewer of them. Narrower groups organized for collective action can, through their market-undermining lobbying, promote policies that advance narrow interests at the expense of the general (and rationally uninvolved) public—the rest of us.

The discussion of the logic and role of interest groups had broad applicability and is now part of the firmament of the public choice literature, but it did not explicitly address the differences that might result from the interaction of those interests with different political systems. Olson's focus on the encompassing interests of autocrats, which may have grown out of a lunchtime conversation in the mid-1970s (McGuire 1998), was developed over the years that followed. History has numerous examples of places ruled quite undemocratically that provide market-augmenting public goods. This observation led Olson to develop his metaphor of the stationary bandit as a proxy for an autocrat who has an incentive to provide for market-enhancing public goods in order to be able to increase tax receipts from the resulting markets. This insight was developed more formally in Olson's collaboration with Martin McGuire (1996) and occupies the first chapters of Olson's *Power and Prosperity* (2000).

Incentives of Regimes to Augment Markets

In his contribution to this volume, Martin C. McGuire extends these ideas, focusing on the complicating reality that majoritarian democracies can establish policies that discriminate against some subsets, isolating themselves from costs that the earlier model assumed they would internalize. McGuire approaches this issue by considering the relation between market augmentation and redistribution in autocracies, majoritarian democracies, and consensual democracies. Authoritarian states are ruled by an autocrat who decides public good provision and tax rates to maximize his or her tax receipts. Consensual democracies, by contrast, set tax rates and the level of public good provision to maximize aggregate welfare. Majoritarian democracies tend to decide on policies that maximize the welfare of the ruling majorities.

The first part of the essay repeats the original McGuire and Olson analysis (1996). In that framework, the government has to charge the same tax rate for the entire population, including the ruling majority. One central insight of that model is that a government representing a large enough majority would choose ideal policies because it would otherwise have to levy distortionary taxes on its own members. Even autocracies would be driven by "the first blessing of the invisible hand" to provide law and order and other market-augmenting public goods and desist from taxing their subjects beyond the top of the Laffer curve. The tone of the analysis is thus quite optimistic.

In the second part of the essay, McGuire analyzes governance under a majoritarian democracy that can set discriminatory tax rates and tax minorities at a higher rate. This leads to less than ideal behavior on the part of the majorities, who are no longer constrained by having to charge themselves the same tax rates as others.

Another direction for research would be to weaken the assumption that all kinds of activities can be easily taxed. The ruler may be able to tax only certain activities, which could lead to large distortions. Also, the provision of some public goods may interfere with tax collection. It would not be rational for a dictator to protect property rights, grant civil liberties, or build good roads if this interfered with tax collection or made revolution more probable.[12] John Hicks (1969) has argued that for much of history the ability to collect taxes has depended upon goods passing through certain well-defined points. Might this have reduced a government's incentive to invest in a dense network of roads? Similarly, in modern times as well as historically governments have found particular economic activities such as international trade much easier to tax than others; as a consequence, even governments convinced of the gains from specialization and technological transfer may impose tariffs to keep the fiscal ship afloat. One serious, and sinister, possibility is that if those in power think that access to economic resources is an important source of power they will want to keep others from becoming prosperous.

Dictatorships may therefore do even worse than the theory predicts. However, history shows us that majoritarian democracies, too, can suffer from similar failures, as illustrated by John Wallis's review of the institution of market-augmenting corporate law in the nineteenth-century United States.

Fiscal Interest, Ideology, and Market-Augmenting Government in Nineteenth-Century America

John Wallis's essay reviews the circumstances that led several U.S. states to modernize their laws relating to the granting of corporate charters. Can government's fiscal interest always account for the adoption of certain policies, as suggested by McGuire? Or did the policies of American states toward incorporation have ideological roots?

Wallis argues that fiscal interest is an important but not a sufficient explanation. In the early years of the American Republic, corporate charters were offered on a case-by-case basis. Between the late 1830s and the 1880s, an increasing number of states employed "general" incorporation rules that allowed specific kinds of firms to become incorporated. For example, the New York Free Banking Law essentially allowed any bank that satisfied certain capitalization requirements to be incorporated. But these acts were restricted to certain kinds of companies—typically, banks, insurance companies, manufacturing companies, and railroads. In the 1880s, several states, led by New Jersey and Delaware, began creating more liberal incorporation acts, essentially allowing corporations to pursue any business they chose. Limits on the voting rights of shareholders were eased, including allowing voting by proxy, which is now considered an important determinant of well-functioning equity markets.[13] Limits on the internal organization of firms were eased, and the idea evolved that "legitimacy would be most fully achieved if the law empowered businessmen to create whatever arrangements they found most serviceable" (Dodd 1936).

These legal reforms established by 1900 the essence of the modern corporation. American commercial law had thus augmented capital markets by the turn of the century. But how did this change come about? What were the political roots of these reforms? Wallis demonstrates not only how American laws augmented markets but the political, ideological, and fiscal roots of market-augmenting government.

Drawing from the arguments of North (1981, 1990), Olson (1993, 2000), and Olson's 1996 paper coauthored with McGuire, Wallis argues that it was in part fiscal interest and in part the demands of ideology that drove American states to adopt or delay the adoption of statutes of incorporation toward financial and manufacturing firms. Those states that taxed *profits* restricted access to incorporation so as to preserve the monopoly profits of the banks in their jurisdictions.

States that taxed the *assets* of banks, however, had an interest in expanding market size and so allowed easier access to incorporation.

Wallis compares the development of the laws of incorporation in New York, Pennsylvania, and Massachusetts. The state of Pennsylvania had part ownership in the existing Bank of North America, and thus resisted the creation of new banks for fear of reducing its dividend flow, but on occasion accepted financial inducements to allow new banks. The creation of new banks in Philadelphia was therefore slow. Massachusetts, in contrast, had a tax on bank capital by 1812. The state thus saw that its fiscal interest lay in increasing market size and began to liberally grant bank charters.

The case of New York is as fraught with ideology and politics as it is with fiscal interest. In 1814, the New York Republican Party had begun granting bank charters for political purposes, and because its supporters now owned the existing banks the government resisted the establishment of a bank capital tax and even changed the "rules of the game" by requiring a two-thirds majority for new incorporations. But the excesses of the Republican administration produced a reaction, and in 1838, when the Republicans were out of office, the "Free Banking" law was passed and a bank capitalization tax was imposed. The law and the state's fiscal interest were now aligned to allow and encourage the growth of the banking sector, and by 1840 both the number and the size of banks had dramatically risen.

Wallis's description of this episode reminds us that democracies also have imperfections, as manifested by the Republican laws that encouraged monopolies. Such use of public office for private gain is all too familiar. But the episode also shows how such excesses can be reversed in a democracy. It was, in our view, not just ideology but ideology *in a democratic setting* that allowed these market-augmenting reforms.

Wallis is onto an important principle here. Taxation and fiscal interest can take on many hues. For reasons of history, ideology, and technological and institutional feasibility, states tax some economic activities and not others, and they tax them in different ways. The Olsonian suggestion (Olson 2000) that "the invisible hand of the left" induces even a cynical government to maximize something close to aggregate income rests on the optimistic assumption that all of the gross domestic product (GDP) is being taxed. If, however, governments own the rights to profits, they may encourage or tolerate monopolies. Is it possible that governments today, nervous about stock market fluctuations, may be wary of undertaking antitrust actions? And how would investing the social security surplus in the stock market affect the U.S. government's interest in maintaining competitive markets?

As for the role played by ideology, Americans had two important sets of apparently conflicting ideological beliefs: a belief in the freedom of assembly and association and a suspicion of special interests and charters. A corporate charter that limited liability and created an institution that could be used (among other things) to lobby for further special privileges invoked both freedom of association and privilege. It seems the logical solution would be to allow this form of association *following general rules.* Indeed, the laws of American states moved to this ideal. Though the early incorporations were based on special charters, by 1940 all but four states had general articles of association whereby any corporation or bank that satisfied some general rules could be incorporated. Wallis argues strongly for the importance of ideology in these legal reforms. Notably, states that had no fiscal interest in allowing for general incorporation also did so, and he demonstrates this reform following the local politics of New York. Although Wallis never quite says so, this seems remarkably similar to Summers's argument that good American commercial laws are the product of a culture that believes in the virtues of laws that are "lawlike," which includes, importantly, that laws be "general and definite."[14]

Incentives of Regimes and Supranational Institutions

As one considers the provision of public goods benefiting several political jurisdictions, a different set of mechanisms comes into play. Under circumstances in which there is neither an autocrat nor a consensual democratic regime, how is it that public goods emerge? This question was an early logical extension of Olson's *Logic of Collective Action* as well as of his first "home run," "An Economic Theory of Alliances" (Olson and Zeckhauser 1966);[15] both studies considered the problems with private provision of public goods.

Todd Sandler's essay extends this reasoning to analyze the rationale for positive development of institutions that would support international commerce. In considering the nature of these cross-national markets, and of a broader set of institutions that might augment them, Sandler argues that some commercial rules are self-enforcing, which makes them more feasible as supranational institutions. Other rules, which are not self-enforcing, may be based on excludability—that is, their benefits might be provided as club goods.

Sandler discusses many supranational institutions that may augment markets. Unified contract law, together with courts in which disputes can be resolved and international crime reduced, may augment international transactions. Intellectual property rights may induce a more rapid rate of innovation, with global payoffs. Reducing the risk of financial crises may encourage more people to participate in financial markets. The allocation of clear property rights, and an infrastructure in which to exchange them, may protect the environment.

The provision of public goods by a group of voluntary agents (in this case countries) is tricky, however, and requires precise knowledge about their private valuations. Uncertainty over agents' valuations can prove fatal, as agents have an incentive to understate their valuations to reduce their own required contribution (see Olson's 2000 paper coauthored with Dixit). This highlights the importance of research in establishing each country's benefits from public good provision; indeed, research was an essential part of such international agreements as the Montreal protocol to reduce levels of atmospheric pollution (Sandler 1997).

Some countries may have genuinely negative payoffs from a global public good like reducing global warming. Why would such countries agree to a global regime to restrict greenhouse gases? We conjecture that one solution to this problem may be to bundle global public goods together. If the expected value of each global public good is positive, and there are a large number of public goods, it may be quite unlikely that any country will have a negative valuation of the entire bundle. This bundle of global public goods could then be provided by unanimous consent.

IV. How Could We Design Government and Its Institutions to Better Augment Markets?

It is important to have a sense not only of what governments do to augment markets, and why they have an interest in doing so, but also how they can go about actually making progress toward this goal. To pose the question succinctly: how is it that polities can organize to pick up the "big bills" left on the sidewalk by poor institutional arrangements? Olson's terse answer was: "The best thing a society can do to increase its prosperity is to wise up" (1996, 21). His more specific thoughts on the matter, as outlined in Olson 2000 and elsewhere, address the design of government.

Robert D. Cooter's essay analyzes the optimal design of government along two dimensions. Along one dimension, government can be "factored" or "spliced." An example of a factored government is that of San Francisco, where voters choose the boards that govern the schools and the police in separate elections. Spliced governments are of the more familiar form, in which voters vote for a president, who then appoints a cabinet across different seemingly unrelated areas (foreign policy and welfare policy). A *factored* government has the advantage that people can decide different political outcomes in separate elections. A *spliced* government, on the other hand, allows bargains among the people's delegates. The representatives of different groups of voters can be flexible on issues on which they have weak preferences in return for support on issues on which they have strong preferences. The trade-offs, then, between independent choices of voters on separate issues and foregone gains from bargaining determine the optimal form of democratic government.

On the other dimension, governments can have either *rules* or *discretion.* Cooter uses a principal-agent framework to decide the optimal amount of rules and discretion. At high levels of politics, Cooter conjectures, politicians are effectively monitored by citizens who follow high-level politics for reasons of general interest or civic virtue. Thus, discretion works well at the top, as the actions of a chief executive appointing a cabinet are monitored by citizens. However, civic virtue may not extend to monitoring each of these cabinet members as they appoint their staffs. Therefore, turnover in the professional civil service should be kept to a minimum. Perhaps we could also argue that, in those developing countries with limited press coverage, there should be more rules and less discretion than in developed countries.

Cooter's intuition is that there is insufficient factoring in developing countries. Take, for example, the question of whether a corrupt though democratic country such as Indonesia should have a separate election for an anticorruption officer. Because corruption is not fundamentally boring, it would not be a drain on civic virtue to ask citizens to focus on this election. And political bargains on corruption are particularly costly. Taken together, these two arguments suggest there should be a separate election for an anticorruption officer in Indonesia and other widely corrupt democracies.

V. Conclusion

Over the past ten years, work by economists with an explicit focus on the links between governance and growth has produced an increasingly persuasive account of the effects of good governance on economic performance. In this effort, Mancur Olson's contribution has been fundamental both in timeliness and in content. Throughout forty years of scholarship, his attention ranged from thinking about basic issues of collective action to thinking about how markets and government interact and addressing the processes of improvement in outcomes. In the essays collected here, we have focused on extending Olson's own thinking to respond to the "sad and all-too-general reality [that] individual rationality is very far indeed from being sufficient for social rationality" (Olson 1996, 23).

Any persuasive account of the causal chain from the quality of government to economic performance must provide details from the study of specific countries. In addition, we must try to understand the components of good government and the specific ways in which each affects economic performance. It was with this need in mind that we sponsored the essays that appear in this volume, with the hope that the research presented here will begin to fill the gaps in our knowledge about the nature of good government and the mechanisms by means of which it promotes prosperity. We would like to reiterate, however, that this is a young field of research in which questions far outnumber answers, and much important and exciting work remains to be done. In his concluding essay for this volume, Roger Betancourt specifies a series of issues that emerge from our efforts here.

A recurring theme in this volume is the importance of democracy in promoting the specific institutions that underlie prosperity. It appears to us that democracy, properly understood to include freedom of the press and the independence of the judiciary, is an important determinant of good government and ultimately of economic performance. Much more work, however, needs to be done on this important subject before a persuasive case can be made for it.

Perhaps it is not the presence or absence of democracy but the *form* of democracy that is most important for establishing good government. Whether proportional representation is better or worse than the Anglo-American "single-member district" system is acutely important but imperfectly understood. Of similar importance may be the separation of powers, both between the executive and legislature and between central and local governments. The assignment of political and fiscal responsibilities for the provision of public services to central or local governments is another important but imperfectly understood subject.[16] Finally, democracy within political parties themselves may have a significant impact on the quality of government.

Much research also remains to be done on narrower subjects like the importance of links between specific commercial laws and economic performance. A reasonable case can now be made for the importance of a certain set of laws in augmenting markets for debt and equity, but (with the possible exception of ensuring that secured lenders are paid first) we cannot state with much confidence that any one particular commercial law is good or bad for debt or equity markets. Additionally, we would like to know whether the impact of these laws increases with the quality of enforcement and whether they have any effect at all if the quality of enforcement is poor.

Economists are—still, to some extent—used to thinking of states and markets as dichotomous variables. The analysis of the optimal role of the state traditionally focused on how the tasks of production and exchange should be *divided* among markets and governments. In 1990, after the collapse of communist governments in Eastern Europe—where the state had clearly overreached its competence—the widespread prescription was to roll back the state. While reasonable people can disagree on the optimal pace at which the state should have withdrawn from the activities of production and exchange, it does appear in hindsight that not enough attention was given in the early years to positive actions that the states must take to augment markets. In the excitement over rolling back the state, and with the presumption that sophisticated market economies would appear soon after the state desisted from its sins of commission, the importance of market-augmenting governance was overlooked. If even a small fraction of the disorganization that characterized the transition in Eastern Europe could have been avoided, this would have meant that the livelihoods of millions would not have deteriorated as far as they did. In monetary terms, reforms that cost millions of dollars might have saved billions of dollars in foregone income.

Among the reasons why reform is so difficult is that it involves convincing a large set of people of the value of some institutional change, such as a change in a particular commercial law. Reform, however, can be blocked by powerful interests, whose representatives either do not believe that the intended reform will be beneficial or find it expedient to pretend not to believe in the benefits. To be effective, therefore, *research must be so persuasive that it makes it politically costly to block the intended reform.* Only research of the highest quality can be effective at promoting reform. We are today still far from achieving this standard for most of the reforms that we have some reason to believe have large positive impacts; to produce such a persuasive account remains an important challenge for social science.

Notes

1. *The Logic of Collective Action* (1965), *The Rise and Decline of Nations* (1982), and *Power and Prosperity* (2000).

2. Olson found this debate off point. See *Power and Prosperity* (2000, chap. 9). In arriving at the precise term *market-augmenting government*, Olson took characteristic care to research any other possible usage of the term for any purpose. His concerns for the correct articulation and the originality of the phrase led him to have his graduate assistants conduct extensive and repeated searches of various social science and press full text data bases. He also made detailed inquiries of many colleagues as he gave talks using his new phrase. Had they ever heard it used? What did it suggest to their ears? Did it prompt a new way of considering a familiar problem? Only after he had satisfied himself on these points did he suggest the effort that led to this book. Indeed, because he was still wrestling with how to put meat on the bones of this term, he did not use this formulation in his final book, the posthumously published *Power and Prosperity*—although the concluding chapter of that volume serves as an excellent introduction to the various parts of the present volume.

3. CIM $= (M_2 - C)/M_2$.

4. The burden of the executive could perhaps be lightened by allowing private repossessions, but in order for a law to have any meaning a creditor who has a lesser capacity for violence than the debtor should be able to appeal for public enforcement.

5. See, for example, Peerenboom 1999, Fuller 1964, or Fallon 1997.

6. In earlier work, Levine and his coauthors also examined the relationship between capital and credit markets and growth (e.g., King and Levine 1993).

7. These measures were collected by La Porta et al. (1998).

8. In other words, $150 billion $\times$ 0.06 $\approx$ $1 billion in the first year. Over ten years, this works out to $1 billion $\times$ 1/2 $\times$ 10 $\times$ 10 $=$ $50 billion.

9. These international arrangements are developed further in Lanyi 2001.

10. As Mancur Olson once stated, there are no property rights without government: "People may have possessions in the sense that a dog possesses a bone, but there is no socially sanctioned right to property without government" (1999).

11. Of course, since this market would not otherwise exist it's not really being replaced.

12. We're paraphrasing Bardhan (2000) paraphrasing Robinson (1998). William Nelson at George Mason University is working on related issues (Nelson 2002).

13. See Lanyi and Lee and (especially) Levine in this volume; La Porta et al. 1997, 1998; and Olson's 1999 paper coauthored with Azfar and Matheson.

14. See Summers's comment on Wallis's essay (this volume) for an elaboration of this point.

15. McGuire in his 1998 paper observe that the "immediate and sensational" attention paid to the Olson and Zeckhauser article differentiates it from the earlier foundational *Logic of Collective Action,* which took root over a longer period of time.

16. Yet again Olson made an important rhetorical contribution on this subject in the idea of "fiscal equivalence"—that public goods should be provided by the smallest political unit that can internalize spillovers (1969). Recent work at IRIS has developed this idea empirically (Azfar, Kahkonen, and Meagher 2001).

References

Works of Mancur Olson Jr.

1963. "Rapid Growth as a Destabilizing Force." *Journal of Economic History* 23 (4): 529–52.

1965. *The Logic of Collective Action.* Cambridge: Harvard University Press.

1969. "The Principle of 'Fiscal Equivalence': The Division of Responsibilities among Different Levels of Government." *American Economic Review, Proceedings* 59 (2): 479–87.

1982. *The Rise and Decline of Nations.* New Haven: Yale University Press.

1987. "Diseconomies of Scale and Development." *Cato Journal* 7 (1): 77–97.

1993. "Dictatorship, Democracy, and Development." *American Political Science Review* 87 (3): 567–76.

1996. "Big Bills Left on the Sidewalk: Why Some Nations Are Rich, and Others Poor." *Journal of Economic Perspectives* 10 (2): 3–24.

2000. *Power and Prosperity: Outgrowing Communist and Capitalist Dictatorships.* New York: Basic Books.

with Christopher Clague, Philip Keefer, and Steven Knack. 1996. "Property and Contract Rights in Autocracies and Democracies." *Journal of Economic Growth* 1 (2): 243–76.

———. 1999. "Contract-Intensive Money: Contract Enforcement, Property Rights, and Economic Performance." *Journal of Economic Growth* 4: 185–211.

with Avinash Dixit. 2000. "Does Voluntary Participation Undermine the Coase Theorem?" *Journal of Public Economics* 76 (3): 309–35.

with S. Kahkonen, eds. 2000. *A Not-So-Dismal Science: A Broader View of Economies and Societies.* New York: Oxford University Press.
with Martin McGuire. 1996. "The Economics of Autocracy and Majority Rule: The Invisible Hand and the Use of Force." *Journal of Economic Literature* 34:72–97.
with Richard Zeckhauser. 1966. "An Economic Theory of Alliances." *Review of Economics and Statistics* 47:266–79.

Other Works Cited

Azfar, Omar, Satu Kahkonen, and Patrick Meagher. 2001. "Conditions for Effective Decentralized Governance: A Synthesis of Research Findings." Unpublished paper, IRIS, University of Maryland, College Park.
Azfar, Omar, and T. Matheson. 2003. "Market-Mobilized Capital." *Public Choice* (forthcoming).
Bagehot, W. [1873] 1991. *Lombard Street.* Reprint, Philadelphia: Porcupine Press, Onon Editions.
Bardhan, P. 2000. "The Nature of Institutional Impediments to Economic Development." In Olson and Kahkonen 2000, 245–68.
Barro, Robert. 1997. *Determinants of Economic Growth: A Cross-Country Empirical Study.* Cambridge: MIT Press.
de Soto, Hernando. 2000. *The Mystery of Capital: Why Capitalism Triumphs in the West and Fails Everywhere Else.* New York: Basic Books.
Demirgüç-Kunt, Asli, and Ross Levine. 1995. "Stock Market Development and Financial Intermediaries: Stylized Facts." *World Bank Economic Review* 10 (2): 223–39.
Dodd, E. 1936. "Statutory Developments in Business Corporation Law, 1886–1936." *Harvard Law Review* 50:27–59.
Fallon, Richard. 1997. "'The Rule of Law' as a Concept in Constitutional Discourse." *Columbia Law Review* 97 (1).
Fuller, Lon. 1964. *The Morality of Law.* New Haven: Yale University Press.
Gastil, R. 1978. *Freedom in the World: Political Rights and Civil Liberties.* New York: Freedom House.
Herodotus. 1987. *The History.* Chicago: University of Chicago Press.
Hicks, John. 1969. *A Theory of Economic History.* London: Oxford University Press.
King, Robert G., and Ross Levine. 1993. "Finance and Growth: Schumpeter Might Be Right." *Quarterly Journal of Economics* 108 (3): 717–38.
Knack, Steve, and Phil Keefer. 1995. "Institutions and Economic Performance: Cross Country Tests Using Alternative Institutional Measures." *Economics and Politics* 7:207–27.
Lanyi, Anthony. 2001. "International Financial Architecture and Domestic Economic Governance." Unpublished paper, IRIS, University of Maryland, College Park.

La Porta, R., F. Lopez-de-Silanes, A. Shleifer, and R. Vishny. 1997. "Legal Determinants of External Finance." *Journal of Finance* 10 (2): 223–39.

———. 1998. "Law and Finance." *Journal of Political Economy* 106 (6): 1113–55.

Levine, Ross. 1997. "Financial Development and Economic Growth: Views and an Agenda." *Journal of Economic Literature* 35 (2): 1688–726.

McGuire, Martin. 1998. "1932–1998 Personal Recollections." *Eastern Economic Journal* 24 (3): 253–63.

Nelson, William. 2002. "Why Dictatorships Keep Their People Poor." Mimeo, School of Business, SUNY Buffalo.

North, D. 1981. *Structure and Change in Economic History.* Cambridge: Cambridge University Press.

———. 1990. *Institutions, Institutional Change, and Economic Performance.* Cambridge: Cambridge University Press.

Peerenboom, Randall. 1999. "Ruling the Country in Accordance with Law: Reflections on the Rule and Role of Law in China." *Cultural Dynamics* 11:315–51.

Rauch, Jonathan. 1994. *Demosclerosis.* New York: Random House.

Robinson, James A. 1998. "Theories of Bad Policy." *Journal of Policy Reform* 2 (1): 1–46.

Rodrik, D., and F. Rodriguez. 1999. "Trade Policy and Economic Growth: A Skeptic's Guide to the Cross-National Evidence." Working paper, University of Maryland, College Park.

Sala-i-Martin, X. 1999. "I Just Ran Four Million Regressions." Working paper, National Bureau of Economic Research, Cambridge, MA.

Sandler, T. 1997. *Global Challenges.* Cambridge: Cambridge University Press.

Summers, Robert S. 1973. "A Formal Theory of the Rule of Law." *Ratio Juris* 6 (2): 127–42.

Temple, J. 1999. "The New Growth Evidence." *Journal of Economic Literature* 37 (1): 112–56.

Some Basic Ways Good Law, Good Legal Institutions, Good Legal Traditions, and Principles of the Rule of Law Can Augment Markets

Robert S. Summers

One kind of good law is good contract law. Contract law and related law, good in form and good in content, can help augment markets. The first part of this essay summarizes the rudiments of how this is so, focusing on contracts of loan (including credits) secured by interests in personal property and identifying eight basic characteristics of a rational system whereby parties may create, through contract and related law, loans and personal property security interests to secure such loans and thereby augment markets for loans. The second part identifies the basic types of good institutions required to facilitate and enforce such contractual and related law. The third part addresses how a society may come to have good contract and related law. There I will single out legal traditions but will concentrate on the extent to which the society subscribes to principles of the rule of law generally. Such a society is much more likely to have good contract and related law than a society that does not so subscribe. This, of course, is not the only factor that can explain the existence of good contract and related law in a society. Yet, as I will argue, because of its fundamental and normative character it is worthy of special emphasis.

I. The Rudiments of Good Contract and Related Law for Secured Loans

A society with good contract law with respect to loans of money would have several important types of good contract law and several important types of related personal property law. Such a society would also have several important types of legal institutions and other basic legal constructs that facilitate and implement secured lending pursuant to contract. As the late Mancur Olson saw clearly, markets for loans also depend on the existence of what he called "third-party enforcement" through appropriate action of courts and other agencies.

One of the most important types of contract is that in which the lender makes a loan secured by an interest in the debtor's personal property, that is, the collateral. If the debtor fails to repay the loan as agreed, the creditor becomes entitled to "realize" on the collateral, either by applying it directly in satisfaction of the debt or by making a public sale and applying the proceeds on the debt, with the debtor remaining liable for any deficiency. Such a security interest in the debtor's personal property is a kind of "insurance" safeguard, and in the Western economies with which I am familiar, creditors generally do not enter into contracts of loan with the expectation that the debtor is likely to default, so that it will be necessary to realize on the collateral. Rather, creditors generally expect repayment in the usual course, without default. The usual decision to lend is therefore largely made on the basis of an independent assessment of the prospective debtor's likely ability to repay the loan without default and so without the need to realize on any collateral.

Still, loans are not self-enforcing trades. Creditors' decisions are frequently based to some degree on specific personal property security, which they know they have a right to realize on if the debtor defaults. Although this point is debated, it seems reasonably certain that even in advanced Western economies many loans might not be made if it were not possible to take security interests in collateral to be realized in event of loan default. It is likely that this is all the more true in some less developed economies.[1]

I will now identify the main characteristics of good contract and related law with respect to contracts of loan to be secured by interests in personal property. I will dwell on the positive and the negative; that is, I will identify not only each of the major positive characteristics of such good law but also the major corresponding deficiency for each characteristic. In many developing economies, it is the deficiencies that stand out.

1. Recognition of contracts for secured loans as valid and enforceable. At minimum, the law must grant and protect *broad freedom of contract* to enter into loan agreements. This type of freedom of contract is, in developed systems, merely one facet of much broader grants of freedom of contract. If the system already has a special body of law on contracts of this general type, legal recognition of their validity should be straightforward. The law governing contract formation with respect to loans ought to be relatively simple, and contract formation ought to be relatively cheap. The relevant criteria of validity ought to require only that contracts of loan be in writing and that there be offer, acceptance, consideration or its equivalent, and due definiteness. The law ought also to include "off the rack" gap fillers providing standard terms in event of omissions in the contract itself.

The main possible deficiencies in such a body of law are simply the negative correlates of the foregoing: undue restrictions on freedom of contract, costly formalities of contract formation, absence of gap fillers, and so on. Another type of deficiency is that the system might fail to provide for the creation of security interests in property *acquired* by the debtor *after* the loan is made, for example, in inventory or equipment. That is, the system may fail to recognize "after-acquired property" clauses in security agreements and therefore may require parties to incur further costs to sign additional security agreements covering such property. The recognition of such clauses at the outset saves these costs.

Similarly, the system might fail to recognize "future advance" clauses in security agreements. Such clauses allow one agreement to provide *now* for a security interest in property currently held by the debtor to secure not only loans *now* but loans to be made in the future. This saves costs, too.

The system might also fail to identify, define, and differentiate clearly the various possible *types of recognized collateral*. Such binding legal definitions are essential. The lender needs to be able to describe the collateral in the security agreement and in any further document that is to be publicly registered. The parties should be able to describe such collateral with legally effective accuracy free of confusion.

Also, if the various types of collateral do not, in the law, have authoritative defining descriptions, this may create an incentive for some lenders to become "collateral hogs" and insist on taking security interests in *all* of a debtor's property. If this occurs, it is likely to limit the flow of financing to the debtor.

The system of definitions should be clear enough, and related types of collateral sufficiently differentiated, so that several different lenders might be willing to share in the overall risk of lending to the same debtor—as when, for example, a real estate lender takes a security interest in the debtor's land, an equipment manufacturer takes a security interest in the debtor's equipment sold to the debtor by the manufacturer, a bank takes a security interest in the debtor's inventory (created through use of the equipment and materials), and so on.

Another possible deficiency is in the rules for *determining ownership* of types of personal property. The law might fail to include definitive rules for determining who has title to what. If it is difficult for a lender to determine with certainty whether a prospective borrower owns a given asset, the lender may be less willing to lend against such collateral. The rules for integrating and coordinating *personal property* security interests with security interests in *land* (and fixtures on the land) may also be deficient and certainly will require special attention.

2. Adequate recognition of types of personal property interests that may be created by contract. The law should allow the creation of security interests in all appropriate types of personal property. This positive characteristic is perhaps best understood by considering what recognition would not be adequate. There might be valuable types of property that the law fails to recognize as possible types of collateral. For example, the system might fail to recognize inventory as potential collateral. Or the system might fail to recognize goods stored in a warehouse, or goods in process of manufacture, as potential collateral. Or the system might fail to recognize certain general intangibles such as intellectual property (copyrights, trademarks, or patents) as potential collateral.

3. Simplified and effective requirements for creating security interests through contract in personal property. The law should provide *simple and effective means* whereby two parties may contractually create security interests. This requirement, too, may be best understood by focusing on the ways in which it can fail to be satisfied. This requirement includes the subject of formalities for creation of a valid contract as such, and since I have already referred to this topic I will confine myself here to the additional steps necessary to create a security interest in personal property.

The rules might fail to specify *clearly* what steps the contracting parties must take to create a valid security interest, for example, what type of language serves to create such an interest and in what property. Further, the legal requirements for creation of a valid security interest might be excessive, unduly formal, or too costly, or they might unjustifiably limit the power to contract to a select class of prospective lenders (thereby inhibiting competition among lenders).

In addition, the rules might lack facilitative gap fillers that impor- tantly supplement the usual security agreement. For example, the rules might not provide that the creditor's security interest in inven- tory attaches to proceeds of its sale in the absence of contrary agree- ment. The rules might also be deficient in a further, major way: they might fail to provide, or fail to provide clearly, the time when a secu- rity interest becomes effective, how long it is to last, and how it may be terminated.

4. Provision for due notice to possibly interested third parties that the creditor and debtor are creating a security interest by contract in per- sonal property of the debtor.   The creditor and debtor do not enter into their contract in a vacuum. There may be interested third parties, including other creditors of the debtor, buyers from the debtor, hold- ers of liens on the debtor's property, and still others who have or wish to assert interests in the same property. All such persons need to be able to make informed decisions. A rational system for contractual creation and enforcement of security interests therefore must gener- ally provide for *public notice* of the creation of security interests.

The rules might simply fail to give adequate public notice to possible lenders and other interested third parties that the creditor and the debtor are creating a security interest. Some systems require that the lender either take possession of the collateral (pledge) or give notice by filing in a public registry in order to "perfect" the se- curity interest and thereby achieve maximum protection against other possible third-party creditors and other claimants. Both pos- session and formal filing in a registry give notice to third parties. Other devices may also be used, such as "field warehousing," the posting of signs on the debtor's property, and the like.

Generally, priority of right as between competing lenders with security interests in the same collateral should date from the time of taking possession or filing, whichever is earlier. So should priority of a secured creditor over unsecured creditors of the same debtor.

To the extent that a system does not require either creditor pos- session of the collateral or public filing in a registry, the system toler- ates "secret liens." In general, this is likely to undermine creditor confidence in the system as a whole. (Of course, many systems do not require possession or filing for every single type of collateral. For ex- ample, neither may be required for security interests in certain con- sumer goods.)

The most fundamental flaw here is simply the failure to provide any kind of public registry in which notice of the contractual creation of a security interest can be filed, with date of filing serving as a basis for determining priority as between competing security interests in the collateral or other competing claims to the collateral. There may be many types of collateral, such as equipment, that cannot be efficiently possessed by the creditor. Hence, there is a basic need for some kind of public registry to put third parties on notice.

Another possible flaw is that the rules governing the operation of the registry might not inspire confidence among creditors as to the reliability of the registry. Also, the costs of filing in the registry may be unduly high. Or there may be several registries in different places, instead of merely one for personal property and one for land interests. This duplication may make search costs by prospective creditors unduly high compared to the cost of searching a single, centralized registry for personal property security interests.

5. Provision of sound rules for determining priority as between different parties claiming rights in the same personal property.   Because of the inevitability of some debtor defaults, with the inevitability that different parties will, in event of such defaults, claim interests in the same personal property of the debtor, a system of contract and related law facilitating the use of personal property to secure loans must also include clear rules determining *who wins in event of priority conflicts.* This fundamental characteristic of a rational system can also best be understood in light of possible deficiencies in the rules.

Thus, the system might not include clear and well-defined priority rules granting priority to specified types of secured creditors in competition with each other or in competition with other third parties such as buyers. In most systems I know, such rules generally grant priority on the basis of who publicly perfected first, as by taking possession or by filing in a public registry.

The system might also fail to give sufficient priority status to a secured creditor over competing *unsecured* creditors or over other third parties claiming against the collateral in the absence of bankruptcy. Or, in event of bankruptcy, the system might fail to give a secured creditor sufficient priority status against competing creditors or other parties represented by a trustee in bankruptcy. If a security interest becomes valueless when the debtor takes bankruptcy, this is a grievous legal flaw.

The priority rules of the system might themselves not be well justified. For example, they might generally disregard the basic justificatory principle of "first in time, first in right," a principle that grants priority to the first creditor to file publicly or take possession. Or the rules might, for example, fail to provide exceptional priority for a "new money" lender, a lender who helps keep the borrower's business going by making new loans regularly, even though second in time.

6. Provision of rules enabling the secured creditor to enforce the loan and the security interest on debtor default. A further major characteristic of a system of contract and related law providing for the creation of security interests in personal property is that such a system includes sound rules enabling the secured creditor to enforce the loan and realize the security interest on default. Again, the possible deficiencies in enforcement rules remind us of the importance of enforcement. A system must, at minimum, define the duties of a creditor seeking to exercise rights on default. What steps must a creditor take to get possession of the collateral or to require a third party owing the debtor to pay the creditor directly? What notice must a creditor give the debtor or others of intent to conduct a foreclosure sale? How must the creditor advertise such a sale of collateral? The law must include definite rules here, yet we by no means always find such rules. Moreover, the rules should not be unduly cumbersome, such as rules requiring judicial approval of any and all foreclosure sales. Of course, the rules must also provide for rights of the creditor to collect any deficiency.

7. Protections of debtors against creditor overreaching and the like. A sound body of law allowing the contractual creation and enforcement of personal property interests to secure loans must also provide specific *protections to debtors.* Fairness to debtors, too, is an important characteristic of a rational body of law in this context. Debtors should be protected against bad faith declarations of default, against creditor repossessions that are not peaceful, against failure of the creditor to take due care of property repossessed, against failure of the creditor to send notice of foreclosure sales, against failure of the creditor to publicly advertise and conduct such sales openly and fairly, and more.

8. Establishment of a unified system for contractual security interests for loans. A rational system for contractual security interests is also a *unified system.* Yet many countries lack such a system; they have different bodies of law, and sometimes even different registries, for contractual security interests in equipment, retail merchants' assets, ship and airplane financing, fixtures on real estate, and on and on. All these separate bodies of law can, however, be efficiently drawn together under one unified system of rules and a single registry. Multiple systems within a single jurisdiction are far more costly to establish and operate.

II. The Rudiments of Good Institutions to Facilitate and Implement Contractual Arrangements for Secured Loans

It is not enough for a developing country to have good substantive law with respect to contracting for loans and with respect to personal property security. We must also have good institutions; the most essential institutional requirements are a well-designed legislature, executive branch, and court system.

1. The need for a well-designed legislature.   There is plainly a need for a well-designed legislative body capable of installing a system of contract law and personal property security for loans in the first place, and capable of amending statutes as required by major economic changes. For example, new forms of personal property security collateral may come into use or potential use, and this may require changes in the existing law.

Moreover, an effective legislative body is required to provide material and other support to the court system, which plays a major role in the authoritative interpretation and enforcement of private contracts. Similarly, the legislature must provide requisite material and other support for the executive branch of government.

2. The need for a well-designed executive branch.   There must also, of course, be an effective executive branch of government. The executive must have the power to appoint judges—and it must allow judges to make decisions independently and impartially. Furthermore, the executive branch and the legislature will have specific roles to play in order for the contractual and related arrangements required for a system of personal property security law to function. A major example is simply that of setting up and administering the central registry for filing security interests in personal property. It must also provide an official agency capable of exercising state power, as ordered by a court, to enforce private contracts and court-awarded judgments. Further, a central banking system will have an important role to play.

3. The need for a well-designed court system. Mancur Olson's concept of "third-party enforcement" is indispensable if contracts of loan secured by personal property collateral are to be at all viable and thus serve to augment markets for financing. A well-designed court system is essential to enforcement of contracts.

The courts should devise rational and consistent *methodologies for interpreting contracts* and for filling gaps in contracts—methodologies that can also be applied to resolve contractual disputes out of court. This will contribute greatly to the certainty and predictability of contract rights generally and more particularly to the efficacy of a system of secured contractual lending against personalty.

Courts must also have efficient and reliable means of *finding facts.* When, in disputed cases, the courts accurately find facts and resolve disputed issues of law, this secures enforcement of contracts of loan against personal property collateral and, just as important, may also induce parties to perform such contracts voluntarily, without intervention by the courts.

Similarly, when courts devise a rational and consistent *methodology for interpretation of statutes* applying to aspects of loan contracts, this, too, contributes greatly to the general reliability and enforceability of contracts.

4. The need for a well-trained and accessible legal profession. A further basic institutional need is for a well-trained and accessible legal profession to draft contracts of loan, interpret and advise on the meaning of contract language, interpret statutes applicable to contracts of loan and personal property security, conduct negotiations in the event of disputes over contract rights and duties, and represent creditors and debtors in disputed cases before courts. Without well-trained lawyers to do these things, the other legal institutions cannot function as they must.

III. Good Legal Tradition as Explanatory of Good Law and Good Legal Institutions

How is it that a society may come to have a good system of contractual and related law for lending and a good basic set of institutions furthering such contractual lending? We can identify several general factors that make for good law and good institutions generally. I will first provide a general review of several basic factors. I will then concentrate on one of these, namely, the extent to which the system generally subscribes to principles of the rule of law.

General Factors of Tradition That May Make for Good Contract Law and Good Legal Institutions

I am often asked the following question when advising on law reform abroad: just what is it that explains the fact that the American legal system is as good as it is? More particularly, why do we generally have such a good body of contract and related law and such a good set of legal institutions—a set that works so well (or at least seems to)? This question is extremely difficult to answer. I am not a legal historian, and I do not have a full or even anything like a final answer, but I will suggest some contributing factors.

Inheritance of English Law

The first factor I would mention is simply our general inheritance. Carried over on the *Mayflower* and subsequent ships were law books as well as people with memories. We directly inherited much from English law, including the idea of contract, the idea of loans of money in return for interest, and the idea of lending money against security, with land being a prominent form of collateral. All these inheritances came to us as early as the seventeenth and eighteenth centuries and so have been with us for hundreds of years. The second major factor is that, given this age-old inheritance, we have had a long time to improve upon it.

Inheritance of Values

Moreover, this inheritance—and the disposition to develop and improve upon it—readily took root in America. Why? For one thing, our inheritance coalesced with *important values* held dear by our ancestors and passed on to their successors, values as elementary as that a promisor should keep a promise and a debtor should repay a debt. The most fundamental value in this context is perhaps freedom: contract is, after all, a powerful instrument of freedom. It is understandable that settlers rejecting restrictions on freedom in the Old World would strive to improve contract as an instrument of freedom. This disposition to improve contract continues to thrive in many fields, including the field that is our subject in this volume. Article 9 of the

Uniform Commercial Code is now being revised in major ways for the third time in fifty years.

Needs of a Developing Society

Just as important, the basic development of a society—economic, scientific, and cultural—requires facilitative law. When our country was first settled, it of course required development, and Americans saw early the connection between economic development and law facilitative of that development, a connection that continues to be emphasized at the beginning of the twenty-first century. The complex needs entailed in current levels of production and exchange would in any case require an equally complex and sophisticated body of law and legal institutions.

A System of Legal Education

Since the end of the nineteenth century, the United States has had a highly advanced and continuously improving system of legal education and has accorded lawyers high social status. This has provided human and other resources not merely to staff our legal institutions and advise private citizens but to pursue continuous efforts to improve our substantive and procedural law, including, of course, our law of contract.

Respect for the Rule of Law

A fundamental factor, worthy of more detailed examination, is the prevailing attitude of general respect for the rule of law, including a recognition of the corresponding set of general principles of the rule of law.[2] American society generally recognizes a widely accepted set of formal standards of what constitutes law-like uses of law, departures from which are apt to provoke criticism. I suspect that our espousal of these, more than any other factor, is what sustains us most in all matters of law, including general contract law and the institutions that facilitate it.

General Principles of the Rule of Law

Even though the principles of the rule of law are not, as such, derived from the idea of market augmentation, they are of fundamental importance for it. Many of the rudiments of good contract and personal property security law identified earlier can be seen as manifestations of the general commitment of society to principles of the rule of law. Certainly without general commitment to these principles the general law of contract in a system could not flourish, nor could any of its special branches.

Ordinary first-order law (as opposed to the rule of law) includes both principles and rules. *Principles* of ordinary first-order law apply directly to determine legal relations between the immediate addresses of such law. (Two examples are the moral principle that "no person shall profit from his own wrong" and the quite different commercial law principle that "a transferee of property takes no better title than the transferor had.") Examples of first-order *rules* include the contractual and security interest rules discussed earlier.

Unlike first-order principles and rules, the principles of the rule of law are what might be called second-order principles. That is, they are *about* first-order law; they are rules *about* rules of first-order law. Principles of the rule of law are general norms that direct and constrain what counts as first-order law and how it is created and implemented. They are also about first-order law in the sense that they specify its general shape and configuration. When the creation and implementation of a first-order principle or rule conforms to these second-order norms, the requirements of the rule of law are met.

Individual principles of the rule of law thus have a far wider scope of application than individual first-order laws. Indeed, principles of the rule of law apply across all the basic operations of a legal system in their full "breadth," and also apply to these operations in their full "length" and so are truly systemic in scope. These (second-order) principles of the rule of law indirectly serve the basic substantive policies and other values incorporated in first-order principles, rules, decrees, and other such law. At the same time, the principles of the rule of law, as applied, serve fundamental political values (such as legitimacy) and general legal values (such as certainty).

What follows is a relatively comprehensive inventory of the second-order principles that govern how first-order law is to be made and implemented, and what shape it is to take if it is to conform to the rule of law.[3] All of these principles are recognized to some extent in developed Western systems of law.

1. That all forms of law be duly *authorized* and thus conform to established criteria of validity

2. That the accepted *criteria* for determining the validity of law generally be clear and readily applicable and include criteria for the resolution of any conflicts between otherwise valid forms of law

3. That state-made law on a given subject be *uniform* within state boundaries and, as far as is feasible and appropriate, take the preceptive form of general and definite rules applicable to classes of persons, acts, circumstances, and so on, and also be applicable to officials and citizens alike, as appropriate

4. That all forms of law be appropriately *clear and determinate* in meaning

5. That state-made law, and other law as appropriate, be in some written form and be promulgated, *published,* or otherwise be made accessible to its addressees

6. That law, and changes in law, generally be *prospective* rather than retroactive (see also [13] and [14])

7. That the behavioral requirements of a law be *within the capacity* of its addressees to comply

8. That the law on a subject, once made and put into effect, *not be changed so frequently* that its addressees cannot readily conform their conduct to it or cannot feasibly engage in long-term planning

9. That purported *changes in the law* be made by duly authorized institutions, officials, or persons and in accordance with known procedures, as appropriate

10. That a form of law be interpreted or otherwise applied in accordance with an appropriate, uniform (for that type of law), and determinate *interpretive methodology,* itself duly respectful of the expressional form and content of that type of law

11. That any possible remedy, sanction, nullification, or other adverse consequence of failure to comply with a form of law be known or *knowable in advance* of the relevant occasions for action or decision under that law

12. That in case of dispute, or occasions for enforcement, a politically independent and *impartial system of courts* and administrative tribunals exist and have power, (a) to determine the validity of the law in dispute, (b) to resolve issues of fact in accordance with relevant procedural and substantive law, and (c) to apply the valid law in accordance with an appropriate interpretive or other applicational methodology

13. That when an interpretive methodology or another applicational methodology does not authorize an outcome under antecedent law, yet a court or a tribunal is urged (sometimes in the guise of such methodology) to modify or otherwise depart from law to achieve such an outcome, courts or tribunals shall have only quite limited and exceptional power thus to modify or otherwise depart from antecedent statute, precedent, or other law, in order that the legal conclusions and any reasons for action or decision on the part of the law's addressees that would otherwise arise under valid law, duly interpreted or applied, generally remain peremptory for the law's addressees, including courts and other tribunals

14. That any exceptional power of courts or other tribunals to modify or depart from antecedent law at the point of application be a power that, as far as is feasible, is itself explicitly specified and duly circumscribed in rules, so that this is a power that is itself law-governed in its exercise

15. That a party who is the victim of an alleged legal wrong (such as a crime, regulatory violation, tort, breach of contract, wrongful denial of a public benefit, or wrongful administrative action) shall be entitled to instigate criminal prosecution, or seek other appropriate redress, before an independent and impartial court or other tribunal with power to compel the alleged wrongdoer or other person responsible to answer for such wrong

16. That except for minor matters no significant sanction, remedy, or other adverse legal consequence shall be imposed on a party for an alleged legal wrong without the party having a fair opportunity to contest its legality and factual basis before an independent and impartial court or other, similar tribunal

17. That a private party who fails to prevail before such a court or tribunal, pursuant to (15) and (16), whether an alleged victim or an alleged wrongdoer, shall have the opportunity to seek at least one level of appellate review, in a court, as a check against legal error

18. That the system and its institutions and processes be generally accessible, that is, (a) that there be a recognized, organized, and independent legal profession legally empowered and willing to provide legal advice and to advocate causes before courts, other tribunals, and other institutions as ap-

propriate; and (b) that where a party is accused of a significant crime or similar violation, denies liability, and is without financial means to pay costs of defense, such party shall be entitled to have defense provided by the state.

This enumeration does not include mere *devices* for implementation of such principles. Not everything that tends to secure the rule of law is itself a principle of the rule of law. For example, the constitutional separation and division of powers in many systems tend to secure against official behavior contrary to the rule of law, but I do not include it as an affirmative principle of the rule of law. Provision for periodic transfer of power from one set of elected officials to a set of newly elected officials also tends to secure against lawless despotism, but this provision, again, is not itself a principle of the rule of law, even though whatever secures against despotism also tends strongly to secure the rule of law. A provision of a bill of rights entrenching freedom to criticize the government tends to secure against lawless rule, but this freedom is not itself a principle of the rule of law. Rather, all the foregoing are merely examples of what I call devices that, among other things, implement the rule of law. Of course, at the borderline there is no sharp line between such devices and principles of the rule of law.

Do the second-order principles of the rule of law apply only to the creation and implementation of first-order law by the state or do they also apply to first-order law created by private parties? Such privately created first-order law includes contracts, including contracts of loan, certain property arrangements, and more. Most of the principles of the rule of law, as they are formulated here, do indeed apply (with appropriate modifications) to privately created law.

Does just any particular departure from any of the enumerated principles always seriously threaten the rule of law? Not at all. Exceptional departures from some of the principles of the rule of law may even be justified. A particular retroactive statute may be justified, for example. Moreover, not all judicial departures even from the explicit text of a statute seriously threaten the rule of law. Thus, a judicial modification that makes a statute clearer in a fashion consistent with the text may even be justified. Also, sometimes a law cannot be made definite, and therefore must in some respect be left vague, given its subject matter.

Yet at the same time complete noncompliance with any single major principle of the rule of law would indeed signify that the system cannot properly be called a legal system. No balancing act could rescue such a "system." It would not be possible, for example, to rescue total abandonment of all rules by formally adopting all the moral principles possibly relevant to any legal matter. Nor, similarly, could we rescue total abandonment of a generally accepted interpretive methodology by somehow designating totally wise and judicious men and women as ad hoc judges. Conformity to the principles of the rule of law is nevertheless a matter of degree, and some systems will conform less fully than others.

Not all of these enumerated principles of the rule of law are fully recognized as binding in the positive law of all developed Western systems. Moreover, a principle may be recognized by different means in different systems: one system may embody a principle in a constitutional provision, while another leaves this matter entirely to judge-made law; one system may recognize a principle directly and explicitly, while another merely adopts a device that, in effect, recognizes it only indirectly and implicitly; or one system may provide real "teeth" for enforcing a principle, while another does not.

The second-order principles of the rule of law, then, direct and constrain how the legal system is to operate at all stages and within each of its basic operational techniques. The directives and constraints of the principles of the rule of law are not, however, merely instrumental means to the ends and values to be served by first-order law. That is, these principles do not merely secure efficacious use of first-order law. A significant violation of principles of the rule of law may signify not only that the first-order use of law in question will be ineffective or less effective but, moreover, that a given first-order use of law *is not really lawlike.* A vague rule regarding who has priority between competing creditors would not merely be ineffective; it would also be less lawlike. A rule that is quite unclear in its meaning is not really lawlike. In the absence of quite special circumstances, a retroactive statute is not really lawlike. In all such instances, it is not only the efficacy of law that is sacrificed but also, possibly, the very claim that this use of first-order law is lawlike.

What should we say if violations of principles of the rule of law were to occur not merely individually here and there but on a major scale across all of the law's primary operational techniques and were to extend to the full length of the linear progressions within each technique? Should we say that such a "system" is not really a system of law at all? Certainly such massive violation would strain our very *concept of a legal system* by failing to conform to its minimal essential form. We might even say that the whole system is at least less truly a system of law, and at most we would say that the system is not a system of law at all. It is characteristic of a true system of law that overall it operates substantially in accord with principles of the rule of law.

A system of law is not, conceptually, merely a system that includes first-order rules (and other first-order law) having the type of substantive content that purports to order human relations. A system of law is, conceptually, a system that actually operates, in its breadth and length, in lawlike ways. That is, it generally operates substantially in accordance with the second-order principles of the rule of law. It is logically possible that a system of law could even have first-order bodies of law that are in themselves just, right, and good in subject matter yet the system itself not be a true system of law because of its general failure to operate sufficiently in accordance with second-order principles of the rule of law. For example, these good laws might be indefinite, retrospective, secret, and generally inaccessible to the citizenry, sprung on citizens at despotic whim. Fundamental fairness, and hence legitimacy, are at stake in departures from principles of the rule of law—even though these principles are all apparently formal!

How Good Law and Institutions Augmenting Markets Instantiate Principles of the Rule of Law

Many examples might be offered to illustrate how good law and good institutions that augment markets may be viewed as instantiations of principles of the rule of law. Each of the following four examples represents a good law or good institution that plays a fundamental role in augmenting markets for secured lending. Each example also instantiates a major principle of the rule of law.

First, it is a major principle of the rule of law that there be clear and readily applicable criteria for determining the validity of newly created first-order law, whether created by state institutions or private individuals or entities. Contracts of loan and the interests in personal property securing such loans, when valid, constitute privately created law. An important relevant law, in this context, is the law specifying what is required for a valid contract of loan secured by an interest in personal property. This is a first-order law specifying criteria of validity, and thus it instantiates a leading principle of the rule of law.

Second, it is a basic principle of the rule of law that all first-order law, as far as is feasible, must take the shape of general and definite rules with clear and determinate meanings; vague or open-ended formulations would afford little guidance to citizens on the front lines of human interaction and in effect would confer on judges vast power to decide disputes however they wish. The eight main characteristics of good contract and related law with respect to loans secured by interests in personal property (enumerated in sec. I) all call for the relevant law to take the form of highly determinate rules, including (e.g.) rules defining and differentiating the various types of property in which security interests may be created. Without such determinate rules, this branch of the law would lack the certainty required for general business confidence that loans will be duly repaid.

Third, it is a further leading principle of the rule of law that for each major variety of law (such as statute, precedent, and contract) there be an appropriate, uniform (for that type of law), and determinate interpretive or other relevant applicational methodology, itself a methodology duly respectful of the special expressional form and content of the type of law to be applied. One of the requirements of good law and good institutions with respect to contracts of loan secured by personal property interests is precisely that there be a rational and consistent interpretive methodology for contracts, and also one for applicable statutes, and indeed further ones for other types of relevant law.

Fourth, it is a vital principle of the rule of law that there be independent and impartial courts with (1) the power to determine the validity of law in dispute, (2) the power to resolve issues of fact, (3) the power to apply valid law in accordance with appropriate interpretive or other applicational methodologies, and (4) the power to grant appropriate remedies. Both the legal and the institutional setups for recognizing and enforcing loan contracts (and interests in personalty securing them) instantiate this vital principle of the rule of law. Credible courts may in fact have farther-reaching influence in the threat of their use, by securing out of court compliance with law, than they have through the specific contractual or other remedies that they grant in actual judicial proceedings.

As this last example illustrates, the principles of the rule of law have relevance also for the institutional requirements discussed in section II. In order to have market-augmenting impact, the principal institutions of governance—legislature, executive, and judiciary— must themselves be informed by respect for the rule of law and its vital principles.

Notes

The author wishes to thank Mrs. Pam Finnigan for assistance and also Ms. Shelley Detwiller, Cornell Law School, Class of 1999; Mr. Steve Greenblatt, Cornell Law School, Class of 1999; and Mr. Ian Johnson, Cornell Law School, Class of 2000, for assistance. The types of law discussed in this essay are treated intensively in White and Summers 1995.

1. This issue is discussed in Harris and Mooney 1994. See also White 1984.
2. For one of the leading general accounts, see Fuller 1969. See also Summers 1984, chap. 3.
3. In this inventory, I do not include specific legal devices for implementing each such principle in the set.

References

Fuller, Lon L. 1969. *The Morality of Law*. 2d ed. New Haven: Yale University Press.

Harris, Steven L., and Charles W. Mooney Jr. 1994. "A Property-Based Theory of Security Interests: Taking Debtor's Choices Seriously." *Virginia Law Review* 80 (8): 2021–72.

Summers, Robert S. 1984. *Lon L. Fuller*. Palo Alto: Stanford University Press.

White, James J. 1984. "Efficiency Justifications for Personal Property Security." *Vanderbilt Law Review* 37 (3): 473–508.

White, James J., and Robert S. Summers. 1995. *The Uniform Commercial Code*. 4 vols. St. Paul: West Publishing.

Comment

Charles A. Cadwell

How Can We Use Robert Summers's Market-Augmenting "Principles of the Rule of Law"?

In one essay, Professor Summers has provided an explanation of both how a particular law interacts with the needs of markets and why narrow legal reform—absent attention to issues of rule-based governance—will fall short in terms of augmenting markets. This he does with the ordered logic of one who has thought deeply about how laws are used by judges, businesses, lawyers, and the rest of us, and as one who has significant practical experience with the laws related to commerce.[1]

The eighteen principles of the rule of law that Summers enunciates in section III could serve well as a cogent standard for those seeking to advance the rule of law in developing polities. Yet the essay stops short of suggesting how we might achieve these goals: it does not attempt to describe the "mere *devices* for the implementation of such principles" (emphasis in the original). Summers has chosen the role of architect rather than that of social engineer. This note offers some ways in which Summers's principles might be put to practical use.

The idea underlying the essay, that there are "first-" and "second-order" principles and laws, may seem to most economists to be a distinction without substantive content. First-order laws determine relations between the immediate addressees of the law—in this case, the relations between borrowers, creditors, and third parties. Second-order principles or rules describe how such first-order rules are made and sustained. They serve as substantive but broad rules that apply to many or all first-order laws. From one perspective, all of the rules or principles described by both first- and second-order principles are simply part of the institutional environment of a particular economic exchange, described with more or less specificity. Economists often assume that these laws regarding contract enforcement are a "black box," easily attached to private transactions and thus not a cause for worry. But exactly what is the function of the distinction between first- and second-order rules? Are rules *about rules* different in some important way?

In terms of their operation with respect to market augmentation, all of the rules, laws, and principles described by Summers are in fact part of a continuum of institutions difficult to distinguish conceptually. As is clear from Summers's essay, the way in which they can be distinguished is in their scope. While a good secured lending law (a first-order rule) affects people interested in credit, a rule about the *regularity* of this law (a second-order principle) applies equally to other laws as well: it has benefits that extend to other areas of law. The message of the Summers essay is that the second-order principles are essential complements, indeed underpinnings. Reformers who focus on first-order reforms, and wish in a vague way for improvements in the "rule of law," can find specifics in the second-order principles identified here. Likewise, those attempting to advance the rule of law by training judges, building bar associations, or expanding information systems can find specific instruction in the real objectives of such activity.

This of course poses a dilemma for reformers in developing countries and for donors seeking to support them. Even though we have the assertion from an author of great experience and ability that the second-order rules are in fact the main thing and not a secondary matter, it is difficult to lay out steps for how to "enact" them. This is so, first, because few will perceive a direct or immediate benefit from steps taken to implement second-order principles. Furthermore, the steps themselves are elusive in terms of what specifically to do and with whom to do it.

If we could enact these principles, the benefits would be highly "democratic" in that they would be accessible to the many, not just the few. But reformers, legislatures, and government administrations ordinarily proceed by proposing, enacting, and enforcing specific measures, not general ones. So the challenge is for us to consider how one might implement these principles, making them not only correct but useful.

There are two ways in which the principles might be useful: first, in developing or assessing particular reform efforts; and, second, in comparing overall rule of law environments. Among those involved in supporting legal reforms in transitional and developing countries, there has been a rush of late to emphasize the importance of "implementation." This may seem a long overdue emphasis to those not involved in this sort of work, but it reflects a new recognition that statutes and rules are not self-enforcing. It reflects an appreciation that institutions—often those of the state—are required if laws affecting private contracting are to have an effect. The second-order principles that Summers has identified are for the most part principles related to the implementation of first-order laws. While an economist might assume that all government has to do is enforce contracts among private parties, the principles here suggest how complex an activity that actually is. Anyone developing a reform of a first-order law who purports to have implementation clearly in view ought to pay attention to the answers to the questions implicit in these eighteen principles.

Often the answers will be that the institutions, entities, and behaviors described in the principles do not yet exist. This gap can be addressed in at least a couple of ways. One is that the content of the laws can be scaled back to account for the gap. If there is no capacity or potential capacity for a national registry of pledged property, then the law ought not to presuppose such a pledge (principle 7: the law ought to be within the capacity of addressees to comply). Appropriate alternatives need to be sought (e.g., provide for local posting of pledges?). If there are no people able to make the kinds of judgments needed for the law to have an effect, then develop simpler rules, even at the sacrifice of precision (principle 2: the law must be appropriately clear;[2] principle 11: remedies and sanctions must be knowable in advance). Work on a first-order rule that took full account of local manifestations of second-order principles would look significantly different from a drafting that assumed that these outcomes, like gravity, exist everywhere on earth.

A significant subset of the principles relate to the authority, autonomy, and constraints of tribunals (principles 12–17). This emphasis might lead one to postpone any first-order reform until the courts are working in accordance with these principles. But this is very often an impractical option. The utility of these principles lies in forcing us to consider how, using alternatives to the regular courts, we might achieve the outcomes described. Is there a set of institutional innovations that will give better effect to the first-order law being considered—that will operate in a more "lawlike" fashion—that we can develop or draw upon for implementation of the proposed rules? Innovations might include: special courts with narrow scope; participation of industry experts; special provisions for transparency; shifting presumptions; bringing in outside, indeed international, participation; and a range of other steps to create an island of lawlike behavior. This of course falls short of achieving the broad lawlike environment that is the objective of the eighteen principles, but it makes use of a particular reform to claim territory for such an environment, yard by yard.

The second way in which these eighteen principles can serve us in addressing how governments actually augment markets is as a comparative standard against which one might usefully measure developing legal systems, serving better than observation of the "mere devices" of the rule of law (such as the formal provision for independent courts or the separation of powers) and better than an arbitrary compilation of the first-order laws.

The several "country risk services" that compile subjective observations of businesspeople have proved both popular and useful in providing studies of comparative institutional development. They do not, however—despite their utility—suggest why it is that contracts are enforceable or why the risk of expropriation is great or small. In order to take from these ratings any direction for reform, we ought to complement them with an understanding of the specifics outlined by the Summers principles. If we had an inventory of how a particular country delivers these second-order principles, we would have a much needed blueprint for advising, whether on investor comfort or essential reforms. Indeed, such an inventory would be a better guide for needed reform than a simple assessment of first-order legal sufficiency or an examination of the formal devices of the legal system, as important as these are. These observations do not, of course, benefit from the broad experience that Summers could bring to the questions he has not had space to address: how these second-order rules evolved in the United States and elsewhere; and, by extension, in places that do not enjoy lawlike systems, what steps can reformers take toward these goals? The few speculations here are intended to prompt readers—and perhaps Professor Summers—to suggest better ways to answer a question important to development in dozens of countries.

Notes

1. For those of us who are lawyers, Professor Summers's work with James White not only helped us through our legal training but stands the test of time and later experience. See Summers and White 1988.

2. This idea is expressed in specific form in Black and Kraakman 1996. It also emerges from conversations with a minister, discussing development of competition law, to wit: "We don't have administrators or judges who can analyze market definition, market shares, or the like, so we need competition rules that avoid standards like 'tend to monopolize' or 'unfair trade.'"

References

Black, Bernard, and Reinier Kraakman. 1996. "A Self-Enforcing Model of Corporate Law." *Harvard Law Review* 109:1911–82.

Summers, Robert S., and James J. White. 1988. *The Uniform Commercial Code.* 3d ed. St. Paul: West Publishing.

Napoleon, Bourses, and Growth, with a Focus on Latin America

Ross Levine

Developing countries' stock markets accounted for a disproportionately large share of the late 1990s boom in global stock market activity. The value of equity market transactions in emerging economies soared from about 2 percent of the world total in 1986 to 12 percent in 1996.[1] This boom was accompanied by an explosion of international capital flows, especially flows into developing country stock markets. Net private capital flows to developing nations had jumped tenfold over the previous decade, exceeding $250 billion in 1996.[2] Moreover, while equity flows had been a negligible part of capital flows to emerging markets in the mid-1980s, equity flows represented about 20 percent of private capital flows to developing nations by 1996. In the late 1990s, however, the dramatic financial disturbances emanating from Asia curtailed some capital flows and raised questions about the role of financial markets.

These developments raise critical questions for policymakers. Are developing country stock markets simply casinos where foreigners place bets? Or do developing countries themselves reap large benefits from liquid equity markets? If better stock markets are important catalysts of economic development, what can policymakers do to improve the functioning of their bourses?

In addressing these policy issues, this essay makes three points.

1. First, stock market development, especially stock market liquidity, exerts a positive, first-order impact on economic development. A growing body of research supports the view espoused by Walter Bagehot more than one hundred years ago: *better-functioning financial markets cause faster economic growth.*

2. Second, particular laws and regulations materially affect the operation of stock markets. Cross-country differences in laws concerning the rights of shareholders—especially minority shareholders—help explain the level of stock market development. Also, countries with

companies that provide high-quality, comprehensive, and comparable financial statements tend to enjoy better-developed stock markets than countries where regulatory systems are less effective in encouraging firms to publish useful information. Thus, governments can augment the functioning of private markets and thereby boost economic growth by effectively protecting property rights and facilitating the dissemination of information. *In sum, countries where legal codes stress the rights of shareholders, and where the regulatory system rigorously encourages corporate information disclosure, tend to have better-developed financial markets.*

3. Third, relatively uninformative financial statements, combined with relatively weak legal protection of minority shareholders, help account for the comparably underdeveloped state of Latin America's stock exchanges and its disappointingly slow growth. These characteristics can in part be traced to the influence of the French legal tradition on Latin America's legal and regulatory systems. The French-Napoleonic legal tradition is in fact strongly associated with relatively underdeveloped financial systems.[3] Once we examine the strong empirical connection between the legal and regulatory environment, the financial system, and growth, *Latin America's legal and regulatory systems stand out as deserving particularly careful scrutiny as it seeks to accelerate economic development.*

Methodologically, the essay primarily uses cross-country comparisons based on data from forty-five countries over the period 1976–94. Each country is one observation. Two major weaknesses of this methodology are that it does not provide a detailed evaluation of the particular circumstances of any individual country and it focuses attention on Latin America as a region instead of on individual countries. The strength of this analysis is that it places Latin America in an international context. The cross-country comparisons suggest an urgency that would not emerge from a country-specific study. Latin America, on average, has notably weaker legal codes in terms of the protection of minority shareholders than does the rest of the world. To an even greater degree, Latin American companies tend to publish lower-quality and less comprehensive financial statements. The results offer a broad reform strategy but not a precise blueprint of how to reform the policies of any particular country.

Sections I and II discuss the theories and empirical evidence regarding the relationship of stock markets and banks with economic growth. The issue here is not whether stock prices efficiently reflect expectations about future corporate profits or whether quickly rising stock prices are good or bad. The issue is whether a well-developed stock market—*a market where it is relatively easy to trade ownership of the country's companies*—helps that country grow faster.

The data summarized in section II show that, even after controlling for many factors associated with growth, stock market liquidity—*as measured both by the value of stock trading relative to the size of the market and by the value of trading relative to the size of the economy*—is positively and significantly correlated with future rates of long-run economic growth. A growing body of microeconomic evidence supports this finding. These results are consistent with the view that a greater ability to trade ownership of an economy's companies facilitates faster economic growth. Moreover, the level of banking development—*as measured by bank loans to private enterprises divided by gross domestic product (GDP)*—also helps in predicting economic growth. Since measures of stock market liquidity and banking development both enter the growth regressions significantly, the findings suggest that banks provide *different* financial services from those provided by stock markets. Banking and stock market development in developing countries tend to complement each other, not substitute for one another.

Since better stock markets seem to boost economic development, policymakers have a responsibility to implement legal, regulatory, and policy reforms that promote healthy stock market development. Researchers similarly have a responsibility to identify such reforms. Thus, section III examines the relationship between stock market development and both the legal rights of shareholders and the degree to which the regulatory regime successfully encourages firms to publish comprehensive financial statements.

The data presented in section III suggest a strong link between stock market development and a country's legal and regulatory environment. Countries where the legal system emphasizes the rights of minority shareholders, and where the regulatory/accounting regime produces high-quality information about firms, have larger stock markets (where size is measured both by market capitalization and by the number of primary market issues). Furthermore, the relationship between accounting standards and stock market liquidity is significant and economically meaningful. The data imply that one standard deviation increase in information disclosure increases liquidity by the median value of the sample.

Next, section III confronts the issue of causality, tracing the impact of the legal and regulatory environment on stock market development and ultimately on economic growth. Specifically, I use as instrumental variables measures of the legal rights of minority shareholders and the regulatory regime's ability to encourage high-quality corporate reports as a way of extracting the exogenous component of stock market development—that is, the component of stock market development that is defined by the legal and accounting environment.

There are good reasons to use measures of the legal and regulatory environment as instrumental variables. First, they are direct policy levers. Second, the current legal/regulatory environment has been heavily influenced by legal heritage. In particular, La Porta et al. (1997, 1998) show that differences in the legal treatment of shareholders as well as in the quality of corporate annual reports are systematically linked to the country's legal origin. Based on the work of legal scholars, they categorize countries as having predominantly English, French, German, or Scandinavian legal origins. Since most countries obtained their legal systems through occupation and colonization, and since these systems vary little over time, the legal variables can be treated as exogenous for the 1976–93 period. Section III shows that the exogenous component of stock market development—*the component of stock market development defined by the legal and accounting regime*—is in fact positively associated with long-run economic growth. (The econometric specification passes the test of the overidentifying restrictions: the specific legal variables used in this essay do not influence growth beyond their influence on financial development, eliminating simultaneity bias as an explanation of the correlation.)

The impact of the exogenous component of stock market development on economic growth is positive, statistically significant, robust, and economically meaningful. The results imply that if Latin America as a whole could implement regulatory reforms that improve the quality of its corporate statements from its current value of 48 to the average for the Organization for Economic Cooperation and Development (OECD [65]) this would boost stock market liquidity and thereby accelerate real per capita GDP growth by 0.5 percentage points per year. This would be a very large impact, considering that median real per capita GDP growth for the whole sample is only about 1.9 percent. The limitations of the study are discussed in section IV.

Section V provides policy recommendations and attempts to go beyond the specific legal and regulatory variables used in this essay. There may be ways to improve the position of minority shareholders and the quality of published information on firms without fundamentally altering legal codes. These suggestions may offer practical avenues for boosting financial system development and growth.

I. Theory: Stock Markets and Economic Development

Finance and Growth: A Theoretical Overview

There are good theoretical reasons for believing that the financial system influences the rate of economic growth.[4] In a frictionless world, capital would flow toward the most profitable activities and it would be easy to write and enforce contracts that align the interests of managers and owners. Similarly, in a frictionless world individuals costlessly diversify and pool risks and easily find buyers or sellers for securities at well-known prices. But the world is not frictionless. There are large costs associated with researching firms. There are large information and contracting costs associated with monitoring managers and encouraging them to act in the best interests of firm owners.[5] It is expensive to mobilize capital from disparate savers. Furthermore, an array of costly contractual and institutional arrangements must arise to reduce the costs to savers and investors of pooling risks and trading securities. Financial contracts, markets, and intermediaries have emerged to mitigate the negative consequences of these information, transaction, and contracting costs.[6] These financial arrangements can reduce the adverse effects of market frictions on resource allocation and growth.

Countries have different financial systems due to differences in legal tradition, politics, policies, natural resource endowments, and perhaps historical accident. Financial systems differ in their ability to identify profitable ventures, mobilize capital to fund those ventures, monitor and create appropriate incentives for corporate managers, facilitate risk management and transactions, and augment the ease and confidence with which agents can exchange assets. These differences may have profound implications for economic growth.

Theoretical Issues: From Stock Market to Economic Growth

An important channel via which financial systems affect economic activity is through productivity. For example, Joseph Schumpeter ([1912] 1934, 74) argued that "the banker, therefore, is not so much primarily a middleman. . . . He authorises people, in the name of society as it were, [to innovate]." Thus, financial markets are not simply pipes via which funds flow. According to Schumpeter, better financial systems will find better-quality investments, so that better financial markets boost overall economic development by boosting productivity growth.

Better-functioning equity markets may also affect productivity. Many profitable investments require a long-term commitment of capital, but investors are often reluctant to relinquish control of their savings for long periods. Liquid equity markets make long-term investment more attractive because they allow savers to sell equities quickly and cheaply if they need access to their savings. At the same time, companies enjoy permanent access to capital raised through equity issues. By facilitating longer term, more profitable investments, liquid markets improve the allocation of capital and thereby boost productivity growth.[7]

Stock markets may also exert a positive impact on productivity growth by stimulating the acquisition of information about firms. Specifically, investors want to make a profit by identifying undervalued stocks and exploiting this information by buying or selling equities quickly and cheaply in liquid markets. If markets are liquid, this will create incentives for investors to evaluate firms energetically. Alternatively, if markets are illiquid, investors have fewer incentives to undertake the costly process of researching firms because they will not be confident about exploiting any information advantage they have garnered in the market.[8] Thus, by stimulating the acquisition of information about firms, liquid stock markets can improve the allocation of capital.

Adverse Implications of Stock Markets

Contentious theoretical debate exists, however, about the impact of financial systems in general and stock markets in particular on economic development.[9] Theory suggests that greater stock market liquidity has ambiguous effects on savings: if greater liquidity boosts the returns to investment, this increase in returns has ambiguous effects on saving rates due to well-known income and substitution effects. So, to the extent that financial development boosts investment returns, it is unclear what will happen to saving rates.[10]

Moreover, theoretical debate exists about whether greater stock market liquidity actually encourages a shift to higher-return projects that stimulate productivity growth. Since more liquidity makes it easier to sell shares, some argue that more liquidity reduces the incentives of shareholders to undertake the costly task of monitoring managers (Shleifer and Vishny 1986; Shleifer and Summers 1988; Bhide 1993). In turn, weaker corporate governance impedes effective resource allocation and slows productivity growth.

Theory: Stock Markets and Banks May Not Be Substitutes

Traditionally, development specialists have focused on banks, viewing stock markets as unimportant sideshows. They note that much more corporate capital is raised from banks than from equity issues. This traditional view ignores an important point: stock markets may provide different financial services from banks. Put differently, stock markets may positively affect economic development even though not much capital is raised through them. For instance, stock markets may play a more prominent role in easing the risk of trading and boosting liquidity. In contrast, banks may focus more on establishing long-run relationships with firms and monitoring managers. To grow, economies need both liquidity and information about managers and projects.

The point is not to draw too sharp a line between banks and markets. Like stock markets, banks help savers diversify risk and provide liquid deposits, which assists economic activity. Like banks, stock markets may stimulate the acquisition of information about firms because investors want to make a profit by identifying undervalued stocks. The point is simply to highlight the empirical nature of the questions at hand. Do stock markets boost economic development? Do stock markets boost economic development independently of the level of banking development? Are there interactions between stock markets and banks?

II. Evidence on Stock Markets, Banks, and Economic Growth

Substantial evidence supports the view that better financial systems in general and stock markets in particular boost economic growth. Levine (1997) compiles and analyzes this evidence. This section presents figures summarizing the main cross-country findings on stock markets and growth based on data on a maximum of forty-five countries over the period 1976–93.[11] The section also presents new evidence on the impact of primary market development on economic growth, in contrast to past work, which has focused exclusively on secondary market development. I also summarize microeconomic and time-series evidence regarding the link between stock markets and growth. Special attention is given to the joint role of banks and stock markets in facilitating economic development.

Measures of Stock Market Development

This essay uses two measures of stock market liquidity. The first equals the total value of the trades of domestic stock on domestic stock exchanges divided by GDP and is called *Value Traded*.[12] While it is not a direct measure of trading costs or the uncertainty associated with trading on a particular exchange, theoretical models of stock market liquidity and economic growth directly motivate Value Traded (Levine 1991; Bencivenga et al. 1995). Value Traded measures trading volume as a share of national output and should therefore positively reflect liquidity on an economywide basis. The value-traded ratio is likely to vary with the ease of trading: if it is costly and risky to trade, there will tend to be less trading.

The second measure of stock market liquidity, *Turnover*, equals the value of domestic shares traded on domestic exchanges divided by the value of listed shares. While Value Traded captures trading relative to the size of the economy, Turnover measures trading relative to the size of the market. Thus, a small, liquid market will have high Turnover but small Value Traded.

To measure the size of the secondary market, I use *Capitalization*, which equals the value of listed domestic shares on domestic exchanges divided by GDP. Although large markets do not necessarily function well, and taxes may distort incentives to list on the exchange, many observers use Capitalization as an indicator of market development.

To measure the size of the primary market, I use IPO, which equals the number of initial public offerings of shares in each country relative to the size of the population (in millions). While initial public offerings may reflect many phenomena, I wanted to get some indication of external equity financing. This measure is taken from La Porta et al. 1997. Whereas the other stock market indicators are available for the period 1976–93, IPO is measured only over the period mid-1995 to mid-1996 due to data availability.[13]

Finally, I use a measure termed stock return volatility. Specifically, *Volatility* is a twelve-month rolling standard deviation estimate that is based on market returns, where the return series is cleansed of monthly means, and twelve months of autocorrelations (Schwert 1989).

Liquidity and Growth

This subsection begins an assessment of whether developing country stock markets are simply casinos where an increasing number of foreigners are coming to place bets or whether the developing countries themselves reap large benefits from having access to liquid stock markets. The data suggest that stock markets are not simply casinos. There is a very strong link between stock market liquidity and future long-run growth.

Figure 1 shows that countries that had relatively liquid stock exchanges in 1976 tended to grow much faster over the next eighteen years. To illustrate this, I use Value Traded for the thirty-eight countries with data in 1976. The countries are first ranked by the liquidity of their stock markets. The first group has the nine most illiquid markets, the second group has the next ten most illiquid markets, the third group has the next ten, and the final group has the nine countries with the largest value-traded ratios. Figure 1 shows there is a systematic relationship between initial liquidity and future real per capita GDP growth.[14]

For developing countries, the returns to boosting stock market liquidity may be large. Here, it is important to note that the strong link between liquidity and growth remains strong even after controlling for cross-country differences in inflation, fiscal policy, political stability, education, the efficiency of the legal system, exchange rate policy, and openness to international trade, as shown in Levine and Zervos 1998a. Thus, it is not that stock market liquidity is merely highly correlated with the nonfinancial factors that are the real causes of economic growth. Raising stock market liquidity may independently produce big growth dividends. For example, regression analyses imply that if Mexico's value-traded ratio in 1976 had been the average of all thirty-eight countries (0.06 instead of 0.01), the average Mexican's income would be 8 percent greater today. This forecast must be viewed cautiously, however, since it does not specify *how* to enhance liquidity. Nevertheless, the example does illustrate the potentially large economic costs of policy, regulatory, and legal impediments to stock market development.

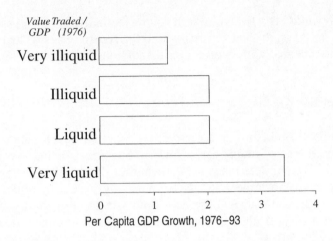

Fig. 1. **Stock market liquidity predicts growth**

Size, Volatility, and Growth

Other measures of stock market development do not tell the same story. For example, stock market size, as measured by market capitalization divided by GDP, is not a good predictor of future economic growth (fig. 2) and greater stock return volatility does not forecast poor economic performance (fig. 3). Countries with large stock markets appear to be no more likely to grow quickly than those with small ones. Nor does there seem to be a strong link between stock market volatility and economic growth. Liquidity—the ability to buy

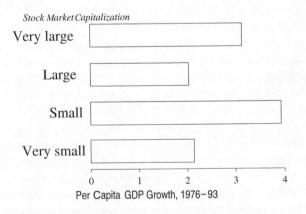

Fig. 2. **Market size does not predict growth**

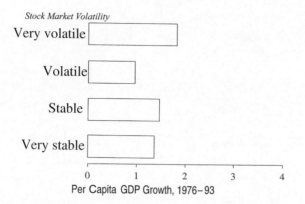

Fig. 3. **Market volatility does not predict growth**

and sell equities easily—is what exhibits the strong connection to long-run growth.

IPOs and Growth

This essay also examines for the first time the relationship between the primary equity market and long-run growth. With the full sample of countries, there is not a clear positive link between IPO and growth, as illustrated in figure 4. This lack of a strong link is supported by regression analyses that control for other country characteristics. However, it is important to note that two countries skew these results. Taiwan and Korea are the fastest growers but have virtually no recorded IPO activity over the limited time period for which there are data. If these two countries are omitted, the positive relationship between growth and IPO becomes stronger, as shown in table 1. Table 1 presents regression results of average annual real per capita GDP growth over the 1976–93 period (GROWTH) on IPO, while controlling for an assortment of other country characteristics. There is one observation per country. I follow the standard cross-country growth literature in controlling for a range of other country characteristics (e.g., Barro and Sala-i-Martin 1995; Easterly and Levine 1997; and Levine and Renelt 1992). In regression 1, I control for the logarithm of initial real per capita GDP (Income), the logarithm of secondary school enrollment (Enrollment), and the number of revolutions and coups per year (Revolutions). Regression 2 also includes the average annual inflation rate (Inflation) and the ratio of central government spending to GDP (Government). Regression 3

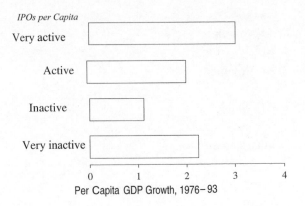

IPOs per Capita

Very active

Active

Inactive

Very inactive

Per Capita GDP Growth, 1976–93

Fig. 4. Primary market activity and growth

TABLE 1. Primary Market Activity and Growth, 1976–93

| | Dependent Variable: Average per Capita GDP Growth, 1976–93 | | |
	1	2	3
c	0.116	0.117	0.124
	(3.43)	(2.89)	(4.23)
Initial Income	−0.017	−0.017	−0.005
	−(2.56)	−(2.24)	−(0.62)
Enrollment	0.012	0.012	−0.012
	(0.98)	(0.97)	−(0.97)
Revolutions	−0.022	−0.022	−0.017
	−(2.74)	−(2.50)	−(2.77)
Inflation		0.000	0.002
		−(0.35)	(2.46)
Government		−0.007	−0.001
		−(0.16)	−(4.60)
Black Market Premium			−0.058
			−(1.32)
IPO	0.004	0.004	0.003
	(2.21)	(2.09)	(1.78)
P-value	{0.035}	{0.046}	{0.087}
R^2	0.38	0.38	0.71

Notes: Number of observations = 34. These regressions omit Korea and Taiwan. IPO = initial public offerings per million population; Initial Income = logarithm of Initial real per capita GDP; Enrollment = logarithm of initial secondary school enrollment; Revolutions = number of revolutions and coups per year; Inflation = average annual inflation rate; Government = central government expenditures as a share of GDP; Black Market Premium = average black market premium.

also adds the average annual black market exchange rate premium (Black Market Premium).

In table 1, IPO is positively and significantly correlated with economic growth in regressions 1 and 2 at the 5 percent significance level when Taiwan and Korea are excluded. When also controlling for Black Market Premium, the *P*-values rise to 0.087. This suggestive though still inconclusive evidence calls for further study of the ties between long-run growth and primary market development. In sum, the above analysis focuses the growth spotlight on stock market liquidity and leaves, at least for now, other characteristics of stock markets in the shadows.

Stock Markets, Banks, and Growth

This analysis may elicit the following skeptical inquiry. Is there really an independent link between stock market liquidity and growth or is stock market development merely highly correlated with banking sector development? Perhaps banks are the real financial engines of growth and stock markets are mere sideshows. Indeed, figure 5 shows that countries with well-developed banking systems—as measured by bank loans to private enterprises as a share of GDP—tend to grow faster than countries with underdeveloped banks.[15]

Empirically, the effect of stock markets on growth can be distinguished from the impact of banking development. To show this, the thirty-eight countries were divided into four groups. The first group had greater than median stock market liquidity (as measured by Value Traded) in 1976 and greater than median banking development. Group 2 had liquid stock markets in 1976 but less than median banking development. Group 3 had less than median stock market liquidity in 1976 but well-developed banks. Group 4 had illiquid stock markets in 1976 and less than median banking development.

Countries with both liquid stock markets and well-developed banks grew faster than countries with both illiquid markets and underdeveloped banks (fig. 6). More interestingly, greater stock market liquidity implies faster growth regardless of the level of banking development. Similarly, greater banking development implies faster growth regardless of the level of stock market liquidity. If one uses Turnover, one gets the same results. Moreover, after controlling for other country characteristics such as initial income, schooling, political stability, and monetary, fiscal, trade, and exchange rate policies, the data still indicate that there is a strong link to growth for each of

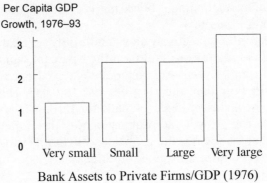

Per Capita GDP
Growth, 1976–93

Bank Assets to Private Firms/GDP (1976)

Fig. 5.   Size of banking sector predicts growth

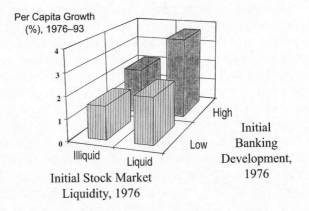

Per Capita Growth
(%), 1976–93

Initial Stock Market
Liquidity, 1976

Initial Banking Development, 1976

Fig. 6.   Growth, stock markets, and banks

the two measures of financial sector development (as shown in Levine and Zervos 1998a).

Growth: Potential Interactions between Banks and Markets

The strong, positive link between economic growth and both stock market and banking sector development suggests a two-part question about the interactions between stock markets and banks.

Will an increase in banking development have a bigger (smaller) impact on growth in the presence of a relatively well developed stock market and will an increase in stock market development have a bigger (smaller) impact on growth in the presence of a relatively well developed banking sector?

To study this question, I used interaction terms. Specifically, let SMI stand for Stock Market Indicator, which can equal Capitalization, IPO, Value Traded, or Turnover. Let Bank equal the bank development indicator, that is, bank credit to the private sector divided by GDP. Finally, let X equal a matrix of control variables such as initial income, the level of schooling, and indicators of political stability as well as monetary, fiscal, trade, and exchange rate policies. Then the following cross-country regressions were run.

$$\text{GROWTH} = a(X) + b(\text{SMI}) + c(\text{Bank}) + d(\text{SMI*Bank}) + u,$$

where u is the regression residual. If the coefficient, d, on the interaction term, SMI*Bank, is positive, this would imply that an increase in stock market development, SMI, would have a bigger positive impact on Growth for a higher level of banking development. This was not the case, however. In all specifications, the coefficient on the interaction term, d, was highly insignificant. Taken together with the findings reported earlier, the data suggest that stock markets and banks are positively associated with growth. The data do not support the view that an improvement in stock market development will positively affect growth *more* in a country with a well-developed banking system. In sum, it is not stock markets *versus* banks; it is stock markets *and* banks. Each of these components of the financial system is an independently strong predictor of growth.

Other Evidence

Although I will present new evidence on causality, it is worth highlighting the results of a growing body of empirical literature. Using different empirical methodologies, a variety of authors present evidence consistent with the view that finance causes growth. Taking a microeconomic approach, Rajan and Zingales (1998) show that, in countries with well-developed financial systems industries that are naturally heavy users of external financing grow relatively faster than other industries. Alternatively, in countries with poorly developed financial systems industries that are naturally heavy users of external financing grow more slowly than other industries. Furthermore, Demirgüç-Kunt and Maksimovic (1988) show that firms in countries with better-developed financial systems grow faster than they could have grown without this access. Also, in an innovative event study, Jayaratne and Strahan (1996) show that when individual states of the United States relaxed intrastate branching restrictions, the quality of bank loans rose and per capita GDP growth accelerated. Furthermore, Levine (1998, 1999), using instrumental variables to extract the exogenous component of financial development, shows that the exogenous component of financial development is strongly, positively correlated with economic growth. On causality, Hansson and Jonung (n.d.), Neusser and Kugler (1998), Rousseau and Wachtel (1998a), and Wachtel and Rousseau (1995) find that financial intermediation Granger-causes economic performance. Levine, Loayza, and Beck (2000) and Beck, Levine, and Loayza (2000) use dynamic panel econometric procedures to control for both potential endogeneity and omitted variable biases. They show that financial development exerts a causal impact on economic growth. Rousseau and Wachtel (1998b) use time-series procedures and show that equity market development causes growth. Finally, the microeconomic studies of Rajan and Zingales (1998) and Demirgüç-Kunt and Maksimovic (1998) also suggest a causal link running from financial development to economic growth. Thus, while there is still some room for skepticism, a growing and diverse literature is consistent with the view that better financial systems cause faster economic growth.

III. The Legal Environment and Stock Market Development

Since the financial system importantly influences economic development, policymakers have a responsibility to implement legal, regulatory, and policy reforms that promote healthy financial sector development. In turn, researchers have a responsibility to identify legal, regulatory, and policy reforms that promote healthy financial sector development. This section examines the relationship between the legal/accounting environment and stock market development. Specifically, I quantify the link between stock market development and (1) measures of the legal treatment of shareholders and (2) the effectiveness of the accounting system in providing comprehensive and comparable information about firms to investors. Finally, I trace the link from the legal and regulatory environment through stock market development and on to economic growth. Specifically, I study whether the exogenous component of stock market development—the component of stock market development associated with the legal and regulatory environment—explains long-run economic growth.

Overview

As described by Glendon et al. (1982) and Berman (1983), Roman law was compiled under the direction of the Byzantine emperor Justinian in the sixth century. As particular problems arose throughout Europe during subsequent centuries, Roman law was adapted and modified. Eventually, individual countries formalized individual legal codes. In the seventeenth and eighteenth centuries, the Scandinavian countries codified their national laws. The Scandinavian legal system has remained relatively unaffected by the sweeping influences of the German and especially English and French legal traditions.

The English legal tradition is not a civil law heritage. Under a civil law system, legal scholars play a leading role in shaping laws. In the Common Law—English—legal tradition, laws are heavily influenced by judges trying to resolve particular cases. Common Law was spread through conquest and colonization to various corners of the globe.

Napoleon directed the writing of the French Civil Code in 1804. The Civil Code is relatively short and meant to be accessible to the general public. Napoleon was very proud of the Civil Code and saw its permanence as more important than the fleeting nature of his military conquests. He made it a priority to secure its adoption in all conquered territories. Thus, the code was adopted in Italy, Poland, the Low Countries, and the Hapsburg Empire. France extended its legal influence during the colonial era to parts of the Near East, northern and sub-Saharan Africa, Indochina, Oceania, French Guiana, and the French Caribbean islands. Furthermore, the French Civil Code shaped the Portuguese and Spanish legal systems, with obvious implications for Central and South America.

Almost a century later, Bismarck directed the writing of the German Civil Code, a massive effort that began in 1871 and was completed in 1896. The German Civil Code has no parallel in terms of comprehensiveness and detail. It shaped the legal systems of Austria, China, Hungary, Japan, and Switzerland. Through China and Japan, it also exerted a powerful influence on the legal traditions of Korea and Taiwan.

La Porta et al. (1998) categorize countries as having predominantly English, French, German, or Scandinavian legal origins, based on the work of legal scholars. Since the English, French, and German systems were spread primarily through conquest and imperialism, I view legal origin as an exogenous "endowment" in studying the relationship between the legal system and financial sector development.

La Porta et al. (1998) show that legal origin materially influences both the legal treatment of shareholders and regulations governing corporate information. English law countries have laws that emphasize the rights of minority shareholders to a greater degree than the French, German, and Scandinavian countries. French civil law countries protect shareholders the least, with German and Scandinavian civil law countries falling in the middle. In terms of regulations governing corporate information disclosure, countries with a French legal heritage have the lowest quality information. La Porta et al. also examine the quality of law enforcement; while legal codes are important, effectively and efficiently enforcing those laws is critical for financial sector operations. They find that countries with a French legal heritage have the lowest quality of law enforcement, while countries with German and Scandinavian legal traditions tend to be the best at enforcing contracts. Thus, legal heritage importantly shapes the current legal/regulatory environment governing financial sector transactions.

1. The legal environment: Data.   Consider the connection between the legal protection of minority shareholders and the liquidity of equity markets. Conceptually, legal systems that protect shareholders, especially minority shareholders, encourage greater participation. Shareholders exercise their power by voting for directors. Thus, to quantify the legal treatment of shareholders I use five measures of their voting rights.[16]

PROXY equals one if shareholders can choose to vote by either showing up in person (or sending an authorized representative) or mailing in their vote. PROXY equals zero if shareholders cannot vote by mail. This can impede shareholder participation because they must either attend the meeting or go through the legal procedure of designating an authorized representative.

CUMULATIVE equals one if the company law or commercial code allows shareholders to cast all their votes for one candidate, and zero otherwise. The ability to vote all of one's shares for one candidate may make it easier for minority shareholders to put their representatives on boards of directors.

BLOCKED equals one if the company law or commercial code

does *not* allow firms to require that shareholders deposit their shares prior to a general shareholders' meeting, thus preventing them from selling those shares for a number of days, and zero otherwise. When shares are blocked in this manner, the shares are kept in custody until a few days after the meeting. This practice prevents shareholders who do not bother to go through this arduous exercise from voting.

MINOR equals one if the company law or commercial code grants minority shareholders either a judicial venue in which to challenge the management decisions or the right to step out of the company by requiring the company to purchase their shares when they object to certain fundamental changes (such as mergers, asset dispositions, and changes in the articles of incorporation). The variable equals zero otherwise.

MEETING equals one if a shareholder is entitled to call for an extraordinary shareholders' meeting with a minimum percentage of ownership share capital of less than 10 percent; it is zero otherwise. The minimum percentage of ownership share capital that entitles a shareholder to call for an extraordinary shareholders' meeting ranges from 1 to 33 percent, with a median of 10 percent. Mexico has the highest value in the sample of countries. Presumably, the harder it is for minority shareholders to call a meeting and contest management the less attractive it will be for agents to participate in equity markets.

SRIGHTS aggregates these five indicators into a conglomerate index of shareholder rights.

2. The regulatory/accounting environment: Data. Besides the legal rights of shareholders, it is important to consider the availability of information about firms. Information about corporations is critical for exerting corporate governance and identifying the best investments. These activities will be facilitated by accounting standards that simplify the interpretability and comparability of information across corporations. Furthermore, many types of financial contracting use accounting measures to trigger particular actions. These types of contracts can only be enforced, and will only be used, if accounting measures are reasonably unambiguous. Since accurate information about corporations may improve financial contracting and intermediation, this section examines the quality, comprehensiveness, and comparability of information disclosed through corporate accounts using a measure from La Porta et al. 1998. Accounting standards differ across countries, and governments impose an assortment of regulations regarding information disclosure and accounting standards.

Thus, measures of the quality of information in corporate financial statements also reflect the regulatory system.

ACCOUNT is an index of the comprehensiveness and quality of company reports. The maximum possible value is ninety and the minimum is zero. The Center for International Financial Analysis and Research assessed general accounting information, income statements, balance sheets, funds flow statements, accounting standards, and stock data in company reports in 1990. Given the importance of information in financial contracting, I expect ACCOUNT to be positively correlated with stock market activity.

3. Summary statistics on the legal and accounting environment. Table 2 provides summary statistics on SRIGHTS and ACCOUNT. The data are sorted by region. There is substantial cross-country variation, where the maximum value is 5, the minimum value is 0, and the standard deviation is about 1.2. Belgium, Italy, and Mexico (all countries with a French-origin legal system) are countries where SRIGHTS equals the minimum value of 0, indicating that their legal systems do not stress the rights of minority shareholders. In contrast, the legal codes of the United States stress the rights of shareholders, such that SRIGHTS = 5.

The French legal tradition is clearly evident in Latin America. This region's legal system places comparatively less emphasis on the legal rights of shareholders, particularly minority shareholders, than those of other regions do (table 2). The average value of the SRIGHTS indicator of the legal protection of shareholders equals two in Latin America, which is the same as in France and about equal to the average of French civil law countries (table 3). It is also important to note the cross–Latin America variation. The legal codes of Argentina, Brazil, and Chile place a comparatively high priority on minority shareholder rights, while Colombia, Mexico, and Venezuela are far below the international average.

As with other French civil law countries, Latin America tends to provide less comprehensive and comparable information about corporations to investors, as shown by the low value of ACCOUNT in table 2. The Latin American average of forty-eight is about the same as the average for all French civil law countries, fifty-one (table 3).

Latin America's comparatively weak legal protection of shareholders and its relatively uninformative accounting systems evidently have a price: comparatively poor stock markets. Latin America's stock markets over the period tended to be smaller (Capitalization,

TABLE 2. Summary Statistics by Country Groups

Region	SRIGHTS	ACCOUNT	ENFORCE	CAPITALIZATION	IPO	VALUE TRADED	TOR[a]	VOLATILITY
East Asia	2.86	69.00	7.44	0.61	2.06	0.36	0.67	0.09
Latin America	2.00	48.43	5.13	0.16	0.11	0.02	0.23	0.14
Argentina	4	45	6.31	0.05	0.20	0.01	0.27	0.31
Brazil	3	54	6.91	0.21	0.00	0.04	0.36	0.20
Chile	3	52	4.55	0.40	0.35	0.02	0.06	0.06
Colombia	1	50	5.95	0.06	0.05	0.00	0.09	0.06
Mexico	0	60	3.59	0.13	0.03	0.04	0.50	0.11
Peru	2	38	6.34		0.13	0.00		
Venezuela	1	40	5.54	0.09	0.00	0.01	0.09	0.08
OECD	2.33	65.48	9.07	0.29	1.17	0.12	0.29	0.05
Sub-Saharan Africa	3.25	64.50	4.82	0.48	0.05	0.02	0.04	0.08
Other	2.67	52.50	4.79	0.21	1.10	0.05	0.30	0.05

[a]Turnover Ratio.

IPO) less active (Value Traded), and more volatile (Volatility) than the markets of other regions of the world, as shown in table 2. Finally, a general index of the efficiency of the legal system in enforcing contracts (ENFORCE) is also notably lower in Latin America. As emphasized by La Porta et al. (1997, 1998), these tendencies can be traced back to Latin America's French legal heritage, as illustrated by table 2.

Regressions of Stock Market Size on Legal and Accounting Variables

Table 3 presents cross-country regressions that examine more rigorously the connection between the legal rights of shareholders, the accounting regime, and stock market size. The dependent variable is either Capitalization or IPO. As regressors, each of the regressions

TABLE 3.   The Legal Determinants of Market Size

	Dependent Variable					
	Capitalization			IPO		
Independent Variable	(1)	(2)	(3)	(1)	(2)	(3)
c	−0.72	−0.28	−0.49	−5.34	−4.82	−5.56
	(0.296)	(0.469)	(0.439)	(2.068)	(2.391)	(2.486)
	{0.020}	{0.556}	{0.276}	{0.014}	{0.052}	{0.032}
INCOME	0.09	−0.04	−0.01	0.58	0.22	0.32
	(0.034)	(0.064)	(0.063)	(0.235)	(0.281)	(0.307)
	{0.011}	{0.534}	{0.818}	{0.018}	{0.444}	{0.309}
SRIGHTS	0.10		0.08	0.59		0.42
	(0.036)		(0.032)	(0.160)		(0.149)
	{0.006}		{0.016}	{0.001}		{0.009}
ACCOUNT		0.02	0.01		0.07	0.05
		(0.005)	(0.004)		(0.019)	(0.019)
		{0.002}	{0.010}		{0.002}	{0.019}
Number of observations	44	39	39	41	37	37
R^2	0.21	0.28	0.36	0.3	0.3	0.38

Note: Standard errors appear in parentheses. *P*-values are in braces.

includes a constant and INCOME. I control for INCOME since the overall level of economic development may influence stock market size. I want to isolate the relationship between market size and both the legal rights of shareholders, SRIGHTS, and the quality of corporate financial statements, ACCOUNT. Regression 1 includes the constant, INCOME, and SRIGHTS. Regression 2 includes a constant, INCOME, and ACCOUNT. Regression 3 includes all of the explanatory variables.

The data indicate a strong link between SRIGHTS and AC-COUNT. Both SRIGHTS and ACCOUNT enter all of the regressions with positive and significant coefficients (at the 0.05 level). Even after controlling for the level of real per capita GDP, countries with legal systems that emphasize the rights of shareholders—especially minority shareholders—enjoy larger markets. Similarly, countries that have regulatory/accounting regimes that produce comparable and comprehensive information about firms tend to have larger stock markets. The data also suggest that the links are economically large. For instance, a one standard deviation increase in ACCOUNT (12) translates into a 0.144 rise in Capitalization ($0.144 = 12 \times 0.12$), which is a bit less than the median value of Capitalization (0.19).

Regression of Stock Market Liquidity on Legal and Accounting Variables

The data also indicate a strong link between stock market liquidity and the availability of high-quality information about firms. As shown in table 4, there is a statistically significant relationship between ACCOUNT and the two measures of stock market liquidity, Value Traded and Turnover, when controlling for the legal rights of shareholders. In contrast, shareholder rights do not have a very robust link with stock market liquidity. This differs from the results reported in table 3, where SRIGHTS were strongly linked to market size. Thus, good information (ACCOUNT) is strongly linked to both market size and liquidity, while SRIGHTS is strongly associated with overall market *size* (table 3) but not with market *activity*. These findings highlight the importance of good regulations governing information disclosure.[17]

Furthermore, the relationship between ACCOUNT and liquidity is economically meaningful. For example, a one standard deviation increase in ACCOUNT (12) increases Value Traded by 0.058 ($0.058 =$

0.0048×12), which is about the median value of Value Traded in the sample (0.054). Although the R^2 in each of these regressions is low, about 10 percent, the legal and accounting variables do help account for cross-country variations in stock market size and liquidity.

Before continuing, it is critical to note that SRIGHTS is not merely a proxy for the overall quality of a country's legal system. As shown by Levine (1998, 1999), legal variables that define the rights of creditors are closely connected to banking sector development. But SRIGHTS is *not* highly correlated with banking sector development, nor are the legal rights of creditors highly correlated with stock market development. Thus, these legal variables are capturing particular aspects of the legal environment. They are not proxying for overall legal efficiency.

TABLE 4. The Legal Determinants of Market Liquidity

Independent Variable	Dependent Variable					
	Value Traded			Turnover		
	(1)	(2)	(3)	(4)	(5)	(6)
c	−0.32	−0.05	−0.11	0.03	0.59	0.60
	(0.172)	(0.320)	(0.308)	(0.379)	(0.594)	(0.585)
	{0.074}	{0.884}	{0.731}	{0.929}	{0.331}	{0.308}
INCOME	0.04	−0.02	−0.01	0.03	−0.08	−0.08
	(0.021)	(0.044)	(0.043)	(0.043)	(0.083)	(0.081)
	{0.058}	{0.651}	{0.765}	{0.504}	{0.349}	{0.327}
SRIGHTS	0.04		0.02	0.02		−0.01
	(0.017)		(0.017)	(0.027)		(0.027)
	{0.037}		{0.194}	{0.567}		{0.786}
ACCOUNT		0.01	0.00		0.01	0.01
		(0.002)	(0.002)		(0.003)	(0.003
		{0.005}	{0.013}		{0.052}	{0.037}
Number of observations	45	40	40	44	39	39
R^2	0.08	0.1	0.12	0.01	0.05	0.05

Note: Standard errors appear in parentheses. *P*-values are in braces. Income = logarithm of real per capita GDP in 1976; SRIGHTS = an index of the legal rights of shareholders, especially minority shareholders, that takes values between 0 and 5; Account = an index of the comprehensiveness and comparability of corporate financial statements; Value Traded = total value of shares traded divided by GDP; Turnover = total value of shares traded divided by Capitalization.

Linking Legal and Regulatory Environment to Stock Market and Then to Growth

Thus far, I have explored two distinct links in the chain running from policy levers to economic growth. First, there is a growing abundance of evidence that better-functioning stock markets are associated with more rapid economic growth. Second, there are particular characteristics of legal and regulatory systems that promote better-functioning stock markets. Latin American countries, perhaps because of their French legal heritage, tend to have legal and regulatory (accounting) systems that discourage stock market development. The general implication of these findings is that policymakers can promote economic development with legal and regulatory changes that bolster the legal rights of shareholders and encourage firms to publish comparable and comprehensive financial statements. The analysis, however, has not yet put the two links of the chain together.

This subsection uses instrumental variable procedures to determine whether the exogenous component of stock market development is linked to long-run growth. Specifically, I examine whether the component of stock market development defined by the legal and regulatory regime is positively associated with economic growth. As instrumental variables, I use the SRIGHTS and ACCOUNT variables defined earlier. The basic regression takes the form:

$$\text{GROWTH} = \alpha + \beta \text{SMI} + \gamma \mathbf{X} + \varepsilon, \tag{1}$$

where the dependent variable, GROWTH, is real per capita GDP growth over the 1976–93 period; SMI is either Value Traded, Turnover, Capitalization, or IPO; and **X** represents a matrix of conditioning information that controls for other factors associated with economic growth. I use SRIGHTS and ACCOUNT as instrumental variables for each of the SMI indicators and use a generalized method of moments (GMM) estimator.

To control for "other factors," I include three different conditioning information sets.[18] Conditioning information set 1 includes a constant plus the logarithm of initial per capita GDP, the logarithm of initial secondary school enrollment, and the number of revolutions and coups.[19] Conditioning information set 2 includes these variables plus the ratio of government spending to GDP, inflation, and the black market exchange rate premium. Conditioning information set 3 includes all the control variables in conditioning information set 2 plus Bank, which equals bank credit to the private sector divided by GDP.

The results indicate a strong, positive relationship between the exogenous component of stock market development and economic growth. Table 5 summarizes the results from twelve GMM regressions: three regressions, based on the three conditioning information sets, for each of the four stock market indicators: Value Traded, Turnover, Capitalization, and IPO. Table 5 presents only coefficient estimates on the stock market indicators and not the results on the other regressors. For the simple conditioning information set (1), table 6 provides the full regression results.

After controlling for a wide array of factors, the exogenous component of Value Traded, Capitalization, and IPO all enter the growth regression with coefficients that are significant at the 0.05 level, and Turnover is significant at the 0.10 level. Tests of the overidentifying restrictions support the econometric specification. Specifically, the tests indicate that shareholder rights and accounting system quality do not affect growth other than through stock market development and the other explanatory variables. I am not claiming that the legal system affects growth only through financial market development. The results do, however, suggest that simultaneity bias is not driving

TABLE 5.   Stock Markets and Growth: Using Instrumental Variables

SMI	Conditioning Information Set 1	Conditioning Information Set 2	Conditioning Information Set 3
Value Traded	0.056**	0.056**	0.060**
	(0.023)	(0.023)	(0.024)
Turnover	0.059*	0.060*	0.059*
	(0.031)	(0.033)	(0.030)
Capitalization	0.03**	0.032**	0.033**
	(0.011)	(0.011)	(0.011)
IPO	0.005*	0.005**	0.006**
	(0.002)	(0.002)	(0.002)

Notes: Growth = a + B[matrix of conditioning information] + c(SMI). Instruments: matrix of conditioning information plus SRIGHTS and ACCOUNT. SMI is alternatively Value Traded, Turnover, Capitalization, and IPO.

Conditioning information set 1: logarithm of initial income per capita, logarithm of initial secondary school enrollment, and number of revolutions and coups. Conditioning information set 2: conditioning information set 1 plus the initial values of government spending divided by GDP, inflation, and the black market exchange rate premium. Conditioning information set 3: set 2 plus initial value of bank credit to the private sector divided by GDP. Estimation was performed using the generalized method of moments.

** indicates significant at the .05 level; * indicates significant at the .10 level.

the strong positive relationship between equity market development and long-run growth.

Moreover, the strong link between the exogenous component of stock market development and growth holds using alternative instrumental variables. Table 7 presents the results of using the dummy variables for legal origin (English, French, or German) as instrumental variables without using SRIGHTS and ACCOUNT. The findings with these alternative instruments are very similar to those reported in table 5, except that IPO no longer enters significantly and Turnover's *P*-value falls below 0.05. The stock market indicators of secondary market development are robustly correlated with economic growth. The exogenous component of stock market development—*the component of stock market development defined by the legal environment*—is positively associated with long-run economic growth. These instrumental variable regressions also pass the test of the overidentifying restrictions, so that the econometric specification is consistent with the data. Simultaneity biases are not driving the results; the data suggest that equity market development exerts a causal impact on economic growth.

The linkages from the regulatory regime through stock market

TABLE 6.   Stock Markets and Growth: Full Instrumental Variable Results Instruments, Conditioning Information Set, Plus SRIGHTS and ACCOUNT

	Regression			
	1	2	3	4
c	0.105	0.095	0.134	0.167
	{0.009}	{0.033}	{0.001}	{0.017}
Logarithm of initial GDP	−0.017	−0.018	−0.023	−0.033
per capita	{0.028}	{0.023}	{0.001}	{0.014}
Logarithm of initial	0.015	0.017	0.021	0.035
secondary school enrollment	{0.107}	{0.081}	{0.010}	{0.053}
Number of revolutions	−0.023	−0.025	−0.029	−0.037
and coups	{0.021}	{0.006}	{0.000}	{0.006}
Value Traded	0.056			
	{0.004}			
Turnover		0.059		
		{0.064}		
Capitalization			0.030	
			{0.009}	
IPO				0.005
				{0.073}

Note: *P*-values are in braces. They were estimated using the generalized method of moments.

liquidity to long-run growth are economically meaningful. For example, the results imply that if Argentina implemented regulatory changes that improved the quality of corporate financial statements from the recorded value of forty-five to the average for OECD countries (sixty-five), the growth would be 0.6 percentage points faster per year. This is quite large, considering that Argentina's real per capita GDP growth averaged only about 0.2 percentage points per year over this period. Furthermore, after a decade, 0.6 percentage points faster per capita GDP growth implies that each Argentinean would be earning 6 percent more *per year*. (This is meant to be illustrative: since the analysis does not consider any country in detail, the coefficients should not be applied to any individual country.) This example serves to demonstrate the large potential costs, measured in slower long-run growth, of permitting poor information disclosure to persist.

IV. Cautionary Notes

It is important to be clear about what these results do *not* show.

First, the essay does *not* show that economic growth does not influence stock markets. The results do not contradict the argument that causality runs in both directions: financial development influences economic growth, and economic growth influences financial

TABLE 7. Stock Markets and Growth: Alternative Instrumental Variables

SMI	Conditioning Information Set 1	Conditioning Information Set 2	Conditioning Information Set 3
Value Traded	0.066**	0.062**	0.063**
	(0.024)	(0.023)	(0.025)
Turnover	0.036**	0.033**	0.032**
	(0.015)	(0.013)	(0.014)
Capitalization	0.023**	0.024**	0.024**
	(0.011)	(0.011)	(0.010)
IPO	0.002	0.001	0.003
	(0.003)	(0.003)	(0.002)

Notes: Growth = $a + B$[matrix of conditioning information] + c(SMI). Instruments: matrix of conditioning information plus legal origin dummy variables. SMI is alternatively Value Traded, Turnover, Capitalization, and IPO.

Conditioning information set 1: logarithm of initial income per capita, logarithm of initial secondary school enrollment, and number of revolutions and coups. Conditioning information set 2: conditioning information set 1 plus the initial values of government spending divided by GDP, inflation, and the black market exchange rate premium. Conditioning information set 3: set 2 plus initial value of bank credit to the private sector divided by GDP. Estimation was performed using the generalized method of moments.

** indicates significant at the .05 level; * indicates significant at the .10 level.

sector development. Rather, this essay provides evidence for the hypothesis that the exogenous component of stock market development itself promotes economic growth.

Second, this essay does not examine a slew of factors that may influence the operation of stock markets. For instance, a wide range of regulations influence stock market activity beyond those summarized by SRIGHTS and ACCOUNT. These range from listing requirements to requirements governing the trading of securities, supervision of broker/dealers, and so forth. Furthermore, the essay does not consider differences in the organization and trading technologies of individual exchanges. Market microstructure may importantly influence stock market development. These factors were omitted due to data availability, not potential relevance.

This essay makes a more limited argument: legal heritage is closely linked to the legal rights of shareholders and the quality of corporate financial statements, legal and accounting characteristics influence stock market size and liquidity, and the exogenous component of stock market development is strongly linked with long-run rates of economic growth.

Third, the empirical results in conjunction with the theoretical overview do not imply that every country needs its own active bourse. Conceptually, firms and savers benefit from easy access to liquid stock markets. It is the ability to trade and issue securities easily that facilitates long-term growth, not the geographical location of the market. Thus, capital control liberalization may improve the ability of firms to raise capital both by improving the liquidity of domestic exchanges and by providing greater access to foreign exchanges.[20]

Fourth, as noted earlier, this essay uses cross-country comparisons; it does not examine any single country in depth.[21] Thus, while the essay has very clear policy implications, these must be viewed as illuminating a reform strategy. It does not offer a precise blueprint. Nonetheless, the results—and therefore the policy implications— jump out. Particular characteristics of the legal and regulatory environment are strongly linked to how well the stock exchange operates, with important spillovers for economic development.

Finally, many things are changing in Latin America, and "Latin America" is of course not a single entity. By making broad international comparisons, I do not focus on inter–Latin American differences. For example, while Mexico has comparatively good accounting standards, the quality of the financial statements for the rest of the countries of Latin America average almost two standard deviations below the international mean. Nevertheless, the strong connections between its Napoleonic legal heritage, its generally weak legal and regulatory framework, its comparatively poorly developed markets, and its less than desirable rate of growth certainly make this analysis as relevant for Latin America as for any other region. It is also true that many countries have engaged in serious reforms so as to improve the operations of their markets. (Nonetheless, the time period does not seem to dictate the results. For example, if one considers only the 1990s, Latin America still suffers in international comparisons.) For those countries that have already implemented reforms to boost shareholder rights, improve information availability, and enhance the operation of stock exchanges, this essay can be viewed as encouragement for an effort already begun rather than suggesting a new direction for policy reform.

V. Conclusions and Policy Tips

The essay shows that particular characteristics of national legal and regulatory systems—the protection of minority shareholders and the quality of corporate financial statements—exert a major influence on stock market development. Stock markets, in turn, help determine the rate of long-run growth. Walter Bagehot argued in the mid-1800s that only an excellent financial system can funnel capital to those enterprises that spur economic growth ([1873] 1962). This essay builds on the work of La Porta et al. (1997) to show that legal and regulatory systems play an enormous role in determining the excellence of a financial system. Thus, governments can augment capital market development by protecting the rights of minority shareholders and by encouraging corporations to publish high-quality, comparable financial statements.

The essay also shows that Latin America stands out. It tends to have relatively weak accounting standards, and its legal systems are comparatively lax in enforcing the rights of minority shareholders. In light of the strong empirical connection between the legal and regulatory environments, the financial system, and growth, Latin America's legal and regulatory systems stand out as deserving careful scrutiny as the region seeks to promote faster growth.

These results also have implications for legal reform in Eastern Europe, the former Soviet republics, and other countries. Laws, enforcement mechanisms, and accounting systems make a significant difference in developing capital markets, with consequent repercussions on long-run growth. Governments interested in economic development therefore have an important role to play in defining and enforcing property rights and encouraging the dissemination of sound information. Legal traditions that stress the rights of shareholders and promote sound accounting standards appear to offer tangible benefits over alternative legal systems.

This analysis supports a two-pronged reform strategy. First, the results motivate a detailed evaluation of the legal treatment of minority shareholders, together with regulatory and policy changes that can improve the quality, comparability, and comprehensiveness of information about corporations. Improvements along these lines may offer substantial growth dividends.

The second prong—since it is very difficult to change legal codes—searches for other means of boosting the position of minority shareholders and fostering better accounting standards. For instance, stock exchanges can promote better corporate governance through their listing requirements. As a condition to having its securities traded on the exchange, a company can be required to adopt more effective means of protecting minority shareholders. These might include (1) requiring greater information disclosure by listed companies (both periodic reporting and timely disclosure of special events, including transactions with affiliates), (2) imposing tighter accounting standards, and (3) creating and promoting standards for arbitration of shareholder claims (and perhaps sponsoring its own arbitration system). Further, regulators and exchange officials could encourage companies to incorporate into their articles of incorporation or by-laws important minority shareholder protections that go beyond those currently required by law. These additional provisions can include (1) outside (nonmanagement) director requirements, (2) disclosure of related party transactions and management compensation, (3) supermajority or outside director approval for transactions with related parties, (4) rotation of outside independent auditors, (5) periodic reporting by outside auditors to shareholders, and (6) mandatory private arbitration of disputes between shareholders and the company/management.[22]

Looking forward, much research remains to be done. This essay's aggregate, cross-country approach should be complemented with detailed case studies. For Latin America, it is unrealistic and probably unwise to toss out the French Commercial Code and start again. Nonetheless, parts of Canada and the United States (Louisiana) have successfully modified their legal approaches to financial contracting;

more recently, Argentina has enacted major changes in its legal treatment of shareholders. Detailed information on successes and failures will help foster more successes in the future. To make sound policy recommendations, we also need more data: comprehensive cross-country data on the costs associated with primary and secondary market activities; extensive cross-country information on listing requirements and the full range of securities markets regulations, so as to compare the efficacy of different approaches; and information on primary market offerings in equity and bond markets, so as to investigate the links between secondary market liquidity and the ability to issue new securities. Finally, we have information on the legal codes governing shareholders for only fifty countries; more comprehensive data would provide more accurate information on the relationship between stock market development and economic growth. Given the importance of financial markets for economic growth, this research agenda should be accorded a high priority.

Notes

Omar Azfar, Paul Holden, and Jennifer Sobotka provided very helpful comments on an earlier draft of this essay.

1. These figures are from the World Bank 1998 and use its classification of emerging and developed markets. Hong Kong and Singapore are classified as developed. Shifting them into the emerging market category makes the disproportionate boom in emerging markets even more noticeable.

2. The capital flow figures are from World Bank 1997.

3. See especially La Porta et al. 1997, 1998, but also Levine 1998, 1999; and section II.

4. See Levine 1997 for a detailed discussion of the links between the financial system and economic development.

5. See Shleifer and Vishny 1997.

6. See, for example, Gale and Hellwig 1985 on debt instruments, Merton 1992 and Crane et al. 1995 on more sophisticated financial contracts, Levine 1991 and Bencivenga et al. 1995 on stock markets, and Boyd and Prescott 1986 on financial intermediation.

7. This has been shown formally by Levine 1991 and Bencivenga et al. 1995.

8. See Kyle 1984. Also, stock market development can promote corporate governance by making it easier to write managerial performance contracts that align the interests of managers and owners. See Holmstrom and Tirole 1993.

9. See Levine 1997.

10. Also, if there are capital externalities a drop in savings could put sufficient downward pressure on growth, so that overall GDP growth falls even as productivity rises.

11. The following countries were used in the analyses: Argentina, Australia, Austria, Bangladesh, Belgium, Brazil, Canada, Chile, Colombia, Cote d'Ivoire, Costa Rica, Germany, Denmark, Egypt, Spain, Finland, France, the United Kingdom, Greece, Hong Kong, Indonesia, India, Israel, Italy, Jamaica, Jordan, Japan, Korea, Luxembourg, Mexico, Malaysia, Morocco, Nigeria, the Netherlands, Norway, New Zealand, Pakistan, Peru, the Philippines, Portugal, Singapore, Sweden, Sri Lanka, Thailand, Turkey, Taiwan, the United States, Venezuela, and Zimbabwe.

12. Stock market data are from the International Finance Corporation's Emerging Market Data Base (electronic version) and the International Monetary Fund's International Financial Statistics.

13. I am in the process of expanding the data to more years and measuring the quantity of funds raised through equity issues.

14. Moreover, countries with the most liquid stock markets in 1976 both accumulated more capital and enjoyed faster productivity growth over the next eighteen years. See Levine and Zervos 1998a.

15. This is shown more rigorously by King and Levine 1993a, 1993b.

16. The variable descriptions that follow are taken directly from La Porta et al. 1998.

17. Recall that the strong relationship between long-run growth and stock market development runs primarily through market liquidity, which highlights the importance of comprehensive and comparable data in facilitating stock market activity.

18. These conditioning information sets reflect the large cross-country growth regression literature. For a discussion of these variables, see Barro and Sala-i-Martin 1995, Easterly and Levine 1997, or Levine and Renelt 1992.

19. The initial income variable is used to capture the convergence effect highlighted by Barro and Sala-i-Martin 1995. As in many cross-country analyses, initial secondary school enrollment is used to control for investment in human capital accumulation, as emphasized by Lucas 1988. Barro and Sala-i-Martin examine the link between political stability and economic growth.

20. See Levine and Zervos 1998b for empirical evidence that countries that liberalize international capital control restrictions see a marked improvement in the functioning of their stock markets.

21. Other essays and comments in this volume do examine individual countries. See those by Holden and Sobotka, Lanyi and Lee, and Wallis.

22. Of course, the exchange will be sensitive to the effects such additional requirements may have on the decision by potential issuers to list

their securities on the exchange. Nevertheless, better corporate governance will, in the long run, increase the financial benefits of listing on the exchange by promoting greater participation by savers.

References

Atje, Raymond, and Boyan Jovanovic. 1993. "Stock Markets and Development." *European Economic Review* 37 (2–3): 632–40.

Bagehot, Walter. [1873] 1962. *Lombard Street.* Homewood, IL: Richard D. Irwin.

Barro, Robert, and Xavier Sala-i-Martin. 1995. *Economic Growth.* New York: McGraw-Hill.

Beck, Thorsten, Ross Levine, and Norman Loayza. 2000. "Finance and the Sources of Growth." *Journal of Financial Economics* 58 (1–2): 261–300.

Bencivenga, Valerie R., and Bruce D. Smith. 1991. "Financial Intermediation and Endogenous Growth." *Review of Economic Studies* 58 (2): 195–209.

Bencivenga, Valerie R., Bruce D. Smith, and Ross M. Starr. 1995. "Transaction Costs, Technological Choice, and Endogenous Growth." *Journal of Economic Theory* 67 (1): 53–177.

Berman, Harold J. 1983. *Law and Revolution: The Formation of the Western Legal Tradition.* Cambridge: Harvard University Press.

Bhide, Amar. 1993. "The Hidden Costs of Stock Market Liquidity." *Journal of Financial Economics* 34 (2): 31–51.

Bonser-Neal, Catherine, and Kathryn Dewenter. 1999. "Does Financial Market Development Stimulate Savings? Evidence from Emerging Stock Markets." *Contemporary Economic Policy* 17 (3): 370–80.

Boyd, John H., and Edward C. Prescott. 1986. "Financial Intermediary Coalitions. *Journal of Economic Theory* 38 (2): 211–32.

Boyd, John H., and Bruce D. Smith. 1996. "The Coevolution of the Real and Financial Sectors in the Growth Process." *World Bank Economic Review* 10 (2): 371–96.

Crane, D. B., K. A. Froot, S. P. Mason, A. F. Perold, R. C. Merton, Z. Bodie, E. R. Sirri, and P. Tufano. 1995. *The Global Financial System: A Functional Perspective.* Boston: Harvard Business School Press.

Demirgüç-Kunt, Asli, and Ross Levine. 1996. "Stock Market Development and Financial Intermediaries: Stylized Facts." *World Bank Economic Review* 19 (2): 291–322.

Demirgüç-Kunt, Asli, and Vojislav Maksimovic. 1998. "Law, Finance, and Firm Growth." *Journal of Finance* 53 (6): 2107–37.

Easterly, William. 1994. "Economic Stagnation, Fixed Factors, and Policy Thresholds." *Journal of Monetary Economics* 33:525–57.

Easterly, William, and Ross Levine. 1997. "Africa's Growth Tragedy: Policies and Ethnic Divisions." *Quarterly Journal of Economics* 112 (4): 1203–50.

Easterly, William, and Sergio Rebelo. 1993. "Fiscal Policy and Economic

Growth: An Empirical Investigation." *Journal of Monetary Economics* 32 (3): 417–57.

Engerman, Stanley L., and Kenneth L. Sokoloff. 1996. "Factor Endowments, Institutions, and Differential Paths of Growth among New World Economies: A View from Economic Historians of the United States." In *How Latin America Fell Behind,* edited by Stephen Haber. Stanford: Stanford University Press.

Fischer, Stanley. 1993. "The Role of Macroeconomic Factors in Growth." *Journal of Monetary Economics* 32 (3): 485–511.

Gale, Douglas, and Martin Hellwig. 1985. "Incentive-Compatible Debt Contracts: The One-Period Problem." *Review of Economic Studies* 52:647–63.

Glendon, Mary Ann, Michael Gordon, and Christopher Osakwe. 1982. *Comparative Legal Tradition in a Nutshell.* St. Paul: West Publishing.

Greenwood, Jeremy, and Bruce Smith. 1997. "Financial Markets in Development and the Development of Financial Markets." *Journal of Economic Dynamics and Control* 21 (1): 145–86.

Hansson, Pontus, and Lars Jonung. N.d. "Finance and Growth: The Case of Sweden, 1834–1991." Mimeo, Stockholm. Stockholm School of Economics.

Holmstrom, Bengt, and Jean Tirole. 1993. "Market Liquidity and Performance Monitoring." *Journal of Political Economy* 101 (4): 678–709.

Knack, Stephen, and Philip Keefer. 1995. "Institutions and Economic Performance: Cross-Country Tests Using Alternative Institutional Measures." *Economics and Politics* 7:207–27.

Jayaratne, Jith, and Philip E. Strahan. 1996. "The Finance-Growth Nexus: Evidence from Bank Branch Deregulation." *Quarterly Journal of Economics* 111 (3): 639–70.

King, Robert G., and Ross Levine. 1993a. "Finance and Growth: Schumpeter Might Be Right." *Quarterly Journal of Economics* 108 (3): 717–38.

———. 1993b. "Finance, Entrepreneurship, and Growth: Theory and Evidence." *Journal of Monetary Economics* 32 (3): 513–42.

Kyle, Albert S. 1984. "Market Structure, Information, Futures Markets, and Price Formation." In *International Agricultural Trade: Advanced Readings in Price Formation, Market Structure, and Price Instability,* edited by Gary G. Storey, Andrew Schmitz, and Alexander H. Sarris. Boulder: Westview.

La Porta, Rafael, Florencio Lopez-de-Silanes, Andrei Shleifer, and Robert W. Vishny. 1997. "Legal Determinants of External Finance." *Journal of Finance* 52 (3): 1131–50.

———. 1998. "Law and Finance." *Journal of Political Economy* 106 (6): 1113–55.

Levine, Ross. 1991. "Stock Markets, Growth, and Tax Policy." *Journal of Finance* 46 (4): 1445–65.

————. 1997. "Financial Development and Economic Growth: Views and Agenda." *Journal of Economic Literature* 35 (2): 688–726.

————. 1998. "The Legal Environment, Banks, and Long-Run Economic Growth." *Journal of Money, Credit, and Banking* 30 (3, pt. 2): 596–613.

————. 1999. "Law, Finance, and Economic Growth." *Journal of Financial Intermediation* 8 (1–2): 8–35.

Levine, Ross, Norman Loayza, and Thorsten Beck. 2000. "Financial Intermediation and Growth: Causality and Causes." *Journal of Monetary Economics* 46 (1): 31–77.

Levine, Ross, and David Renelt. 1992. "A Sensitivity Analysis of Cross-Country Growth Regressions." *American Economic Review* 82 (4): 942–63.

Levine, Ross, and Sara Zervos. 1998a. "Stock Markets, Banks, and Economic Growth." *American Economic Review* 88 (3): 537–58.

————. 1998b. "Capital Control Liberalization and Stock Market Development." *World Development* 26 (7): 1169–83.

Lucas, Robert. 1988. "On the Mechanics of Economic Development." *Journal of Monetary Economics* 22:3–42.

Mauro, Paolo. 1995. "Corruption and Economic Growth." *Quarterly Journal of Economics* 110 (3): 681–712.

Merton, R. C. 1992. "Financial Innovation and Economic Performance." *Journal of Applied Corporate Finance* 2 (winter): 12–22.

Neusser, Klaus, and Maurice Kugler. 1998. "Manufacturing Growth and Financial Development: Evidence from OECD Countries." *Review of Economics and Statistics* 80 (4): 638–46.

North, Douglas C. 1981. *Structure and Change in Economic History*. New York: Norton.

Patrick, Hugh. 1966. "Financial Development and Economic Growth in Underdeveloped Countries." *Economic Development Cultural Change* 14 (2): 174–89.

Rajan, Raghuram G., and Luigi Zingales. 1998. "Financial Dependence and Growth." *American Economic Review* 88 (3): 559–86.

Rousseau, Peter L., and Paul Wachtel. 1998a. "Financial Intermediation and Economic Performance: Historical Evidence from Five Industrial Countries." *Journal of Money, Credit, and Banking* 30 (4): 657–78.

————. 1998b. "Equity Markets and Growth: Cross-Country Evidence on Timing and Outcomes, 1980–1995." Working paper S/98/29, New York University, Salomon Center.

Schumpeter, Joseph A. [1912] 1934. *The Theory of Economic Development*. Trans. Redvers Opie. Cambridge: Harvard University Press.

Schwert, G. William. 1989. "Why Does Stock Market Volatility Change over Time?" *Journal of Finance* 49 (5): 1115–53.

Shleifer, Andrei, and Lawrence Summers. 1988. "Breach of Trust in Hostile Takeovers." In *Corporate Takeovers: Causes and Consequences*, edited by A. Auerbach. Chicago: University of Chicago Press.

Shleifer, Andrei, and Robert W. Vishny. 1986. "Large Shareholders and Corporate Control." *Journal of Political Economy* 96 (3): 461–88.

———. 1993. "Corruption." *Quarterly Journal of Economics* 109:599–617.

———. 1997. "A Survey of Corporate Governance." *Journal of Finance* 52 (2): 737–84.

Summers, Robert S., and Allan Heston. 1991. "The Penn World Table (Mark 5): An Expanded Set of International Comparisons, 1950–1988." *Quarterly Journal of Economics* 106 (2): 327–68.

———. 1993. "Penn World Tables, Version 5.5." National Bureau of Economic Research. Diskette.

Wachtel, Paul, and Peter Rousseau. 1995. "Financial Intermediation and Economic Growth: A Historical Comparison of the U.S., U.K., and Canada." In *Anglo-American Financial Systems,* edited by M. D. Bordo and R. Sylla. Homewood, IL: Business One Irwin.

World Bank. International Finance Corporation. 1998. *Emerging Markets Factbook.* New York: World Bank.

World Bank. 1997. *Private Capital Flows to Developing Countries.* New York: Oxford University Press.

Comment

Paul Holden and Jennifer Sobotka

Levine's essay is an in-depth analysis of a topic that should be at the forefront of development studies. Institutional weakness is at the root of many of the economic problems in developing countries, and in spite of a growing recognition of the importance of a sound institutional framework to support economic transactions detailed analysis is still relatively scarce. The essay makes a significant contribution, expanding on the detrimental effects of financial market deficiencies on long-term economic growth. The focus on stock markets is a refreshing change from previous efforts directed solely at the banking sector.

It is particularly important to emphasize the link between financial development and growth in view of the backlash again reforms instituted in the early 1990s. In many countries in Latin America, people appear to be losing patience with the slow pace of reform and the lack of substantial improvements in their personal economic positions. Evidence showing that slow progress is due to *insufficient* rather than *incorrect* reform programs could allow governments to continue on the path to improved markets.

After testing many variables, Levine concludes that the most important determinant of long-term growth rates is stock market turnover; next in importance (excluding Taiwan and Korea) is IPOs. Other variables, such as market capitalization, that would appear ex ante to be important did not show any statistical relationship with long-term growth rates.

We would have liked, however, to see more explanation of the link between stock market turnover and growth. From the perspective of the firm, stock markets should provide a "one-shot" capital injection into a business at the time of the IPO and at other times when the company sells more shares. Is it these cash infusions that then allow for future company growth? The data do support this hypothesis (if one removes Taiwan and Korea from the sample). As more data become available, it would be interesting to know if the trend holds.

Market capitalization in Latin America grew at a much faster rate than the world average during the period 1990–97. For the region as a whole, it was four times higher, as a percentage of GDP, in 1997 than it was in 1990. In comparison, market capitalization slightly more than doubled in the United States and increased by 50 percent for the world as a whole. In some countries, the multiples by which the stock markets expanded were remarkable — by a factor of eight in Brazil and Peru and six in Argentina and Columbia. Market capitalization doubled, from a much higher base of 44 percent, in Chile, the country that has had the most macroeconomic stability and has registered the highest growth rates in Latin America over a prolonged period.

To look at how the relationship between market capitalization, turnover, and GDP evolved over the recent time period, we did some simple correlations for the 1990–97 period. There is evidence of a positive relationship between market capitalization and growth in Brazil and Peru and a weak one in Argentina. Interestingly, the correlation in Brazil is highest, even though the overall growth rate was lower than in the other countries in the sample during this period.

How reliable these relationships are is another matter. In the early part of the decade, several countries in the sample were experiencing or just emerging from hyperinflation. This was also a period during which there was substantial privatization, much of which occurred through the stock markets. We suspect that if one were to

TABLE 1. Financial Development in 1990 and 1997

	Market Capitalization as % of GDP	
Country	1990	1997
Argentina	2.3	15.2
Brazil	3.4	29.0
Chile	44.9	88.8
Colombia	3.5	20.1
Mexico	12.5	31.8
Peru	2.5	20.2
Latin America	7.4	27.4
United States	55.1	115.6
World	51.7	70.6

**TABLE 2.   Correlations of Stock Market
Capitalization, Stock Market Turnover, and Growth**

Country	Market Capitalization Correlation (1990–97)	Turnover Correlation (1990–97)
Argentina	.20	.63
Brazil	.69	.62
Chile	.09	.20
Colombia	.05	.44
Mexico	.03	.66
Peru	.52	.86

control for privatization inflows from the purchase of state-owned enterprises (and the accompanying increase of market capitalization, as the new companies appear on the domestic stock exchange) these figures might look quite different.

Since the correlation between liquidity (turnover) and growth is positive for current years as well as future ones (see tables 1 and 2), there is one additional possibility that we would like to see examined. Could not liquidity be an *indicator* of future growth without any inference of a causal relationship between the two? Assume, for example, that foreign investors carefully monitor developments in international economies. When these investors see a sufficiently convincing sign of growth potential, foreign investment begins to flow into the economy and stock market turnover rises sharply. In this case, we would witness an increase in stock market liquidity and subsequently higher growth, but the latter would not have been caused by the former.

Nonetheless, to discount the relevance of the connection between stock markets and growth in development considerations would be foolhardy. Further research needs to be done to determine the exact nature of the connection, and to suggest whether the remedies for underdeveloped markets are legal, economic, or technical in nature.

The Role of Governance Failures in the East Asian Financial Crisis

Anthony Lanyi and Young Lee

Before June 1997, many economists (notably Stiglitz) were invoking successful governance—especially in relation to capital markets—as a principal factor underlying the so-called East Asian economic miracle. Since mid-1997, conversely, poor governance—especially in relation to capital markets—has been frequently mentioned as a major cause of the so-called East Asian financial crisis. These apparently conflicting views raise important questions about the optimum role of government in developing economies.

In general, there are two conflicting interpretations of the Asian financial crisis, emphasizing, respectively, either economic causes or elements of political governance. Those observers emphasizing economic factors tend to believe that this crisis is just another of the "manias, panics, and crashes"[1] that have marked the history of capitalism since its earliest days. According to this line of reasoning,[2] the most seriously affected countries (MSAs) in Asia, Eastern Europe, and Latin America were essentially victims of the herd mentality of international investors and (in better-informed versions of this view) domestic investors as well.

Several points are evident: financial panic was triggered by excessive short-term foreign borrowing in the immediately preceding years; the panic was exacerbated by fixed exchange rates that were maintained even after regional currencies had become seriously overvalued: and global financial market liberalization, in combination with capital account liberalization during the previous decade (and technological and financial innovations over the past quarter century) served to overwhelm central banks' attempts to intervene in foreign exchange or financial markets in order to stem destabilizing capital movements. It is equally evident that emerging market economies, with their relatively incomplete and poorly supervised financial sectors, have been more vulnerable to such capital movements than the advanced industrial countries, with their deeper and wider markets for goods and services and more fully developed and better-supervised capital markets. It seems clear in hindsight that it was a mistake for the emerging market countries to remove most of their controls on inward and outward capital flows in the 1980s and 1990s, and to liberalize domestic financial markets as rapidly and broadly as they did, without corresponding improvements in the supervision and regulation of those markets.

Key questions, however, remain unanswered regarding the contribution of governance failings to the financial crisis in Asia. Radelet and Sachs (1998, 44–49) analyze econometric evidence regarding the contributing factors; "corruption" variables, they report, do not account for much of the differential impact of the crisis on different Asian economies. This does not mean, however, that governance issues are irrelevant in this context. Indeed, some "economic factors"—such as the excessive accumulation of short-term foreign currency liabilities by banks and large corporations, and weak prudential supervision of financial institutions—far from being explanatory variables, are themselves phenomena requiring explanation, often in terms of governance differences.

In our view, governance issues were indeed important in the East Asian crisis. We hypothesize that transparency and accountability in macroeconomic policy-making, in the operation of the financial system, and in corporate governance lessen a country's vulnerability to financial crises and strengthen its ability to deal with crises when they occur. We hypothesize further that a democratic political system in which leaders are accountable to the electorate—with direct election of the executive as well as an elected legislature and with an independent judiciary and a free press—is less likely to collapse in the face of economic and financial difficulties than is a country with an autocratic government that imposes severe restraints on the public expression of opinion and dissemination of information.[3] The former type of government is more likely than the latter to reach consensus on, and to implement, a painful but necessary program of economic stabilization and restructuring.

The focus of this essay is specifically on various aspects of "economic governance," that is, the way in which economic life is governed and regulated. We understand economic governance to include not only government activity, including macroeconomic policy (sec. II), but also structured arrangements between private principals and agents (sec. III). Section IV analyzes proposals and current realities relating to international macroeconomic and financial governance. While some empirical evidence is presented, the authors' main aim is to point to issues for further research rather than to provide conclusive answers.

I. The Political Basis of Economic Governance

Economic governance in a market economy consists in part of direct control or indirect influence exerted by the government and in part of governance exercised within markets themselves, but even self-governance by markets operates within the legal, judicial, and regulatory framework that has been erected and is supported by the government. When both of these aspects of government activity are used to foster market-based economic growth, one has what Mancur Olson called "market-augmenting government." Market-augmenting government, as discussed in essays by Olson and his colleagues,[4] includes not only the creation of institutions fostering growth and investment but the maintenance of a proper macroeconomic environment. Turning to the East Asian financial crisis, we encounter the dilemma (which Olson himself puzzled over in his last weeks) of how the same governments that were praised for propagating the "East Asian miracle" are now held equally responsible for the East Asian crash. What was before perceived as the careful government direction of investment resources is now being seen as self-interested speculation and predation; the formerly extolled networking among economic players—an essential aspect of the "Asian" or "Japanese" model of economic management—is now derided as "cronyism."

This puzzle of East Asian economic governance suggests, upon reflection, three very different and independent dimensions of economic governance and its political basis. All three were indicated by Olson in his initial reflections on the problem. First, there is the question of the *economic governance regime:* what are the relative costs and benefits of a system that depends on discretionary decisions by the government, compared to those of a system in which the government operates in an arm's length mode through impartial rules and regulations? Second, there is the *time dimension:* does the nature of the ideal market-augmenting government change as the economy develops, so that the kind of government intervention that works very well in the early stages of development works less well with more advanced markets, which are better integrated with the world economy? Are different types of government intervention called for at a more advanced stage of development? Finally, there is the issue of *political regime:* can we say anything about the ideal degree of autocracy or democracy in a market-augmenting government, given that most countries in the East Asian region have elements of both types of regime in their systems? And is one type of government or another better suited to earlier or later stages of development?

Economic Governance Regimes

There is little debate about the desired outcomes of governmental interaction with the economy. A stable macroeconomy, human capital development, openness to international trade and investment, and market-determined prices, together with high rates of saving and investment, are understood to foster sustainable economic growth and provide the basis for a rise in living standards for the broad mass of the population.[5] What, precisely, should be the role of government in achieving these outcomes? We propose to discuss this issue by considering two polar alternatives: a regime that depends on a high degree of direct intervention in the economy by the government; and a regime in which government operates at arm's length from individual enterprises, setting and enforcing rules and creating a general environment for business rather than directly conducting business itself. In discussing the alternatives of discretionary and arm's length regimes, we recognize that in the real world all governments to some extent employ both of these governance techniques but with a wide range of relative emphases between the two.

To analyze the relative costs and benefits of these two approaches to economic governance, it is helpful to employ the concept of market-augmenting government. The key point here is that market-augmenting government has a different meaning in an environment of nonexistent or poorly developed markets than in an economy of highly developed markets. In the latter instance, there is wide consensus that the role of government is to provide a secure, stable setting for private enterprise, under the rule of law, with appropriate regulations to protect the public (including private businesses) from private predation or negative (e.g., environmental) externalities. In the case of poorly developed markets, however, there is a strong argument that governments need to take positive steps to create special inducements for the private sector to initiate certain economic activities that would otherwise not come into being. Although the need for such government action is far from universally accepted,[6] there can be little doubt that as a historical fact the creation of basic infrastructure has normally required government initiative and that proactive government interventions of various types have frequently contributed positively to economic development. The latter point is demonstrated by the record of the East Asian countries and other evidence, which are discussed in the following section.

A cost-benefit calculus of discretionary government intervention in the economy might begin with the following benefits.

1. Creating (or inducing the creation of) missing or barely existing markets
2. Mitigating collective action problems—for example, by government action to create the infrastructure necessary for further market-based development
3. Mitigating information and insurance problems by collecting and disseminating information

At the same time, a great deal of modern economic literature has discussed the various costs and distortions created by discretionary government intervention, which can be summarized as follows.

1. Creating rents for private sector entities and inducing the latter to engage in rent-seeking behavior
2. Encouraging soft budget constraints for favored industries and firms
3. Distorting resource allocation by substituting political rather than strictly economic criteria for channeling resources to particular sectors or activities
4. Creating greater opportunities for government failure (e.g., poor decisions or corruption)

The balance of costs and benefits of government intervention will depend on the particular circumstances of a country during a particular period of time. We examine next, therefore, how the optimum mode of market-augmenting government might change as an economy develops over time.

The Time Dimension of Economic Governance

It appears evident from the foregoing enumeration of costs and benefits that the marginal benefits of discretionary government intervention decline as the stock of infrastructure grows and markets develop. At the same time, the costs of such intervention remain at least constant with growing infrastructure and markets and possibly may rise (as a growing private sector competes for rents). Nevertheless, as domestic markets become more complex and linked to those abroad, more carefully articulated and effective means of arm's length government intervention (e.g., the legal and regulatory framework) may well be needed. Thus, while economists are in the habit of regarding economic systems as ideal types, the reality of both economic and political life is one of evolution.

Market-augmenting government is commonly defined as providing the setting in which existing markets can function successfully.[7] At an early stage of development, however, particular markets may be nonexistent, and at any given point of time different markets may be at different stages of development. The policy implications of this developmental pattern are complicated, and the following suggestions should be regarded as preliminary hypotheses.

As a general rule, more proactive government intervention may be called for at early stages of economic development in order to establish or develop particular markets—intervention of a sort that at later stages of development would be considered counterproductive. At the earlier stages, it may be less costly and more efficient for governments to substitute directly for missing markets than to build up supporting institutions and wait for markets to arise.[8] As markets develop, however, the optimal market-augmenting policies may be those that enhance market-supporting institutions, keeping an arm's length relationship with the private sector; as seen earlier, the enumeration of the costs and benefits of government intervention implies a rise in the ratio of costs to benefits of proactive government intervention as markets develop. Thus, as an economy grows and price systems become more informative and effective, there will be less need for, and greater distortions arising from, *discretionary* state intervention, even as there may be a growing need for *arm's length* government regulation.

The potential time dependence of optimal government policies is not a new idea in economics. The old infant industry argument is based on the notion that government intervention to compensate for market failure is justified at an early stage of development but should be withdrawn at a later stage. A more recent example of this idea is the growing acceptance of privatizing state-owned enterprises, even if it is acknowledged (by some, not all, observers) that the original involvement of the state in creating or taking over such enterprises might have been justified or even necessary. Another example is the argument, which has become popular in the recent financial crisis, that restrictions on international capital movements that might be inappropriate for advanced industrial countries are needed for countries with incompletely developed and poorly regulated financial systems.

Rajan and Zingales (1998) have examined the potential time dependency of optimal systems in the context of firms rather than governments. They argue that as markets develop optimal systems for transactions change from "relationship-based" to "arm's length" systems. (Rajan and Zingales's treatment of institutions differs from the approach in our essay. They treat institutions as a semiexogenous variable and a determinant of optimal systems for transactions in the private sector.) At early stages of market development, they report, institutions for third-party enforcement (in their terminology, "contractual infrastructure") are very weak and prices are not very informative, so that relationship-based systems—for example, a universal banking system—could work better than arm's length systems that require contract enforcement and rational prices. They argue that as the contractual infrastructure develops and prices become more informative, arm's length, competitive, Anglo-Saxon systems become increasingly preferable for private transactions. This conclusion implies that an interventionist approach by the government, based on selective encouragement of particular sectors and firms and involving direct relationships between government officials and favored private sector players, is more consistent with optimal systems at an earlier stage of development than at a later stage.

Another example of the time dependence of government intervention is provided by Wallis (this volume), who shows how, in the early to mid–nineteenth century, American states began to move from restrictive chartering practices—for example, granting operation rights to only a handful of banks—to liberal incorporation laws. Wallis argues that this move laid the basis for an efficient economic system, especially in the financial sector, and, while the timing of this move from relationship-based to arm's length systems depended critically on the fiscal interest of each state, the initially more interventionist policies may well have been necessary for creating financial and transportation systems.

In East Asia, there were many examples of proactive intervention by national governments at early stages of development. Examples of such intervention include: the Korean government's big push, from the 1960s on, to build heavy and chemical industries through a variety of subsidies, preferences, and special financing arrangements, which were often directed at individual firms; Taiwan's import-protective policies in the 1950s and Thailand's similar policies in the 1970s; and state industrial investment in Indonesia both under Sukarno (up to 1966) and again starting with the oil boom of the 1970s. Japan, of course, provided an example with its apparently successful use of directed credits and a protected domestic market, as well as the discretionary assistance rendered by the Ministry of International Trade and Industry (MITI) with regard to foreign exchange allocation[9] and the acquisition of foreign technology. Such policies were widely followed in other developing countries, too, but the fast-growing Asian economies were distinguished by their flexible response to internal and external changes, switching at later stages of their development to an export-promoting strategy that required broad liberalization of their financial, international trade, and foreign exchange regimes. It should be added that the influence of selective government intervention at both earlier and later stages of development is a hotly debated issue, inherently difficult to resolve, as it involves not only comparative statics but dynamic issues with regard to saving and investment incentives.[10]

The question of the appropriateness of particular policies to a given stage of economic development is broadened in the following section to encompass two further issues: whether a particular type of political regime is especially appropriate at a particular stage of development and whether the authoritarian regimes that proved successful in past decades in East Asian countries may become less appropriate as markets in those countries become more developed.

Political Regime

There is no necessary correspondence between the type of economic governance regime and the type of political regime: discretionary and arm's length approaches can each be found among autocratic and democratic regimes. The autocratic-discretionary combination is exemplified both by the Stalinist regimes (and some of their less oppressive successors) and by some of the relatively market-oriented Asian regimes of past decades, such as those of Soeharto in Indonesia or Chung Hee Park in Korea. The autocratic–arm's length combination is less common, but it has occasionally been found in Latin America — for instance, in Chile under Pinochet. The democratic-discretionary combination flourished for decades in South Asia—India and Sri Lanka—and also arguably in postwar Japan, while the democratic–arm's length mode is typified by the United States, the United Kingdom in recent years, and to a lesser extent by the other Western European democracies.

As Rodrik and others have noted, economists and donor-country politicians in the 1980s often viewed good economic policy as requiring "strong" and "autonomous" (not to say authoritarian) leadership. Anyone associated with the International Monetary Fund (IMF) or the World Bank during this period can testify to the admiration of those organizations' staffs for the regime of General Pinochet in Chile and their relief that it was he and not Allende that had been at the helm there since 1974. Likewise, the World Bank's 1993 study, *The East Asian Miracle,* is fulsome in its praise of Asian national leadership in the period from the 1960s to the early 1990s. Technocrats found authoritarian regimes appealing during this period because for the most part those regimes chose proper macroeconomic policies, and to some degree institution-building activities as well, and were able to impose their will unhampered by the party conflicts and special interests that often stifle economic policy formulation and implementation in democracies.

These views were in general informally held. In their writings, economists were generally agnostic with respect to the relevance of political regimes to economic reform. Only since the financial crisis does one occasionally encounter advocacy of going beyond the "first-generation reforms" (reforms in fiscal, monetary, exchange rate, pricing, and subsidy policies) and "second-generation reforms" (institutional improvements in such areas as tax administration, budgetary formulation and monitoring, state enterprise privatization, strengthening regulation of financial institutions, and civil service reform).[11] There is now vague talk especially in the Indonesian context, of the importance of political reforms, or what might be called "third-generation reforms," ostensibly to strengthen the long-term sustainability of the other reforms.

As Gourevitch (1993) has trenchantly observed, over the years theories have been propounded, and evidence accumulated, that could be used to support any one of the following conflicting propositions: markets require democracy, markets require authoritarianism, democracy requires markets, and democracy requires centralized planning and public ownership. In fact, one can find instances of both democratic and relatively authoritarian regimes that have supported sustained market-oriented development. Conversely, one can find instances of both democratic and authoritarian regimes under which the economy has been stifled by excessive controls, inefficient state enterprises, and pervasive official corruption. The challenge is to find the right match, in Gourevitch's terms, of "form and content": form of government and content of economic policy. In the East Asian case, the question arises: how did relatively authoritarian regimes that successfully supported essentially market- and outward-oriented economic development, prove unsustainable, either in the positive sense that they evolved into democratic systems (as in Korea) or in the negative sense of encountering economic and political collapse (as in Indonesia).

Mancur Olson was one of the few economists to tackle the question of why autocracies provide good market-augmenting governance in some circumstances and not in others. In his last months, he was in the process of developing the notion that a market-augmenting, growth-promoting autocracy might evolve into a market-inhibiting, growth-deterring government. While it is certainly possible for an autocrat—or "stationary bandit"—to conduct economic policy in accordance with the encompassing interest of the society, this depends ultimately on his time horizon. If he expects to enjoy a long rule, it is in his interest to conduct policies, and create and maintain institutions, that serve to strengthen the economy and thus induce his subjects to engage in productive economic activity while avoiding overtaxation.[12]

Nevertheless, in comparing dictatorships and democracies, Olson finds two serious flaws in the former. First, one of the main features of market-augmenting government is the rule of law and, in particular, clearly defined and firmly enforced property rights. But without democracy property rights are never entirely free of possible violation by an autocratic government—after all, the most exemplary autocratic government may be succeeded by a less exemplary one. And this brings us to the second problem of autocracy: it lacks mechanisms of orderly succession, and consequently, under autocracy, economic progress can occasionally be set back by succession crises that occur when an autocrat dies or is forcibly removed from power.[13]

In his last oral remarks on the East Asian financial crisis, Olson observed that autocrats long in power may themselves (or through their families) be drawn into rent-seeking activities. This is hardly original as an anecdotal observation—there is, after all, Lord Acton's famous (and often misquoted) statement that "power tends to corrupt, and absolute power corrupts absolutely"—but the motive for such corruption is ambiguous. At first glance, it might seem to be straightforward self-enrichment; that is, as the time horizon for the remainder of the autocrat's rule grows shorter, his strategy for self-enrichment shifts to one of short-term gains, behavior more typical of a roving than a stationary bandit.

But the acquisition of economic assets may also be related to succession, Olson's second major problem of autocracy. If the autocrat is concerned about remaining in power, or keeping his own family in power, then extending family control over major economic entities is a likely strategy since economic power can be a means of achieving or at least sharing in political power. Such a strategy would also explain the tendency of autocrats to seek direct control over economic activity through personal involvement in production or regulation or through such involvement by family members or close personal friends. Such a strategy runs counter, however, to the standard prescription for market-oriented growth, which involves establishing an arm's length relationship between government and business (and by the 1980s this prescription, which underlies the "Washington consensus" of that period [Williamson 1993], would have been well known to the technocrats involved in formulating economic policy in the East Asian countries).

Once this extension of Olson's analysis is accepted, some interesting conclusions follow.

1. To the extent that economic power is dispersed among the ruler's family and friends, *the economic policy aims of the government also became dispersed.* At first, the ruler may give control of some major state enterprise to a sibling or child or spouse, and that economic entity continues to be managed in line with the encompassing interest as conceived by the ruler, with the help of his or her technocratic advisers. The autocrat may even be genuinely convinced that the ruling family control of the enterprise facilitates economic progress for the country. But eventually the economic creature of the government takes on a life of its own, and its aims diverge from that of the encompassing interest. Little by little, as economic power is parceled out to family and friends, operation of each entity is pursued for the self-interest of the individual(s) in control. (This, could, no doubt, be analyzed in terms of typical principal-agent problems [see sec. III]). The network of relationships, including ties to the mechanisms of government, creates overwhelming temptations to self-enrichment by subordinates and associates through every conceivable form of favoritism and corruption. Thus, the evolution of a long-term ("stable")

autocracy parallels that of a stable democracy as described by Olson in *The Rise and Decline of Nations* (1982): the gradual accumulation and growing influence of particular interests, together with a diminished weight given to the society's encompassing interests in the making of economic policy.

2. At the same time, *the process just described tends to undermine the technocratic basis of economic decision making,* which was cited in *The East Asian Miracle* (World Bank 1993) as a reason for the superior performance of these countries since the 1960s. As considerations of the society's encompassing interest increasingly give way to the interests of the corporations and financial institutions run by the ruling family and its friends, the technocrats either find their views overridden by the political authority or are themselves co-opted by those special interests through threat of losing their jobs or through financial incentives. Where there are, moreover, restrictions on freedom of the press and speech, even those technocrats who have not been corrupted have little scope for expressing their views, let alone organizing opposition to government policies.

3. To some extent, the preceding analysis may also apply to the state's economic activities in a genuinely democratic setting, where the government has established state enterprises and state-run banks. Initially, state-owned enterprises (SOEs) are created in order to facilitate encompassing national objectives like economic development, growth, and income stability. But eventually the managements of the state enterprises create the kinds of special interest groups described by Olson (1982), and *the encompassing interest gives way to economic policies geared to protecting particular state-owned sectors or industries.*

4. Olson argued that even in those autocracies where a rule of law protects property rights in order to encourage market-oriented development there is the threat of arbitrary seizure—if not by the current autocrat then possibly by a successor. Thus, in the long run democratically based government, compared to autocracy, has a superior capacity to give individuals greater confidence in the enforcement of property rights. Moreover, the broader framework of law provided by market-augmenting government entails not only enforcement of property rights but also enforcement of contracts, regulation of natural monopolies (and nonfavoritistic auctioning of natural monopoly concessions, like use of frequencies in telecommunications), and regulations protecting the public against exploitation of labor or the environment. Again, *the long-term tendency for autocrats (and their fam-*

ilies and entourage) to acquire economic power could be expected eventually to undermine the execution of such a market-augmenting legal and regulatory framework. Under an autocratic regime, regulations will tend not to be enforced when the autocrat's family businesses are involved, the judiciary will tend to settle contract disputes in favor of those politically best connected, and eminent domain will tend to be exercised arbitrarily when the autocrat's family and friends can benefit thereby. This will tend to be more true the longer the autocrat has been in power.

Mixed Regimes

The stylized description of autocratic government fits some cases—such as the Soeharto era in Indonesia—better than others. In many countries, elements of democracy and autocracy are intermingled. In others, autocracies may be of special types. For example, an autocrat may come to power through a military coup and thus represent the military as such rather than personal or family dynastic ambitions.[14] A military dictatorship can evolve toward personal dictatorship or a form of oligarchy, which is intermediate between autocracy and democracy. In an oligarchy, any individual's attempt at self-enrichment or an undue expansion of power leads to that person's being unseated by the other members of the group *unless* the other oligarchs are given direct or indirect economic rewards.[15] One might expect that under such an arrangement market-augmenting government would flourish if, for example, the wealthy supporters of the regimes are convinced that this approach will lead to their own enrichment. Some Asian countries with limited democracy may well be described as informal oligarchies rather than pure autocracies, and in some cases they were able to spread economic benefits to a broad range of the population, thereby obtaining not only oligarchic but popular support. This approach to market-augmenting government does not, however, eliminate the possibility of a long-ruling autocrat seeking extension of economic control for family members and close associates.

An extreme case of the latter is provided by Indonesia's President Soeharto. It is perhaps not a coincidence that Indonesia is the country that suffered the greatest economic, social, and political disruption due to the Asian financial crisis once the credibility of its leadership was destroyed. When he came to power in the mid-1960s, Soeharto was supported by the Indonesian military not because they saw him as a Napoleon-like ruler who would stay in power for more than three decades but because they saw him as a representative of their group and savior of the country from chaos and communism. Eventually, Soeharto was able to transform this role into long-term power, avoiding removal by his military colleagues by sharing the economic pie with key individuals. But this was at the eventual expense of further undermining the quality of macroeconomic, financial, and corporate governance prevailing in the economic system (see secs. II and III).

In certain Asian countries that have oligarchic regimes combined with democratic elements, "cronyism" developed through complex networks involving politicians, government officials, banks, and other businesses; in this networking, family and friendship relations undermined the impersonal calculations and transactions that characterize a true market system.[16] In some of these countries, however, countervailing tendencies have been substantial: the gradual strengthening of democracy in Korea resulted in the election of a president determined to reduce the monopoly power of the *chaebols*. Such cases, however, may be qualified by path dependencies: a democracy that until recently had strong autocratic elements—as in Korea—may still suffer from inadequately developed supporting institutions, thereby allowing elements of the former leadership to hold on to some degree of their former economic and political power.

Further research is needed to determine to what extent cronyism (and other forms of favoritism and corruption affecting economic decision making) can arise in countries with ostensibly democratic institutions and how these phenomena can be measured and compared across countries and time periods. As an initial hypothesis, we suggest that cronyism and corruption have tended to flourish in countries with a strong executive and relatively weak checks and balances from the legislature or civil society and that this pattern might be expected to be especially strong where one chief executive (e.g., Soeharto) or one party (e.g., the ruling party in Malaysia) holds power for a long period of time. This pattern would, of course, be consistent with the model of autocracy outlined earlier. Another pattern of corruption, consistent with democratic institutions, arises from a heavy degree of government intervention in the economy, with state ownership of banks, public utilities, and manufacturing corporations; this, too, can breed cronyism and the temptation for politicians and government officials to enrich themselves illegally. In a democratic society, however, such scandals tend to come to light— as in France in recent years.

Finally, to return to the evolutionary model discussed in section I, it appears that the development of more sophisticated financial markets, accompanied by integration into the global economy, strengthens the case not only for a more arm's length approach to economic governance but also for democratization. In the first place, autocracy tends ultimately to favor a discretionary approach to government economic policy and resists creating a level playing field for all market participants. In the second place, the types of financial and corporate governance that foster a properly functioning market economy require levels of transparency and accountability that are more likely to be found in a democratic environment than under an autocratic regime (see sec. III).

II. Macroeconomic Governance

By "macroeconomic governance," we mean the political and administrative processes by which macroeconomic policies are formulated, implemented, and evaluated. From a purely technical standpoint, the same policies can be carried out with equal effectiveness by either an autocratic or a democratic government. Indeed, as already noted, officials in international financial institutions tended for many years to suppose that autocrats, if supported by well-trained technocrats, were likely to come up with first-class macroeconomic governance, in part because they could avert the Olsonian collective action problems arising from special interests in established democracies. But there appear to be factors that lead to deterioration over time in the quality of these policies in an autocracy, as well as problems in the ability of such governments to adjust policies in response to changes in economic circumstances.

The international financial community placed great faith in the local technocrats of the East Asian countries, who rightly stressed conservative fiscal and monetary policies. Prior to the crisis, all the most seriously affected countries had participated in the "East Asia miracle." All participated in the global economy, and all had had to deal with the mixed blessing of large-scale capital inflows, which grew to especially high levels in the late 1980s and early 1990s.

Despite their excellent track record up to 1997, Indonesia and Thailand, and perhaps also Korea, are believed by many economists to have hung on too long to what had become overvalued exchange rates. It is generally agreed that all three countries experienced inflated property and stock prices, that all had poorly regulated and poorly supervised financial and corporate systems, and that areas of nontransparency in both official and private financial dealings indirectly exacerbated the crisis when unfortunately timed "revelations" occurred. In particular, all had depended on Japan for large-scale direct investment and trade and consequently suffered in later years from the twin problems of an appreciating dollar (to which all their currencies were pegged) and a stagnating Japanese economy. The decision to stick with a fixed exchange rate was perhaps understandable in view of the great desire for stability and maintaining policy credibility. Less excusable was these governments' unwillingness to submit financial institutions to stricter and more impartial regulation, especially in the face of liberalizations of both financial markets and the capital account of the balance of payments (see Krugman 1998). Both exchange rate and regulatory policies disregarded many years of sound international advice.

The growing problems with macroeconomic policies in these countries were therefore fairly clear, certainly by the early 1990s. Why was nothing done about them at that time? Perhaps the international advisers pressed less hard than they might have because they shared the widespread belief that the Asians "knew better"— that the "Asian way" or "Asian model" (sometimes the "Japanese model") was superior. It is not clear to what extent the international civil servants (notably in the World Bank and IMF) perceived and communicated these problems to political authorities in the MSAs. However, the Mexican crisis of 1994–95, and the literature growing out of it, gave plenty of advance warning of the dangers posed by large capital inflows, fixed exchange rates, poorly supervised banking systems, and volatile international capital markets. It seems unlikely that at least some of the technocrats—both domestic and international—were not aware of these problems. The fact that little or no action was taken (e.g., that large foreign liabilities of banks and corporations were allowed to develop) does suggest ulterior motives on the part of the political authorities.

In particular, the inflexibility of macroeconomic policies may in part be accounted for by the special interests of banks and corporations owned by family or friends of the head of the government. This seems to have been especially true in Indonesia, where, for example, the attempt to establish a currency board in early 1998—at a time when no one knew what an equilibrium exchange rate for the rupiah might be—seems in part to have been intended to protect the interests of those with large foreign liabilities.[17] Such policies might also indicate that the human capital required for effective macroeconomic policies, and the incentives to give objective advice to the political leadership, were less well developed in Indonesia than in, say, Korea and Thailand.

Organizational Issues

A broader question, for both autocracies and democracies, is how to organize macroeconomic governance in a way that is technically competent, coordinated, sensitive to international developments relevant to the home country, and accountable to the political authority. Another broad question is whether the nature of political governance (the regime) matters in this regard: the conventional wisdom formerly held that authoritarian governments may be more effective in "getting the job done" in the macroeconomic realm; the current conventional wisdom is that democratic governance may after all work better in dealing with a major macroeconomic crisis.

Both of these questions require deeper study than can be given here, but the following considerations seem relevant.

1. *In countries with autocratic rule or only partial democracy, the formulation and implementation of budgets is fraught with opportunities for poor governance.* Channeling funds to pet projects and favored enterprises can be regarded initially as a source of *microeconomic* distortion, but in the long run such practices take on *macroeconomic* dimensions, as certain types of expenditures become quasi entitlements and fiscal deficits begin to develop. This is why it is vital to have politically independent auditing and program evaluation units separate from the budgeting ministry or agency. It would be naïve, however, to expect such units to do their job properly, independent of interference from the executive, without the types of safeguards normally found in democratic societies. These include a popularly elected legislature; freedom of speech, press, and assembly; freedom for nongovernmental organizations (NGOs) to organize and operate; and, not least, the rule of law, enforced by an independent, impartial, and competent judiciary.

2. *A key factor in the effectiveness and accountability of macroeconomic policy, and its independence from special interests, is the degree of independence of the central bank.* A relatively depoliticized and independent central bank can be a highly effective means of keeping a country on a stable macroeconomic track—although this cannot be accomplished without a responsible fiscal policy, which

requires political support. Conversely, political pressure on a central bank can lead to distortions in the allocation of credit and to excessive credit expansion generally. While it is certainly possible to encounter such pressures in a democratic setting, an authoritarian government runs a greater risk of nontransparent decision making and favoritism toward government cronies and therefore is more likely to undermine the prudential position of the financial system.

3. There is a widespread historical tendency (having some administrative justification) to divide the responsibility for macroeconomic governance along sectoral lines: the central bank deals with the banking/monetary/financial sector; the ministry of finance (or treasury) deals with fiscal management;[18] another ministry or agency is devoted to international trade agreements and policies (usually coordinated with the Ministry of Finance, which collects customs tariffs); and the ministries with responsibilities for foreign affairs negotiate international agreements having budgetary, monetary, or macroeconomic implications. *Successful macroeconomic policies therefore require coordination among the agencies responsible for their formulation and implementation.* Such coordination requires the existence, somewhere in the government, of a small, highly qualified group of economic analysts who provide a comprehensive view of how monetary, fiscal, and external economic policies are linked in an economic package.[19]

4. *Under an autocrat (or a strong elected executive with weak checks and balances), the coordination of macroeconomic policy is likely to be controlled directly by the ruler and his immediate staff,* without a truly independent central bank or autonomous coordinating agencies, councils, or think tanks. Effective coordination of policies is as necessary for this kind of regime as for others: it is certainly possible for autocracies to be badly run (as in numerous cases in Africa and Latin America). But even compared to a relatively efficient autocracy, and assuming comparable circumstances (per capita income, education levels), in a democracy with checks and balances, and with reasonably effective policy coordination, the quality of macroeconomic advice coming to the chief executive is likely to be superior to that arising from a top-down, manipulated process of policy formation. Wise autocrats have no doubt been known to seek expert, disinterested advice. But the danger of such advice being tarnished by corrupting political processes is greater in an autocracy than in a democracy and (for reasons explained in sec. I) tends to become greater the longer the autocracy has been in power.

Coordinating Governance Policy

In some countries, a coordinated view of macroeconomic and fiscal policy comes chiefly from the central bank, which tends to have better-qualified (because better-paid) staff than the government ministries. In other countries, it comes from a policy group of advisers in the ministry of finance or, possibly, a ministry of economics or planning ministry or agency. Alternatively, there may be a special unit attached directly to the presidential office that can serve as secretariat to a special economic cabinet (like the National Economic Council in the United States). Further support might come from a council of economic advisers, as in the United States or Germany.

The preferable modality of macroeconomic coordination depends on the institutional and political setting as well as available human resources. For example, where skilled human resources are sufficient, two poles of policy coordination (in the central bank and in the ministry of finance, planning, or budget) can work quite well, with strong and properly motivated political leadership. Likewise, in a parliamentary system, where a coordinating policy mechanism already exists in the cabinet, and in countries where skilled personnel are plentiful, a relatively fragmented system of policy-making units based in different government entities may actually work better than concentrating the coordinating power in the office of a president or prime minister.

Coordinating mechanisms can obtain useful support from a strong legislature, with specialized committees (backed by their own, independent, and well-qualified staffs) focusing on budgetary management, tax policy, and overall economic policy. While legislatures often also serve as conduits for the views of special interests, this is at least done under public scrutiny, and legislatures with more than rubber-stamp powers to shape budgets and economic policies can effectively check any tendencies in an autocratic executive to use political power for the benefit of private economic interests. Independent oversight of executive policies is, of course, greatly strengthened by a truly independent and legally protected civil society and a free press.

International influences—including the IMF, World Bank, and regional development banks—can also be helpful in galvanizing and improving faulty coordinating mechanisms as well as bringing pressure to bear on local authorities to follow correct policies. Their influence is necessarily limited, however, in a world of sovereign nation-states (as discussed in sec. IV).

III. Financial and Corporate Governance

It is hardly news that the way in which financial institutions are run, including their supervision and regulation, has much to do with the economic success of a country. It is obvious that when financial institutions are operated imprudently they can engender periodic financial crises; the resulting boom-bust cycle creates economic insecurity, especially for the poor, as well as an investment climate that over the long run may lead to slower growth than in a more stable environment. A less obvious implication of proper management of the financial sector is that when credit is available to *all* potential entrepreneurs—not just the rich and well connected but also new, small businesspersons—economies tend to acquire a more buoyant growth dynamic.

The topic of corporate governance, which has received special attention since the beginning of the Asian crisis, is so closely related to financial governance in these (and many other) countries that it seems useful to discuss these topics together. Moreover, financial and nonfinancial operations tend to be subject to a similar structure of governance—from creditors, shareholders, and markets. The governance of both types of organization is closely linked to the nature of the political regime and its mode of intervention in the economy.

In the United States, nonfinancial and financial corporations apparently exist in different worlds, sharply separated by function and law. This was not the case before the legal separation of such institutions was accomplished through the "trust-busting" legislation of the Progressive era. While this trust-busting was motivated by different considerations than those related to the Asian financial crisis, it reminds us that the close linkage between financial power and the nonfinancial sectors may both serve useful purposes in earlier stages of economic development and create relatively greater problems at later stages. Such problems—including large-scale, inadequately hedged, foreign borrowing—may be especially great when there is a close relationship between economic and political power; it was, in fact, the perception of such a nexus in the United States that led to public enthusiasm for trust-busting.

Definition of Governance

The working definition of *governance* used here is based on a key distinction between *principals* and *agents*. Most economic entities are

operated by agents, not principals, but even principal-operated entities are in some respects carrying out the functions of agents. For example, the daily operations of all but small firms are typically carried
out by managers who are not the main owners; at the same time, most
firms borrow money from lenders whose objectives are different
from those of the borrowers, who thus must act to some extent as the
lenders' agents.

In this context, governance is defined as "the legal and institutional arrangements governing the behavior of an economic entity, by
which owners, creditors, markets and the government compel or induce agents to behave according to the interests of the principals or
those of the broader society." Two key elements of governance are
discussed here. First, agents are confronted with a structure of incentives and rules with regard to such matters as granting and terminat-
ing lending, bankruptcy, the rights of boards of directors, compensation structure, and the termination of employment. Second, the
information flow from agents to principals is structured by the rules
and incentives affecting accountability, transparency, and disclosure
of information. In both cases, the government plays a key role in setting the rules under which private actors operate.

Sources of Governance

There are five main channels through which corporate and financial
governance operate.

1. *Governance by creditors.*   In a typical loan contract, failure of the
debtor to service a loan and repay the principal allows creditors to
force the debtor either to pay or declare bankruptcy. Bankruptcy is
therefore a key element of governance imposed by creditors and has
the economic effect of preventing inefficient overinvestment. The
loan selection process provides another important governance mechanism, determining the granting, renewal, or termination of loans
based (ideally) on a careful evaluation of each borrower and project.
Improper functioning of these mechanisms intensifies problems of
moral hazard and adverse selection and can result in overinvestment
in risky projects, as well as underinvestment in more justified ones.
Suppose that firms failing to service loans could avoid bankruptcy,
and that loans were granted according to criteria other than profitability and riskiness—for instance, by means of discretionary government intervention. In such cases, one would expect to observe

overinvestment and the accumulation of nonperforming loans. These phenomena were, in fact, observed in the Asian MSAs, Korea, Thailand, and Indonesia.

It follows that the positive contribution of the financial sector to governance of the nonfinancial sector is determined at least in part by the quality of political governance. If the government interferes with loan allocation decisions in order to favor particular firms, governance by creditors cannot function as intended. When the selection of loan recipients is based not on economic fundamentals but on ad hoc criteria imposed by the government, favoritism is fostered, and, to make matters worse, when favored firms fail to service loans the government will tend to take measures—bailouts, subsidies, and so on—to help these firms avoid bankruptcy. By the same token, the government may avoid setting up proper bankruptcy procedures in order to restrict the range of nondiscretionary decision making within the economic system.

Finally, the government's direct involvement in loan allocation tends to hamper the orderly development of human capital in financial institutions, that is, the capacity of the staff of those institutions to evaluate, thoroughly and objectively, the expected returns and riskiness of projects proposed in loan applications as well as the track record of the borrowers. Developing such capacity requires "learning by doing," and this will not occur unless the officers of financial institutions are given incentives to carry out these functions properly. Such incentives must be based on accountability (both positive and negative), which in turn requires a profit function that factors in the risk element. If the government directs loan allocations and bails out both financial and nonfinancial corporations that encounter difficulties as the result of poor, politically motivated decisions, such incentives are at best weak.

2. *Governance by owners.* For corporations, there are typically two main sources of principal-agent problems: the separation of management from ownership and management by a key owner who owns only a small fraction of total shares. In the first case, the problem is to restrict empire building and improper personal enrichment by professional managers (a particularly acute problem in Soviet and post-Soviet economies); in the second case, the problem is how to restrict expropriation of minority shareholders by the key owner(s). Of these two problems, management of firms by key owners is reported to be the more common (La Porta et al. 1998a).

The usual mechanisms to deal with these principal-agent problems are boards of directors, an incentive-based compensation structure for managers, the stock market, and the market for corporate control. The first two mechanisms operate directly on the internal governance of a firm. The stock market exercises indirect governance through the continual evaluation of performance implicit in stock price adjustments, which effectively provide the market with information about that evaluation. Various legal and institutional arrangements can be set up to facilitate shareholder control and protect against abuse by insiders, such as the right to call emergency shareholder meetings, penalties for insider trading, and mandatory disclosure of financial and nonfinancial information. Related to the stock market is the market for corporate control, that is, the existence of potential buyers who can take over and restructure a firm (including dismissal of managers) when the firm is performing under its potential.

State-owned enterprises create special problems of corporate governance. Even in a democratic setting, and in a largely market-oriented economy, privatization strengthens governance by owners because private owners are much more active in checking management than is the government. In an autocratic setting, the potential benefits of privatization are still greater. SOEs provide great opportunities for direct government intervention in the economy as a means of securing the power of the regime, for instance, by providing key positions for placing members of the autocrat's family and allies. In the worst case, SOEs can become part of a network of government-directed credits and investments, squeezing out nonfavored private enterprises and thereby weakening the influence of market-determined allocations of resources. In this case, while the power and political support of the regime are ostensibly strengthened, macroeconomic governance tends to be undermined through both the distortion of credit markets and the fiscal burdens that typically result from a large SOE sector.[20]

3. *Government regulation.* When the incentives of financial institutions and nonfinancial corporations deviate from those that lead to socially desirable results, the government may intervene so as to compel or induce these entities to behave in more socially desirable ways. Such regulation may range from environmental regulations to minimum wage legislation. Prudential regulation of financial institutions is the type of regulation most relevant to the Asian financial crisis.

There are several reasons why governments might wish to impose relatively stringent regulations on financial institutions, as opposed to other kinds of businesses. First, regulation aims to ensure the stability of the financial sector, to which a large part of the nonfinancial economy is linked. Second, regulation is necessary because the government, as the lender of last resort, must be concerned with moral hazard and adverse selection problems. Third, information problems are particularly acute in financial markets because financial transactions take place over time, therefore involving more uncertainty and risk than the (usually) shorter-term trade of goods and services.

Fourth, and particularly relevant, is the problem of limited risk. Since financial institutions have limited liability and usually operate under a combination of explicit (e.g., deposit insurance) and implicit guarantees, they may be tempted to reckon on capturing upside potential gains while keeping the downside limited to the amount of their net worth and so may tend to undertake riskier lending and lower capitalization than the public interest would dictate. To deal with these problems, governments impose capitalization and risk-taking guidelines on financial institutions. Overguaranteed and underregulated intermediaries have been blamed—for example, by Krugman and the IMF—as a major cause of the Asian financial crisis.[21] (Related explanations—such as Radelet and Sachs's (1998) emphasis on the accumulation of short-term foreign currency borrowing—may also be ultimately linked to the weakness of government regulation of the financial system.)

The key elements of effective banking legislation and prudential regulation are contained in the Basle Committee's *Core Principles for Effective Banking Supervision.*[22] First, capital adequacy ratios should ensure that banks maintain a minimum amount of capital to absorb unanticipated losses and that managers and owners have incentives to operate banks safely (IMF 1998a, 74–75). Second, risk should be diversified, avoiding excessive lending to a single borrower or connected group of borrowers, or a single sector of the economy. Third, supervisory authorities must have sufficient autonomy, authority, and capacity. With regard to capacity, supervisory agencies need to attract and retain employees of high skill and provide them with ongoing training to keep pace with the growing sophistication of financial sector activities.

Effective government regulation of financial institutions depends on the principle of preserving an arm's length relationship between the government and the financial system. When government becomes directly involved in loan allocations or state-owned banks engage in operations dictated by the state of the government's finances rather than the banks' own business interests, it may be impossible to properly enforce a system of prudential regulation. There is thus a structural tendency for countries with authoritarian, nontransparent, political governance to perform poorly in the field of prudential regulation of financial institutions, and even in more democratic political systems problems may arise in the context of a large state-owned share in the banking system. Establishing a more precise linkage between political regime and the quality of financial regulation would require detailed investigation.

4. *Market competition.*   Market competition puts managers of both financial and nonfinancial corporations under continual pressure to minimize costs and innovate. Furthermore, market competition renders measures of performance, such as profitability, more informative than when there is a lack of competition. In the latter instance, market power can make firms financially successful even in the face of poor investment decisions and resource allocation. Some of the policy conditions in IMF programs for the Asian MSAs—import liberalization, antitrust policy, and allowing foreign banks to enter the domestic market—were intended to improve corporate governance by promoting competition, although these measures were sometimes criticized as imposing the interests of major IMF shareholders (the United States, Japan) on the program countries.

5. *Internal organization.*   The structure within an organization also helps determine the quality of governance. Making managers more accountable for a firm's performance and providing checks and balances within an organization would strengthen internal governance. In this case, outside monitoring—by a board of directors or an outside accountant—lowers the chance that a manager at any level can hide poor performance by nonreporting of information. While management consultants and business schools throughout the world have developed models and techniques of effective internal corporate management, there are still quite large international and interfirm differences—in part cultural, in part individual—among the safeguards used to ensure good internal governance of enterprises.

Corporate and Financial Governance in East Asia

Is there evidence to suggest that a financial crisis is more likely to occur in countries with relatively weak corporate and financial governance? Johnson et al. (1998) provide empirical evidence that governance is more important than macroeconomic conditions in explaining the extent of financial crisis in East Asia. Using data from twenty-five emerging markets, they show that measures of corporate governance—particularly the effectiveness of protection for minority shareholders—explain the extent of currency depreciation and stock market performance better than macroeconomic measures. Instead of conducting regression analysis on data from just a handful of countries, this section presents data for several measures of corporate and financial governance, which clearly indicate that MSAs have weak corporate and financial governance.

1. *Governance by creditors and owners.* The *World Development Report* for the crisis period (World Bank 1998b) assesses the legal infrastructure for creditors' and shareholders' rights for more than fifty countries (table 1). Interestingly, MSAs generally receive a low score for shareholders' rights and especially for law enforcement, suggesting that lack of enforcement was an especially serious problem. The *World Competitiveness Yearbook, 1998* (IMD International 1998), which is based on subjective evaluations by foreign investors, reports a similar pattern: MSAs scored very low in the effectiveness of corporate boards to prevent improper practices and in the protection of the rights and responsibilities of shareholders.

Another World Bank report (World Bank 1998d) provides a more detailed and objective measure for governance by creditors and owners. It reports that the most severely affected countries have relatively poor protection of shareholder rights. Indonesia, Thailand, and Korea receive scores of 1 or 2 for antidirector rights, while Singapore, Hong Kong, Japan, and the United States scored 4 or 5 (table 2). For creditor rights, the MSAs score as high as other countries (table 3). In this case, too, the problem seems to be less a matter of laws on the books than a matter of poor enforcement.

2. *Government regulation.* How well were financial institutions regulated in the MSAs? Did they perform worse than other countries? *The World Competitiveness Yearbook, 1998* (IMD International 1998) ranks Korea, Indonesia, and Thailand among the worst five countries in terms of legal regulation of financial institutions. To some

extent, this ranking simply represents hindsight, but the precrisis (1996) ranking still gives the three countries mediocre rankings: forty-second, thirty-third, and twenty-third out of forty-six countries, respectively.

3. *Market competition.*   Table 4 presents proxies for competition among nonfinancial companies: the number of listed firms per 1 million population, and a trade openness measure. The MSAs tend to have a smaller number of listed firms, suggesting that weak competition in goods markets is related to the occurrence of a financial crisis. A problem in interpreting these data is that they may show not only the degree of market competition but also the availability of business information, since listed firms would tend to face a stronger information disclosure requirement than nonlisted firms.

Restructuring in the Most Severely Affected Countries

The data reported in the previous section suggest that the MSAs have generally had poor corporate and financial governance. Have governance-strengthening measures taken since the onset of the crisis been more effective in some countries than in others and has responsiveness to the crisis itself reflected the quality of political governance?

TABLE 1.   Assessment of Legal Infrastructure

Country	Creditors' Rights	Shareholders' Rights	Enforcement	Origin of Legal Systems
Indonesia	1	2	5.04	French
Thailand	1	3	6.91	English
Korea	1	2	6.97	German
Malaysia	1	3	7.11	English
Philippines	−2	4	3.77	French
Taiwan	0	3	8.84	German
Singapore	1	3	8.72	English
Hong Kong	1	4	8.52	English
Japan	0	3	9.34	German
United States	−1	5	9.50	English
Sample average for forty-nine countries	−0.27	2.45	7.21	

Source: Data from La Porta et al. 1998b; Knack and Keefer 1995; World Bank 1998b.

Note: Scores for creditors' rights range from −2 to 1; scores for shareholders' rights range from 1 to 5; values for enforcement range from 1 to 10.

TABLE 2. Shareholders' Rights

Country	One Share, One Vote	Proxy by Mail Allowed	Not Blocked before Meeting	Cumulative Voting/ Proportional Representation	% of Shares Needed to Call an Extra Meeting	Pre-emptive Right to New Issues	Oppressed Minority	Anti-director Rights
Indonesia	0	0	1	0	0.10	0	0	2
Thailand	0	0	1	1	0.20	0	0	2
Korea, Republic of	1	0	0	0	0.05	0	1	2
Malaysia	1	0	1	0	0.10	1	1	4
Philippines	0	0	1	1	open	0	1	3
Taiwan, China	0	0	0	1	0.03	0	1	3
Hong Kong	0	1	1	0	0.10	1	1	5
Singapore	1	0	1	0	0.10	1	1	4
Japan	1	0	1	1	0.03	0	1	4
United States	0	1	1	1	0.10	0	1	5
Sample average (fifty countries)	0.22	0.18	0.71	0.27	0.11	0.53	0.53	3

Source: Data from La Porta et al. 1998b.

Definitions:

(1) One share, one vote: Equals 1 if the company law or commercial code of the country requires that ordinary shares carry one vote per share, and 0 otherwise. Equivalently, this variable equals 1 when the law prohibits the existence of both multiple-voting and nonvoting ordinary shares and does not allow firms to set a maximum number of votes per shareholder irrespective of the number of shares owned, and 0 otherwise.

(2) Proxy by mail allowed: Equals 1 if the company law or commercial code allows shareholders to mail their proxy vote to the firm, and 0 otherwise.

(3) Not blocked before meeting: Equals 1 if the company law or commercial code allows shareholders to require that shareholders deposit their shares prior to a general shareholders meeting, thus preventing them from selling those shares for a number of days, and 0 otherwise.

(4) Cumulative voting: Equals 1 if the company law or commercial code allows shareholders to cast all of their votes for one candidate standing for election to the board of directors (cumulative voting) or if the company law or commercial code allows a mechanism of proportional representation in the board by means of which minority interests may name a proportional number of directors to the board, and 0 otherwise.

(5) Percentage of shares needed to call an extra meeting: It is minimum percentage of ownership of share capital that entitles a shareholder to call for an extraordinary shareholders' meeting. It ranges from 1 to 33 percent.

(6) Preemptive right to new issues: Equals 1 when the company law or commercial code grants shareholders the first opportunity to buy new issues of stock and this right can only be waived by a shareholders' vote, and 0 otherwise.

(7) Oppressed minority: Equals 1 if the company law or commercial code grants minority shareholders either a judicial venue in which to challenge the decisions of management or of the assembly or the right to step out of the company by requiring the company to purchase their shares when they object to certain fundamental changes, such as mergers, assets, dispositions, and changes in the articles of incorporation. The variable equals 0 otherwise. Minority shareholders are defined as those shareholders who own 10 percent of share capital or less.

(8) Antidirector rights: An index aggregating the shareholder rights, which we labeled "antidirector rights." The index is formed by adding 1 when: (1) the country allows shareholders to mail their proxy votes to the firm; (2) shareholders are not required to deposit their shares prior to the general shareholders' meeting; (3) cumulative voting or proportional representation of minorities on the board of directors is allowed; (4) an oppressed minorities mechanism is in place; (5) the minimum percentage of share capital that entitles a shareholder to call for an extraordinary shareholders' meeting is less than or equal to 10 percent (the sample median); or (6) shareholders have preemptive rights that can only be waived by a shareholders' vote. The index ranges from 0 to 6.

Although it may still be too early to judge the effectiveness of these measures (summarized in the appendix to this chapter), it is useful to briefly review them. The stronger democratic base in Korea and Thailand has apparently produced a more effective response than in Indonesia, which was hampered by continued autocratic rule until May 1998 and has been plagued with political uncertainties and social instability since then.[23]

TABLE 3.   Creditors' Rights

Country	Restrictions for Going into Reorganization	No Automatic Stay on Assets	Secured Creditors First Paid	Management Does Not Stay in Reorganization	Creditors' Rights
Indonesia	1	1	1	1	4
Thailand	0	1	1	1	3
Korea, Republic of	0	1	1	1	3
Malaysia	1	1	1	1	4
Philippines	0	0	0	0	0
Taiwan, China	0	1	1	0	2
Hong Kong	1	1	1	1	4
Singapore	1	1	1	1	4
Japan	0	0	1	1	2
United States	0	0	1	0	1
Sample average (fifty countries)	0.55	0.49	0.81	0.45	2.30

Source: Data from La Porta et al. 1998b.

Definitions:

(1) Restrictions for going into reorganization: Equals 1 if the reorganization procedure imposes restrictions, such as creditors' consent, to file for reorganization. It equals 0 if there are no such restrictions.

(2) No automatic stay on assets: Equals 1 if the reorganization procedure does not impose an automatic stay on the assets of the firm upon filing the reorganization petition. Automatic stay prevents secured creditors from gaining possession of their security. It equals 0 if such a restriction does not exist in the law.

(3) Secured creditors first paid: Equals 1 if secured creditors are ranked first in the distribution of the proceeds that result from the disposition of the assets of a bankrupt firm. Equals 0 if nonsecured creditors, such as the government and workers, are given absolute priority.

(4) Management does not stay in reorganization: Equals 1 when an official appointed by the court, or by the creditors, is responsible for the operation of the business during reorganization. This variable equals 1 if the debtor does not keep the administration of its property pending the resolution of the reorganization process, and 0 otherwise.

(5) Creditors' rights: An index aggregating different creditors' rights. The index is formed by adding 1 when: (1) the country imposes restrictions, such as creditors' consent or minimum dividends, to file for reorganization; (2) secured creditors are able to gain possession of their security once the reorganization petition has been approved (no automatic stay); (3) secured creditors are ranked first in the distribution of the proceeds that result from the disposition of the assets of a bankrupt firm; and (4) the debtor does not retain the administration of its property pending the resolution of the reorganization. The index ranges from 0 to 4.

1. *Governance by creditors.*   All three MSA countries overhauled their bankruptcy systems and adopted workout procedures for insolvent corporations and banks. Indonesia attempted to overhaul its bankruptcy system by introducing procedural rules both to ensure certainty and transparency and to provide greater protection against insider and fraudulent transactions. Indonesia also introduced a Special Commercial Court with jurisdiction over bankruptcy proceedings.[24] Thailand was required to pass a strengthened bankruptcy law.[25] Korea has also improved bankruptcy procedures.[26] Nevertheless, the experience of Indonesia shows that bankruptcy laws alone do not change the business environment overnight: bankruptcy courts are inadequate in number and thousands of bankruptcy cases were still pending at the end of 1998.[27]

Interestingly, Thailand also reformed secured lending laws, from expanding collateral assets to strengthening security rights. Secured lending, in contrast to unsecured lending, provides a better incentive (less moral hazard) to borrowers and a better screening device (less adverse selection) for creditors because collateral implies a higher bankruptcy cost for borrowers. Therefore, strengthening commercial registries leads to financial deepening and a more efficient allocation of funds.

TABLE 4.   Output Market Competition

Country	Domestic Firms/Population	Years Open
Indonesia	1.15	0.56
Thailand	6.70	1.00
Korea, Republic of	15.88	0.60
Philippines	2.90	0.78
Malaysia	25.15	1.00
Taiwan, China	14.22	0.71
Hong Kong	88.16	1.00
Singapore	80.00	1.00
Japan	17.78	0.73
United States	30.11	1.00

Source: Domestic firms/population data from World Bank 1998d. Years open data from Sachs and Warner 1995, 1–95.
   Definition:
   Domestic firms/population: Ratio of the number of domestic firms listed in a given country to its population (in millions) in 1994.

2. *Governance by owners.*   Privatization is included in all the re-structuring plans of the three countries. The Indonesian government was slated to divest its large state enterprises as well as some smaller ones. Thailand prepared a privatization action plan and developed a legal framework for privatization that includes a regulatory frame-work and new corporatization law. The Korean government an-nounced immediate privatization of five SOEs and their twenty-one subsidiaries and gradual privatization, by 2002, of six other SOEs.

In Korea, several measures meant to strengthen the accountabil-ity of boards of directors have been taken, such as introducing a re-quirement that there be outsiders on boards. To better protect the small shareholder, the Korean government allows cumulative voting and the possibility of class action suits against a corporation's execu-tives and its auditors. Also, there must be a separation of the evaluation function from the executive function of boards of directors, thereby providing more effective monitoring of manager's performance.

All three MSAs have enacted laws requiring mandatory regular disclosure of financial and nonfinancial information according to in-ternational accounting standards. Interestingly, the role of the Ko-rean Institute of Certified Public Accountants (KICPA), which is a nongovernmental organization, has been strengthened for the pur-pose of providing accounting standards according to international best practices.

3. *Government prudential regulation.*   From the onset of the crisis, the Asian MSAs had to deal with two problems associated with finan-cial governance: excessive government guarantees to, and deficient regulation of, financial institutions. Allowing the closure of nonviable banks strengthens governance over financial institutions by introduc-ing the possibility that banks can fail, although the desirability of in-stituting this approach in the middle of a financial crisis has certainly been controversial.[28] The appendix indicates the number of banks closed since the onset of the crisis; those numbers are especially high in Thailand, where 53 out of all 142 banks were closed.

All three MSAs have begun to improve the regulatory and su-pervisory framework for financial institutions. Improvements have been made in the standards for capital adequacy and loan classifica-tions, while the independence of supervisory agencies has been strengthened, disclosure requirements have been made more strin-gent, and the responsibilities and duties of managers of financial insti-tutions, as well as the role of outside investors, have been increased.[29]

4. *Competition in goods markets.*   All three countries have committed themselves to taking measures to increase the external openness of their economies by undertaking tariff reductions, phasing out quota restrictions, and opening more markets to foreigners, among other measures. Indonesia has also taken several steps to increase domestic competition, such as abolition of the monopoly of the State Logistics Agency (BULOG) and elimination of provincial and local export taxes. One interesting reform implemented in Korea is forcing each *chaebol* to focus on its chief products by selling other parts of their businesses to other *chaebols*. The effectiveness of this so-called big deal is critically dependent on foreign trade liberalization because it decreases domestic market competition, thereby leading to monopolistic behavior by the *chaebols* unless the latter face greater competitive pressure from abroad.

There seems to be little doubt that all three MSAs suffered serious weaknesses in the areas of financial and corporate governance. Interesting questions for further research are whether meaningful strengthening of financial and corporate governance is more likely to be carried out in a relatively more democratic setting and whether, when the starting point is a relatively more autocratic regime (like Indonesia's), the process of strengthening financial and corporate governance will be enhanced by simultaneous political reforms or indeed will even contribute to those reforms. Korea, which has perhaps the most democratically accountable government among the MSAs, has also made the most rapid recovery since late 1997, although some of this may have been due to its initially more advanced economy and to such exogenous factors as the official pressure on foreign private creditors to roll over the debts of troubled Korean conglomerates. The nature of political governance seems to have important effects on the effectiveness of financial and corporate governance. In good times, weaknesses in these areas are offset by high investment and growth rates; in times of crisis, the weaknesses become fatal.

IV. International Financial Arrangements and Domestic Governance

We have discussed so far, in the context of the East Asian financial crisis, the political roots of the government's role in economic governance and the interaction of that role with the forms of governance exercised within the financial and nonfinancial corporate sectors. The third and final element of the analysis is international mechanisms of economic governance. In discussing this topic, we shall focus solely on international financial arrangements, which have been extensively debated since the onset of the East Asian crisis in July 1997.[30]

There has been a tendency in this debate—though not by its most insightful participants[31]—to assume that international mechanisms of financial governance operate basically as intergovernmental arrangements. Since the signing of the Bretton Woods Agreement in 1944, the IMF has operated on a model in which each government—with variable amounts of skill and determination—pursues the encompassing interest of its polity and financial policies are in the hands of an elite with strong international links, ensuring consistency of viewpoints and policies across countries. Even within the IMF, this has been the explicit or implicit view of its staff, which deals largely with top central bank and ministry of finance officials who are largely technocrats, often with foreign education and international experience.

The reality, however, has proved much more complex. Over the years, policymakers have tended to be guided, in the first instance, not by international financial agreements but rather by their ideologies, party or interest group agendas, political calculations (winning elections or support of key groups), or personal interests. Indeed, as Dahl has pointed out, there is an inherent tension between decisions stemming from international agreements and the processes of democratic government.[32] As a result of these political realities, many countries have tended to diverge from the international norm of prudent macroeconomic policies and gradual foreign trade and exchange liberalization.[33] However, since the early 1980s most of these countries, often under financial and political duress created by their external debt problems, have pursued policies in accord with the "Washington Consensus":[34] prudent fiscal and monetary policies, removal of government controls on both domestic and external markets, privatization of large parts of the state-owned enterprise sector, land reform and privatization of agricultural marketing, and greater openness to foreign direct investment.

But while policymakers were starting to conform more closely to the IMF ideal of a technocratic elite following similar policies throughout the world, the global financial market was acquiring a hitherto unimagined power to overturn even properly formulated economic policies of governments. For example, sudden, unexpected inflows of capital can put irresistible inflationary pressure even on an economy governed by prudent fiscal and monetary policies. East

Asian countries in the early 1990s tried to solve the problem through a fixed exchange rate and rapid productivity growth. This allowed them to remain competitive in traded goods markets for a while but at the eventual price of inflation in the form of real estate and stock market bubbles, which in turn contributed to the financial market crisis in these countries.

It is clear, then, that more must now be demanded of international financial arrangements than simply inducing governments to pursue the right policies and promoting multilateral commerce. The challenge now is to constrain the operation of increasingly powerful and liberalized markets in order to avoid massive economic disruptions in emerging market economies but to do so in ways that do not greatly impede foreign trade and investment. To put the problem in practical terms, how can market players participate in international financial cooperation? Or—in the terms of this essay—how can international governance mechanisms interact with *both* the domestic political economy underlying a government's policies *and* its domestic economic governance mechanisms? Governance mechanisms in *creditor* countries are also relevant here.

Efforts to meet this problem date back to 1982. While big banks and big business have from time to time been mobilized to help deal with crises in individual countries, the first time this was done on a global scale was in reaction to the failure of Mexico to keep up with its external debt service payments, a failure that was made public in the summer of 1982. Late that year, Jacques de Larosiere, the IMF's Managing Director, realized that saving Mexico—and containing contagion to other countries—would require a joint effort by both official and private financial institutions. He informed representatives of the leading commercial banks that the IMF would refuse to undertake a program unless Mexico could demonstrate a feasible balance of payments outcome, which in turn would require rollovers and rescheduling of the government's debt to foreign commercial banks. This approach, though involving painful stabilization programs and lengthy negotiations between the banks and a number of debtor countries, proved to be a successful first step in dealing with the debt crisis.[35]

Another eventual effect of the debt crisis was the intensification of efforts to establish international standards for banking and capital markets. Initial efforts among the Bank of International Settlements (BIS)—starting with the establishment of the Basle Committee on Banking Supervision in 1975, whose members were the Group of Ten countries[36]—culminated in the establishment of international standards for capital adequacy in 1988. Ten years later, the standards have been extended to include all areas of banking supervision, summarized in the so-called Core Principles for Effective Banking Supervision, which have been adopted not only by the G–10 countries making up the Basle Committee but by a large number of other countries that are members of sixteen regional supervisor groups throughout the world.[37] A parallel development concerns the regulation of securities markets: here, too, initial efforts among the major industrial countries, through the International Organization of Securities Commissions (IOSCO), have been extended to other industrial and developing countries.

Against this background, then, the financial crisis of 1997–98 spawned new proposals for a revamped "international financial architecture." This fashionable jargon suggests a lack of understanding of the underlying political and economic processes. As Stanley Fischer correctly noted at a recent seminar in Washington,[38] the older term, *international monetary system,* represents a more realistic description, since it suggests a vast number of players operating in complex interaction with each other, while the architectural metaphor misleadingly suggests a simple, clear, mechanistic, fully controllable structure—hardly representative of the reality of 180–odd countries with a wide variety of political regimes, thousands of banks, millions of firms, and hundreds of millions of individuals directly or indirectly involved in international trade and investment. In line with the architectural metaphor, proposals often seem to focus on *content*—various kinds of ideal mechanisms—while stopping short of analyzing the *process* by which they would actually be put into effect.

Let us then look briefly at the main proposals that have been made and assess them on the basis of the processes that would be necessary to make them meaningful. The proposals for international arrangements to prevent future financial crisis fall into six categories.

1. Improving prudential and supervisory standards for both lending and borrowing countries and institutions (this includes improved risk management in private global financial institutions)
2. Establishing an international lender of last resort
3. Strengthening policy surveillance by international institutions
4. Imposing a set of restrictions and taxes on certain types of capital movements

5. Enforcing better transparency and disclosure in international financial markets
6. Improving debt rescheduling procedures and reducing existing moral hazards in domestic and foreign borrowing operations

Each of these recommendations embodies a number of propositions and must be examined for its feasibility in view of the domestic political incentives and institutions in the affected countries. In short, what incentives do governments and private market participants have to comply with international rules and guidelines and what institutions support compliance? How is international collective action fostered and how is it limited by problems of domestic governance?[39]

1. *Prudential and supervisory standards for financial markets.*   It is well known that a properly functioning banking system—more generally, the financial system—requires a set of regulations that are properly enforced. Efforts to subject such regulations to international guidelines have been described. From the standpoint of this study, the key questions of interest are whether an interventionist government is more or less likely to ensure compliance with international standards and whether compliance is more or less likely under a democratic or autocratic regime. To date, countries with highly developed financial systems have tended to comply with standards promulgated by the Basle Committee and the IOCSO because the principles underlying such standards have already been largely accepted in such countries.

The problem in debtor countries is for the technocratic elite (in the government and central bank) to persuade politicians and well-connected businessmen to accept more stringent standards for capitalization of banks and prudential supervision of financial institutions. Incentives for inducing "countries" to accept such standards have been discussed, for example, IMF publication of the list of countries that have accepted such standards or eligibility for certain kinds of financial assistance from the IMF. But such schemes may be viewed skeptically by countries that were previously able to attract foreign investment without these incentives being present, and there is the further obstacle that the leadership may not be able to persuade its political supporters and the private sector to cooperate. One must therefore conclude that countries tend to carry out reforms only in the midst of an economic crisis, with the strong push of IMF (or World Bank) conditionality. This is unfortunate, because certain reforms, such as financial sector restructuring, are much more costly when carried out during a crisis than during normal periods.

Another important question, which bears further investigation, is whether a political system with democratic checks and balances provides, over the long term, a stronger base for adherence to international standards of financial sector and corporate governance than does a relatively autocratic regime, with its penchant for nontransparent decision making and informal links between government and business.

2. *Establishing an international lender of last resort.* The drive for international standards in banking and securities markets suggests the analogy between national and international supervision. The Mexican crisis of 1994–95 and the Asian crises of 1997–98 have raised another aspect of the analogy between domestic and international markets, namely, whether the established central bank function of "lender of last resort" can be translated into an international counterpart. The IMF appeared to assume a role of this sort in its management of the huge bailouts of Mexico in 1995 and of Indonesia and Korea in 1997–98,[40] which were made up of both IMF resources and loans contributed bilaterally and by the World Bank. Yet even these financial packages were viable only if foreign creditors and wealthy residents also showed a willingness to roll over debts and keep their capital in the affected countries. However, the emergency nature of the bailouts made it difficult to organize the private creditors—who were more dispersed than in 1982—in a timely fashion,[41] and the behavior of residents depended, in a sensitive and hard-to-control manner, on the credibility of the government.

This experience led a number of observers to propose development of an international analogue to central monetary authority safeguards.[42] In a mature, properly managed, national financial system, banking collapse is avoided by a judicious combination of, on the one hand, bank regulation and supervision and, on the other hand, safeguards like deposit insurance and the willingness of the central bank to act as lender of last resort. The regulations and supervision serve to mitigate the moral hazard created by the safeguards. In this way, even though individual financial institutions occasionally go bankrupt, overall confidence in the banking system is maintained and there is no systemic breakdown while deposit insurance protects small and medium-sized depositors.

On an international plane, a lender of last resort would require a large fund available at short notice to provide rescue operations to countries facing sudden foreign exchange crises. Ad hoc rescue operations of the IMF, backed by loans from other international financial institutions (IFIs) and from some wealthy countries, currently serve this purpose, albeit imperfectly.

To analyze this analogy, let us first see what political economy considerations underlie arrangements for ensuring financial stability within a typical industrial country. The main task of the central bank and the bank regulatory authority, which are usually publicly appointed, is to support and maintain the stability and efficiency of the financial system.[43] If, instead, these authorities diverge from fulfillment of those objectives and their actions seem to be motivated by the private interest of particular individuals or firms, their leaders are subjected to attack by a free press and democratically elected legislators and face possible removal from their positions by the political authority.

The incentives and penalties in an international version of this structure are quite different. There are, of course, incentives for a national government to comply with international agreements, as well as disincentives for not complying, and the proposals for an international lender of last resort have focused on setting up such incentives and disincentives. But these incentives and disincentives are limited compared to those on the national level. For one thing, since international rescue operations are motivated by avoidance of "contagion effects" and thereby an international financial crisis, it is unlikely the IMF and G–10 could refrain from assisting a country that has not met the required standards for macroeconomic policies and supervision of financial institutions.[44] For another thing, national governments face not only international incentives but also their own domestic priorities, the interests of their supporters, the sentiments of their electorates (including specific interest groups), and media opinion. A national government therefore has much less incentive to follow international rules than does a domestic commercial bank. Furthermore, a government's ability to misinform an international agency may be greater, at least in the short run, than the scope for a domestic bank to hide information from a national banking authority. An international lender of last resort is therefore likely to face greater problems of asymmetric information than does a domestic central bank—although recent efforts by the IMF to improve reporting by member countries may have narrowed this gap in some cases.

It is debatable whether an international lender of last resort would be better off dealing with national governments that are democratically based or with those that are autocratic. On the one hand, an autocratic government, convinced of the potential benefits of adhering to an international code of good behavior, might find it easier than a democratic government to overcome domestic opposition. On the other hand, a democratic government is likely to promote greater transparency of banking information because this is insisted upon by national legislators and is therefore less likely than an autocratic government to be able to hide relevant information from an international authority.

3. *Strengthening policy surveillance by international institutions.* Surveillance by the IMF consists of a process of consultation with all member countries, involving data collection and discussions with member country authorities carried out by the IMF staff and discussion of reports by its Executive Board. The impact of such consultations, however, is generally thought to be minimal, except in those cases in which the country has a program with the IMF, is in the process of negotiating a program, or is likely to enter into a negotiation.

Restricting the discussion to cases in which IMF policy advice has some impact, the question arises as to the political process by which this advice is translated into practice. The ideal scenario goes something like this: the IMF staff, backed by the management of the relevant area department as well as by the Managing Director, interacts with country officials to produce a consensus solution, which is then explained to and accepted by the political authorities, who (in a democratic system) explain it to and receive at least majority political support from the public. Finally, civil servants translate the agreed policy measures into effective practice.

There are numerous and fairly obvious ways in which reality may fall short of this ideal scenario. In practice, quite apart from problems of competence and available information at the levels of both the IMF staff and the member country government, there is a whole string of principal-agent relationships. A major relationship of this sort is that between the IMF's shareholders—of which the G–10 countries have 50 percent of the votes on the Executive Board—and the IMF management, which must carefully take into account the views of the major countries.[45] Without discussing principal-agent problems within the IMF—although these can be nontrivial—the relationship between the member country government and the IMF staff is itself complex and fraught with lack of transparency on both sides. Such nontransparency can reach the point where—as in Russia, Korea, and Thailand recently, and in Hungary, Mexico, and the Philippines in well-known episodes of earlier years—the member country central bank hides crucial information from the IMF staff. Serious problems of transparency and communication can also arise between the country's own technicians and its political leadership—sometimes simply through the difficulty of explaining technicalities to economically unsophisticated leaders—and between the political authorities and the electorate (even assuming some degree of democracy), where the leaders tend to accentuate the positive and downplay the painful aspects of an economic program. Further problems relate to the relationship between the government and the private sector, where the government is often unwittingly guilty of poor communication with regard to the regulations and taxes it imposes on the private sector, while the latter, often quite wittingly, is nontransparent about the information yielded to the authorities regarding company accounts and operations.

The consequence of this chain of asymmetric information and different principal-agent relationships is that policies "agreed" upon by the IMF staff and the country authorities may be only partially carried out by the latter—sometimes with the tacit compliance of the IMF, which seeks to avoid upsetting a delicate domestic political balance, disturbing financial markets, or damaging the relationship between the IMF staff and the national government. Even when a government is honestly trying to carry out an agreed upon program, its relationship with its electorate and the private sector may constrain its ability to accomplish what it intends. It is noteworthy that despite these difficulties genuine agreement on IMF-supported adjustment programs is often achieved, and such programs are often, at least in good part, actually carried out. Such outcomes are testimony to the professionalism and diplomatic skills of both IMF staff and their member country counterparts, in the context of decades of experience with international monetary cooperation; impressive amounts of technical assistance and training provided by the IMF, World Bank, and other donors; and successful efforts by the emerging market country governments themselves.

4. *Restrictions and taxes on capital movements.* A prominent international economist recently cited as the main argument against restrictions on international capital movements that he himself would

not want to live in a country that had such restrictions (Cooper 1998). This shrewd observation underlines the point that policies with regard to capital account liberalization are in practice based not on standard macroeconomic reasoning but on two other main considerations: first, the path-dependent status quo ante; and, second, the interests of the business community and the relevant players in the government. The reason the first is important is because changing an existing system always involves difficulties and risks. The second reason, related to the first, requires more detailed analysis.

Who are the winners and losers in a system of capital controls? With regard to controls over *capital inflows,* the winners are clearly those domestic financial institutions or investors who are protected—in the same sense as import tariff protection—from market entry by foreign financial institutions or investors. Other winners include those market players who, in a system where certain types of capital inflows are allowed, gain rents from being permitted to borrow or receive investments from abroad. The losers are those who are excluded from the domestic credit market but might be able to obtain credit if foreign funds were allowed to flow in—mainly because this is likely to raise the overall availability of credit. The losers might also include the government because if it must borrow to finance fiscal deficits, the cost of such borrowing is likely to be larger if bank borrowing abroad is prohibited or restricted.

With regard to *capital outflows,* those who lose from restrictions are clearly those who have capital to invest abroad, that is, enterprises and wealthy individuals. The government may gain from the greater policy freedom provided by capital controls and from the possibly lower interest rates resulting from the greater availability of local capital, but most economists would argue that the long-run costs of such restrictions are greater, that is, less investment from abroad (because of possible difficulties in repatriating funds) and consequently less economic growth (see Tamirisa 1999).

Like Keynes, many economists now believe that it might be possible to discourage "bad" capital movements—short-term speculative purchases of equities by nonresidents and short-term foreign borrowing by domestic banks—while continuing to encourage "good" capital flows such as foreign direct investment. This is a technical issue beyond the scope of this essay. The relevant question here is whether the "good" and "bad" capital flows are seen as such by the policymakers and their private-sector (or SOE) constituents; recent evidence is in fact mixed. As long as this remains a politically ambivalent issue, collective action to impose a "rational" international regime in this area is exceedingly unlikely.[46]

5. *Better transparency and disclosure of financial information.* There has been widespread agreement that lack of transparency with regard to the financial position of the government and the central bank, and with regard to commercial banks and nonbank corporations as well, has contributed negatively to financial difficulties, not just in the MSA countries but also in Japan and Malaysia. While this general perception may be supportable by analysis, it needs to be dissected into its several parts, as each information asymmetry involves different incentives and consequences. The chief asymmetries involved are between the international official community (represented by the IMF) and the national government, between the private sector and the national government, and between individual private sector entities and "the market" as a whole.

As suggested earlier, the withholding of key information by national authorities has been a perennial problem faced by international organizations. Incentives for better reporting by IMF member countries—for instance, making timely and complete information a condition for emergency financial assistance—are both weak and noncredible: weak because a determined government with an apparently successful economy knows that market participants will overlook pedantic details like statistical reporting, and noncredible because emergency assistance may be given even to an undeserving member country if the alternative is global financial contagion. While international financial institutions should not be discouraged from announcing and attempting to impose statistical standards and privately remonstrating with central banks and other responsible agencies, the best guarantee of statistical transparency is domestic political transparency. Since the latter can hardly be imposed in any direct way from abroad, the international community needs to continue to preach the benefits of democratic institutions through any media and political channels possible, at the same time not expecting overnight changes in previously authoritarian polities and societies.

A national government's ability to comply with international data disclosure requirements depends crucially on the disclosure of information by the private sector to the national government. It is the authors' view that such disclosure is more likely to be comprehensive and accurate in democratic than in authoritarian regimes and, among the latter, in those regimes (usually with democratic or oligarchic elements) that are committed to market-augmenting government. This is because the greater commitment of democratic regimes to the rule of law will tend to build stronger moral authority for national governments to demand correct information from firms. The greater likelihood of direct links between government officials and financial or corporate entities under an authoritarian regime also implies greater discretionary exemption and shielding of such entities from data-reporting requirements. An authoritarian government, moreover, implies a more restricted scope for independent monitoring, by civil society and the media, of data reporting by enterprises. A political commitment to market-augmenting government tends to lead to greater availability of enterprise data to the market as a whole and therefore also to the government.

Finally, the accuracy and completeness of reported earnings, profits, and other financial data by private sector entities *to the market* is a function of the extent of market development and, both directly and indirectly, market-augmenting government.[47] The latter, for instance, determines the extent of shareholders' rights, disclosure requirements in stock and bond markets, collateral registries, and other public sources of data on individual firms. It also helps determine the overall development and sophistication of markets, one aspect of which is the existence of specialized firms dedicated to collecting and providing (for a price) data on particular markets and individual firms. Since market-augmenting government is more likely to be fostered in democracies—although there are exceptions—one may hypothesize a tendency for the prevalence and strength of democratic institutions in a country to be correlated with private sector reporting. Future research should seek to test this proposition.

6. *Improved rescheduling procedures and reduced moral hazard in domestic and foreign borrowing operations.* There is both an international and a related domestic question to this issue—actually, two domestic questions, one related to the creditor country and one to the debtor.

1. The international question is how to compel creditors, in the wake of a crisis, to take an active part in rescheduling operations, so as to reduce the impact of the crisis on both the financial sector and real activity. Being able to do so would reduce

the moral hazard of lending abroad from the standpoint of the creditor country.

2. Closely related to this question is how creditor countries, through the instrumentality of normal prudential supervision and regulation of financial institutions, can induce or compel such institutions to exercise restraint in their buildup of short-term asset positions in emerging market countries.

3. Finally, there is the question of how to reduce moral hazard with regard to foreign borrowing by financial institutions and nonfinancial corporations in the debtor countries. One of the most harmful features of the financial systems in the MSA countries of Asia was the explicit or implicit guarantee to bail out banks that could not meet their debt-servicing obligations. Not only did this lead to the normal lender of last resort function by the central bank, but it was complicated by the foreign currency denomination of the debt, implying that such debt was backed not only by the central bank's power to create domestic money but by its international reserves (see Goldstein 1998, 46–53).

The Basle Committee is working on the second problem; it is surely within the committee's scope, and that of domestic financial regulatory authorities in creditor countries, to work on the first. The greater difficulty, from a political-economic standpoint, is with the third aspect. Here, the ability of debtor countries to reduce moral hazard within their systems depends to some degree on issues already discussed, for example, the transparency of financial data vis-à-vis both the central bank and the market and the arm's length relationship between the government and individual financial institutions or nonfinancial corporations. Without reliable data, the government is unable to monitor the overall situation and may suddenly find itself in the midst of a crisis that it has no choice but to battle as best it can, including bailouts of banks and other entities. Cronyism between government and the private sector reduces the credibility of any policy that denies even implicit guarantees to banks or corporations in trouble. Here, too, the effectiveness of any scheme that posits possible future international assistance on maintaining a preferred financial regime in a debtor country depends crucially on the governance characteristics of the existing regime in that country.

V. Summary and Conclusions

At the outset, we warned the reader that this essay would raise questions rather than answer them. In conclusion, then, we would like to summarize some of the questions we believe need further investigation.

On the *relative role of governance factors in explaining the East Asian crisis,* there is still a lack of empirical proof that domestic governance problems peculiar to the East Asian countries, rather than a typical financial panic of international origins, was responsible for the sudden outward flows of capital and other monetary disturbances of 1997–98. While the authors believe that the differing abilities of the MSA countries to deal with the crisis clearly demonstrate differences in the quality of governance, more work would be needed to give rigorous empirical support to this proposition.[48]

On the *political basis of economic governance,* we have only suggested a few hypotheses regarding the kind of political regimes likely to produce an effective, growth-enhancing, market-augmenting government. One is that the type of political regime that is especially effective in the early stages of economic development may be less suited to fostering the creation of a full-fledged, sophisticated, market economy at a later stage. There certainly seems to be some indication of this in the Asian experience, in which authoritarian, paternalistic regimes fostered rapid growth when these economies were at relatively low income levels but seem to be evolving toward more democratic models to deal with demands for greater market autonomy. But even if a case can be made for the desirability of democratization as a market economy becomes more sophisticated, the varied historical examples suggest the need to find out more about the conditions under which either an autocratic or a democratic government can be market augmenting or not. It would also be useful to look at the historical evidence for the transition from discretionary to arm's length approaches to state economic governance, and to define the most effective ways in which the international community might assist with this transition.

Empirical work on *macroeconomic governance* would need to tap into the huge literature on macroeconomic policies and their effects and link existing work to variables that reveal the quality of governance. Unfortunately, such variables are hard to quantify, but perhaps a taxonomy of regimes (democratic vs. authoritarian, discretionary vs. arm's length), together with a taxonomy of the way macroeconomic policy is organized (as discussed in sec. II), could yield ways of exploring the relationships between the political and administrative variables, on the one hand, and the more familiar economic ones on the other.

In section III of our essay, preliminary attempts are made to trace the relationship between empirical indicators of *financial and corporate governance* and some governance variables that have been developed by others. But these attempts are hardly the last word on the subject; one needs to look more carefully, perhaps through case studies, at the realities of financial and corporate governance in particular cases. And, again, what is lacking is a linkage between indicators of these types of governance and the more carefully articulated taxonomy of political regimes alluded to earlier. Specifically with regard to the adjustment of MSA countries to the East Asian crisis, it would be interesting to examine the reasons why recovery in Korea has been more rapid than in Indonesia and Thailand.

Finally, one of the authors is at work on a more detailed examination of proposals for improving the *governance of the international monetary system* from the standpoint of how realistically these proposals are related to the actualities of domestic economic governance, especially in emerging market countries.[49] Because of the growing power of global financial markets, and their linkages to effective domestic financial governance in both the major industrial countries and the emerging market economies, the international financial institutions have become increasingly interested in domestic governance issues. One research topic that might be especially interesting in this context would be to look at the quality of data about private-sector financial and nonfinancial activity across different countries and whether there are institutional factors (such as the type of political regime) that are statistically related to variations in data quality.

Appendix

(see following page)

Reform Measures Taken since the Crisis

Governance Mechanisms	Governance-Enhancing Measures	Indonesia	Korea	Thailand
		Structural Reform Measure: Governance from Creditors		
Bankruptcy law	Overhaul of bankruptcy law	Strengthening of the laws in April 1998; transparent court fee system; appointment of ad hoc judges; effective enforcement; training of judges	Strengthening of the laws in February 1998; creation of bankruptcy commission; study to examine setup of additional bankruptcy courts; creation of bankruptcy commission to assist Seoul District Court in insolvency litigation	Overhauling of bankruptcy law in October 1998; allowing unsecured creditors to file their claims; provision of voting on a reorganization proceeding; specific rules on rejection of outstanding contracts
Enhancing accounting standards and requiring information disclosure[a]	International accounting standards	Accounting standards consistent with international standards by December 1998	Accounting standard complying with IAS 30	In process based on the new law
	Information disclosure		Chaebols required to disclose all liabilities to their major creditor banks; biannual audited financial statements by August 31, 1998, and quarterly unaudited financial statements by January 1, 2000; consolidated statements; disclosure of transactions by large shareholders	
	Strengthening nongovernmental self-regulatory institutions		Strengthening of KICPA, nongovernmental regulatory body	

Secured lending				Increase and improve collaterable assets; strengthening of security rights
Arbitration law			A new arbitration law consistent with international standards by December 1998	

Structural Reform Measure: Governance from Shareholders

Enhancing minority shareholder rights	One share, one vote	No	Yes	No
	Cumulative voting/ proportional	No	No; to be introduced in second half of 1999	Yes
	Penalties for insider trading	Yes	Yes	Yes
	Class action suits		Class action suits against executives and auditors	
Enhancing accountability of corporate boards	Outsider on board or audit committee		Listed companies require a minimum of 25% outsiders on board	Setup of an audit committee for each listed company by end of 1999
Capital market development			Creation of mutual funds; expansion of sovereign debt; issue and implement comprehensive M&A guidelines	
Privatization		Divestiture of 12 SOEs by March 1999	Privatization of 5 SOEs; privatization of additional 6 by 2002	Strong emphasis given to privatization; privatization of infrastructure firms

Structural Reform Measure: Prudential Regulations

Consolidation of financial institutions	Initial number of financial institutions	222	169	142

(continues)

Reform Measures Taken since the Crisis—Continued

Governance Mechanisms	Governance-Enhancing Measures	Indonesia	Korea	Thailand
	Closure	59 (26.6%)	10 (5.9%)	56 (39.4%)
	Nationalization or under supervision	43 (19.4%)	2 (1.2%)	18 (12.7%)
	To be merged	4 (1.9%)	5 (3.0%)	0
	Bought by foreigners, joint venture	0	2 (1.2%) in process	4 (2.8%)
Mechanisms dealing with nonperforming loans (NPLs)	Definition of NPL	3 months. Overdue by 2001.	6 months. Overdue, moved to 3 months.	3 months. Overdue by 2000.
	General provision (% of loans)	1%	0.5%	1%
Capital adequacy and loan classification	Capital adequacy requirements	9%, 12% by 2001	8%	8.5%
	Tightening of loan classification standards	Lagged behind relative to capital adequacy	Lagged behind relative to capital adequacy	Lagged behind relative to capital adequacy
Strengthening supervisory authority	Independence	Draft law to institutionalize Bank Indonesia's autonomy	Unification of supervisory organization by January 1, 1999	In process with help from the World Bank New Financial Institutions Law to be enacted by mid-1999
	Upgrading supervisory skills	In process	In process	In process based on the new law
Risk management	Risks associated with short-term foreign borrowing	Setup of foreign exchange monitoring system	70% of short-term loans matched by short-term assets	
	Risks associated with a single borrow		From 45% to 25% in July 2000	
Deposit insurance scheme		Did not exist before the crisis; deposit insurance covering all bank depositors for a period of 2 years was introduced in January 1998	Existed before the crisis; broad-based guarantees to calm depositors; will be replaced by a funded and more limited deposit insurance system	Did not exist before the crisis; broad-based guarantees to calm depositors; will be replaced by a funded and more limited deposit insurance system

Structural Reform Measure: Promoting Market Competition

Structural Reform Measure			
Trade liberalization			
Reduction of trade barriers	In process	Phase out Import Diversification Program	Reduction of tariff to a maximum of 10% for nonfood agricultural products by 2003; reduction of tariffs on chemicals and steel to 5–10% by 2003; phase out quota and nontariff barriers
Elimination of restrictions on foreign investment	Conversion of the Alien Business Law into a new and more liberal Foreign Investment Law; amendment of the land code to allow ownership of residential land	Enact the Foreign Investment Promotion Act; open markets for security dealings, insurance, and leasing	Elimination of restrictions in retail and wholesale trade
Competition law			
Promotion of domestic competition			In process
Elimination of monopoly			Abolition of the monopoly of the State Logistics Agency (BULOG) over the importation and distribution of essential food items
Promotion of mobility of commodities within the country			Elimination of provincial and local export taxes

Source: Government of Thailand, Letter of Intent, various issues; government of Korea, Letter of Intent, various issues, and 1998d; government of Indonesia, Letter of Intent, various issues; IMF 1999a; J. P. Morgan, 1998. *Asian Financial Markets*, various issues.

[a] This is related also to governance from other channels, especially governance from shareholders.

Notes

The authors dedicate this paper to the memory of Mancur Olson, who encouraged them to study this topic and who contributed intriguing suggestions at seminars held at the Center for Institutional Reform and the Informal Sector (IRIS) and the United States Agency for International Development (USAID) in January and February 1998. This essay represents an attempt to extend the analysis he began to develop during those weeks; the process of writing it was immeasurably impoverished by his absence.

The authors are indebted to Omar Azfar, Charles Cadwell, and Todd Sandler for helpful written comments and have also benefited from the oral comments of various economists attending a workshop on this essay at USAID headquarters (January 20, 1999) and the IRIS conference on market-augmenting government (March 26–27, 1999).

1. This is the title of Charles Kindleberger's (1996) excellent book on financial crises.

2. See Radelet and Sachs 1998.

3. Such restraints include parties that are outlawed; controlled media; restrictions on freedom of public assembly; the lack of an independent judiciary; and, in general, no enforced constitutional protection of individuals against arbitrary imprisonment and property seizure by the government.

4. See Olson 2000 and 1998, as well as Lanyi et al. 1997 and Cadwell 1999.

5. For evidence on this point, see Azfar 1999.

6. Some economic thinkers, following Adam Smith, are skeptical about proactive enterprise and market creation by governments even at early stages of economic development. Smith, mirroring primarily the British experience, believed that infrastructure should normally be self-financing through tolls and fees ([1776] 1950, bk. 5, chap. 1, pt. 3). Of course, such infrastructural development utilizing private resources presupposes adequately functioning markets and a stable polity.

7. Olson 2000, 1998; Lanyi et al. 1997; Cadwell 1999.

8. This proposition might be testable on a cross-country basis but possibly not for individual countries, where counterfactuals would be involved.

9. This was in the period before foreign exchange liberalization.

10. A discussion of selective government intervention strategies can be found in World Bank 1993; Krugman 1994; Radelet, Sachs, and Cook 1999; and Porter and Takeuchi 1999.

11. See World Bank 1997, 152, for a standard definition of *first-* and *second-generation reforms.*

12. See Olson 1993, 567–76; 2000. See also Olson and McGuire 1996 for the argument that the optimum tax rate for an autocrat is at the point where the marginal cost of public goods provided through additional tax-financed

government activity is equal to the marginal revenue (derived at the hypothesized tax rate) from the additional output induced by the additional public goods. They further argue that in a democratically governed society the optimum tax rate is likely to be regarded as lower than under an autocratic regime.

13. See, again, Olson 1993. DeLong and Shleifer (1993) assert that, for example, the troubled history of succession in medieval and Renaissance England would naturally have led the "princes" of that time to tax their subjects to the hilt and therefore discourage the growth of trade and manufacturing; it was not until the Glorious Revolution of 1688 that parliamentary supremacy was assured and British trade and manufacturing could "take off." While we do not find this interpretation of English history entirely convincing, to explain why would go far beyond the scope of this essay. Suffice it to say that in England, as in the Asian MSAs, one can find long episodes of "despotic" rule (actually, rarely truly despotic either in England or in most Asian countries) in which commerce flourished for reasons both related and unrelated to government intervention.

14. As an interesting counterexample to Indonesia's Soeharto, General Pinochet not only launched Chile in the right direction economically but also eventually transferred power to a democratically elected government. Pinochet's apparent lack of dynastic ambition may also be related to the relatively low level of personal "corruption" in the Pinochet regime: there was no political motive to extend personal economic control. However, in the historically parallel case of the Argentinian military regime of 1976–84, the military as a group took over a number of large enterprises in order to assure its own continued financing. This type of military involvement in the economy is, like the pure autocratic case, likely both to lead to massive inefficiency in the management of SOEs and to undermine essential central government functions: conducting prudent fiscal policy, ensuring efficient credit allocation by financial institutions, and maintaining arm's length regulation of nonfinancial institutions. It may also lead to a kind of decentralized personal corruption, as individual managers of SOEs are tempted to use their positions for personal enrichment.

15. As Tanzi (1995, 1998) has pointed out, government power may be employed for the benefit of various groups included in the social network of leaders and officials: "the abuse of public power is not necessarily for one's private benefit but for the benefit of one's party, class, tribe, friends, family, and so on" (1998, 564).

16. A description and analysis of these networks can be found, for instance, in Landa and Huang 1999.

17. Some economists, however, were sincerely convinced that this was a legitimate policy intended to stabilize the economy.

18. The latter responsibility is sometimes split, as in Mexico, between the revenue collection/borrowing side (Ministerio de Hacienda y Crédito Publico)

and the budgetary side (Ministerio de Presupuesto y Planeación), or, as in the United States, between a treasury and a budgeting agency (Office of Management and Budget).

19. This topic is discussed further in section III.

20. For elaboration of these problems, see World Bank 1995. The possible need for SOEs, as one form of direct government intervention at an early stage of development, is mentioned in section I. Moreover, as explained, for example, in the World Bank report just cited, mechanisms can be devised to create rules and incentives such that SOEs are run efficiently. But such rules and incentives are more likely to be established and properly implemented in a democratic setting, with public oversight, than in an autocratic regime.

21. See Krugman 1998; IMF 1997b, 1998a; and other IMF publications.

22. It is reproduced in Folkerts-Landau and Lindgren 1998, and discussed in detail in Goldstein 1997.

23. Stiglitz (1998) has argued that autocratic regimes may be more successful in steering economies in good times than in responding quickly and effectively to economic crises.

24. Letter of Intent with the IMF, April 10, 1998 (Government of Indonesia 1998a). See also Lane et al. 1999.

25. Letter of Intent with the IMF, December 1, 1998 (Government of Thailand 1998d). See also Lane et al. 1999.

26. Letter of Intent with the IMF, July 24, 1998 (Government of Korea 1998c). See also Lane et al. 1999.

27. Radelet and Sachs 1999; talk by Steven Radelet at USAID, Washington, DC, January 7, 1999.

28. For instance, see Radelet and Sachs 1998.

29. See World Bank 1998a, 41; and Lane et al. 1999, chap. 8.

30. This section is based on a separate essay by Anthony Lanyi, presently in draft form, entitled "International Financial Architecture and Domestic Economic Governance."

31. For example, there is certainly due regard taken of domestic governance in the excellent surveys conducted by Goldstein (1998) and Eichengreen (1999), but these analyses stop short, for example, of looking at the interaction between different types of political regimes and forms of financial and corporate governance.

32. See Dahl 1998, 114–17.

33. The reasons for the frequent failure of countries to comply with international commitments is discussed in World Bank 1997, 131–42.

34. See Williamson 1993.

35. To put the 1980s debt crisis into present-day perspective, it should be noted that its impact will in all likelihood prove to be more widespread, deeper, and longer in duration than the crisis that began in 1997.

36. The countries are Belgium, Canada, France, the Federal Republic of Germany, Italy, Japan, Luxembourg, the Netherlands, Sweden, Switzerland, the United Kingdom, and the United States—actually twelve, not ten.

37. The core principles are reproduced in Folkerts-Landau and Lindgren 1998. Some of the earlier history of the Basle Committee can be found in the IMF's *International Capital Markets* reports of April 1989 and April 1990. The sixteen regional supervisor groups include: Arab Committee on Banking Supervision, Caribbean Banking Supervisors Group, Association of Banking Supervisory Authorities of Latin America and the Caribbean, Eastern and Southern Africa Banking Supervisors Group, Executives Meeting of East Asia and Pacific Central Banks (EMEAP) Study Group on Banking Supervision, Group of Banking Supervisors from Central and Eastern European countries, Gulf Cooperation Council Banking Supervisors' Committee, Offshore Group of Banking Supervisors, Regional Supervisory Group of Central Asia and Transcaucasia, South East Asia, New Zealand, and Australia (SEANZA) Forum of Banking Supervisors, and the Committee of Banking Supervisors in West and Central Africa.

38. See Fischer 1998b.

39. On this general issue, see Sandler, this volume.

40. The Mexican, Korean, and Indonesian bailout packages were $48, $58, and $40 billion, respectively. The Thai bailout was much smaller, $17 billion, although this was still large relative to the size of the Thai economy.

41. See Goldstein 1998, 37–44, 50–53.

42. See, for instance, President Clinton's address to the annual meetings of the World Bank and International Monetary Fund, October 6, 1998 (see IMF 1999b). Recently, Fischer has provided a thorough analysis of this analogy (1999).

43. The chains of command and responsibility are especially complex in the United States, where there are several supervisory authorities and an independent central bank based on quasi-independent regional Federal Reserve Banks, which appoint their own boards. But the bottom line is that the Federal Reserve system derives its authority from Congress, and is institutionally obligated to work in close coordination with the president and the secretary of the Treasury.

44. It may be argued that fear of contagion may also induce a national central bank to bail out one of its domestic banks—especially a large one—but in the national case the national government has more varied and powerful policy instruments for dealing with a national liquidity crisis than in the analogous international case.

45. Discussion of the IMF as if it were an autonomous agent—saying that "the IMF decided this" or "the IMF imposed that"—is unrealistic to the point of absurdity. Nevertheless, this is the standard format of the criticism of IMF policies. It would be much more interesting to examine, say, the roots of American (or European or Japanese) views vis-à-vis IMF-supported programs and also the sometimes nontransparent ways in which these views are brought to bear on the IMF's management.

46. Of course, these chances are not improved by the fact that economists themselves disagree sharply about what constitutes a rational regime!

47. When such data are reported, they are more firm specific than data that governments make public, which tend to be aggregated so as not to reveal data on individual firms or persons. For instance, tax statistics from the Internal Revenue Service and bank statistics published by the Federal Reserve Board are structured carefully so as to make it impossible to discover data for very large entities that are well known in the market.

48. A good deal of information that supports this belief has been collected recently by Haggard (2000), who finds that democratic government serves better to stabilize financial expectations than does a dictatorship in which succession problems are arising, hence one important reason for the difference between the Korean and Indonesian experiences.

49. Lanyi 2002.

References

Azfar, Omar. 1999. "Sufficient Conditions for Rapid Convergence." IRIS Working Paper. Originally presented at the IRIS conference Market-Augmenting Government, March 26–27, Washington, DC.

Cadwell, Charles. 1999. "Developing Egypt's Financial Markets: The Role of Market-Augmenting Government." Paper presented at the conference Growth beyond Stabilization: Prospects for Egypt, Egyptian Center for Economic Studies, Cairo, February 3–4.

Cooper, Richard. 1998. Panel discussion on policies dealing with international capital movements (October). International Monetary Fund. Annual Meetings of IMF and World Bank, Washington, DC.

Dahl, Robert. 1998. *On Democracy.* New Haven: Yale University Press.

DeLong, J. Bradford, and Andrei Shleifer. 1993. "Princes and Merchants: European City Growth before the Industrial Revolution." *Journal of Law and Economics* 36 (2): 671–702.

Eichengreen, Barry. 1999. *Toward a New International Financial Architecture: A Practical Post-Asia Agenda.* Washington, DC: Institute for International Economics.

Fischer, Stanley. 1998a. "Economic Crisis and the Financial Sector." Mimeo.

———. 1998b. "On Reshaping the International Financial Architecture." Paper presented at the Brookings Institution Roundtable, Washington, DC, October 27.

———. 1999. "On the Need for an International Lender of Last Resort." Princeton Essays in International Economics, no. 220 (November 2000). Princeton, NJ, International Economics Section.

Folkerts-Landau, D., and C.-J. Lindgren. 1998. *Toward a Framework for Financial Stability.* Washington, DC: International Monetary Fund.

Goldstein, Morris. 1997. *The Case for an International Banking Standard.* Washington, DC: Institute for International Economics.

———. 1998. *The Asian Financial Crisis: Causes, Cures, and Systematic Implications.* Washington, DC: Institute for International Economics.

Gourevitch, Peter A. 1993. "Democracy and Economic Policy: Elective Affinities and Circumstantial Conjunctures." *World Development* 21 (8): 1271–80.

Government of Indonesia 1998a. Letter of Intent, July 29. Available at <www.imf.org>. Accessed February 12, 2002.

———. 1998b. Letter of Intent, September 11. Available at <www.imf.org>. Accessed February 12, 2002.

———. 1998c. Letter of Intent, October 19. Available at <www.imf.org>. Accessed February 12, 2002.

———. 1998d. Letter of Intent, November 13. Available at <www.imf.org>. Accessed February 12, 2002.

Government of Korea. 1997. Letter of Intent, December 24. Available at <www.imf.org>. Accessed February 12, 2002.

———. 1998a. Letter of Intent, February 7. Available at <www.imf.org>. Accessed February 12, 2002.

———. 1998b. Letter of Intent, May 2. Available at <www.imf.org>. Accessed February 12, 2002.

———. 1998c. Letter of Intent, July 24. Available at <www.imf.org>. Accessed February 12, 2002.

———. 1998d. Letter of Development Policy, September 24. Available at <www.worldbank.org>. Accessed February 12, 2002.

———. 1998e. Letter of Intent, November 13. Available at <www.imf.org>. Accessed February 12, 2002.

Government of Thailand. 1998a. Letter of Intent, February 24. Available at <www.imf.org>. Accessed February 12, 2002.

———. 1998b. Letter of Intent, May 26. Available at <www.imf.org>. Accessed February 12, 2002.

———. 1998c. Letter of Intent, August 25. Available at <www.imf.org>. Accessed February 12, 2002.

———. 1998d. Letter of Intent, December 1. Available at <www.imf.org>. Accessed February 12, 2002.

Haggard, Stephan. 2000. *The Political Economy of the Asian Financial Crisis.* Washington, DC: Institute of International Economics.

Horsefield, J. Keith, ed. 1969. *The International Monetary Fund, 1945–1965: Twenty Years of International Monetary Cooperation.* Washington, DC: International Monetary Fund.

IMD (Institute for Management Development) International. 1998. *The World Competitiveness Yearbook.* Lausanne, Switzerland: IMD.

IMF (International Monetary Fund). 1989. *International Capital Markets: Development and Prospects.* Washington, DC: International Monetary Fund.

———. 1990. *International Capital Markets: Development and Prospects.* Washington, DC: International Monetary Fund.

———. 1995. *International Capital Markets.* Washington, DC: International Monetary Fund.

————. 1997a. *World Economic Outlook (1997)*. Washington, DC: International Monetary Fund.

————. 1997b. *International Capital Markets: Developments, Prospects, and Key Policy Issues (1997)*. Washington, DC: International Monetary Fund.

————. 1998a. *International Capital Markets: Developments, Prospects, and Key Policy Issues (1998)*. Washington, DC: International Monetary Fund.

————. 1998b. *World Economic Outlook (1998)*. Washington, DC: International Monetary Fund.

————. 1998c. *Toward a Framework for Financial Stability*. Washington, DC: International Monetary Fund.

————. 1998d. *Summary Proceedings, Fifty-Third Annual Meeting*. Washington, DC: International Monetary Fund.

————. 1999a. *IMF-Supported Programs in Indonesia, Korea, and Thailand: A Preliminary Assessment*. Washington, DC: International Monetary Fund.

————. 1999b. *Summary Proceedings: Annual Meeting, 1998*. Washington, DC: International Monetary Fund.

Johnson, Simon, Peter Boone, Alasdair Breach, and Eric Friedman. 1998. "Corporate Governance in the Asian Financial Crisis, 1997–98." SITE Working Papers, no. 137, Stockholm, Stockholm Institute of Transition Economics.

J. P. Morgan. 1998a. *Asian Financial Markets, Second Quarter*. New York: J. P. Morgan.

————. 1998b. *Asian Financial Markets, Third Quarter*. New York: J. P. Morgan.

————. 1998c. *Asian Financial Markets, Fourth Quarter*. New York: J. P. Morgan.

Kindleberger, Charles. 1996. *Manias, Panics, and Crashes*. New York: Wiley.

Knack, Stephen, and Philip Keefer. 1995. "Institutions and Economic Performance: Cross-Country Tests Using Alternative Institutional Measures." *Economics and Politics* 7 (3): 207–27.

Krugman, Paul. 1994. "The Myth of Asia's Miracle." *Foreign Affairs* 73: 62–78.

————. 1998. "What Happened to Asia?" Mimeo.

Landa, Janet, and Peter Huang. 1999. "Asian Business Networks and Forms of Business Organization: A Psychological Game-Theoretic Approach." Paper presented at the IRIS conference "Collective Action and Corruption in Emerging Economies, May 14, 1999, Washington, DC.

Lane, Timothy, Atish Ghosh, Javier Hamann, Steven Phillips, Marianne Schulze-Ghattas, and Tsidi Tsikata. 1999. *IMF-Supported Programs in Indonesia, Korea, and Thailand: A Preliminary Assessment*. Washington, DC: International Monetary Fund.

Lanyi, Anthony. 2002."International Financial Architecture and Domestic Economic Governance." Mimeo, IRIS, University of Maryland, College Park.

Lanyi, Anthony, Neil McMullen, and Patrick Meagher. 1997. "Reform and Modernization of the State: An Institutional Framework for Reform of the Executive Branch with Indicators and Questionnaires for Diagnosis and Project Design." Mimeo, IRIS Center, University of Maryland, College Park.

La Porta, Rafael, Florencio Lopez-de-Silanes, and Andrei Shleifer. 1998a. "Corporate Ownership around the World." NBER Working Papers, no. 6625, National Bureau of Economic Research, Cambridge, MA.

La Porta, Rafael, Florencio Lopez-de-Silanes, Andrei Shleifer, and Robert W. Vishny. 1998b. "Law and Finance." *Journal of Political Economy* 106 (6): 1113–55.

Olson, Mancur. 1982. *The Rise and Decline of Nations.* New Haven: Yale University Press.

———. 1991. "Autocracy, Democracy, and Prosperity." In *Strategy of Choice,* edited by Richard Zeckhauser. Cambridge: MIT Press.

———. 1993. "Democracy, Dictatorship, and Development." *American Political Science Review* 87 (3): 567–76.

———. 1998. "Market-Augmenting Government." Note for IRIS research program.

———. 2000. *Power and Prosperity: Outgrowing Communist and Capitalist Dictatorships.* New York: Basic Books.

Olson, Mancur, and Martin C. McGuire. 1996. "The Economics of Autocracy and Majority Rule: The Invisible Hand and the Use of Force." *Journal of Economic Literature* 34:567–76.

Political Risk Services. 1998. *Transparency International: Corruption Rankings in 1998.* East Syracuse, NY: International Country Risk Guide.

Porter, Michael, and Hirotaka Takeuchi. 1999. "Fixing What Really Ails Japan." *Foreign Affairs* 78 (3): 66–81.

Radelet, Steven, and Jeffrey D. Sachs. 1998. "The East Asian Financial Crisis: Diagnosis, Remedies, Prospects." *Brookings Papers on Economic Activity,* no. 1:2–74.

———. 1999. "What Have We Learned, So Far, from the Asian Financial Crisis." Mimeo.

Radelet, Steven, Jeffrey D. Sachs, and Lisa Cook. 1999. "Manufactured Exports, Export Platforms, and Economic Growth: Insights from Asia for Egypt." Paper presented at the conference Growth beyond Stabilization: Prospects for Egypt." Egyptian Center for Economic Studies, Cairo.

Rajan, Raghuram G., and Luigi Zingales. 1998. "Which Capitalism? Lessons from the East Asian Crisis." *Journal of Applied Corporate Finance* 11 (3): 40–48.

Sachs, Jeffrey, and Andrew Warner. 1995. "Economic Reform and the Process of Global Integration." *Brookings Papers on Economic Activity,* no. 1:1–95.

Shleifer, Andrei, and Robert W. Vishny. 1997. "A Survey of Corporate Governance." *Journal of Finance* 52 (2): 737–83.

———. 1998. *The Grabbing Hand: Government Pathologies and Their Cures.* Cambridge: Harvard University Press.

Smith, Adam. [1776] 1950. *The Wealth of Nations.* Edited by Edwin Cannan. 6th ed. London: Methuen.

Stiglitz, Joseph E. 1998. "Towards a New Paradigm for Development: Strategies, Policies, and Processes." Prebisch Lecture at United Nations Conference on Trade and Development, Geneva.

Tamirisa, Natalia T. 1999. "Exchange and Capital Controls as a Barrier to Trade." *IMF Staff Papers* 46 (1): 69–88.

Tanzi, Vito. 1995. "Corruption: Arm's-Length Relationships and Markets." In *The Economics of Organised Crime,* edited by Gianluca Fiorentini and Sam Peltzman. Cambridge: Cambridge University Press.

———. 1998. "Corruption around the World: Causes, Consequences, Scope, and Cures." *IMF Staff Papers* 45 (4): 559–94.

Williamson, John. 1993. "Democracy and 'The Washington Consensus.'" *World Development* 21 (8): 1329–36.

World Bank. 1993. *The East Asian Miracle.* New York: Oxford University Press.

———. 1995. *Bureaucrats in Business.* New York: Oxford University Press.

———. 1997. *World Development Report: The State in a Changing World.* New York: Oxford University Press.

———. 1998a. *East Asia: The Road to Recovery.* New York: Oxford University Press.

———. 1998b. *World Development Report: Knowledge for Development.* New York: Oxford University Press.

———. 1998c. *Financial Sector Reform.* New York: Oxford University Press.

———. 1998d. *Institutions Matter.* New York: Oxford University Press.

Comment

John Joseph Wallis

Lanyi and Lee's very ambitious essay tackles a number of important and interesting issues and poses some big challenges, worthy of future work.

We do need an endogenous model of government behavior. For example, if we suspend disbelief for a moment and assume that the macro- and international finance economists at the International Monetary Fund (IMF) actually know what is best for an economy, precisely how do those policy recommendations get implemented? Even a simple political economy model suggests that, unless it is in the government's interest to promote a given policy, it won't happen. (This applies to both autocracy and democracy.) There exist two distinct policy sets: the recommended policies and the feasible policies, with no necessary intersection between the two. The best policy recommendations, therefore, will not identify the best policies but rather the best policies *within the feasible set.*

But what determines the feasible set and how do we know what is in it? This, it seems to me, is where the concept of market-augmenting government comes into play. We would need to know about the structure of the economy, the alternatives facing residents, and the structure of the government's fiscal system—particularly how and where it gets its revenues. Ceteris paribus, governments will tend to shade their regulatory policy toward increasing revenues.

How would this apply to the East Asian financial crisis?

First, we need a schematic overview of the East Asian situation. Asian economies had been growing rapidly, fueled, in part, by infusions of foreign capital. Foreign lenders were increasingly willing to lend to Asian businesses but had concerns about exchange rates and default risks. Asian borrowers therefore agreed to loan arrangements in which debt service would be in dollars (or another foreign currency), thus eliminating the exchange rate risk for the lenders. Of course, the risk didn't go away; it was transferred completely to the borrowers. This, in turn, however, increased the default risk faced by the creditors. The Asian borrowers addressed the default risk by guaranteeing the debt in two ways: shifting the borrowing entity from firms to banks and providing direct guarantees from the government.

If this schematic summary is accurate, the authors might consider that *these credit arrangements may in fact have been market-augmenting rather than simply flawed.* (Asian economies in the 1990s should not be compared to contemporary developed economies; a better comparison might be the Western economies of the late nineteenth and early twentieth centuries, when financial panics were endemic in the "developed world.")

Given that you cannot develop a panic-proof financial system in a developing country without substantial costs, what are the benefits of different arrangements, apart from their impact on panic proneness? The *benefit* of the Asian arrangements was access to foreign capital at lower costs by denominating loans in foreign currencies and providing government guarantees. The first-order effect is thus market augmenting: this must have been a policy that the IMF and World Bank liked, since it improved access to capital and in the process made financial markets marginally more active.

Of course, once the loans are in place, the entire economy is held hostage to exchange rate fluctuations. The cost of repaying foreign loans is now dependent on both internal economic and international conditions. The logic of market-augmenting government suggests, however, that once these debt arrangements were entered into the governments would go to great lengths to maintain stable currencies. If Indonesia could have stabilized exchange rates with its currency board, might this have eliminated the root cause of the panic?

This no longer becomes a question of absolutes (i.e., "fixed exchange rates are bad"). If debt denominated in a foreign currency buys significant benefits in the international credit market, then fixed exchange rates may simply be the price a country has to pay to get those advantages. The research on Asian financial markets needs to consider the Asian debt crisis from an ex ante as well as an ex post perspective. If this conference had been held in 1989 instead of 1999, would we be saying that these Asian policies were good rather than bad?

Second, it seems to me that the idea of endogenous government policies—that is, supportable policies—implies that the market knows what is best, taking into account the state of government policies. The tenor of most of the essay, however, is that the IMF knows best. The six proposals presented here are all good ideas, but how can they be made to grow indigenously?

Let me give an example from Robert Gallman and Lance Davis's manuscript (1999), "Tides, Waves, and Sand Castles." Gallman and Davis report that American states performed so badly in the 1840s and the 1870s—defaulting so often on foreign debts—that the American interest rate for British loans was a full percentage point higher than the Canadian or Australian rate. When Americans wanted foreign capital to finance their extensive railroad system (and it was the biggest in the world by a large margin), what developed was an extensive monitoring system undertaken by British and American investment banks (creditor governance). The British limited their investments in America to essentially three forms: government bonds, commercial bank stocks and bonds, and railroad bonds (and later stock). Thus, although governments certainly worried about the exchange markets, private markets in Britain and America emerged to provide five of the six points mentioned in the essay. (The one that wasn't provided was an international lender of last resort.)

What we really need to know, then, is how the *private sector* financial system will change to adapt to the current crisis. Private financiers will be willing to live with some risk of a financial panic if the rewards are high enough. We need to know what makes it in their best interests to pursue more stable policies before we can adopt intelligent government strategies to augment that outcome. Private actors in the financial system will not automatically adopt institutional arrangements that "maximize stability"; they want to maximize net present value. Since in the end it is private decisions that determine the shape of the financial system, we should start with private behavior first.

Market-augmenting government will emerge when governments have an incentive to follow policies—fiscal, monetary, and regulatory—that augment private financial sector arrangements. Market-augmenting government will *not* occur if governments must force "good policies" on financial markets. When the IMF goes to a country and says, "if you want this bailout package, change these institutions," the policy is—almost by definition—politically unsupportable in the adopting country. I would like to see more work on the question of how the six points could be implemented in a market-augmenting way. That is, what institutional structures have to develop, domestically and internationally, to ensure that both private participants and domestic officials will *want* to follow the policies?

Reference

Davis, Lance, and Robert Gallman. 1999. "Tides, Waves, and Sand Castles: The Impact of Foreign Capital Flows on Evolving Financial Markets in the New World, Britain, and Argentina, Australia, Canada, and the United States 1870–1914." Manuscript, California Institute of Technology and University of North Carolina at Chapel Hill.

Biosphere, Markets, and Governments

Geoffrey Heal

Human economic activities are forcing changes in the biosphere, the thin, habitable layer at the surface of the planet and just above it.[1] This is where we live and die, the environment to which millions of years of evolution have adapted us. Significant changes in this environment can have far-reaching implications for human life and welfare.

Human impacts on the biosphere at a global level are a new phenomenon. For most of history we have had local rather than global impacts on our planetary environment. In contrast, over the last half century we have begun to affect the operation of the basic bio-geochemical cycles that support life on earth: the carbon cycle, the hydrological cycle, the nitrogen cycle, and the composition of the web of species that accompany us. Because these impacts are new, we have not yet developed institutions that can mediate between human activities and the biosphere.

In many cases, the important aspects of the biosphere are common property resources: in some cases they are systems and commodities that are not even recognized as resources. We currently recognize the need to mediate our impacts on the stratospheric ozone layer and the carbon cycle. These concerns will no doubt be followed by similar needs relating to the loss of biodiversity and to the planet's nitrogen cycle.

In the two cases in which we have taken action, or at least are beginning to take action, we have chosen two very different routes, the Montreal and Kyoto protocols. The former embodies the classic regulatory approach, dictating what can and cannot be done. The latter is centered much more on economic incentives generated by a market. It seeks to internalize externalities by creating and distributing property rights where none previously existed and then allowing these to be traded. The market here is central and government created. The same is true of the markets in the United States for sulfur dioxide (SO_2) emissions.

There is an alternative market-based approach that is less

153

dependent on government activity—though not independent of it, for in this area (and arguably in all areas) markets depend on the government for an infrastructure of property rights and contract enforcement. This alternative approach involves privatizing and securitizing the biosphere. To be precise, it derives from the observation that the natural world provides many important services to human societies, termed by biologists *ecosystem services.*[2] These services are fundamental to human life and comfort and are generally taken for granted. They include climate stabilization, pollination, renewal of soil fertility, cleansing of water and control of floods, and control of pests.[3]

If the natural environment provides a range of important services to human societies, might it not be possible to charge for the provision of these and in the process provide incentives for their preservation and encourage efficient use? The idea would be to set up markets in environmental services, thus enlisting the price mechanism and the invisible hand in the goal of mediating human interactions with the biosphere. The distinguished biologist E. O. Wilson once wrote of the need to "give the invisible hand of market economics a green thumb."

The prerequisite for this approach is a system of property rights in the natural capital that supplies the ecosystem services. Such approaches are already working and are having a dramatic effect. The best example, to which I shall return, is the Conservation Corporation (ConsCorp) in South Africa. ConsCorp is making profits by restoring degraded natural ecosystems from low-grade farmland and then using them for ecotourism and hunting. In the process, it is both improving the lot of the local populations and conserving important elements of biodiversity. In effect, it is selling ecosystem services. Many water companies are now doing the same: they are conserving the watersheds that provide them with drinkable water as a part of their business strategies. In selling water, they are in effect selling the water collection and purification services of natural watersheds—in many cases, of forests that support considerable biodiversity.

To summarize, there are two basic and quite distinct strategies for using markets to mediate human interactions with the natural environment. One is to establish markets for tradable permits in the use of common property resources, as is done with markets in pollution rights. This approach is in part conventional economics, in that it establishes a market, and in part unconventional: the goods concerned are public goods, and for economists public goods are a classic example of market failure. The atmospheric concentration of carbon dioxide (CO_2) is a global public good; the concentration of SO_2 is a regional public good. But these are unusual public goods in that they are privately produced, the result of individual decisions about heating and transportation choices. The use of markets to manage the provision of public goods that are privately produced is central to the strategies of both the Kyoto protocol and the 1990 Clean Air Act of the United States, which is widely thought to have been successful at managing a reduction in sulfur dioxide emissions.

The other strategy for using markets is to use them to sell the services—ecosystem services—provided to human societies with natural assets. For this approach to be successful, these services must be excludable and property rights must be established.

In both of these approaches, there is a central role for the government in augmenting the market. The roles are similar in the two approaches—establishing property rights and markets, as well as the contractual frameworks on which they depend. In some cases, this can happen in a decentralized fashion: privatization and securitization of ecosystem services has not, to the best of my knowledge, been on any government agenda, yet it has occurred in important contexts, using particular legal infrastructures already in place.

In the remainder of this essay, I review both of these alternatives: the use of permit markets to control the provision of a privately produced public good and the potential development of markets for goods and services provided by natural ecosystems. Although both are relatively new developments, the former is better established and better understood. While we know enough about the latter to realize that it has the potential to contribute a great deal, we still lack a comprehensive understanding of its potential for conservation of the natural environment.

I. Permit Markets and Public Goods

The use of tradable permit markets is being increasingly adopted as a mechanism for controlling human interactions with the biosphere, and to date this approach seems to have been successful. To understand the issues that this raises, consider this example. Carbon dioxide—the principal gas responsible for global climate change—is very stable, remaining in the atmosphere for about sixty years after emission. It mixes well, and within a matter of months the carbon dioxide emitted in New York or Beijing will be diffused around the globe. The concentration of this gas in the atmosphere is thus rather uniform around the world, and the atmospheric concentration of carbon dioxide is a global public good.

How is all this CO_2 being produced? It is produced as a result of billions of decentralized and independent decisions by private households regarding heating and transportation—as well as by corporations for these and other activities—all outside the government's sphere. The government can influence them, but only indirectly, through regulations or incentives. The same holds for other atmospheric pollutants. Sulfur dioxide is likewise produced by the home-heating and power-generation choices of people the world over, and ozone-depleting chlorofluorocarbons are produced for use in the refrigerators and air conditioners of millions of private households. Similarly, the loss of biodiversity results from myriad independent decisions about changes in land use (which inevitably destroy previous habitats) and from pollution-generating activities that affect the climate. Farmers, ranchers, vacation homeowners, suburban homeowners—all have a direct impact on biodiversity loss through their lifestyles and land use choices.

The foregoing observations introduce a new element into the provision of public goods. For traditional public goods, three questions are to be answered.

- How much should be provided?
- How should this be financed?
- How can the state obtain the information needed to answer these questions?

(The last point relates to the famous free-rider problem. Anyone who is asked how much she or he is willing to pay for a public good—and who expects their payment will be affected by the response—has an obvious incentive to give a response that understates the true preference.) For privately produced public goods, however, we have to ask a fourth question.

- Given a desirable target level of production, how do we attain it and how is this target production to be divided between all of the potential producers?

For example, in the case of cutting back the emission of greenhouse gases, this takes a very specific and difficult form: which countries should cut back emissions and how much? The same question will then be repeated within the country and indeed probably within individual organizations and firms.

This new question—how the production of the public good should be distributed among agents—has surprising and interesting implications for the equity-efficiency dichotomy that has been traditional in welfare economics. In principle, there are several ways of deciding how the production or abatement should be distributed between agents.

1. The traditional "command and control" approach: take the total, divide it in some way among the possible producers, and instruct each of them that this is what they will produce. In the most common case of privately produced public goods— environmental pollution—this approach typically takes the form of deciding that there will be an X percent reduction in the output of the pollutant and instructing everyone to reduce pollution by X percent.
2. The pollution can be reduced by taxation, by picking a tax rate that will bring about just the desire pollution level.
3. A market can be used to decide who produces how much by allocating pollution rights and allowing them to be traded.

Standard arguments indicate that either of the last two approaches—taxation or permit markets—is more cost effective than command and control. *Cost effective* here means that a given abatement level is achieved at a lower total cost. Of the two cost-effective approaches, markets are a better way of attaining a given target total pollution level, for the obvious reason that we can pick the total volume of pollution permits to equal the target pollution level. The idea of trading rights to pollute goes back at least to Dales 1968, although it could be argued that it has origins in Coase 1960 or even in Lindahl's work on public goods (see Foley 1970). For a general review of the issues, see Chichilnisky, Heal, and Starrett 1999 and Chichilnisky and Heal 1999.[4]

It is important to understand exactly how the market in pollution rights will work. A total production level is chosen for pollution, equal to the total permissible pollution level. The next step is to allocate tradable rights to pollute—also known as tradable emission quotas—equal to the chosen total production target. These rights are divided among potential polluters according to a procedure chosen by the authority controlling the pollution.

To make this concrete, consider sulfur dioxide emission permits in the United States. The Environmental Protection Agency sets limits on the total emission of sulfur dioxide in a region, issues permits to emit SO_2 that add up to this limit, and then allocates these permits between potential polluters. Once this is done, the potential polluters are free to pollute up to the limit set by the permits that they have received. Alternatively, they can pollute less and sell the permits for which they have no need, or they can purchase additional permits from other potential polluters and then pollute up to a level given by their initial allocation of permits plus their purchases. The incentive to cut back on pollution is provided by the fact that an unused permit can be sold and an additional permit will cost money; the higher the market price, the stronger the incentive.

How would this work for a *global* public good such as CO_2? In other words, what are its implications for the Kyoto agreement on greenhouse gas emission? To introduce a regime of tradable emission quotas, we have to create property rights where none previously existed. These property rights must then be allocated to countries participating in the CO_2 abatement program in the form of quotas. Such quotas have market value, perhaps very great market value. The creation and distribution of quotas could therefore lead to a major redistribution of wealth internationally. This means that it is economically and politically important to understand fully the issues that underlie an evaluation of alternative ways of distributing emission quotas.

A clear precedent for the redistributive effect of the international assignment of property rights can be seen in the Law of the Sea conference and the introduction of two hundred-mile territorial limits in the waters off a nation's coast. These limits established national property rights where none previously existed, rights that could be (and frequently were) distributed by governments to domestic firms. The creation of property rights in offshore water thus effected a very substantial redistribution of wealth internationally.

There is no way to restrict countries' emissions of greenhouse gases without altering their energy use—and without altering their overall production and consumption patterns. The implementation of measures to decrease carbon emissions will thus have a significant impact on the ability of different groups and countries to produce goods and services for their own consumption and for trade. Because of this, the distributional impact of environmental policy—the choice of who will bear the adjustment costs—is of major import. Under a tradable quota regime, payment for the provision of a public good—in this case, payment for an atmosphere containing fewer greenhouse gases—takes the form of bearing the economic costs of adjusting to the quota regime and its prices. This makes the analysis of environmental policy particularly difficult because distributional considerations are typically the ones on which consensus is most difficult to achieve.

Distribution and Efficiency

Competitive markets are intellectually attractive because of the efficiency of the resulting allocations. Market efficiency requires three key properties.

1. Markets must be competitive.
2. There must be no external effects: in the Pigouvian terminology, private and social costs must be equal; in the Coasian terminology, there must be property rights in the environment.
3. The goods produced and traded must be private.[5]

In this framework, the efficiency of market allocation is independent of the assignment of property rights. Ownership patterns are certainly of great interest for welfare reasons, and they may have consequences for allocations (where traders achieve varying levels of consumption and there are different distributions of income). Nevertheless, ownership patterns have no impact on market efficiency. The efficiency of the market *independently of distribution* is a crucial property underlying the organization of most modern societies.

Yet the efficiency properties that make the market so valuable for the allocation of private goods fail when the goods are public. *With public goods, it is not possible to separate efficiency from distribution.* For public goods, market solutions are efficient only with appropriate distributions of initial property rights.

As this is not a familiar result, let me state it formally and precisely.[6] Consider a world economy with I regions, $I > 1$ indexed by $i = 1,...,I$. Each region has a utility function u_i, which depends on its consumption of a vector of private goods $c_i = (c_{i1}, c_{i2},...,c_{iM})$, where M is the number of private goods (indexed by m), and also on the quality of the world's atmosphere, a, which is a public good. Formally, $u_i(c_i, a)$ measures welfare, where u_i is a continuous, strictly concave and increasing function assumed to be twice-continuously differentiable. The quality of the atmosphere a can be thought of as a measure of abatement. It could be measured by, for example, the reciprocal or the negative of the concentration of CO_2: the more abatement there is, the lower is this concentration. The concentration of CO_2 is "produced" by emissions of carbon, which are positively associated with the levels of production of private goods. Let y_i be a vector in R^M giving the production levels of the M private goods in country i. The "production functions" or "abatement functions" f_i are continuously differentiable and strictly concave and show the trade-off between the level of abatement or quality of the atmosphere and the output of consumption. Then

$$a = \sum_{i=1}^{I} a_i, \, a_i = f_i(y_i) \quad \text{for each country } i = 1,...,I \quad \text{and} \quad \frac{\partial f_i}{\partial y_{i,m}} < 0 \quad \text{for all } i.$$

An allocation is feasible if it satisfies the preceding constraint as well as the condition that the total consumption of each private good worldwide be equal to the total production.

In this framework, one can prove the following theorem.

THEOREM 1 (*Chichilnisky, Heal, and Starrett*). *Let* E* *be the level of total emissions at a Pareto-efficient allocation of resources in the economy described earlier. Assume that regions maximize utility subject to the budget constraint given by the ability to trade emission permits:*

$$c_i = y_i - p_e(E_i + a_i).$$

Here p_e *is the market price of an emission permit in terms of consumption, and* E_i *is the quantity of emission permits allocated to region* i. *Assume that a regularity condition is satisfied.*[7] *Then, of all possible ways of allocating the total emission* E* *among the regions as initial endowments, only a subset of measure zero will lead to market equilibria that are Pareto-efficient. Alternatively, almost every allocation of permits between regions will lead to inefficient outcomes. If the inequality*

$$(I - 1) + M \le (I - 1) \times M$$

holds, then only a finite number of ways of allocating the emission rights lead to efficiency.[8]

In words, this result states what was implied earlier. Whether a market in emission permits will lead to an efficient allocation of resources depends on the initial allocation of emission permits among the traders. Only some, indeed a few, ways of allocating these permits will lead to efficiency.

Why does this result occur? When all goods are private, different traders typically end up with different amounts of goods at a market-clearing equilibrium because of their different tastes and endowments. The flexibility of the market in assigning different bundles of goods to different traders is crucial for efficient solutions. But traders with different preferences should reach consumption levels at which economywide relative prices between any two goods are both (1) equal to the marginal rate of substitution between those goods for every trader and (2) equal to the rate of transformation between the two goods for every producer. This is an enormous task, and it is a testament to the decentralized power of markets that this coincidence of values emerges at a market-clearing allocation.

When one good is public, however, there is a physical constraint: all traders, no matter how different, must consume the same quantity. This imposes a restriction that does not exist in markets in which all goods are private. Because of this restriction, some of the adjustments needed to reach an efficient equilibrium are no longer available in markets with public goods.

The number of instruments the market uses to reach an efficient solution—the goods' prices and the quantities consumed by all traders—is the same with private or public goods. But with a public good these instruments must now do more: at a market equilibrium, the quantities of the public good demanded independently by each trader must be the same, no matter how different the traders are. As a result, in addition to equalizing price ratios to every trader's marginal rates of substitution and transformation, an additional condition must now be met for efficiency.

The physical requirement of equal consumption by all thus introduces a fundamental difference between efficiency with public goods and efficiency with private goods. All this must be achieved by the market in a decentralized fashion. Traders must still be able to choose freely, maximizing their individual utilities, and therefore the previous condition of equating each trader's marginal rates of substitution and transformation to prices must still hold. (Otherwise the market-clearing allocation would not be efficient.) In other words, with public goods the market must perform one more task. A Lindahl equilibrium provides extra instruments for this task, namely, extra prices, by considering personalized prices for public goods. Our earlier result says that *redistribution of endowments* can substitute for the extra prices in a Lindahl equilibrium.

Since the markets with n private goods has precisely as many instruments as tasks, with public goods new instruments must be enlisted. The Lindahl equilibrium uses extra prices. In the present case, some of the economy's characteristics can be adjusted to meet the new goals. The traders' property rights to the public good—for example, their rights to emit gases into the atmosphere—are a natural instrument for this purpose because they are in principle free and undefined until the environmental policy is considered. By treating the allocations of quotas as an instrument—by varying the distribution of property rights on the atmosphere—it is generally possible to achieve a market-clearing solution in which traders choose freely to consume exactly the same amount of the public good. Market efficiency can be achieved with public goods but only with the appropriate distribution of property rights. Again, distribution and efficiency are no longer independent.

To summarize, markets for emission permits have many advantages as mechanisms for controlling the use of atmospheric (or possibly aquatic) common property resources. Government action is a prerequisite for their effective introduction, as they require that property rights be established where typically there were previously none. Government action is also needed in allocating these newly established property rights. This allocation clearly has an impact on the distribution of benefits arising from the use of the market; it also affects the total of the benefits since it affects the efficiency of the market outcomes.

II. Privatizing and Securitizing the Biosphere

I turn now to the second route by which markets can mediate between humans and the biosphere. The issue here is the following: can we establish markets in ecosystem services? If so, we will in effect extend the scope of the market mechanism, in the process internalizing many of the external effects imposed by humans on the natural environment and associated with the present institutional structure (or lack of it). This approach is in the classical tradition of internalizing externalities by establishing markets and property rights. I begin with a review of four cases in which this approach is at least potentially effective and then will move on to a more general context.

Watersheds

Ninety percent of New York's water comes from a watershed in the Catskill Mountains. Until recently, a purification process carried out in the soil by roots and microorganisms as the water percolates through, assisted by filtration and sedimentation occurring during this flow, was sufficient to cleanse the water to U.S. Environmental Protection Agency (EPA) standards. Recently, however, sewage, fertilizer, and pesticides in the soil have reduced the efficacy of this process to the point where New York's water no longer met EPA standards. The city was faced with a choice: restore the integrity of the Catskill ecosystems or build a filtration plant at a capital cost of $6 to $8 billion, plus running costs of the order of $300 million annually. In other words, New York had to invest in either environmental conservation or treatment facilities.

Which was more attractive? Investment in conservation in this case meant buying land in and around the watershed so that its use could be restricted, subsidizing the construction of better sewage treatment plants, and buying conservation easements in the region. The total cost of measures of this type needed to restore the watershed is expected to be in the range of $1 to $1.5 billion. So investing $1 to $1.5 billion in conservation could save an investment of $6 to $8 billion in treatment facilities, giving an internal rate of return of between 90 and 170 percent.[9] This return is an order of magnitude higher than is normally available, particularly on relatively safe investments. These calculations are in fact conservative, as they consider only one watershed service, while watersheds, typically forests, often provide other important services.

In 1997, New York City floated an "environmental bond issue," earmarking the proceeds to restore the water purification function of the watershed ecosystems. The cost of the bond issue will be met by the savings produced, arising from the avoidance of a capital investment of $6 to $8 billion plus the $300 million annual running costs of the plant. The cash that would otherwise have gone to these will pay the interest on the bonds.

The market could have handled a similar transaction by using the technique of securitization. This involves issuing tradable contracts, securities, entitling the owners to a fraction of the benefits from a venture. In this case, the securities would entitle their owners to a fraction of the cost savings resulting from watershed restoration:

they would be "watershed securities." In exchange for the securities, investors would contribute the capital needed for restoration. In effect, they would invest in the restoration and receive in return a share of the benefits from restoration. Securitization is a technique extensively used for attracting investors into a venture and is already used environmentally in securitizing the savings from increased energy efficiency in buildings by issuing securities entitling their owners to a specified fraction of the savings. Typically these contracts are tradable and can be sold by investors even before the savings are realized. This is simply a way of making investments in saving energy attractive to the investing public and institutions: it does not imply any transfer of ownership of the underlying asset. The U.S. Department of Energy has a standard protocol for estimating the savings from enhanced building energy efficiency, and several financial agencies are willing to accept these estimates of energy savings as collateral for loans.

In the New York watershed case, the city could have opened a "watershed savings account" into which it would pay a fraction of the costs avoided by not having to build and run a filtration plant; this account would pay investors for the use of their capital. The purpose of securitization is to make it possible to finance projects such as New York's watershed restoration without using the credit of the city itself—an important issue in developing countries whose metropolitan areas may not have credit ratings comparable to New York's.

One could take the introduction of market forces a step further. Imagine a corporation hired to manage the restoration of New York's watershed. It has the right to sell to New York City the services of the ecosystem, that is, the provision of water meeting EPA standards. Ownership of this right would enable it to raise capital from capital markets to be used for meeting the costs of conserving New York's watershed. Of course, some regulation would be needed: for example, the corporation would be a natural monopoly, and it would be appropriate to regulate its prices. It would also be reasonable to place some restrictions on the modifications that it could make to the natural ecosystems in the watershed area.

Analytically, what is the general point illustrated by this example? It is that water is a good for which individuals or municipalities are willing to pay. They are willing to pay for quality as well as quantity, and this in effect puts a *price* on the water management and purification services provided by a watershed. It generates a derived demand for watersheds. In this case, there is a possible replacement for the ecosystems services provided by the watershed: this is the filtration plant. The cost of this—in the New York case, $8 billion plus—puts an upper limit on what it would make sense to spend on restoring the watershed, looked at only from the water management and purification perspective. Of course, the watershed may have many other values to society: in this case, the Catskills are a much-valued recreational area, and society has a substantial willingness to pay for this in addition to the watershed services. An important aspect of this story is that by improving sewage systems in the Catskills and other measures to reduce pollution there, and by buying conservation easements, the city of New York has improved the quality of life and injected a considerable amount of income into the Catskills community. It has therefore provided some financial compensation to the residents of the area to be conserved and given them a direct financial stake in the conservation.

Ecotourism

Another powerful example comes from South Africa, in the form of the Conservation Corporation, or ConsCorp, a company started as a private venture and recently floated on the London Stock Exchange.[10] This imaginative venture has capitalized on the demand for ecotourism and hunting: this demand is such that land yielding $25 per hectare annually for ranching and $70 per hectare in cropping can yield between $200 and $300 per hectare as part of a reserve managed for tourism or hunting. ConsCorp contracts with landowners to incorporate their land in its reserves; it does not buy the land outright. Landowners have to maintain their land in accordance with tightly specified regulations and to stock it with specified animals. ConsCorp manages the business part of the operation: bringing in tourists and hunters, building facilities, and providing guides and vehicles. To date, it has restored several hundred thousand hectares of farmland to their original ecosystems. An interesting detail is that the presence of lions will add about 30 percent to the revenues from an area, so the incentive to restock with these is great.[11] Supporting lions at the top of the food chain requires restoring most of the rest of the food chain as well: what the lions eat, what the lions' food eats, and so on. There is a strong economic incentive to do a thorough job of restoration, as reflected in the very explicit rules used by ConsCorp. The articles of association for one reserve state that its aims are "to provide and conserve endemic wildlife within the confines of the area . . . to establish the Reserve as a sanctuary in perpetuity for endemic wildlife and habitat so as to ensure sustainable resource utilization . . . to endeavor to increase the area of the Reserve; and to maximize the long term economic and ecological value of the properties." Landowners even agree not to keep any domestic animals, including dogs and cats. An interesting quote from a South African writer captures some of what is happening in this movement.

> The interesting thing is that untold hundreds of thousands of hectares and morgen that even a few years ago were scrub grazing for a mixture of game and cattle have now been entirely allocated to game. Why? Economics, as always. Game pays its own way, eats nearly anything, is more resistant to disease and predators and generally produces a higher and better use for the land. . . . Even the old enemies become assets to the farmer who switches from cattle to game. One friend of mine used to lose as many as thirty calves a season to leopards. . . . Now those same leopards are worth a cool $3000 to $4000 to sport hunters, not a bad trade-off for animals that caused a liability of well over ten grand and had to be poisoned! Tell me, is that bad for leopards?[12]

Similar developments are occurring in Kenya. The land there is less productive and the country has less infrastructure, so the numbers are all lower. But they tell the same story in terms of incentives: in the Laikipia region of Kenya, ecotourism can bring $5 to $30 per hectare per year, compared to less than $2 per hectare per year for traditional livestock husbandry.[13] In fact in the whole of southern Africa (Namibia, Zimbabwe, Botswana, South Africa, and Mozambique), about 18 percent of the land area is now devoted to game management, that is, to the management of naturally occurring wildlife, largely because of the economic returns that this provides.[14]

Prospecting for Pharmaceuticals

Bioprospecting is another activity that can yield cash for conservation. Bioprospecting means seeking for leads in the development of new drugs, or new chemicals for use in agriculture, by looking at biological resources. As a matter of fact, over 60 percent by value of prescription drugs in the United States are or were initially derived from plants and insects, so this is a reasonable place to start looking. The key point is that certain plants and animals are known to produce substances that are highly active pharmacologically. Plants that live in insect-infested areas produce substances that are poisonous to insects, and these have been used as the basis for insecticides. Some snakes produce venom that paralyzes parts of the nervous system, and others produce venom that reduces blood pressure. Other insects produce anticoagulants. All of these have been adapted for medical use. Observations of this type have led most major drug companies to pursue bioprospecting as a way to find new pharmacologically active substances to serve as a basis for drug development. Typically they have sought these compounds in the tropics, in areas where there is extensive interspecies competition, or in other extreme areas. They have been willing to pay quite substantial sums for access to these regions and have made deals with host countries that involve giving them a royalty on the products that might eventually be based on this prospecting.

Such royalties may be very large relative to the incomes of the countries concerned. Two concrete examples will illustrate the potential salience of this point. The key enzyme in the polymerase chain reaction (pcr), a reaction central to much modern genetic testing and indeed to a broader range of biotechnologies, was discovered in one of the hot springs at Yellowstone National Park, where it had evolved the resistance to heat that is critical to its role in pcr. By now, virtually every biotechnology laboratory uses derivatives of this enzyme, whose commercial value is immense. Merck, Inc., one of the largest pharmaceutical companies in the United States, has an agreement with a Costa Rican agency called InBio (Institute Nacional de La Biodiversidad) for bioprospecting rights in Costa Rica. The terms of the agreement required Merck to pay InBio a fixed sum, to be used for forest conservation, in exchange for the right to receive samples collected by InBio and to use these as the basis for new product development. Should any of them prove commercially successful, Merck will also pay InBio a royalty on the revenues generated. Similar agreements are in place between other U.S. pharmaceutical companies and other regions of Central and South America.

There has been some controversy about the potential value of bioprospecting to developing countries. The discovery of the enzyme for the pcr reaction and the agreement between Merck and InBio (as well as several other drug discoveries based on plants from developing countries) led to a wave of optimism, sometimes perhaps excessive, about the potential commercial value of in situ biodiversity in developing countries. After a reaction, a more balanced position is emerging, although we still lack extensive practical experience. Real data will emerge only slowly, as the development and testing of drugs is a slow process, taking at least ten years. However, recent calculations have suggested that in some of the world's biodiversity hot spots the right to bioprospect may be worth as much as $9,000 per hectare—about a century's worth of ranching income.[15] The key insight in these calculations is that prior knowledge of the nature of the ecosystems in a location can improve estimates of the probability of finding commercially interesting compounds there. In practical terms, developing countries can clarify the commercial attractions of their biodiversity by doing preliminary research on the ecosystems of which it is a part. This is rather like a country with potential oil reserves engaging in basic geological prospecting before seeking to negotiate leases for oil development. The results may be positive or negative, but either way they will give it a better view of its prospects.

Here the economic point is recognizing the value of the knowledge that can be derived from natural systems and then establishing intellectual property rights in that knowledge. The property rights are needed to ensure that some of the value ultimately created by that knowledge returns to the country from which it derived.

Growing Carbon and the Kyoto Protocol

The Kyoto protocol negotiations provide an interesting example of how markets might provide powerful incentives for environmental conservation. One innovation under discussion entails carbon sequestration credits: countries that remove carbon from the atmosphere (e.g., by growing trees) would receive credits in the form of tradable greenhouse gas emission permits. We can't know the exact value of these permits until markets for carbon emission permits become active, but preliminary economic calculations[16] suggest that their market value could be in the range of $15 to $100 per ton of carbon or equivalent. What would this mean for the economics of conserving tropical forests? We can do some rough preliminary calculations. Moist tropical forests remove carbon from the air at a rate in the range of five to fifteen tons per hectare per year, possibly more.[17] Taking these two ranges of numbers together, we see that growing forests could be remunerated by carbon sequestration credits at a rate of $75 to $1,500 per hectare per year. This is a lot of money: ranches in Costa Rica, for example, make profits of at most $100 to $125 per hectare per year. Reforesting has a one-time cost of planting the seedlings, which can be as high as $900 per hectare.[18] Even with this initial cost, it seems possible that if the world as a whole pays for just one of the many services of tropical forests, this could change radically the economics of forest conservation. On a very small scale, some of this is already happening through the schemes for joint implementation encouraged by the Global Environment Facility and the World Bank.

Analytically, this example demonstrates the following point. The sequestration of carbon by forests is a global public good. By stabilizing the climate, it benefits all of humankind. Typically it is difficult for the providers of such a service to appropriate all or even a significant part of the benefits, so that it is underprovided, as noted earlier. A combination of a tradable permit system for greenhouse gas emissions with a regime of giving permits for sequestration may allow ecosystems that provide sequestration services to capture the full economic value of what they provide.[19]

Privatization and Securitization: Conclusions

These examples—carbon sequestration and the Kyoto protocol, the New York watershed, and ConsCorp and bioprospecting—make two points. One is that, with the right institutional structures and property rights in place, the market can be used to realize some of the value inherent in certain natural assets. The second is that, if this is done, incentives for conservation can be generated. If the market will yield a higher return through conservation than through any other use, then entrepreneurs will find a way to conserve.

Of course, these particular examples are not meant to imply that *all* valuable natural capital can be conserved this way. What they do suggest is that we should explore the potential benefits of this approach. Preliminary estimates suggest that up to 10 percent of the land area of the United States, and a comparable or greater area worldwide, could be economically conserved on the grounds of watershed protection.[20] I am not aware of comparable studies for ecotourism, but this has certainly become a major industry in several regions of the world, including Central America and East and southern Africa. As noted earlier, in southern Africa an area approaching 20 percent of the land area is now conserved because of the economic incentives provided by ecotourism. Some countries in these regions are now earning about one-third of their foreign exchange from ecotourism.

What is the potential for application of privatization or securitization to a broader range of ecosystems? Daily (1997) identifies the following social and economic functions of ecosystem services: purification of air and water, mitigation of floods and droughts, detoxification and decomposition of wastes, generation and preservation of soils, control of the vast majority of potential agricultural pests, pollination of crops and natural vegetation, dispersal of seeds, cycling of nutrients, maintenance of biodiversity, protection of coastal shores from erosion, protection from harmful ultraviolet rays, partial stabilization of the climate, and provision of aesthetic beauty and intellectual stimulation that lift the human spirit.

Which of these are amenable to the approach that we have indicated? One clear prerequisite is that the ecosystem to be conserved must provide goods or services to which a commercial value can be attached. Watersheds satisfy this criterion: drinkable water is becoming increasingly scarce, and indeed the availability of such water is one of the main constraints on health improvements in many poorer countries.

Commercial value of an ecosystem service is necessary but not sufficient for privatization: some portion of that value has to be *appropriable* by the producer. A critical issue in deciding whether ecosystem services can be privatized is the question of the extent to which they are public goods. Pure public goods are challenging to privatize. It is hard (though not necessarily impossible) to exclude from benefiting from their provision those who do not contribute to their costs; thus, their providers cannot appropriate all of their returns. Water quality is a public good in the sense that if it is improved for one user of a watershed it is improved for all. But the consumption of water itself is excludable, so the watershed case involves bundling a public with a private good. Knowledge, an intermediate category (and one of the services of biodiversity), has to be commercialized with care, as shown by the need to protect it with patents, copyrights, and other supports of intellectual property rights. Many of the examples that I have cited—watersheds, carbon sequestration, and ecotourism—have the characteristics of what have been termed club goods, goods that can be provided as public goods to a select group of people who agree to finance their provision. This is the kind of arrangement often used to finance the provision of facilities such as tennis or golf clubs, and indeed it represents a particular way of privatizing the provision of certain public goods.[21]

I have a final observation on the privatization approach: the different ways of obtaining a return described in our examples are not mutually exclusive. A forest could obtain returns from carbon sequestration, bioprospecting, managing a watershed, *and* ecotourism. In fact, the region of the Mata Atlantica (a Brazilian coastal rain forest inland from Rio de Janeiro) is in a position to do exactly this. It manages the watershed for Rio in much the same way that the Catskills region does for New York. It also manages the stream flow of the Rio Paraibo do Sul, the river that provides most of the hydropower for Rio de Janeiro. These two services make it truly a major utility for Rio, with great economic value. Additionally, it supports a wide range of endemic species, sequesters carbon, and acts as a magnet for tourists. Currently, however, the region obtains a financial return on only one of these activities, ecotourism.

III. Conclusions

There are two routes via which markets can contribute to environmental conservation. One is the route marked out by the 1990 Clean Air Act in the United States, followed by the Kyoto protocol. The formula here is to note that many environmental goods and bads are public goods or bads and then to use permit markets to control their production. The public nature of the goods, coupled with the use of a market, introduces some novel features into the analysis concerning the links between efficiency and distribution.

The alternative route is simultaneously more traditional and more novel. It is more traditional in that, from an economic perspective, it breaks no new conceptual ground; it is more innovative in that only very recently have there been any concrete cases of this method being applied successfully. This approach involves establishing markets in the services provided to human societies by natural ecosystems and thereby bringing many externalities within the domain of the market.

Neither of these approaches will emerge naturally. The former clearly requires a particular legal infrastructure, in particular, the establishment of transferable property rights in a good that was previously common property. The latter approach is perhaps more capable of spontaneous emergence, as illustrated by the case of ConsCorp and the activities of various water companies in putting pressure on government for control over watershed areas. But this approach, too, will clearly benefit from government actions to establish a favorable legal regime. In the case of ConsCorp, the existence of private property rights in fugacious animals was important in ensuring the full benefits from a growing market for ecotourism and hunting. For either of these approaches, governments need to take positive steps to augment (if not to create) and efficient market providing public benefits.

Notes

I am grateful to Todd Sandler for very insightful comments. The subject matter of this essay is elaborated upon in Heal 2000.

1. See Vitousek et al. 1997 for details.
2. See Daily 1997.
3. Daily (ibid.) provides a comprehensive list of ecosystem services and an analysis of how human societies depend on the natural environment.
4. Good general references are Tietenberg 1980 and Atkinson 1983.
5. A fourth requirement is a complete set of markets for securities, present and future. This is a critical requirement in the context of managing risks through a market system.
6. The formalization comes from Chichilnisky, Heal, and Starrett 1999.
7. See ibid. for details.
8. For a proof, see ibid.
9. The discussion of the New York watershed case is taken from Chichilnisky and Heal 1998.
10. Their web site is <http://www.world-travel-net.co.uk/conscorp>. For more discussion see the International Union for the Conservation of Nature (IUCN) web site, <http://economics.iucn.org>. Anderson 1996 provided most of the material on ConsCorp used here. Also of interest is 't sas-Rolfes 1996.
11. Craig Packer, personal communication.
12. Peter Capstick, cited in Heal 1998.
13. Rubenstein 1993.
14. D. Cumming (World Wildlife Federation, Zimbabwe), personal communication.
15. See Rausser and Small 2000. These figures apply only to selected locations recognized as rich in biodiversity and should not be taken as typical of tropical regions.
16. The range of $10 to $50 emerges from simulations conducted by the Program on Information and Resources at Columbia University using a modified version of the Organization for Economic Cooperation and Development's GREEN computer model of the global economy. W. D. Nordhaus of Yale has reported estimates as high as $100 (personal communication).
17. Steve Pacala, Ecology Department, Princeton University, personal communication.

18. Daniel Botkin, personal communication.
19. The assertion that markets can give appropriate incentives for providing public goods is a surprising one to most economists in view of the free-rider problem. For a detailed analysis, see Chichilnisky and Heal 1998.
20. These numbers come from Reid 1998. In this essay, Reid begins to explore the scope for generalizing the New York case to other regions.
21. On clubs, see Cornes and Sandler 1996.

References

Anderson, Terry. 1996. "Enviro-Capitalists: Why and How to Preserve Their Habitat." <http://economics.iucn.org/96-01-14.pdf>.
Atkinson, Scott E. 1983. "Marketable Pollution Permits and Acid Rain Externalities." *Canadian Journal of Economics* 16:704–22.
Chichilnisky, G., and G. M. Heal. 1998. "Economic Returns from the Biosphere." *Nature* 391 (February 12): 629–30.
Chichilnisky, G., and G. M. Heal. 1999. *Environmental Markets.* New York: Columbia University Press.
Chichilnisky, G., G. M. Heal, and D. A. Starrett. 1999. "Equity and Efficiency in Environmental Markets: Global Trade in CO_2 Emissions." In *Environmental Markets,* edited by G. Chichilnisky and G. M. Heal. New York: Columbia University Press.
Coase, Ronald. 1960. "The Problem of Social Cost." *Journal of Law and Economics* 3:144.
Cornes, Richard, and Todd Sandler. 1996. *The Theory of Externalities, Club Goods, and Public Goods.* New York: Cambridge University Press.
Daily, G. C. 1997. *Nature's Services: Societal Dependence on Natural Ecosystems.* Washington, DC: Island Press.
Dales, J. H. 1968. *Pollution, Property, and Prices.* Toronto: University of Toronto Press.
Foley, Duncan K. 1970. "Lindahl's Solution and the Core of an Economy with Public Goods." *Econometrica* 38 (1):66–72.
Heal, Geoffrey. 1998. "Markets and Sustainability." Working paper PW-98-02, Columbia Business School.
Heal, Geoffrey. 2000. *Nature and the Marketplace.* Washington, DC: Island Press.
Rausser, G. C., and A. A. Small. 2000. "Valuing Research Leads: Bioprospecting and the Conservation of Genetic Resources." *Journal of Political Economy* 108 (1):173–206.
Reid, W. V. 1998. "A Business Plan for Ecosystem Services: Extending the New York City Watershed Model to Other Geographic Regions and Other Ecosystem Services." Paper presented by the World Resources Institute at the conference Managing Human-Dominated Ecosystems, Missouri Botanical Gardens, St. Louis, Missouri, March.

Rubenstein, D. I. 1993. "Science and the Pursuit of a Sustainable World." *Ecological Applications* 3:585–87.

Tietenberg, T. H. 1980. "Transferable Discharge Permits and the Control of Stationary Source Air Pollution: A Survey and Synthesis." *Land Economics* 56:391–416.

't sas-Rolfes, Michael. 1996. "The Use of Auctions as an Incentive Measure for Wildlife Conservation." <http://economics.iucn.org/96-03-16.pdf>.

Vitousek, P., Harold Mooney, Jane Lubchenco, and Jerry Melillo. 1997. "Human Domination of Earth's Ecosystems." *Science* 277 (25 July): 494–99.

Comment

Todd Sandler

The essay is an interesting and useful exploration of market-augmenting government policies with respect to ecosystems. In particular, the essay examines two market-based approaches: (1) the use of tradable permits to control pollution levels in a least costly fashion, and (2) privatizing and securitizing some aspects of ecosystems.

Tradable permits are gaining great favor as a means of controlling sulfur dioxide and other emissions under the Clean Air Act. When property rights to pollute are assigned, firms with low marginal abatement costs can sell some of their rights to firms with high marginal abatement costs and, in so doing, would reduce overall costs. Eventually, a given (desirable) pollution level would be achieved, determined by the fixed number of permits, at the point where marginal abatement costs are equal across firms. Emissions trading had its roots well before the 1990 amendments to the Clean Air Act, dating to 1977 when the act was amended to permit a policy of emission offsets known as the "bubble policy." Firms with multiple plants in a given region—the "bubble"—could increase their pollution from some plants if they made even larger reductions in pollution at other plants.

Emission trading at the national level depends on a central government that can issue these rights and establish the necessary market. At the supranational level, however, as for the Kyoto protocol, things are not so simple. A supranational government that might both issue and enforce permit rights does not currently exist and may not exist for the foreseeable future.

While this first market-based approach is well understood and by now commonplace in the literature, the second approach—involving trading claims to services of the ecosystems—is more radical and avant-garde. Though a fascinating idea, this approach needs further clarification. First, the differences between the two approaches need to be better drawn. In many ways, issuing pollution permits *is* selling services of the ecosystem to absorb pollution. Second, the necessary

175

features needed to allow this privatizing and securitizing need to be identified. Some of the examples—ecotourism, watershed protection—are really "club goods": excludable, easily monitored, and subject to congestion (on clubs, Cornes and Sandler, 1996). Other useful examples are the electromagnetic spectrum and orbital bands,[1] and here again excludability, monitoring, and crowding are key ingredients. Such goods can be securitized and traded, as shown by Sandler (1982, 191–208).[2]

The "growing carbon" example is more troublesome from the point of view of determining the true shadow price. The problem is the nonexcludability and nonrivalry of sequestration benefits. I don't see how one can establish a market when what is really being traded has these two properties. Sequestration might be a cheaper alternative to emission reductions, and therefore cost minimizing, but I am not convinced that a true shadow price can be established for this example.

Notes

1. See Sandler and Schulze 1981; Wihlborg and Wijkman 1981; Macauley 1998; and the symposium issue "Property Rights to Radio Spectrum" 1998.
2. Prospecting for pharmaceuticals also has strong elements of excludability, but not necessarily crowding. Here again there are some useful references. If I had to pick just one, then it would be Roger Sedjo's "Genetic Resources and Biotechnological Change" (1992).

References

Cornes, Richard, and Todd Sandler. 1996. *The Theory of Externalities, Club Goods, and Public Goods.* Cambridge: Cambridge University Press.
Macauley, Molly K. 1998. "Allocation of Orbit and Spectrum Resources for Regional Communications: What's at Stake?" *Journal of Law and Economics* 31 (October): 737–64.
"Property Rights to the Radio Spectrum." 1998. Special symposium issue, *Journal of Law and Economics* 31 (October).
Sandler, Todd. 1982. "The Theory of Intergenerational Clubs." *Economic Inquiry* 20 (2): 191–208.
Sandler, Todd, and William Schulze. 1981. "The Economics of Outer Space." *Natural Resources Journal* 21 (2): 371–93.
Sedjo, Roger. 1992. "Genetic Resources and Biotechnological Change." *Journal of Law and Economics* 35 (April): 199–213.
Wihlborg, Clas C., and Per Magnus Wijkman. 1981. "Outer Space Resources in Efficient and Equitable Use: New Frontiers for Old Principles." *Journal of Law and Economics* 24 (April): 23–43.

Failures in Governance and the Dominion of Markets

Martin C. McGuire

I. Olson's Idea of Market Augmentation

Two singularly lucid articles, written forty years ago, summarized the accumulated wisdom[1] of welfare economics as to when and whether a government should intervene in the allocative workings of the private economy. Paul Samuelson (1954) showed that allocative efficiency required the government to accept sole responsibility for providing some types of goods for which markets were *absent* altogether—"public goods," which the market economy would neglect virtually entirely. In "The Anatomy of Market Failure" (1958), Francis Bator established for an entire generation of economists the parameters for judging the private allocative effects of government intervention in *existing* markets. He identified four systematic deficits in markets: *failure by enforcement, failure by incentive, failure by signal,* and *failure by structure.* Each was occasioned by a specific fault, to be corrected with a specific mechanism.[2] While there have been many important advances[3] in our understanding of these categories of government activity, economists continue to divide the allocative role of government into the same two categories to this day: *provision of public goods* by the government and government *regulation of private-good* markets.

Into this picture place Mancur Olson. Forty years later, Olson called our attention to the idea that *effective functioning of private markets is itself a collective good:* the better functioning they are, the more public benefit they provide (1997).[4] It follows that increasing the proper reach and effectiveness of markets provides a return for *all* in the society, especially (but by no means solely) for those who participate directly in each private market. This benefit constitutes a substantial augmentation of welfare and therefore a worthy objective of government—hence his turn of phrase as well as the title of this volume. While Olson would, in all likelihood, have wanted to include our other modern prescriptions for correcting market failure under the umbrella of "market augmentation," his approach extended the term beyond mere corrections of market failure, recognizing that our accepted classification was leaving out something important.

Completely and Perfectly Augmented Markets

To bring this idea into focus, we might ask ourselves, "What constitutes a perfect or ideal market?" From a welfare and developmental viewpoint, a perfect market permits all voluntary exchanges—however indirect or intermediated (by other voluntary exchanges)—that are of mutual benefit to buyers and sellers: all kinds of exchanges of goods, assets, and services and of promises to perform or refrain from performing. Not only this, a perfect market would also allow or ensure that all the *relevant marginal benefits and costs* occasioned by each voluntary transaction would figure in the decisions of buyers and sellers (in the vocabulary of economics, would be "internalized" in the decision calculus of buyers and sellers). This scenario might be achieved by various types of government actions: definition of property rights, imposition of externality taxes, and so on. Moreover, a truly ideal market would also have the property of costing no more to establish, operate, and maintain than the amount of aggregate surplus benefit it allows to buyers and sellers, *as well as to others who may benefit from the existence and operation of markets, in addition to the buyers and sellers in any one market.* That is, a market itself conveys an external economy to society over and above the benefit it procures for those who make immediate use of it.

It is precisely the uniform nonindividualized, institutional nature of ideal markets that constitutes such a powerful public good for so many, far beyond the individuals who actually participate directly in buying and selling. It is this institutional character that allows markets to announce information about others' wants and needs, inform about scarcities, and permit planning as well as decentralized coordination. This is precisely the public-good benefit that market augmentation seeks to procure. And, because it is a public-good benefit shared by all, private efforts to supply it will always be insufficient and suboptimal; riven by free-rider conflicts, "market augmentation" is essentially and necessarily a collective, government function.

II. Private Benefits, Government Failure, and the Forces that Limit Market Augmentation

Although the public benefits of market augmentation may be vast, it is unlikely that they will be unalloyed with redistributions of private benefits. If we ask, "Why are markets truncated, restricted, and falling short of the ideal?" we will frequently find that the answer is, "On purpose!" If the limitation on markets is deliberate—effected, for example, by manipulation of government power—then there are, ipso facto, private parties who benefit from these restrictions, and opening up the markets would harm them, at least insofar as first-round effects are concerned. That is, *distribution of benefits* is a central factor in the creation of impediments in the first place, and the *resistance to private loss* is the central explanation for the failure to correct truncation of the market. So one crucial effect of market augmentation will be not only to create value for everyone in the society but also to redistribute income or welfare from some to others within the society.

This essay will consider three categories of "government failure" to promote ideal market augmentation, all deriving from a special redistributive benefit that a particular private interest obtains by inducing the failure. In the first category, "failure in representation" and "failure by redistribution proper" are really two sides of the same coin; the second and third categories are "failure by predatory discrimination" and "failure by corrupt implementation."[5]

Failure in Representation

Under this category, I will show how the desire of a government's supporters to redistribute income *to* themselves *from* the society at large will cause a government to restrict its market-augmenting action (thus, failure by redistribution). As I will demonstrate presently, if the government represents the entire society, and this society accepts the market distribution of income as optimal, then redistribution will not be desired and all tax collections will be allocated to market augmentation. But if, on the contrary, only a subset of those citizens who actually work and produce control the government, then (as I shall also demonstrate) redistribution that can help that subset will provide the government with an incentive to suppress market augmentation (thus, failure in representation). The real source of this failure is that market augmentation requires resources that may need

to come from resource pools that the government has already reserved for the privileged and powerful. We need to ask, therefore,
how the interaction of wealth redistribution and productivity en-
hancement (by virtue of market augmentation) will vary, *depending
on whom the government represents.*

Failure by Discrimination

Under this category, I identify how the market-augmenting behavior
of a governing majority (or any subset in power) will change when
that group can discriminate between *its own sector* and the remainder of the economy. Such discrimination is possible both in the provision of market-augmenting effort to different sectors of the economy and in the taxation imposed on different sectors. This merely
extends the assumption that the rulers can tax and redistribute to
themselves. Now we will assume that they can not only discriminate
in the taxation they impose on themselves versus others but can also
discriminate in their provision of market augmentation as between
their "home" economy and a colony or satellite economy. This suggests how ethnic identities or rivalries, and the consequent creation
of explicitly disadvantaged minorities, provide both the opportunity
and the rationale for restricting market augmentation.

Corruption: Failure in Implementation or by Competition

Here I will compare the effects of erosion of a government's monopoly tax power with the effects of degradation of its ability to deliver
market-augmenting public goods. How do these *different categories
of corruption* change the performance and outcome under *different
forms of governance?* For example, is an autocratic form of governance more vulnerable to corruption in its tax collection system or its
market-augmenting public-good provision?

Building on earlier work coauthored with Mancur Olson
(McGuire and Olson 1996, 1994, 1993), this essay will focus on the allocative consequences of these three types of government failure,
comparing them in all cases with the *optimal* amount of market augmentation that a nonredistributive, nondiscriminatory, noncorrupt,
utopian/consensus democracy would implement. I first will summarize the basic McGuire and Olson model, which provides a structure
for further analysis, making special use of their theorem that every

realistic, semidemocratic government can be modeled as a linear combination of a perfect consensual democracy and a perfect enduring autocratic government that desires to maximize its redistribution.

III. McGuire and Olson: "Economics of Autocracy and Majority Rule"

McGuire and Olson considered how a perfectly efficient, utopian, consensual democracy would supply productivity-enhancing public goods—the resources, institutions, policies, and rules for market augmentation. *Utopian democracy* was defined as a democracy in which all questions of redistribution among individuals had been settled so that the society could be modeled as a monolithic benevolent dictator. They next asked how this provision would compare with that of an enduring autocrat with an infinitely long-lived dynasty and then how it would compare with the provision under other forms of governance such as majoritarian or oligarchic elite governance or an interest-group-driven, modern, semidemocratic society. Concrete examples of public goods in McGuire and Olson include property right definition, contract enforcement, and protection against theft, as examples of market augmentation that expand the productivity of the private economy. Of special relevance here is their notion that the incentives facing all of these many forms of government can be shown by a system of two simple (proportionately) independent relationships plus a descriptive parameter.

Market Augmentation

The first of these relations gives "market augmentation" in the creation of national income/product, modeled as a production function $Y = Y(L,G)$,[6] which serves as numeraire with price $p = 1$. See figure 1, where

$Y =$ aggregate output lumped into a single variable. The function $Y(G,L)$ shows the net effect of increases in market augmentation (which might derive from sources listed in section III, paragraph 1), with all effects or transfers among citizens that might be concomitant with G being netted out;

$L =$ labor force and all other inputs to production assumed to be constant;

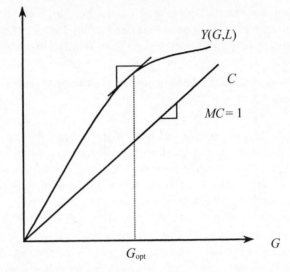

Fig. 1. The optimal level of government provision under lump sum taxes

G = public factor inputs, including for our purposes all market-augmenting efforts/expenditures to be undertaken exclusively by the government. When convenient, G is assumed to be essential for any positive output, as illustrated.

As figure 1 shows, if nondistorting lump-sum taxation were possible the optimal provision of market augmentation would occur at G_{opt}, where its marginal contribution to production equaled its marginal cost of unity.

Tax Distortions

The second McGuire and Olson relationship reflects an assumption that lump-sum, nondistorting taxation is impossible and thus that some sacrifices of market augmentation, in at least some sector(s), is necessary to collect revenues—revenues that are used in turn for market augmentation elsewhere in the economy. This assumption leads to a tax-induced "efficiency loss function" or "deadweight loss function." See figure 2, where

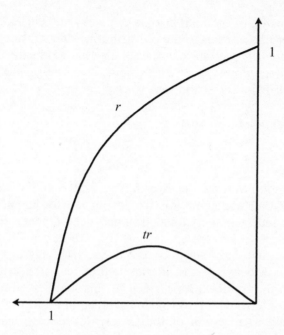

Fig. 2. Deadweight losses and the Laffer curve

$1 - r(t) =$ the *proportion* of Y lost due to incentive distorting taxation;

$t =$ the constant uniform average (equal to marginal) rate at which output is taxed to obtain resources for tribute to the government and to finance the supply of G;

$r(t) =$ the proportion of Y remaining after deadweight losses.

Figure 2 also shows $tr(t)$, the proportion of national income collected in taxes. When $t = 0$ or $r = 0$, total collections are nil, which implies that tr reaches a maximum in the interior.

Overlap between Economic Ownership and Political Power

The third innovation in the McGuire and Olson analysis is to devise a parameter to represent the form of governance on a spectrum ranging from perfect democracy to pure dictatorship—a parameter describing the relation between economic ownership and political power. To do this let

F = the fraction of the total income produced and earned in the market that accrues to the redistributive ruling interest;

S = the *proportionate* share of the total actual production, rY, that the ruling interest receives, including its earnings and its receipts from redistribution.

The formula for its share is

$$S \doteq F + (1 - F)t. \tag{1}$$

The assumption that the deadweight loss from taxation and productivity of market augmentation are proportionally independent[7] allows aggregate actual national product, net of deadweight losses from taxation, to be written as $r(t)Y(G)$, where the L in $Y(G,L)$, being a constant, has been suppressed. Similarly, aggregate tax revenues can now be written as the simple product $tr(t)Y(G)$.

Within the framework provided by this simplification, McGuire and Olson infer how a government's choice of t and G depends on the political organization of the society. Moreover, this neat $r(t)$, $Y(G)$, $S(F,t)$ framework allows a simple graphic exposition of the incentive structures and relative outcomes of different forms of governance. Most importantly, the analysis implies:

1. That modern semidemocratic regimes can be analyzed as a simple linear combination of the two extreme cases: purely selfish autocracy and purely selfless representative utopia.
2. That an inherent tendency exists for all regimes—autocratic, oligarchic, or majoritarian—to limit taxation because it erodes both the efficacy of markets and the productivity of public-good capital (G). It therefore erodes the return to the ruling interest's own labor along with other private inputs.

These models and insights bear directly on the analysis of failures of governance, to which we now turn.

IV. "Government Failure by Representation/Redistribution": Trade-Offs between Market Augmentation and Income Redistribution

Here I want to show how government's incentive to redistribute conflicts with the incentive to provide for market efficiency by summarizing and extending certain portions of the McGuire and Olson model.[8] I begin with an analysis of a society in which there is no re-distribution—a "perfect society" in one sense—which we can use as a basis for comparison.

A Consensual Society: A Benchmark for Ideal Market Augmentation

Consider a society with a given distribution that enjoys unanimous consensus. Assume that in this society each citizen pays a share of the cost of market-augmenting public goods that is exactly proportional to his or her share of the gains (marginal and average) from the social order. We can use this ideal to examine public-good provision in a Pareto-efficient society with no coercive redistribution of income and to make welfare comparisons across regimes.[9] It would be feasible for this "Lindahl consensus" to collect more taxes than needed to finance public goods and redistribute the surplus to itself, but because it already has agreement about its income distribution doing this would cause deadweight losses from incentive-distorting taxation for no purpose. Accordingly, the Lindahl consensus society will choose to collect taxes only to provide the public good. We can therefore describe the Lindahl society as always proceeding on the boundary of the constraint $tr(t)Y(G) - G = 0$. This determines G as a function of t: $G = G(t)$, or $t = t(G)$. The dual relationships $t(G)$ and $G(t)$ are derived graphically in figure 3.[10] Each common value of $tr(t) = G/Y(G)$ shown in the third quadrant implies a specific G-t combination.

The welfare of the consensus society depends on *posttax* income. One approach to its allocation problem is to ask the optimal value of t, with G thereby determined by $G(t)$, derived earlier; under this approach, our benchmark society maximizes equation (2):

$$W = \text{Max}_{t}(1 - t)r(t)Y[G(t)]. \qquad (2)$$

It chooses a tax rate so that, with all tax proceeds spent on G, the marginal *social* benefit of the tax just equals its marginal *social* cost. Because it represents the entire society, this government includes *all* social costs and benefits in its decision calculus.

An alternative way to characterize the consensual society is to focus on its optimal provision of G. This calls for formulating its social welfare maximization as

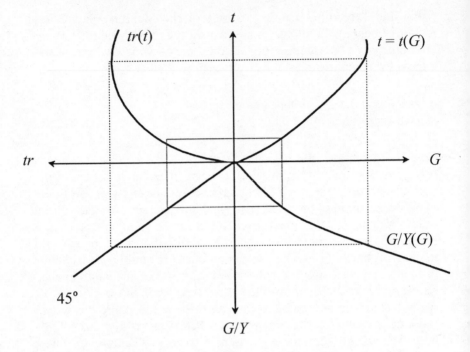

Fig. 3.   Derivation of $t = t(G)$ from the given production and tax efficiency loss functions

$$U = \underset{G}{\text{Max}}\{[r[t(G)]Y(G)] - G\}. \tag{3}$$

Here the variable of choice is G, with $t = t(G)$ implicit from the constraint, and therefore $r = r(G)$. Either formulation, eq. (2) or eq. (3), is sufficient to solve the entire problem for the consensual society, but with equation (3) the marginal resource costs and marginal deadweight losses show up explicitly. The derivative of equation (3) with respect to G yields

$$rY' + Yr'\frac{dt}{dG} - 1 = 0. \tag{4}$$

The marginal (pretax, in this case) social cost of G consists of the direct unit resource cost plus $Yr'\,dt/dG$, the marginal deadweight loss of the tax necessary to net a unit of resources. Equation (4), therefore, shows how a consensus society takes account of *all* of the benefits of the public good. It is clear from equation (4) that the marginal costs of financing G themselves depend upon $Y'(G)$. When the constraint $tr(t)Y(G) = G$ is totally differentiated, solved for $dG/dt = -Y(r + tr')/(trY' - 1)$, substituted into equation (4), and then simplified, we obtain the details of marginal benefits and cost and the relation between t and G that must obtain at the consensus optimum.[11] Here *MSB* stands for the marginal social benefit of one unit of G, while *MSC* stands for the marginal cost of obtaining one dollar of resources and includes all deadweight loss effects:

$$\frac{MSB}{r} = Y'(G) = \frac{r(t) - (1 - t)r'(t)}{r^2} = \frac{MSC}{r} \tag{5}$$

or

$$MSB \equiv rY'(G) = 1 - (1 - t)\frac{r'}{r} \equiv MSC. \tag{6}$$

These relationships are shown in figure 4.

This analysis is a necessary beginning for understanding how market augmentation and income redistribution interact. In a consensual society, distribution and market augmentation do not compete, so failure by redistribution is ruled out. Although the public good has a price or resource cost of 1, that is *not* its marginal cost to the Lindahl democracy. For this society—for *any* society that does not redistribute income, and that therefore must raise the tax rate in order to obtain more of the public good—its marginal cost includes the marginal deadweight losses from the additional taxation needed to finance more of the public good. *It follows that the more easily taxation can be evaded, and therefore the greater the deadweight loss to generate any given level of taxes, the lower is the incentive to augment markets, even in a perfect Lindahl consensus.* As will be evident from the next section, this is *not* the case for any regime that redistributes—for example, an autocratically ruled society.

Autocratic, Majoritarian, and Semidemocratic Regime Incentives

Every redistributive regime will choose a higher tax rate than needed to finance a social order, including market augmentation. Therefore,

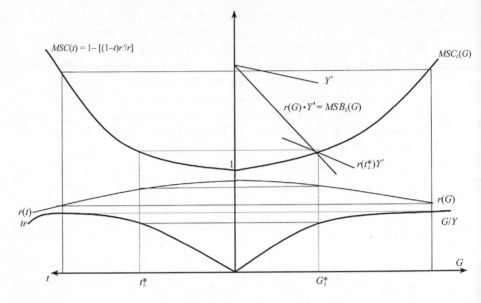

Fig. 4.   Equilibrium in a consensual society

The second quadrant shows $r(t)$ ($r'' < 0$ assumed), tax shares $tr(t)$ at each tax rate as before, as well as MSC from equation (6) and MSC from equation (7); for illustration, these are drawn as increasing throughout. The first quadrant shows Y' and derives the two functions $r[t(G)]$ and $MSC[t(G)]$, which must obtain for every society that spends all its revenues on public goods like the Lindahl society. For each value of t, and therefore of $r(t)$ and $MSC(t)$ in the second quadrant, the corresponding value of G is read from $tr = G/Y(G)$ in the first quadrant, with $r(G)$ and $MSC(G)$ thereby constructed. The first quadrant also shows the marginal social benefit of a balanced budget provision of G, that is, $r[t(G)]Y' = MSB(G)$. The Lindahl society's optimum, then, is identified at the intersection of $MSB(G)$ and $MSC(G)$. The figure also shows for reference a marginal social benefit curve r^*Y', where r^* is evaluated at the optimum value of $t = t^*$. This reference curve r^*Y' is flatter than the MSB curve; that is, $r[t(G)]Y'$ is steeper because it includes the effects of G upon r by way of the budget balance requirement. The curve $r(G)Y'$ is steeper than $r(t^*)Y'$ because to increase G taxes must be raised and deadweight losses increased. But with t fixed at its optimal value t^* the consensus society's choice of G will occur where $r^* = r[t^*(G^*)]$, so the curves intersect at the optimal value. With the consensus society's choice of t and G so determined where $MSB(G) = MSC(t)$, the division of national product between tax collections which equal expenditures on G and citizens' consumption follows.

when the government taxes to redistribute, redistribution and market augmentation necessarily compete for resources. As I will demonstrate, unlike the case of consensual societies, this competition for resources brings about a failure in governance via failure by distribution.

Consider the problem faced by the elite rulers or redistributing majority. Using the S, F, t parameter notation developed earlier, I represent the optimization problem of a governing interest as

$$\underset{t,G}{\text{Max}}(1 - t)r(t)FY(G) + [tr(t)Y(G) - G]; \qquad s.t.\ G \leq tr(t)Y(G), \qquad (7)$$

which is equivalent to

$$\text{Max } Sr(t)Y(G) - G; \qquad s.t.\ G \leq trY(G). \qquad (8)$$

The first term of this objective function in equation (7) shows the market income of the ruling majority after both deadweight losses and taxes, and the second term is the surplus that the majority transfers to itself. To generalize for both positive and zero redistribution, the appropriate Lagrange function is

$$(1 - t)r(t)FY(G) + tr(t)Y(G) - G + \lambda[tr(t)Y(G) - G], \qquad (9)$$

with Kuhn-Tucker conditions $\lambda[tr(t)Y(G) - G] = 0$, $\lambda \geq 0$, and $[tr(t)Y(G) - G] \geq 0$. First assume positive redistribution, that is, that $trY > G$. Then $\lambda = 0$ and the first-order conditions are

$$F[-r + (1 - t)r'] + (r + t'r) = 0 \qquad (10)$$

and

$$[(1 - t)rF + tr]Y' - 1 = SrY' - 1 = 0. \qquad (11)$$

Equation (10) requires that the marginal cost of the tax (of dt) to the ruling or majority party—the negative of the first term in equation (10)—be equal to the marginal benefit from redistribution—the second term. That is, the majority/elite limits the deadweight losses it imposes on society because it bears some of these losses. Rearranging gives equation (12): as the tax rate is increased from $t = 0$, $R(t)$ tends to fall;

$$F = \frac{r + tr'}{r - (1 - t)r'} \equiv R(t) \qquad (12)$$

deadweight losses at the margin (the denominator) increase; marginal gains from redistribution (the numerator) decrease. The majority/elite increases its tax rate until $R(t)$ falls to where it equals F. For

t such that $R > F$, the marginal benefits of further redistribution to the rulers exceed the marginal costs, and therefore taxes are increased. For $R < F$, the opposite holds.

The redistributive majority's incentives are pictured in figure 5, illustrating the tendency for governments that are beholden to interest groups to limit taxation short of complete confiscation. The majority's total income is given by adding its market income, $FrY(G)$, to the redistribution it exacts from the minority, $(1 - F)trY(G)$, giving a combined income share of $Fr + (1 - F)tr = rS = \mathcal{S}$. The redistributive majority maximizes its proportionate share of realized output irrespective of the amount of public good it decides to supply. This maximum of $\mathcal{S}$ and the optimal redistribution from the minority to the majority occur at the tax rate, t_R^*, which we derive from equation (10):

$$t_R^* = -\frac{r}{r'} - \frac{F}{(1 - F)}; \qquad F \neq 1. \tag{13}$$

Equation (13) implies that the larger a majority's fraction, F, the lower will be its optimal tax rate. It also shows that a majority or other ruling interest that earns some of the society's market income necessarily levies lower taxes than an autocrat does, since $F = 0$ for an autocrat. Observe also that every redistributive regime — an autocrat or a ruling elite — will choose an optimal tax rate independently of its decision on how much G to provide. Because we have assumed that the proportional deadweight social loss, $1 - r(t)$, is independent of public-good supply, this market augmentation does not enter into equations (10), (12), or (13).

Having chosen the tax rate to give optimal redistribution, the ruling interest then chooses its optimal public-good level.[12] That is, having taxed, a redistributive regime will provide G out of its inframarginal tax receipts. Therefore, the marginal private cost of G to a redistributive regime does not include deadweight losses from taxation; for every redistributive majority, including autocrats, its marginal *private* cost of G is simply the direct unit resource cost. This decides how much market-augmenting public good a redistributive interest will provide. The majority's marginal *private* benefit from G is given by equation (11) as SrY', which it equates to its marginal *private* cost of 1.

With this model, we can now understand how a redistributing

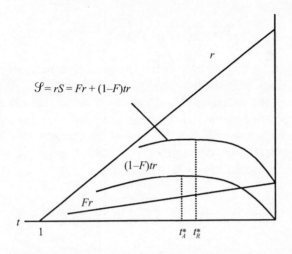

Fig. 5. Equilibrium tax rates in redistributive societies

elite's reduced provision of market-augmenting public goods represents a *failure* in governance. To appreciate this, consider the relation between marginal social/private benefits (MS/PB) and marginal social/private costs (MS/PC) when the resource allocation agenda is controlled by a ruling interest—smaller than the total society that obtains under a Lindahl consensus—a ruling interest that makes allocations based on its own private benefits and costs rather than social benefits or costs. At this majority's optimal value of G marginal private benefits $MPB = SrY'(G) = 1$—or equivalently marginal social benefits $MSB = rY'(G) = 1/S$. That is, when the majority provides G until its marginal *private* benefit (MPB) equals its marginal private costs, or 1, at that same point, rY' (i.e., society's marginal social benefit [MSB] $= 1/S$. But at its optimal tax rate the majority's chosen $1/S$ also equals marginal social costs (MSC)—consistent with equation (14)—because the redistributing majority also nets S percent of tax revenues. This follows from combining equations (10) and (11) to obtain (14) and (15) (note that eq. (14) for the majority elite has the same functional form as (5) for the Lindahl consensus):

$$\frac{MSB}{r} = Y' = \frac{r - (1 - t)r'}{r^2} = \frac{1}{rF + (1 - F)tr} = \frac{MSC}{r} \qquad (14)$$

or

$$MSB = rY' = \frac{1}{F + (1 - F)t} \equiv \frac{1}{S} = \text{MSC.} \tag{15}$$

A ruling elite, acting strictly in its private selfish interest, chooses a value of G such that the marginal *social* benefits of G, *given* the tax rate t_R^*, equal the marginal *social* costs of G, which the tax rate t_R^* imposes on the entire society. That is, at its optimal tax rate, the majority's chosen $1/S$ also equals MSC, so that we can generalize equation (15) as applicable to all regimes, consensual, autocratic, or in between. This is shown as

$$\text{Marginal Social Benefit} = \frac{1}{S} = \text{Marginal Social Cost.} \tag{16}$$

The Lindahl consensus chooses a *lower tax,* $t_L^* < t_R^*$, and therefore generates a lesser MSC of resources than does a ruling elite: $MSC_L < MSC_R$. But the Lindahl consensus also provides *more* of the market-augmenting public good even at this lower tax, so that the marginal social benefit of G is less than under a ruling elite: $MSB_L < MSB_R$. Figure 6 shows the choice of G by the ruling elite, and illustrates how it implicitly chooses: (1) a higher MSC than the Lindahl consensus, (2) a higher MSB, and (3) a lower value of G. (A striking implication of this model is that ruling elites with sufficiently broad ownership stakes in their economies will undertake no redistribution whatever and will allocate resources the same as would an idealized consensus democracy. For further discussion see the appendix to this essay.)

The foregoing extensions of the McGuire and Olson model demonstrate how the incentive to redistribute from the powerless to the powerful creates a *failure in governance.* This is the first of the three governance failures to be identified here—a failure by redistribution—and a suboptimal provision of those public goods that support a social order by enhancing the private economy.

We can now use the methods just developed to extend the model. We will find that the $t, r, Y(G), F, S$ framework has a direct application to the two other sources of government failure—failure by predatory discrimination and failure by corruption.

V. Tax Differentials and Failure by Discrimination

First, we extend the foregoing argument to readdress intergroup discrimination in taxation and public-good provision within a single

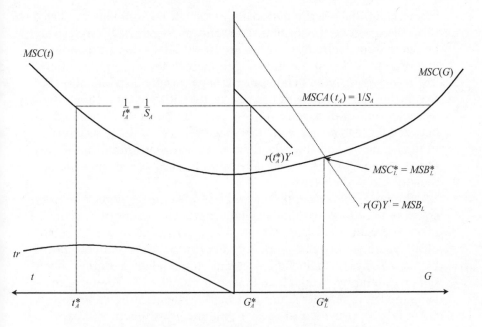

Fig. 6. An autocrat's choice of *G* and of *t* compared to the choices of a Lindahl consensus

political economy. The majority elites described earlier, although "predatory" in some sense, are restricted in their predation by technology and information. Because the basic McGuire and Olson model assumes one integrated economy, a predatory elite or a predatory majority cannot differentiate among various beneficiaries of the market-augmenting public goods. Thus, the provision of *G* in the basic model benefits everyone indivisibly—a technological limitation that prevents the rulers from applying selective market augmentation to their favored support. Similarly, the basic model precludes discriminatory taxation by assumption. Because of lack of information, the ruling elite is unable to tax its own support less than that of others.

This section corrects these two shortcomings because, especially in environments where economies are driven by ethnic divisions and the ruling elites are drawn from one ethnic group at the expense of others, it may be easily possible for the ruling classes to discriminate both in taxation and in public-good provision. (This point is developed further in Omar Azfar's comments on this essay.)[13]

We will specifically focus on an extreme case—"internal colonization," which is used as a first proxy for the many cases of national, ethnic, and tribal discrimination under a single government. Typically, this will be a government that represents or is controlled exclusively by one national, ethnic, or tribal group yet has tax and expenditure authority over one or more distinguishably different subpopulations. The term *colonization* denotes an extreme form of discrimination between the elite group and the rest of the citizenry and thus establishes a point of departure for less clear-cut cases of discrimination between those in power, who own a share of the productive resources of the economy, and the remainder of the citizens, who own the rest of the economy but have no power to tax, sustain a social order, or redistribute to themselves.

Suppose, therefore, that a unified, consensual "home" country controls a "colony" within its own borders. All citizens of the colony taken together are assumed to be a unit. Production in each sector of the country's economy—denoted H for the home country and C for the colony—is assumed to depend on the labor and other material private inputs available in that sector and on the degree of market-supporting infrastructure and market-augmenting expenditure, $G^k = G^H, G^C$, provided to each. The home government will provide both G^H and G^C from the taxes it imposes on the home population and production in the colony. The provisions of G^H and G^C apply strictly within each subeconomy. (Presently, we will postulate G^N, which augments both home and colonial economics indivisibly, but we begin with only local public goods, G^H and G^C). The elite governments can also tax each subpopulation differently—determining $t^k = t^H, t^C$—collect the aggregate tax revenues, and then allocate them among three purposes: (1) provision of G^H, (2) provision of G^C, and (3) transfers to the home population. As in McGuire and Olson, assume that average and marginal tax rates imposed on either population, though different for different populations, are constant within each. Moreover, take $Y(G)$ as the numeraire and assume that the price of G, G^H, and G^C are constant at unity. For simplicity and to avoid prejudicing the results, it is assumed that the production $Y(G^k)$ and deadweight loss functions $1 - r(t^k) : k = (H, C)$ are the same in the home sector and the colony—that is, the functions are the same although the realized values will differ. Market augmentation in both sectors—represented by expenditures on G^H and G^C—may increase trade between the two sectors, integrating their economies, but that aspect is only implicitly modeled in this first stage. Later we will explore the implications if some types of public good or market augmentation are nonexcludable and nonrival *across* sectors. Our initial setup resembles two isolated economies governed by the same authority.

Comparisons between the home government's treatment of its own citizens and those of its colony will naturally depend on the type of governance at home. For example, if the home government were a selfish autocrat (with $F = 0$) then its treatment of its colony would be no different from treatment of its own population, since the home population is in effect just another colony. Therefore, to make the problem interesting and the contrast more stark, we will assume that the objective of the home government is to maximize the welfare of its own home population. If it taxes its own people, excess burden or deadweight loss will inevitably follow, directly reducing home income and consumption. If the home government taxes the colony, the colony's product will decline through the vehicle of deadweight loss and the home government's tax base in its colony will become eroded and its tax revenue will decline. The optimal level of taxation, and the optimal investment in market augmentation at home and in the colony, therefore depend on how all of these factors interact. To capture this idea, we write W for the home government's welfare objective:

$$\text{Max}_{t^H, t^C, G^H, G^C} \quad W = r(t^H)Y(G^H) - G^H + t^C r(t^C)Y(G^C) - G^C. \quad (17)$$

Here W consists of home production eroded by efficiency losses from home taxation (if there is any positive taxation), plus tax collections from the colony, whose production has also been eroded by taxes—reduced by expenditures on home and colony market augmentation. This objective function is maximized subject to the constraint that revenues equal or exceed outlays on market augmentation, written with the Lagrange coefficient, λ:

$$\lambda[t^H r(t^H)Y(G^H) + t^C r(t^C)Y(G^C) \geq G^H + G^C]. \quad (18)$$

The sum of terms on the left are tax revenues and on the right expenditures on G. The home government will distribute any surplus directly to its citizens. Kuhn-Tucker conditions yield $\lambda = 0$ if tax collections exceed ΣG^k. In this case, it must be that $t^H = 0$ because for $t^H > 0$ the home government is simply taxing its own citizens and distributing the proceeds straight back to them. But this would be wasteful because of the deadweight losses caused by taxation; taxes could be reduced keeping ΣG^k at the same value, which would increase H's net income because of a reduction in the deadweight loss of self taxation, that is, because

$$d[r(t^H)Y(G^H)]/dt^H < 0. \tag{19}$$

Accordingly there are two cases of interest:

1. When the home government taxes its own people, $t^H > 0$, then no direct tribute is collected from the colony, that is, $\Sigma G^k = \Sigma R^k$, where R^k indicates tax revenue obtained from sector $k = H,C$
2. When the home government imposes no tax on its own citizens, that is, $t^H = 0$, and $\Sigma G^k < \Sigma R^k$, meaning that excess revenue is collected from the colony over and above that needed for public-good provision there, so that a surplus remains to transfer directly to home citizens

We now compare values of t and G chosen for home and the colony in each of these two situations.

Case 1. Indirect cross-subsidy from the colony to home, balanced allocative budget, and no direct income transfers: $\lambda > 0$; $t^H > 0$; $\Sigma G^k = \Sigma R^k$. Here the home country taxes itself to contribute partially to the provision of market-sustaining public goods. Necessary conditions for a maximum for each indicated variable in equations (18) plus (19) are

$$t^H: \quad r_t^H + \lambda(r^H + t^H r_t^H) = 0, \tag{20}$$

$$t^C: \quad (1 + \lambda)(r^C + t^C r_t^C) = 0 \Rightarrow (r^C + t^C r_t^C) = 0; \\ \text{autocratic taxation}, \tag{21}$$

$$G^H: \quad r^H Y_G^H - 1 + \lambda(t^H r^H Y_G^H - 1) = 0, \tag{22}$$

$$G^C: \quad t^C r^C Y_G^C - 1 + \lambda(t^C r^C Y_G^C - 1) = 0 \Rightarrow t^C r^C Y_G^C = 1: \\ \text{autocratic provision of } G^C. \tag{23}$$

First, note that at this level of aggregation *the home country treats its colony the same way an autocrat would treat a subject population,* assuming an enduring permanent colonial status. With respect to taxation of the colony, we can see this equivalence from equation (21); the home country extracts the maximum share possible from its colony's economy. It should not overtax the colony; this would destroy the tax base. Instead, the home country places its colony (as far as taxation is concerned) at the peak of its "Laffer curve." Similarly, the home country underinvests in the colony, as shown by equation (23); it invests the same amount as a selfish dictator would invest in his or her subjects. But this investment in market augmentation in the colony is not zero; rather, it is sufficient so that the home country receives back in taxes at the margin just the amount of outlay required to support market augmentation—*just as would an autocrat in a single home domain.*

Equations (20) and (22) show tax and expenditure policies applied to home citizens. First, from

$$(r^H + t^H r_t^H) = -r_t^H/\lambda > 0 \tag{24}$$

or

$$\lambda r^H = -r_t^H(1 + \lambda t^H), \tag{25}$$

we infer that the home country taxes itself less than would an autocrat since $-r_t^H > 0$ and therefore $t^H(*)$ (i.e., the equilibrium or maximizing value of t^H) falls short of the value of t^H, which an enduring autocrat would choose for home (because an autocrat's value of t^H would be such as to set eq. (24) equal to zero). The exact amount of home taxation depends on the productivity of public goods/market augmentation. The effects of $G, Y(G)$, and $Y'(G)$ are buried in the parameter λ for determining the home country's Lindahl-like selection of t^H and provision of G^H. But with identical deadweight loss (DWL) functions and identical $Y(G)$ functions both at home and in the colony the tax rate at home is less than in the colony even while the provision of market-augmenting public goods is greater at home than in the suppressed, colonial sector. We can see this from combining equation (22) with equation (25).

$$\frac{\lambda}{1 + \lambda} Y_G^H = -\frac{r_t^H}{(r^H)^2} : \lambda > 0, r_t^H < 0. \tag{26}$$

Since $\lambda > 0$, it follows that $0 < \lambda/(1 + \lambda) < 1$. Contrast this with Y_G^C, obtained from equation (23), that is, $Y_G^C = 1/t^C r^C$ and $t^C = -r^C/r_t^C$ from equation (21). Combining these for comparison gives

$$Y_G^C = -\frac{r_t^C}{(r^C)^2} \, . \tag{27}$$

Although the Lindahl home government will tax its own citizens less than its colony, inferences as to the effect of discrimination against a colony on the provision of *self-funded* G at home are ambiguous. Home's autocratic, surplus-maximizing choice with respect to its colony procures for it a lump-sum start-up endowment of G, for which it pays nothing. To see the effect of this endowment on home's self-funded provision of G, one must begin with the prediscrimination supply of G by home's government. This will depend on the organization of home's society—whether it is an autocracy; a utopian consensual government; or a mixed, interest-group-driven semidemocracy characterized by parameters F and S. Figure 7 gives a diagrammatic solution for this problem, starting with the baseline case where Home is a utopian consensus with no colony. The figure then shows the effect of a lump-sum grant from a colony, G_o^H, on the consensus society's choice of self-funded G and G_s^H and therefore on its choice of total $G^H = G_o^H + G_s^H$. The lump-sum transfer from the colony reduces Y_G^H, the marginal productivity of G_s^H in H, but at the same time (because it boosts output in H) it lowers the tax rate necessary to finance a given G_s^H. These two effects work in opposite directions, so that a lump-sum receipt of G_o^H may increase G_s^H or decrease it. In fact, if the surplus that can be extracted from the colony is great enough—depending on productivity of G there and on the deadweight loss function $1 - r(t)$—home may reduce its self-financed provision of G even below the amount a Home autocrat would provide (from eq. (26); if λ is sufficiently small the equation may be satisfied at a value of $G^H = G_o^H + G_s^H$, smaller than would obtain under a home autocracy). Nevertheless, the home country will definitely increase its aggregate provision of public-goods/market-augmentation capital over its Lindahl provision as a result of exploitation of its interior colony, and that domestic colony will definitely enjoy a lesser amount of market-augmenting public goods than it would if it were independent and separate, ruled by anything better than a totalitarian autocrat.

Case 2. Cross-subsidy from the colony to home, allocative budget in surplus; positive direct income transfers to home: $t^H = 0$; $\Sigma G^k < \Sigma R^k$. In this second case, taxation of the colony is so effective that home producers are not taxed at all by their consensual representative government. The revenue income from the colony is greater than the

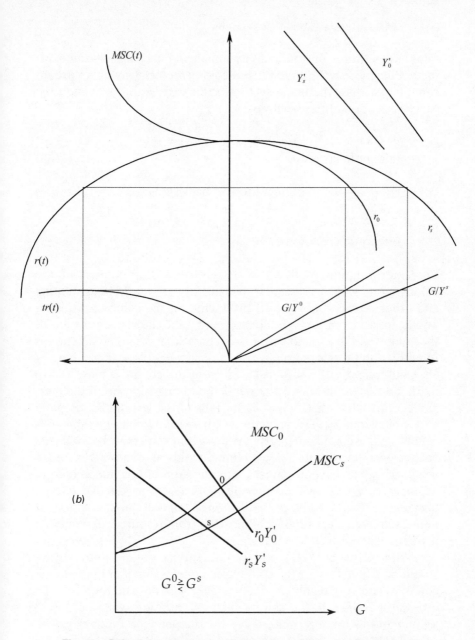

**Fig. 7. Colonial revenues and the size of home government:
a, baseline case—Home is a utopian consensus with no colony;
b, effect of a lump-sum grant from a colony**

The endowment of public good financed by revenue from the colony lowers deadweight losses for any amount of self-financed public good but also lowers productivity of self-financed G because of diminishing returns to G. Therefore, the prediscrimination (0) outcome under a Lindahl consensus government may entail greater or less G than after the home country has taxed its colony (s).

total expenditures on productivity-enhancing and market-augmenting public goods in both home and colony sectors, leaving a pure income transfer for the home sector. In this case, with $\lambda = 0$ and $t^H = 0$, necessary conditions become

t^C: $(1 + \lambda)(r^C + t^C r_t^C) = 0 \Rightarrow (r^C + t^C r_t^C) = 0$:
autocratic taxation,   (28)

G^H: $Y_G^H - 1 = 0$:   perfect utopian provision of G^H,   (29)

G^C: $t^C r^C Y_G^C - 1 + \lambda(t^C r^C Y_G^C - 1) = 0 \Rightarrow t^C r^C Y_G^C = 1$:
autocratic provision of G^C.   (30)

The interpretation of these is straightforward. Treatment of the colony is the same as in case 1, but in this case market-augmenting and other public goods are so productive in the colony, and deadweight losses from taxation are so small, that autocratic taxation of the colony yields a grand surplus—so great that no home taxation is required and therefore no tax-driven deadweight loss arises there at all. Consequently, the surplus taken from the colony is allocated to market-augmentation or other public-good provisions until the marginal contribution of G^H, that is, Y_G^H, falls to the level of its marginal cost, which equals 1. Thus, equation (29) shows $Y_G^H = 1$, the same outcome as pictured in figure 1. By avoiding all taxation and deriving its entire revenue from its colony, Home avoids all deadweight losses, which therefore have no effect on its decision of how much market augmentation to provide. Ironically, sufficiently productive foreign taxation supports truly perfect *utopian* market augmentation at home, that is, perfect support of markets from resources extracted at zero efficiency loss (home DWL).

With identical $Y(G)$ and $r(t)$ functions, colonization always would be a bad deal for the colony, but conceivably if G in the home country were very highly productive and t very destructive, while the opposite obtained in the colony, then colonization could be potentially Pareto-superior (materially) to independent Lindahl governance! (Of course assuming home to have no altruistic motives the implied Pareto improvement would be strictly potential.) As unlikely as this conclusion may seem, it does suggest that simulation analysis may be a rich source of insight into the relative effects of punishing efficiency loss and productive market augmentation in countries at various stages of development.

VI. Cross-Sectoral Market Augmentation

The foregoing model treats the home country (or ruling sector) and the colony (or exploited sector) as two separate economies. No private-good trade gains nor common collective-good investment benefits are modeled explicitly between them. This is a fair representation of a country with an exploited and a governing class—or at least it is a first step toward having differential taxation between the rulers and the ruled, in the Y, r, t, G, F, S setup. A more complete model would allow for the F-majority to be drawn from both sectors, some from Home's ethnic citizenry and some from the foreign ethnic group. This would allow derivation of the tax rules and market augmentation provision to change smoothly with the proportions F_H and F_C, where the subscripts indicate F-values of home and colony populations represented by the elite.

A less complicated representation of a common interest between the ruling classes in H and the colonized groups in C is to assume some common public goods or market augmentation along a common dimension among or between them. To capture this, we rewrite the production function of each as $Y^k(G^k,G^N)$, where $k = H, C$. This allows G^k to differ between sectors or regions but requires G^N to be the same nonexcluded, nonrival public good that both share. This might be a common set of contract laws, police enforcement, financial system or regulation, or even a common defense, to the extent that such measures count to secure markets and allow transactions that otherwise would not occur.

With this change, the welfare objective of the Lindahl consensual home government becomes

$$\text{Max} \atop t^H, t^C, G^H, G^C, G^N \qquad W = r(t^H)Y(G^H,G^N) + t^C r(t^C)Y(G^C,G^N) \qquad (31)$$
$$- G^C - G^H - G^N$$

subject to

$$\lambda[t^H r(t^H)Y(G^H,G^N) + t^C r(t^C)Y(G^C,G^N) \geq G^H + G^C + G^N]. \qquad (32)$$

The sum of terms on the left within the constraint are tax revenues and on the right expenditures on G. This extension of the model to include economywide public factor inputs has no effect on the classification made earlier into two classes of solutions (1) with $\lambda > 0, t^H > 0$, and $\Sigma G^k = \Sigma R^k$, and (2) with $\lambda = 0, t^H = 0$, and $\Sigma G^k = \Sigma R^k$. So with the addition of an economywide public good we must deal with two cases once again. The details with respect to the home government's choice of t^k and G^k for $k = (H,C)$ are not qualitatively changed by the introduction of the common production factor, so they are omitted. The interesting difference concerns provision of G^N, the joint public factor input. The home country's best choice of G^N is neatly summarized.

$$\text{For} \quad t^H > 0, \; \frac{Y_N^H}{Y_G^H} + \frac{Y_N^C}{Y_G^C} = 1. \tag{33}$$

$$\text{For} \quad t^H = 0, \; Y_N^H + \frac{Y_N^C}{Y_G^C} = 1. \tag{34}$$

Thus, the efficient home country ensures that the total value of G^N measured in each domain relative to the alternative investment of G^H or G^C and then summed across domains equals its marginal cost. Really, equation (34) is a special case of equation (33), since when $t^H = 0, Y_G^H = 1$. First of all, either of these conditions is to be compared with the truly optimal provision of G^N. Both equations (34) and (35) show underprovision of G^N, since utopian optimality requires $Y_G^H = 1, Y_G^C = 1$, and $Y_N^H + Y_N^C = 1$. Comparison between these conditions shows that a Lindahl home government has an incentive to do a better (though still not an ideal) job of providing for the joint common production economy when it is so successful in extracting a monetary surplus from its colony that it need not tax itself at all. This follows from $Y_G^H > 1$ when $t^H > 0$, but, when $t^H = 0, Y_G^H = 1$.

VII. Corruption: Failure of Governance by Competition

We now come to the third of the failures in economic governance that erode the provision for markets and their efficient operation. This is failure by corruption, in this essay viewed strictly and solely as it pertains to the public sector. At this stage, I adopt a naive definition of *corruption* as illicit or unsanctioned private intervention into the privileged/reserved activities of the state for private gain. I say naive because I will not delve into questions of when such intervention is really just another example of redistribution from the powerless to the powerful. Instead I will focus on one sweeping distinction in the theory and practice of corruption, namely, the divide between taxation and expenditure activities of the government. Accordingly, we will delve into the comparative economics of corruption in the tax sector versus the expenditure sector.

- Is corruption in the *tax system* or the *provision of public goods* more damaging to an economy?
- How do the incentives that lead to corruption determine the final equilibrium of the political economy, including the incidence and the redistributive effects of corruption's benefits and costs?
- Do the costs of corruption in taxation versus expenditure vary systematically with the form of governance?

To my knowledge, despite their importance, these questions have not been posed in the literature, nor has this approach to the analysis of corruption been forwarded elsewhere. One reason for this may be a latent presumption that it will not matter whether unwelcome, corrupt intrusion is imposed on the demand or the supply side of the market—such being the received wisdom of partial equilibrium tax analysis in public finance. We will see that in the analysis of corruption—to be defined for now as an additional tax paid to a tax collector/entrepreneur or an additional bribe/cost for G paid to the government's expenditure agent—it in fact matters a great deal which side of the market this corruption tariff is imposed upon and what the form of governance is.

Mancur Olson was among the first to recognize the efficiency benefits to a society of granting exclusive power to tax to one single taxation authority. One wants the entity with authority to tax to act as a monopoly—in Olson's charming terminology, a *stationary* bandit rather than a *roving* bandit—because this reduces the opportunities for excessive tax theft. The monopoly *tax authority* will internalize in its benefit-cost calculus the losses its taxation imposes on the entire society because the entire society creates the tax base on which the monopolist subsists. Similarly, monopoly power on the *expenditure* side concentrates the incentives to invest in the provision of market-augmenting public goods for the economy; it gives the government monopoly the maximum incentive to expand, through rational investment, the economic base on which it and its tax collections depend. Accordingly, the failure in governance represented by corruption really results from a breakdown in these monopoly powers. Because loss of monopoly power is similar to corruption, we have called this a failure by competition.

The extensions of McGuire and Olson sketched earlier, in fact, apply directly to this issue of comparing corruption on the tax and benefit sides, allowing a direct comparison of the effects of these two types of corruption under alternative forms of governance. This will uncover the incentives corruption generates to tax too much or too little and to under- or overprovide market-sustaining social overhead capital. In particular, a redistributive government perceives a differential between the marginal cost of tax resources, which include deadweight losses, and the marginal cost of a unit of public good (which is simply its unadulterated resource cost of 1), while a consensual, nondistributive government does not perceive any such difference. Because of this crucial distinction, the effects of tax corruption and expenditure corruption differ in principle between the two types of politico-economic regimes.

To be concrete, we first must decide how to characterize "corruption." Here I assume the very simplest form—a constant percentage markup in taxes or in costs of public-good provision. So for any net tax rate, t, I will assume that corruption in the tax system adds a constant percentage markup of B. Thus, for the government to collect t percent, the tax on the citizens becomes $t(1 + B)$ percent, with the purveyors of corruption obtaining trB percent of national income. In the same fashion, I assume that corruption in the provision of public goods adds a constant markup to the unit price of G, so that, in order to obtain one unit of G at a resource cost of 1, the government must pay $(1 + A)$ units of Y, with A dollars going to a corrupt agent. Next, in order to pursue the comparisons among different regimes evenhandedly, I will assume that the corruption markup is the same whether it is applied to taxation or expenditure. That is, I will assume $\beta = (1 + B) = (1 + A) = \alpha$. Any other assumption would prejudice the analysis from the start.

Now we introduce corruption into the decision framework of the Lindahl consensus and the redistributive elite, including the special case of an autocrat. Objective functions and constraints now change as

For the Lindahl Consensus: $W = \underset{t}{\mathrm{Max}}(1 - \beta t) \cdot r(\beta t) \cdot Y[G(t)]$

$$s.t. \ tr(\beta t) \cdot Y(G) - \alpha G = 0, \tag{35}$$

For the Redistributive Elite: $\underset{t,G}{\mathrm{Max}}(1 - \beta t) \cdot r(\beta t) \cdot FY(G)$

$$+ [tr(\beta t) \cdot Y(G) - \alpha G]; \quad s.t. \ \alpha G \le tr(\beta t) \cdot Y(G), \tag{36}$$

that is,

$$\text{Max } S(t,B,F) \cdot r[\beta t] \cdot Y(G) - \alpha G; \qquad s.t. \ \alpha G \leq tr(\beta t) \cdot Y(G). \quad (37)$$

This arrangement now allows us to compare the effects of positive A,B on a government's decision to tax and to supply market-augmenting public goods. It will allow us to study whether one avenue of corruption or the other is more profitable under different forms of government, for example, whether tax corruption is more or less profitable than expenditure corruption under an autocracy versus a utopian ideal such as a Lindahl consensus. Moreover, this analytic tool will help us to better understand the channels by which corruption spreads throughout the political economy of a country, passing infection from one sector to another. Last, one might hope to learn where corruption might be most easily isolated or controlled.

Effects of Corruption on the Behavior of a Ruling Majority

Following the same procedure for the S-majority as was reported in the derivation of equations (9) through (15), one finds that corruption does not alter the decision sequence for the ruling elite: the rulers first choose a value of t to maximize their share and then choose a value of G such that the marginal private benefit of the last increment of G equals the marginal private cost. In other words, neither tax nor expenditure corruption changes the fact that *the level of taxation is determined independently of how much of a public good to provide.* Assuming positive redistribution to the elite gives $R(B,t)$ in place of the $R(t)$ of equation (12), and $t(F,B)$ in place of equation (13), as follows.

$$F = \frac{r + \beta tr}{\beta r - (1 - \beta t)\beta r'} = R(t,B) \qquad (38)$$

$$t^* = -\frac{r}{\beta r'} - \frac{F}{1 - \beta F}. \qquad (39)$$

When $B = 0$ or $\beta = 1$, these reduce to equations (12) and (13), respectively. Equation (39) suggests that tax corruption reduces the tax rate of the ruling majority for given F and increases the total tax burden on the citizenry. The most notable feature of the redistributing elite's optimum choice is that the tax rate is affected only by B plus the $r(t)$ function. That is, while *tax corruption* influences the chosen tax rate, *expenditure corruption* does not—a corollary of the independence of tax and expenditure decisions.

Expenditure corruption—represented by the parameter A or a—of course influences the amount of a public good provided. The expression for the optimum choice of G, corresponding to equations (14)–(15), is derived as

$$rY' = \frac{\alpha}{S} = \alpha \, \frac{\beta[r - (1 - \beta t)r']}{r(1 + \beta tB)} = - \frac{\alpha r' \beta}{r(1 - F\beta)} \, . \tag{40}$$

It is clear from equation (40) that a redistributing majority's marginal private benefit rY' is degraded by tax corruption, since $r = r(t,B)$. Moreover, the ruling elite's "share," S, is also eroded by tax corruption; not only is there an indirect effect on S (because r declines with B), but there is a direct effect, since the agents of corruption exact their own share, thereby directly reducing the share of the ruling interest—a double whammy that the optimal choice of t^* only partially offsets. Equation (40) shows these dual impacts of B on the choice of G by the terms in the numerator and denominator, showing also how the entire society suffers from corruption on the expenditure side: by raising the price of public goods, the agents of expenditure-corruption further reduce the incentive of the ruling elite to provide them. I will give a numerical example of these effects presently for the special case of autocracy, when $F = 0$ and $S = t$ in the preceding equations. (To determine more precise insights, the system of equations (38) and (40) should be differentiated totally with respect to A and B.)

Figure 8 gives a picture of these multiple effects. Notice that the $MSC(t)/r$ both shifts up (because of B) and rotates clockwise. At the same time, we can show the independent effect of expenditure corruption by showing the equilibrium choice of G using $Y'(\alpha) = 1/rS$ as in equation (40). Under this convention, the marginal product curve of G rotates downward to Y'/α, as shown, and the overall effect of corruption on the choice of social capital or market-augmentation effort is shown to result from the two simultaneous shifts.

Effects of Corruption on the Behavior of a Lindahl Consensus

To maximize its welfare, the Lindahl consensus government considers alternative balanced-budget provisions of G. We can no longer

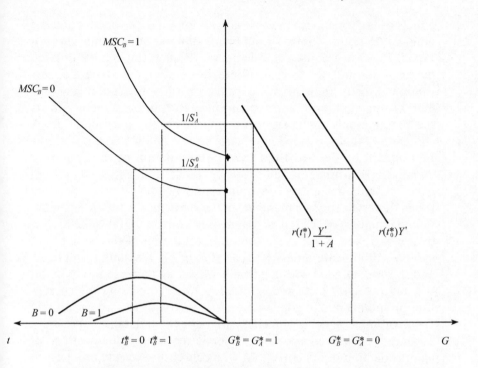

Fig. 8. Effects of expenditure corruption (*A* = 1) and tax corruption (*B* = 1) in an autocracy

separate the decisions to tax from those to provide public goods, as the balanced budget constraint now becomes $\alpha G = tr(\beta t)Y(G)$. The outcome that simultaneously combines best choice of t and of G reduces to equation (41), where $r(\beta t)$, and so on, are to be understood as a function of $t(1 + B)$. Equations (41) and (42) are to be compared to equation (14) as the case of zero corruption:

$$Y' = \alpha \frac{r(\beta t) - [\beta(1 - t)]r'(\beta t)}{[r(\beta t)]^2} \tag{41}$$

or

$$\frac{Y'}{\alpha} = \frac{r(\beta t) - [\beta(1 - t)r'(\beta t)]}{[r(\beta t)]^2}. \tag{42}$$

In the case of a redistributive democracy, equations (39) and (40) indicate that one can separate out, in the sense explained earlier, the effects of tax versus expenditure corruption on the economy and the political economic choice of public-good/market-augmentation provision. But, for a consensual democracy that taxes only to provide public goods and not to redistribute, this is no longer true. Tax corruption directly influences the provision of public goods such as market augmentation, and expenditure corruption directly affects the requirements for taxation to support market augmentation. A complete evaluation of the interactions between the two types of corruption will be derived from total differentiation of the system of equations consisting of the first-order condition in equation (41), together with the resources constraint $t \cdot r(\beta t) \cdot Y(G) - \alpha G = 0$. Some rough generalizations can, however, be extracted from an examination of equation (42). First, if A increases from an initial value of $A = 0$, or $\alpha = 1$, and $B = 0$, then total differentiation of the equilibrium system will indicate a new higher value of Y', meaning lowered G, and this is combined with a partially offsetting increase in t to maintain tax revenues to finance more expensive (including the corruption premium) public goods in an economy with lesser cooperating G-factor input. Specific outcomes will depend on details of $Y(G)$, Y', Y'', and so on, as well as on r, r', r''. Similarly, the systematic effects of an introduction of tax corruption in a consensual society are derived assuming $A = 0$ and considering an introduction of $B > 0$. First-order effects of this change indicate $\partial Y'/\partial B > 0$, provided $r'' < 0$. This implies that tax corruption will indeed reduce the Lindahl society's market-augmenting investment in itself and will therefore dampen overall production.

Figure 9 gives a general idea of these outcomes for the Lindahl consensus democracy, to be compared with redistributive regimes. One sees that expenditure corruption has a progressively declining effect as the optimal value of G increases (which would be the case, for example, if G in $Y(G)$ becomes more productive). This follows from the fact that the difference between $Y'(G)$ and $Y'(G)/\alpha$ grows progressively smaller as G increases. At the same time, the numerator of equations (41)–(42) shows that the tax corruption effect on the choice of t also declines as t increases and disappears altogether when $t = 1$. Both of these factors therefore indicate a particular vulnerability of small and low-technology economies to corruption. With a powerful incentive to invest in its economy (suppose $Y = 100G^{0.8}$), a government is less affected proportionally than is a less advanced economy with, say, $Y = 10G^{0.4}$.

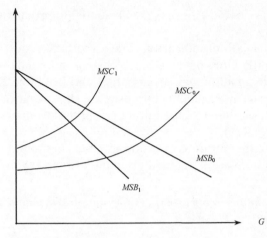

Fig. 9. Effects of expenditure corruption ($A = 1$) and tax corruption ($B = 1$) under a consensual government. (Lindahl consensus: before corruption = 0; after corruption = 1.)

Numerical Examples

Table 1 summarizes in a general way what this analysis indicates about how the expected incentive effects of corruption vary with the form of governance.

For understanding the general r, t, G, Y, S, F case, it will be helpful to make some simplifications and to calculate the resulting implications of tax versus expenditure corruption (see tables 2 and 3). The purpose here is to show the power of this model to compare different types of corruption. These special assumptions will include

- The ruling elite is an autocrat. $F = 0$, $S = t$.
- $A = B = 1$. The implicit tax/price increase of corruption doubles costs.
- $r(t,B) = 1 - t(1 + B) = 1 - 2t$. The erosion of product due to taxation is linear.

Society's or citizens' consensual, optimum optimorum
No corruption, no DWL, lump-sum taxation:
Max $64/G - G \Rightarrow G = 1{,}024$; $Y = 2{,}048$;
Citizens' consumption $= Y - G = 1{,}024$

- $Y(G) = 64\sqrt{G}$. This makes G essential to production.

These calculations indicate several important trends. Corruption overall is slightly more devastating to citizens in a Lindahl consensus society than in an autocracy (from parts 1 and 2 of table 3: $106/432 < 32/128$). Citizens in a Lindahl consensus are slightly more vulnerable to tax corruption than to expenditure corruption compared to an autocracy ($216 > 212$).

Tax and expenditure corruption interact/compound with devastating effects on market augmentation under both regimes, although

TABLE 1.   Expected Incentive Effects of Corruption Depending on the Form of the Government

Venue for Corruption	Decision Structure of Autocracy: Max$tr(t,B)$ Budget Surplus $= trY - (1 + A)G$ $G: Y' = (1 + A)/t^*R(T^*,B)$ (choice of G and t separated)	Structure of Lindahl Consensus: Max: $r(G)Y(G) - (1 + A)G$ Balanced Budget: $tr(t,B)Y(G) = (1 + A)G$ $G = f(t,B,A)$ (single choice of $G \Leftrightarrow t$)
Government supply cost rip-offs $A > 0$ price of $G = (1 + A)$	No direct effect on tax revenue t and $S(t)$ not changed directly but only by the autocrat's choice. Opt G declines and $\therefore Y(G)$ declines and therefore tax revenues and autocrat's tribute decline. Citizens' after-tax income declines because of lower G and $Y(G)$ even though t is not changed directly.	The choice of public goods supply and taxes to collect are made together, since the only reason for taxation is to supply public goods. Therefore, one should expect the effects of tax corruption and expenditure corruption to be more or less qualtitatively similar. Expenditure corruption which raises the price of G creates incentives to lower taxes since the DWL of taxes brings reduced productive benefit. But lower taxes further reduce tax revenues, leading to compounded incentives to further reduce public-goods supply.
Tax-inflation Rake-offs $B > 0$ tax rate $= t(1 + B)$	Government tax revenue declines for two reasons: a. Increases of DWL in economy. b. Leakage from treasury reduces opt t and $S(t) = tr$. Lower Share reduces opt G and $\therefore$ $Y(G)$ and $\therefore$ optimum collections $trY(G)$. Therefore, citizens lose both because of less G (due to lower S) and because of reduction in their share to $[1 - t(1 + B)]$.	Tax corruption raises the marginal DWL cost of resources. Therefore the required social payoff to marginal G must increase, and with this the incentive to invest in G must decline.

TABLE 2. Effects of Corruption

Tax B	Expenditure A	t	r	G	Y	rY	Citizens' Consumption	Tax Revenues	Total Graft	Tax Graft	Expenditure Graft
							Lindahl Consensus				
0	0	.25	.75	144	768	576	432	144	0	0	0
0	1	.25	.75	36	384	288	216	72	36	0	36
1	0	.1464	.7071	44	424	300	212	44	44	44	0
1	1	.1464	.7071	11	212	150	106	22	33	22	11

B	A	t	r	G	Y	rY	Autocrat's Consumption	Citizens' Consumption	Tax Revenues	Total Graft	Tax Graft	Expenditure Graft
							Autocracy					
0	0	.50	.50	64	512	256	64	128	128	0	0	0
0	1	.50	.50	16	256	128	32	64	64	16	0	16
1	0	.25	.50	16	256	128	16	64	32	32	32	0
1	1	.25	.50	8	128	64	8	32	16	20	16	4

it is even worse under an autocracy than under a consensual society (from part 3 of table 3: 4/64 < 11/144).

Tax graft is more lucrative than expenditure graft under both regimes, but the superiority of corruption in the collection of taxes under an autocracy is proportionally much greater than it is under a consensual government (from part 4 of table 3: 44 > 36 and 32 > 16).

Tax plus expenditure graft, as a proportion of citizens' consumption or of national income, is far greater in an autocracy than in a Lindahl democracy (from parts 1 and 4 of table 3: 20/32 > 33/106). The inevitable conclusion is that if one must have a graft-ridden government it is much better if it is democratic rather than autocratic. Or, put otherwise, the monopoly graft of a single autocrat is much worse for everyone (including the corrupt independent agents of graft as well as citizens).

VIII. Conclusions

The best measure of a society's economic success derives from its achievements in inducing collaboration among its members, encompassing as many as possible in such cooperation, and distributing the immense gains of this economic cooperation in a just fashion. As Mancur Olson so clearly saw, a unifying thread wound through the many instances of social failure in this realm—the unifying thread of necessity for collective action and the myriad ways that failure to overcome problems of free riding can be manifest.

TABLE 3. Summary Comparisons

A	B Lindahl	0 Autocracy	1 Lindahl	Autocracy
Part 1. Citizen's Consumption				
0	432	128	212	64
1	216	64	106	32
Part 2. Tax Collections				
0	144	128	44	32
1	72	64	22	16
Part 3. Social-Overhead Provision				
0	144	64	44	16
1	36	16	11	4
Part 4. Graft				
0	0	0	44	32
1	36	16	33	20

Early principles in economists' thinking about systemic failures of economic organization identified so-called "market failures" in the private economy. In these cases, various portions of the private economy have already overcome the collective action problem *within* their fields of control but at a higher level, coordination between or among these sectors has failed. Thus the anatomy of private market failure (including its more modern developments), actually represents a failure of collective action no less than more conventional failures to achieve efficiency in the provision of a pure Samuelsonian public good. In both cases the culprit is individual free riding. The efficient organization of markets, in other words, is in fact a public good, and a paramount example of one at that. It is this lasting insight of Olson's on which I have based this essay. For just as markets may fall short because of a coordination failure among their parts, similarly governments and entire systems of governance can fail for the same reason. In this essay I have focused on one particular cause of such "failures of governance." These are the failures which arise from conflicts between the efficiency opportunities that a society as a whole will have to grow its economy, by way of market-augmenting investments, versus the opportunities some groups within the society may have to redistribute to themselves for their own selfish benefit.

This conflict between market augmentation and redistribution is highly germane to the present. The past generation has seen massive increases in government enforced redistributions within countries throughout the world. In the United States, fully two thirds of federal outlays are for redistribution and it is not at all unusual for 25 percent of the entire GDP of industrialized countries to be redistributed through its tax system. These redistributions, which play so crucial a role in the political economy of the modern state, are undertaken by governments, which exact taxes from some groups and make transfers for the benefit of other groups. The beneficiaries in this process are in general the groups to whom governments are beholden, and the taxpayers those to whom they are not.

But redistribution is not the only economic function of government. Concurrently with it, governments use taxes for allocative purposes, to invest in their economies. Year by year, empirical research substantiates that by investing in certain "Public Goods" including, market augmentation, governments can increase the productivity of their societies dramatically, and that this benefits everyone in the society. This means that public good allocation and group discriminatory redistribution are conflicting resource use options between which any government must choose. Irrespective of its political make up this is a choice every government must make.

This line of reasoning compels a conclusion: the true cost of social investment—and of the gigantic gains it produces—is the redistribution from the powerless to the powerful which a society pays as a bribe for imperfect governance instead of anarchic impoverishment. This essay has explored one dimension of the dilemma.

Appendix: Majorities That Provide Ideal Market Augmentation

A striking implication of the model is that ruling elites with sufficiently broad ownership stakes in their economies will undertake no redistribution whatever and will allocate resources the same as would an idealized consensus democracy. To see why, consider the two opposing incentives in the McGuire and Olson theory. First, the greater a ruling interest's market fraction, F, the larger its share of the deadweight loss of taxation and the *lower* the tax rate it desires. This follows from equation (11). Second, the greater the value of S, the larger the elite's share of the benefits from market augmentation and the *more* it wants to provide, which follows from equation (12). The public good is needed to produce output and, as F—and therefore S—goes up, those in political power obtain a larger share of the benefits of G, which makes them want to provide more, thereby requiring that more taxes be allocated to the provision of G. Equation (12) shows that, as F and thus S increase, the solution value of Y' declines and therefore G_R^* increases. Thus, as a ruling elite's ownership stake in the economy grows, it wants to tax less and, at the same time, spend more of the taxes it does raise on the provision of G. Once F reaches a high enough value, t_R^* will be so low and G so great that *all* tax revenues will be needed to pay for public goods and there will be no redistribution.[14] Now consider a society in which the $r(t)$ and $Y(G)$ functions remain unchanged and where market-sustaining social order is essential for production of any output at all [$Y(0) = 0$]. As F increases, and with it S, a point $\hat{F}$ will be reached at which the ruling elite allocates all taxes to public-good provision. At this point, government represents such a high fraction of the economy that it ceases redistributing and treats the minority as well as it treats itself. If the government reflects this fraction, $\hat{F}$, or any greater fraction, it will *not* redistribute to itself. It will, in fact, act in exactly the same way that the consensual democracy does.

We derive this conclusion by returning to the Lagrange function (eq. (11)), but now we assume that $trY = G$. Then $\lambda > 0$ and the first-order conditions with respect to t yield

$$\frac{F}{1 + \lambda} = \frac{r + t'r}{r - (1 - t)r'} \equiv R(t) \tag{A1}$$

or

$$F = (1 + \lambda)R(t), \tag{A2}$$

and, with respect to G, we obtain

$$\frac{F}{1 + \lambda} = \frac{1 - trY'}{(1 - t)rY'} . \tag{A3}$$

Equation (A1) or (A2) gives the condition for optimal distribution when the majority just supplies the public good out of tax collections with nothing left over for redistribution and $\lambda > 0$. Under these conditions (evaluated at zero redistribution), the majority's marginal costs of redistribution exceed the marginal benefits that it would gain. Equation (A1) says that, if it were possible to reduce taxes toward equality of their marginal costs and benefits, the ruling interest would do so. Lower taxes, however, would cut into the revenue needed to finance the desired level of the public good. Analogously, equation (A3) indicates that at the constrained optimum of G the marginal benefits of G exceed marginal costs. Equations (A1) and (A3) also indicate that every ruling majority with an F so high that it rejects redistribution behaves just like a majority with $F = \hat{F}$. All ruling interests that are forced not to redistribute, by the constraint $trY = G$, behave as if their $F = \hat{F}$ and as if they had *chosen* $trY = G$. That is, for all $F > \hat{F}$, $F/(1 + \lambda) = \hat{F}$.

One implication of this equivalence is that every nonredistributive ruling interest, whatever its F, will make the same decisions about public-good provision that it would have made had its F been $\hat{F}$, and all will have the same tax rate, $\hat{t}^*$. It also means that such a "superencompassing" majority will provide the same level of G and have the same tax rate as a consensual democracy. Thus, when $F \geq \hat{F}$, the absence of redistribution implies that both the majority and the minority each pay their proportional share of the tax burden. The majority receives F percent of the benefits of the public good and pays F percent of the tax. It therefore chooses exactly the same level of public-good provision as does the consensual democracy. Thus, the society ruled by a superencompassing majority not only abstains from redistributive taxation but chooses an ideal[15] level of public-good provision that reflects the minority's interests as its own. This can be seen by comparing the net income of the redistributive majority at $\hat{F}$, where it redistributes nothing, to its welfare if it had no separate power and were just $100 \hat{F}$ percent of a consensus democracy.

Redistributive majority's net income $= SrY - G$ \hspace{2em} (A4)

Majority's fraction of society's net income $= F(rY - G)$. \hspace{2em} (A5)

When all taxes are spent on G, then $trY = G$, and the two incomes of the $\hat{F}$-majority are the same, and all failure of governance by redistribution vanishes.

Notes

I thank Jongseok An, Omar Azfar, Roger Betancourt, and Ke-Young Chu for helpful comments.

1. Accumulated from debates on the price system, regulation (Pigou 1920), and the socialist economy (Lerner 1944).

2. "Failure by structure" is monopoly, correctable by increases in numbers of firms or by regulation that attempts to mimic the effects of increased numbers. "Failure by enforcement" refers to unpriced common assets such as highways or common resources, correctable by congestion or externality taxes, subsidies, marketable permits, and the like. "Failure by signal" identifies the problem of insufficient size of demand relative to cost and is to be corrected by subsidy or multipart tariff. "Failure by incentive" refers to non-convexities that preclude attainment of profit maximization by means of marginal cost pricing.

3. Notably, advances in mechanisms for collective-good provision (particularly in the realms of incentive compatibility and honest preference-evoking mechanisms) and discoveries about asymmetric information, self-selection, and moral hazard in understanding private markets.

4. This idea was implicit in Olson's early observation that price—in any ordinary, atomistic, competitive market—is a public good for the individual buyers and sellers in that market (1965, 9).

5. Not all limitations on the optimal reach of markets are determined by design. Some market augmentation will simply arise through identification and exploitation of previously unrecognized opportunities to extend markets. These might include: property definitions, contract enforcement mechanisms, and other requisites to exchange; lack of knowledge that underlying wants exist; lack of technology with which to create market institutions (e.g., communications technology); the existence of legitimate costs that overwhelm private benefits from market operations; and cultural or conventional habits that reduce communication and interfere with market-sustaining expectations. These defects might be labeled "failure by ignorance."

6. An extension of McGuire and Olson to allow variation in the private resource input (L to include labor and other private inputs) is accomplished in McGuire 1998a.

7. The introduction of a second variable factor input, which is supplied subject to the choice of the citizens—for example, labor input—will violate proportional independence and cause t to influence directly the productivity of G. The advantage of this elaboration is to introduce income effects that

are absent from the McGuire and Olson model by assumption. See McGuire 1998a.

8. This section draws extensively on McGuire and Olson 1993.

9. Note that under Lindahl tax shares, every voter wants the same socially efficient amount of the collective good. To maintain an assumption of a simple linear tax, we also assume either that all individuals are identical or that Lindahl tax shares do not change as more or less of the public good is provided.

10. Mathematically this is done by equating successively $h(t) = tr(t) = G/Y(G) = f(G)$, to give $t = h^{-1}[f(G)]$ or $G = f^{-1}[h(t)]$, and $dG/dt = -Y(r + tr')/(trY' - 1)$.

11. Second-order conditions require $d^2[(1 - t)r(t)Y(G)]/dt^2 < 0$; s.t. $tr(t)Y(G) = G$. Utilization of the expression for dG/dt, its derivative, and equation (13) simplifies this condition to: $-2(r')^2 + rr'' + YY''[(r)^2/(1 - t)]^2 < 0$. Evidently, $r'' < 0$ may be sufficient but not necessary to ensure a maximum. Note that, in the marginal social benefit (MSB), r is constant, evaluated at the optimum value of $t = t_N^*$, and, in the marginal social cost (MSC), $r' = dr/dt$, *not* $dr[t(G)]/dG$.

12. Of course, the best tax rate and best public-good provision depend also on the specifics of $Y'(G)$ and $1 - r(t)$. For an analysis that incorporates the interdependence between allocation and redistribution, see McGuire 1998a.

13. For further analysis of this idea, see Azfar and McGuire 2002.

14. The existence of ruling interests that leave out part of society yet act in the interest of all is not only a possibility but (with incentive-distorting taxation) a necessity. For $F = 0$, the autocrat obtains a positive surplus for himself while providing G_A^* of the public good. By equation (15), there is also a value of $F = F^0 < 1$ that entails that $t_R^* = 0$. At this tax rate, there is no revenue for G. It follows that some value of $F(0 < F < F^0)$ will entail a positive tax rate just sufficient to pay for the optimal provision of G. I designate the "crossover" values at this point as $\hat{F}, \hat{t}^*, \hat{G}^*$. A value of $\hat{F}''F^0$ must exist where the rulers are best served by a tax rate just sufficient to finance optimal provision of public goods: at $\hat{F}$, by definition $\hat{t}^*\hat{r}^*Y(\hat{G}^*) = \hat{G}^*$. That is, ruling interests must abstain from redistribution before $F = F^0$ and therefore *before* $F = 1$, which proves that when a majority or other ruling interest is sufficiently encompassing it will not redistribute any income and will treat those subject to its power as well as it treats itself.

15. Public-good provision is "ideal" but still subject to deadweight losses from taxation.

References

Azfar, O., and M. C. McGuire. 2002. "The Natural Advantage of Dictatorship over Democracy: A 'Gresham's Law' of Governance." *International Tax and Public Finance* 9: 451–63.

Banfield, E. 1958. *The Moral Basis of a Backward Society.* Glencoe, IL: Free Press.

Barro, R. 1990. "Government Spending in a Simple Model of Endogenous Growth." *Journal of Political Economy* 98 (5, pt. 2): S103–25.

Barzel, Y. 1997. "Property Rights and the Evolution of the State." Manuscript.

Bator, F. 1958. "The Anatomy of Market Failure." *Quarterly Journal of Economics* 72:351–79.

Brennan, G., and J. M. Buchanan. 1977. "Toward a Tax Constitution for Leviathan." *Journal of Public Economics* 8:255–74.

Engineer, M. 1989. "Taxes, Public Goods, and the Ruling Class: An Exploration of the Territory between Brennan and Buchanan's Leviathan and Conventional Public Finance." *Public Finance* 44: 19–30.

———. 1990. "Brennan and Buchanan's Leviathan Models." *Social Science Journal* 27 (4): 419–33.

Hirshleifer, J. 1994. "The Dark Side of the Force." *Economic Inquiry* 32:1–10. Western Economic Association presidential address.

Hobbes, T. 1651. *The Leviathan.* Reprint, Harmondsworth, Eng.: Penguin, 1985.

Karras, G. 1996. "The Optimal Government Size: Further International Evidence on the Productivity of Government Services." *Economic Inquiry* 34:193–203.

Lerner, A. 1944. *The Economics of Control.* London: Macmillan.

McGuire, M. C. 1982. "Regulation, Factor Rewards, and International Trade." *Journal of Public Economics* 17 (3): 335–54.

———. 1998a. "Redistribution, Political Power, and Public Goods." Paper presented at the *Journal of Public Economic Theory* Inaugural Conference. University of Alabama, Mobile.

———. 1998b. "The Security Factors in Economic Development." *International Monetary Fund Working Papers* 98 (33): 1–41.

McGuire, M. C., and M. L. Olson. 1993. "Social Capital Formation, Income Redistribution, and the Form of Governance." Paper presented at the Western Economics Association Meeting, Department of Economics, University of California, Irvine, June.

———. 1994. "The Economics of Autocracy and Majority Rule." Working Paper, Department of Economics, University of California, Irvine.

———. 1996. "The Economics of Autocracy and Majority Rule: The Invisible Hand and the Use of Force." *Journal of Economic Literature* 34: 72–97.

Niskanen, W. A. 1997. "Autocratic, Democratic, and Optimal Government." *Economic Inquiry* 35 (3): 464–79.

Okun, A. M. 1975. *Efficiency and Equity: The Big Trade-off.* Washington, DC: Brookings Institution.

Olson, M. L. Jr. 1965. *The Logic of Collective Action.* Cambridge: Harvard University Press.

———. 1982. *The Rise and Decline of Nations.* New Haven: Yale University Press.

———. 1991. "Autocracy, Democracy, and Prosperity." In *Strategy and Choice,* edited by Richard J. Zeckhauser. Cambridge: MIT Press.

———. 1993. "Dictatorship, Democracy, and Development." *American Political Science Review* 87 (3): 567–76.

———. 1997. "Why Some Nations Are Rich and Others Poor." Ernest Sturc Memorial Lecture presented at the Johns Hopkins University School for Advanced International Studies, Washington, DC. Transcribed as "Market-Augmenting Government," IRIS, University of Maryland, College Park.

Pigou, A. 1920. *Economics of Welfare.* London: Macmillan.

Samuelson, P. 1954. "The Pure Theory of Public Expenditure." *Review of Economics and Statistics* 36:387–89.

Usher, D., and M. Engineer. 1987. "The Distribution of Income in a Despotic Society." *Public Choice* 54 (3): 261–76.

Wintrobe, R. 1990. "The Tinpot and the Totalitarian: An Economic Theory of Dictatorship." *American Political Science Review* 8:49–72.

———. 1998. *The Political Economy of Dictatorship.* New York: Cambridge University Press.

Comment

Omar Azfar

Martin McGuire's essay highlights the two main failures of market-augmenting government—sins of omission and sins of commission that prevent markets from attaining their potential. The essay examines how different governments, governing states with different social structures, fail on two counts.

1. They may tax at high rates, destroying the incentives to produce.
2. They may fail to provide public goods, including social peace, law and order, and transport networks that augment exchange.

In the McGuire and Olson framework, governments are classified as autocratic, consensual and democratic, or majoritarian and democratic. Authoritarian states are ruled by an autocrat who attempts to expropriate as much as he can from the economy. The autocrat sets taxes and public-good provision (which augments markets and thus enhances the appropriable amount) to maximize this expropriation. Consensual democracies, in contrast, set public-good provision and the taxes needed to finance it at levels that maximize production and welfare. This comparison already yields a useful insight: the quality of governance should be higher in democracies. And, indeed, Clague et al. (1996) find that it is. (Possibly this is conventional wisdom now, but a few years ago it wasn't. Indeed, Mancur's earlier works, such as *The Rise and Decline of Nations,* may have contributed to the prevailing skepticism about democracies.)

But the most realistic and interesting part of the McGuire and Olson framework, further developed in the essay, is the analysis of majoritarian democracies ruled by predatory coalitions that prey on minorities. Majoritarian democracies set taxes and choose spending levels (which may include redistributions to members of the ruling coalition) to maximize the welfare of members of the ruling coalition.

Such expropriatory majoritarian democracies may characterize the governments of countries that are made up of more than one ethnic group. If a group leader feels that by mobilizing his or her ethnic group he or she can prey on others, then such a group may be mobilized to form a predatory coalition. (There is no inevitability about such an eventuality, of course; such a mobilization is a complicated coordination problem, and there is a large variance in the expropriatory behavior of majority ethnic groups.)

In the current essay, McGuire offers two formulations of how such a government would behave.

1. In the first formulation, the predatory coalition is disciplined by having to set similar tax rates and provide similar public goods to the entire population. If majorities are large enough, in fact, the government may mimic the behavior of consensual democracies due to a desire to avoid distortionary taxes on members of its own coalition.
2. In the second formulation, the government can set different taxes and levels of public-good provision for members and nonmembers of the ruling coalition. Minorities are treated worse in this world, where governments can discriminate in taxes and spending.

An increasing number of the world's countries may now be ruled by majoritarian democracies, and this framework may offer important insights into the failures of governance that keep much of the world in poverty. Suggestions of rules, like common tax rates, that may constrain a state's ability to prey on its population would be invaluable.

Ethnic Federalism: A Remedy to Majoritarian Predation?

Could ethnic federalism remedy majoritarian predation? The central idea of ethnic federalism is that the devolution of the authority to tax and spend to democratic local governments would improve the quality of governance. In subsequent work, Azfar and McGuire (2002) have evaluated this remedy using the McGuire and Olson framework, with stark results.

Almost all federations do allow the federal government to tax and thus give it the freedom to prey on minorities. Federalism merely allows local governments to raise revenues and provide public goods in their jurisdictions. But even predatory central governments have incentives to provide public goods, if only to raise the appropriable income of minorities. The formal analysis of McGuire and Azfar shows that there are in fact no gains arising from the devolution of the authority to tax and spend, even in the transition from a pure dictatorship to a consensual democracy. Other remedies to ethnic predation, such as improved minority representation in central decision making, may hold more promise.

References

Azfar, Omar, and Martin McGuire. 2002. "The Natural Advantage of Dictatorship over Democracy: A 'Gresham's Law' of Governance." *International Tax and Public Finance* 9:451–63.

Clague, Chris, Phil Keefer, Steven Knack, and Mancur Olson. 1996. "Property and Contract Rights in Autocracies and Democracies." *Journal of Economic Growth* 1 (2): 243–76.

Market-Augmenting Government?
States and Corporations in Nineteenth-Century America

John Joseph Wallis

> The reader does not require to be told that we have in our country an infinite number of corporations aggregate, which have no concern whatever with affairs of a municipal nature. These associations we not only find scattered throughout every cultivated part of the United States, but so engaged are they in all the varieties of useful pursuit, that we see them directing the concentration of mind and capital to the advancement of religion; to the diffusion of literature, science and the arts; to the prosecution of plans of internal communications and improvement; and to the encouragement and extension of the great interests of commerce, agriculture, and manufactures. There is a great difference in this respect between our own country, and the country from which we have derived a great portion of our laws. What is done in England by combination, unless it be the management of municipal concerns, is most generally done by a combination of individuals, established by mere articles of agreement. On the other hand, what is done here by the co-operation of several persons, is, in the greater number of instances, the result of consolidation effected by an express act or charter of incorporation.
> —Joseph K. Angell and Samuel Ames, 1832

I. The Problem

By 1830, Americans were aware that their attitude toward business incorporation was something new in the world. They had departed from the model of the British and were seeking out new ways of combining individual effort, in both public and private forms, that would allow their new society to expand and grow. By 1900, Americans had in place the outlines of the modern corporation that would dominate manufacturing and finance throughout the global economy in the twentieth century.

Over the last decade, Mancur Olson became interested in the reasons why governments might pursue policies that promote, rather than

223

retard, economic growth. In a series of essays, he presented a framework in which a state's economic policies depended on its fiscal interest. Governments have a simple goal: maximize revenues. States will sometimes find it in their fiscal interest to augment market exchange because the resulting economic growth increases the ruler's revenue. They are unconcerned whether they fulfill their goals by stealing, taxing, or providing market infrastructure. The results are as likely to be policies that retard growth as those that promote it. Market-augmenting government policies include defining and enforcing property rights, providing and supporting an efficient and fair judicial system, and regulating and supporting various forms of business organization.

The development of American policy toward corporations is a natural venue in which to understand how market-augmenting government evolves. The corporate form is one of the central institutions of modern economies, and the American experience offers several advantages for the study of government creation and regulation of corporations. First, the American experience was not derivative. Hurst noted that "both in the colonial years and after independence, corporation law was homemade product."[1] Americans were creating an institution out of whole cloth, not following an English example. Second, corporations were almost exclusively the creations of states. The First and Second Banks of the United States were the only corporations chartered by the federal government before the Civil War. The variety of government policies toward corporations provides an unusual opportunity to see widely different policy outcomes within an institutional environment that was fairly homogeneous.

This relative homogeneity was abetted by the Supreme Court's decision in *Dartmouth College v. Woodward,* when John Marshall wrote in his decision that

> a corporation is an artificial being, invisible, intangible, and existing only in its contemplation of law. Being the mere creature of law, it possesses only those properties which the charter of its creation confers upon it, either expressly, or as incidental to its very existence. (*The Trustees of Dartmouth College v. Woodward,* 4 Wheaton 518, 636 [U.S. 1819])

By rendering the decision in this way, the court ensured that corporations would be treated as artificial *persons* at law, cloaking corporations in many of the constitutional protections provided to persons.[2] The homogeneity was in fact an underlying principle, however, not an outcome. In 1839, in *Bank of Augusta v. Earle,* the court placed a major limit on the constitutional protection available to corporations when it delineated that, while corporations were "persons," they were not "citizens." Thus, a corporation did not enjoy a constitutional right to do business in a state other than the one in which it was chartered, nor was it entitled to all the privileges and immunities of citizens in the several states.

If we want to understand when and why governments will pursue and support market-augmenting policies, it is hard to imagine a better historical situation. The wide variety of outcomes from state to state produces a wealth of variation to explain. While we cannot test directly whether some state policies were better than others at promoting income growth, we can *observe* directly the effect of policies on the number of corporations and, with somewhat more difficulty, the capital of those corporations.[3] To the extent that we can measure the sophistication of a financial network by the density and specialization of financial intermediaries, we can directly observe the effect of state policies on market development.

There are other benefits of examining American corporations and state governments. Incorporated banks were the most important financial intermediaries in the early nineteenth century, and the United States possessed a sophisticated financial system by 1830 (Sylla 1998). Although banks account for less than a quarter of the corporate charters issued in any state, charters for banks were typically the most valuable charters issued and, as a result, the most hotly contested.[4] The banking system was a critically important part of the financial markets in the individual states and throughout the country. Government regulation and incorporation of banks were the aspects of market-augmenting government with the most direct impact on capital markets, and the discussion of early-nineteenth-century chartering will therefore focus almost exclusively on banks.

Finally, corporations were enormously important to state finances and, again, important in ways that varied widely between states. Revenues derived from specific corporate revenue sources, such as capital taxes and charter fees, often provided 20 to 50 percent of state revenues. It easy to see and count corporations, and it is equally easy to observe a state's fiscal interest, since the financial returns from a state's corporate policies show up in the financial records of state governments. States taxed corporations in a number of ways, each with a different implication for state revenues. States with revenue systems that shared in corporate *profits* (e.g., state ownership of stock) tended to limit the number of corporations and therefore to increase the profitability of the few businesses that were chartered and increase state revenues correspondingly. States with revenue systems that taxed the *number* or *size* of corporations (e.g., a tax on capital stock) tended to maximize the number of corporations, foster more competition, lower aggregate profits, and thus increase state revenues. There is clear evidence that fiscal interest did shape the way in which states chartered corporations. Some states chartered more corporations, encouraged entry, and promoted competition because it was in their fiscal interest to do so.

Since the revenue structures of American states were fairly simple, and corporate revenues were so important in a number of states, it is relatively easy to observe the relationships between fiscal interest and corporate policy. Section II presents a brief overview of corporate policy in the nineteenth century and identifies three periods and two transitions that we would like to be able to explain. Section III discusses some general ways in which fiscal interest may or may not lead a state to pursue market-augmenting government policies. The rest of the essay looks more closely at state regulation of banking before 1860, the rise of general incorporation acts and free banking laws after 1840, the transition to national chartered banks during the Civil War, and finally the development of more general corporate forms by New Jersey and Delaware at the end of the century.

II. The History

The seed for this essay was Oscar and Mary Flug Handlin's book *Commonwealth: A Study of the Role of Government in the American Economy, Massachusetts, 1774–1861* (1969). The Handlins' book was one of a number commissioned and supported by the Committee on Research in Economic History (CREH) to investigate the role of the government, particularly the importance of laissez-faire policies, in promoting economic development in the early nineteenth century.[5] The Handlins quickly discovered that states did not in fact follow laissez-faire policies in Massachusetts or anywhere else. States everywhere deliberately and actively promoted development. Their book examines the role of association, organization, and incorporation in the economy of Massachusetts and the role of government in promoting organizations as well as restricting and shaping them. The Handlins found that the state's most important role was helping the economy to organize itself.

The public purpose which justified extension of government powers to a bank, to bridges, and to a factory soon comprehended a wide and ever widening circle of enterprises. The Commonwealth's concern with the entire productive system, its solicitude for the welfare of many diverse activities, all interdependent and all adding to the strength of Massachusetts, quickly put the corporate form to the use of many new ventures. The political balance defeated any notion of keeping the device exclusive; the expansive thinking, the excited spirits of the young state, brooked no casual denial. Charters in steadily mounting volume clothed with living tissues the skeletal hopes for an economy to serve the common interests. (1969, 106)

One of the most consistent themes in Mancur Olson's scholarship is the role that self-organized groups played in determining the workings of the economy. I was deeply intrigued by the notion that the primary contribution that the states had made to early economic development was organizational, as I most often think of the government's primary contribution in terms of internal improvement investment, improved financial markets, and property rights in general.

Massachusetts was something of an outlier with regard to corporations. Corporations were not welcomed with open arms in all states, nor were all states willing to make the corporate form available to everyone. The intellectual heritage of the Revolution contained two strong, but contradictory, ways of thinking about corporations. On the one hand, Americans believed strongly in the right to freely associate and organize themselves voluntarily into groups to pursue common goals. The corporation was one of the ways in which people could organize, and in most states the earliest corporations were eleemosynary: charitable corporations like libraries, hospitals, schools, funeral societies, and fire companies.[6] The boundaries between charitable, public service, and business corporations were not clear, and public support for most types of incorporation was strong.

On the other hand, the revolutionary generation also left a legacy of suspicion of special interests, parties, and factions. A significant portion of the colonial complaints against the English had, at their root, the claim that the king's corrupt ministers represented the "monied interest."[7] This interest was composed of those politicians, bankers, merchants, and manufacturers whose prosperity was so closely tied to the expanding British state.[8] The British themselves had questioned the wisdom of granting corporate status to the monied interests, as evidenced in the Bubble Act of 1719, which made incorporation more difficult. With a consequent lack of British precedents, the Americans would ultimately set off on their own corporate road after independence. When American states began operating as independent governments in the 1770s, among the first groups to approach them for corporate status were those same monied interests—in the form of banks.

Americans began their republican experiment with an expansive and positive view of association and incorporation, and they viewed their right to peaceable assembly as an inherent part of their rights as citizens. At the same time, they brought from their English and revolutionary tradition a hatred and suspicion of special interests, combinations, and conspiracies. They had learned to fear the power of special monied interests to corrupt the independent legislative process, short-circuiting the constitutional design of both the unwritten English constitution and the new, written state and national constitutions. At the very heart of the American form of political economy, then, there was a profound tension between the positive and negative potential of corporate forms of business organization. The corporation epitomized the dangers of well-organized interest groups that Americans saw everywhere in the perils of party and faction. This tension would steadily increase, fueled by the constantly growing economic interests at stake as well as by the continuing political disagreement over the appropriate role of special interests and elites in what was becoming an increasingly democratic government.

It is not surprising, then, that for the first sixty years of the nation's history states granted corporate charters on a case by case basis. With a few notable exceptions, 1774 to 1838 can be considered the period of incorporation by special charter. Each corporation was created individually by a deliberate act of a state legislature, and only two corporations were chartered by the national government, the First and Second Banks of the United States. Beginning in the late 1830s, general incorporation acts became popular. Under these acts, the most famous of which was New York's Free Banking Law, any group that met minimum standards, primarily for capitalization, could obtain a corporate charter administratively by applying to the appropriate state office or official. By the 1870s, incorporation under general acts had become the norm throughout the country. General incorporation acts, however, typically placed well-defined limits on the capitalization, structure, and functions of corporations. States often had several general incorporation acts in force at any one time.

In New York, for example, there were more than twenty general incorporation acts for banks, insurance companies, cemetery associations, manufacturing companies, railroads, and so on (Seavoy 1982).

In 1880, several states, led by New Jersey and Delaware, began creating much more liberal general incorporation acts. Under these statutes, corporations were allowed to pursue almost any business they chose. Corporations were allowed to own stock in other corporations, including corporations charted in other states. Limits on capitalization were raised and eventually eliminated. Restrictions on the internal structure of corporations—such as boards of directors, the voting rights of shareholders, the use of proxies, and the like— were eased or eliminated, and corporations were allowed to structure their own internal organization through corporation articles and bylaws. Incorporation acts continued to be liberalized into the 1930s (Dodd 1936). The movement to liberal incorporation acts allowed businesses to become self-organizing and removed the regulation of business activity from the chartering process.

> The movement of policy from the 1890's into the 1930's carried the utilitarian attitude [toward the corporations] about as far as it could go: if the law of corporate organization was legitimated by its utility to business enterprise, legitimacy would be most fully achieved if the law empowered businessmen to create whatever arrangements they found most serviceable. . . . [The] regulation of business activity was no longer to be deemed a proper function of the law of corporate organization. The function of corporate law was to enable businessmen to act, not to police their action. (Hurst 1970, 70)

The 1880s saw the end of corporate regulation by internal devices such as corporate charters, and internal regulation was thereafter steadily replaced with external regulation of corporate actions by states and the national government.

This three-period division is based on Hurst 1970, but its outlines are so clear in the historical record that this periodization is found in almost every history of corporate policy. There are, however, a variety of exceptions; indeed, exceptions are rather the rule. Since this essay will focus on the transition from special charters to general incorporation acts, and from general acts to liberal general acts, a more explicit treatment of the exceptions is in order.

States varied in the rate at which corporations were created.

Table 1 presents information on average annual incorporations per decade from 1800 to 1839 for New York, Ohio, Maryland, Pennsylvania, New Jersey, and Maine. These were relatively developed states (with the exception of Maine) and showed active levels of incorporation in every decade. The three most common types of business incorporations (in descending order of importance) were: public utilities engaged in transportation (bridges, turnpikes, roads, canals, and, at the end, railroads); manufacturing concerns, and banks. While numbers varied considerably from year to year, in no state did incorporations for either banks or manufacturing concerns comprise more than one-quarter of the total incorporations, while public utilities account for more than half.[9]

Most of these corporations were created by special acts of state legislatures, but how special were these special charters? Hurst argues, in detail, that despite their unique passage, special charters quickly fell into standardized patterns.

> Typical—and at first appearance contrary to the idea of standardization—was the growth in the amount of detail put into special charters by mid-century. The combined evidence of hundreds upon hundreds of special charters with the elaboration of provisions on organization and powers written into these charters might be read as showing that the moving impulse was to tailor each charter to the particular desires of particular promoters. But closer reading shows relatively little variety spawned by all of this print. The bulk of the content of special charters tends to fall quickly into stock patterns. The practical impulse behind the continued increase in number and detail of special charters seems to have been mainly the wish to avoid certain features of the optional general incorporation acts, which were becoming more common by mid-century—tight limits on capitalization, for example, and requirements that certain facts about the firm's operations be made a matter of public record. But whatever it was

TABLE 1. Average Incorporations per Year, Decade Averages

Decade	New York	Ohio	Maryland	Pennsylvania	New Jersey	Maine
1800–1809	17.9	0.875	2.0	5.6	4.2	
1810–19	42.6	5.0	9.6	21.9	6.5	
1820–29	35.4	4.3	7.3	13.1	6.9	13.2
1830–39	57.3	43.0	17.8	37.9	18.2	43.3

Source: Data from Evans 1948.

that they did not like about the available general incorporation acts, promoters and their lawyers did not strive for much variety in the internal organization of the companies. (1970, 29)

Hurst was undoubtedly right for the "hundreds and hundreds" of special charters that fit standard forms.[10] But here is what Cadman has to say about New Jersey.

Whatever the reasons for New Jersey's failure to adopt general regulating statutes during the pre-1845 years, the absence of such laws had considerable significance. When a group approached the legislature for a charter of incorporation, there was no general legislation to hamper them in pressing for any special privileges they desired. The road was open to secure a charter with as few or as many provisions and with as liberal terms as they had influence or tactical ability to obtain; there were no statutory obstacles to getting favors that would put the petitioning group at an advantage with respect to competitors or even with respect to the general public. In the absence of general regulating statutes, particular groups could obtain special assistance from a legislature that would have been unwilling to go so far as to change a general statute for their benefit.... The wide variety of privileges and restrictions appearing in business corporation charters granted by New Jersey bear testimony to the results of treating each charter as a separate and independent grant without the salutary influence of statutes of general applicability. (1949, 17–18)

The differences between Cadman and Hurst are extremely relevant to the argument that follows. Special acts of incorporation that confer special privileges on well-organized special interest groups are prominent examples of phenomena in which Mancur Olson was interested; it would be useful to determine how important such truly special acts of incorporation were.

While there is, unfortunately, no organized body of data that allows us to address the question, there were certainly numerous instances of very special charters being granted. There were charters for monopoly state banks in Indiana and Missouri; the New Jersey charter to the Camden and Amboy railroad, which, in its amended form, guaranteed the railroad a monopoly of through traffic between New York and Pennsylvania (more on this later); and charter renewal for five banks in Baltimore that guaranteed that the state would charter no more banks in the city provided that the banks built a road to Hagerstown. Instances like these are quite common in the historical record. There is little reason to doubt that the drive for general incorporation acts in and after the 1830s, which was politically motivated as a way to eliminate special privilege, was fueled by reaction to such truly special charters. All charters for railroads, turnpikes, and bridges that included the right of eminent domain necessarily included a special privilege that could not be generalized. Special charters must have conveyed some privileges. In New Jersey between 1845 and 1875, it was possible to obtain a charter through either a general or a special act. Of the 2,049 corporations chartered in those years, only 494, or 20 percent, used the general incorporation procedure (Cadman 1949, 206–8).

It would be inappropriate to assume that most special charters were simply standardized duplicates of one another without careful examination of a state's chartering practice.[11] Undoubtedly many states did move toward standardized patterns even in the period of special chartering, and some states used patterns almost from the beginning. But the possibility of granting a truly special charter existed as long as there was no prohibition against special charters.

This raises the corollary question: how general were general incorporation acts? We must remember that there were many types of corporations other than business corporations, and within the category of business corporations there were many types of charters. Seavoy (1982, 5–8) identifies five stages in the development of corporate law. First, all corporations are granted special charters. In the second stage, a general incorporation statute is passed for benevolent organizations: schools, churches, funeral societies, and so on. In the third stage, a general regulatory statute is passed, governing the shape of corporate charters for particular purposes, but the legislature still incorporates individual businesses by special act within the framework of the general regulation. (This was the model followed by Massachusetts, discussed later.) The fourth stage was a general incorporation act for a specific type of business, which created an administrative mechanism for issuing charters to all applicants who met the stated qualifications, and stipulated specifically what the terms of the charter would be. This was the type of act that became more widely adopted in a number of states around and after 1840, although the first instances were earlier. A stage four and a half, not identified by Seavoy, occurred when states created constitutional requirements that all corporations be created under general incorporation acts and specifically *prohibited* incorporation by special act.[12] The fifth stage was reached when a liberal, general incorporation code was created, which extended the corporate form to a wide variety of functions and did not place limits on the activities, internal structure, or capitalization of individual corporations. This type of act was not adopted until the 1880s and 1890s.

General incorporation acts usually applied to specific business functions, not to incorporations in general. New York created a general incorporation act for manufacturing firms in 1811 but for banks only in 1838. By 1855, New York had created general incorporation acts for roughly twenty types of business activity.[13] But until the constitutional revisions of 1846 New York firms could still obtain a charter through special act, and many did.[14] Massachusetts established a series of general regulatory acts that governed the structure of charters (for banks in 1829) but continued to issue charters individually through the legislature. Massachusetts effectively guaranteed to charter any corporation that met the terms of the regulatory statutes long before it had general incorporation acts that provided for an administrative mechanism (what Massachusetts would call in several cases "self-incorporation").[15]

So the answer to both questions—how special was special and how general was general?—is that it depends. It depends on the particular state and time under consideration. Hurst's periodization still holds, however. Until 1838, when New York passed its Free Banking Act, every state was effectively a special charter state. This was even true for manufacturing in New York, since the General Act of 1811 did not preclude an interested group from obtaining a special charter. Some states, such as New Jersey, had very special chartering, with each charter unique and special privileges and accommodations the norm. Other states, like Massachusetts, had essentially standardized charters, adopting a general regulatory statute or issuing standardized charters in practice.

The transition to general incorporation acts was accomplished in two stages. First, incorporation in a standard form through an administrative mechanism became possible. At this stage, groups could choose to obtain a charter through a special act or by administrative arrangement. Second, incorporation by special charter was prohibited. Strict general incorporation was accomplished by constitutional amendment or revision. Most, but not all, states had constitutional restrictions in place by 1880. In 1780, most state constitutions did not mention corporations at all, and the few that did placed little or no restriction on the legislatures' ability to create them at will.

The movement toward liberal general incorporations laws after 1880 is easier to document because it developed essentially in two states, New Jersey and Delaware, and spread to other states through interjurisdictional competition. The next section outlines some general issues to be considered.

III. Some Theory

Throughout most of his academic career, Mancur Olson was steadfast and clear about whether governments augmented markets: they didn't. The logic of the *Logic of Collective Action* (1965), and the extension of the argument in the *Rise and Decline of Nations* (1982), left little or no room for positive action on the part of government.[16] It was only in the absence of government redistributive policies that economies would grow. The inexorable tendency was for redistributive coalitions to accumulate, to accrete additional layers of government programs to redistribute income and wealth, and ultimately to slow growth. Only in the last decade had Mancur come to seriously ponder the question of how and why governments might act to promote the development of markets and economies.

The intellectual context for Mancur's work is neoclassical economic theory, in which economies automatically allocate resources to the highest valued use and grow until they have exhausted profitable investment of capital or investment in new technologies.[17] What economic history clearly required, however, was something completely different. It required a model of economic development in which economies usually didn't grow and when they did grow were unable to sustain growth over long periods of time. The level of population and the level of income in, say, 1700 was not consistent with sustained rates of growth in per capita income for any substantial period of time.[18] At the same time, growth had to be possible but generally reversible. In other words, economies occasionally rose, but they always (until recently) declined. Mancur Olson wanted to explain to neoclassical economists why economies failed to grow, and the explanation needed to be consistent with individual rationality and other neoclassical assumptions. Long-run technological change (generally irreversible) was not a good candidate for the driving force in this theory. A good theory would also be capable of explaining the sustained growth of industrial economies since the eighteenth century. Even with their ups and downs, they have been remarkably vigorous in their growth. Of all the possible causes that could explain both the positive and negative episodes in a long run of history, only govern-ment—the state—seems to be a likely candidate.

Although Mancur came rather late to theorize about the positive role that government might play in economic growth, he brought a characteristic vocabulary to the task.[19] Beginning with a predatory state that would rob from its constituents whenever it was profitable to do so and had only its own wealth and utility in mind, Mancur pos-tulated two kinds of bandit states: roving and stationary. Roving ban-dits took what they could get in the short run, regardless of the long-run consequences for their victims. Stationary bandits were settled, and their thieving had to be more systematic. Destroying property today would reduce the economy's potential in the future; indiscrim-inate robbery weakened property rights and therefore the incentive to produce in the present and to invest in the future. The farsighted ruler would be willing to sacrifice revenue today for more revenue in the future.

To determine exactly how much the ruler would be willing to in-vest in the economic well-being of the general populace, Mancur brought in an old friend, the concept of encompassing interest.[20] Rulers that taxed all of their citizens had an interest in increasing the income of all of their citizens since it increased their tax haul, and the rulers' incentive to promote growth was increasing with the tax rate. Rulers who taxed only some of their subjects or a portion of eco-nomic activity, because some subjects were powerful or some activi-ties were difficult to measure and/or tax, would have a less encom-passing interest in promoting higher incomes. The willingness of rulers to pursue market-augmenting government policies would de-pend, ceteris paribus, on the extent to which their economic interests were encompassing. Potentially, this model would allow for rising and declining economies as the degree of the government's encompassing fiscal interest rose or fell. Ultimately, political democracies would cre-ate governments with larger encompassing interests (even if their governments were still predatory). The growth of modern nation-states with a modicum of representation, then republican govern-ments, and finally fully democratic systems of government moved progressively toward economic policies that enhance everyone's in-come and thus government revenues. These economies, of course, could still not avoid the problem of redistributive coalitions and groups promoting destructive rent-seeking policies, but the growth-enhancing effects of the government's fiscal interests outweighed, on balance, the growth-retarding effects of the government's fiscal interests. Essentially, as long as the government finds that it can get more revenues from supporting market-augmenting institutions than it can from creating special privileges, there is a dynamic, driving force to counterbalance the creeping institutional sclerosis caused by a buildup of redistributional coalitions.

While the vocabulary and conceptual apparatus of the stationary bandit is pure Mancur Olson, the logic is pure Douglass North. In chapter 5 of *Structure and Change in Economic History* (1981), North lays out exactly the same logic, although he presents it in a slightly different manner. North places more emphasis on the effect that transaction costs have on the ruler's ability to tax different groups, suggesting that it can be in the ruler's interest to confer a monopoly, or a tax farm, on a group or individual in return for a low-cost source of revenue. North also emphasizes the importance of competing rulers (either actual external competitors or potential internal ones) limiting the ability of the ruler to extract rents.

Both Olson and North build a theory of state behavior around the fiscal interest of the state. The theory is "neoclassical" in the sense that states are understood to have a well-defined objective function—to maximize the present value of their net revenue streams—and really don't care whether they achieve their goals by promoting secure private property rights or through brigandage.

The theory has three attractive features. First, it is indeterminate with respect to growth. The institutions that emerge from a state's maximizing its fiscal interests are never a priori good or bad for growth. Indeed, the same state may simultaneously promote growth by creating better property rights in one sector of the economy while it retards growth by creating the wrong incentives for investment in another.

Second, while North and Olson provide very limited empirical and historical studies, the notion of fiscal interest is quite easy to operationalize. Fiscal interests can be readily identified by careful study of government budgets and tax policies. ("Thick description" is necessary to make the explanations plausible, but it is feasible.) While the theory does not make predictions about the growth-enhancing or retarding effect of state policies, it does make predictions about fiscal structures and policy outcomes. We should be able to predict some government policies simply by paying close attention to revenue structures.

Third, fiscal interest can readily be incorporated into a more general, if less well defined, model of state behavior. For example, we may be interested in what determines the number of businesses and the degree of competition in an industry. Directly observing the interests of potential competitors, as well as existing businesses, is extremely difficult. But we may be able to determine the fiscal interest that the government has in allowing entry, and indirectly we may get a handle on the value of entry by examining the entry fee charged by the government as well as the number of businesses willing to enter.

The ideas that I will use in the remainder of the essay are very simple and can be explained verbally, but it may help to translate them into a formal model.

The basic policy I wish to explain is the degree of entry allowed by the state, specifically, how many charters it issues. Suppose that one state taxes the output or an input of the chartered firms, a second state owns stock in a chartered firm, and a third state sells charters outright. The states derive revenues from the existence of the chartered companies and charter the number of firms that will maximize their revenues.

The state that taxes inputs or outputs has an incentive to maximize output. Output, Q, is a function of the number of firms allowed in the industry, N, and the tax rate, t.

$$Q = f(t,N), \tag{1}$$

where $f^t < 0$, $f^N > 0$, and $f^{NN} < 0$. So revenues, V, are given by

$$V = t^* f(t,N). \tag{2}$$

The first order conditions are

$$dV/dt = f(t,N) + tf^t = 0 \tag{3}$$

and

$$dV/dN = tf^N = 0. \tag{4}$$

Equation (3) is straightforward: raise the tax as long as the increase in revenues on units that are produced is greater than the loss in total tax revenue of the units lost because of the tax increase. Equation (4) is of primary interest because it implies that for any given tax rate the optimal number of firms is as many as will enter, that is, allow entry until $f^N = 0$. A state that taxes output, or the corollary case in which a state taxes an input, should follow a chartering policy that allows free entry into the industry.[21]

On the opposite end, suppose that the state owns a firm outright. Now the objective function is

$$V = PQ - C(Q),$$ (5)

where $P = d(Q)$. If this is a competitive firm ($d^Q = 0$), the firm is a price taker. Profits, however, will be maximized when the firm is a monopolist and

$$dV/dQ = d(Q) - d^QQ - C^Q = 0$$ (6)

or

$$d(Q) - d^QQ = C^Q.$$ (7)

In other words, profits are maximized when marginal revenue equals marginal costs. The firm has no revenue incentives to allow entry since entry will reduce profits.

An intermediate case can be described in which there is limited entry. The state charges an entry fee to obtain a charter. This is more complicated, since the entry decision has to be explicitly modeled. In general, the amount that a firm is willing to pay to enter will be positively related to the firm's profitability and negatively related to the number of firms allowed in. The number of firms allowed to enter at the revenue-maximizing entry fee will usually be more than one and less than the competitive market would support. A limiting case occurs with one firm, where the entry fee exhausts the firm's profit— and we are back in the extreme examples used by North and Olson.

Table 2 shows how fiscal structure is related to regulatory policy. The left side of the table lists three types of fiscal regimes: inputs, entry fees, and monopoly. Along the top of the table there are the

TABLE 2.   Outcome

Fiscal Regime	Free Entry	Limited Entry	No Entry
Tax inputs	X		
Entry fees		X	
Monopoly			X

three regulatory policies on entry associated with the fiscal regimes: free entry, limited entry, and no entry. There is nothing in the model to suggest which fiscal regime a state will adopt. Fiscal structure, tax rates, and entry are all endogenous. It remains to show how fiscal interest helps us to understand whether and how early American governments augmented the development of financial markets by encouraging or discouraging the chartering of corporations.

IV. Taxation and Regulation of Banks before 1860

The discussion of early-nineteenth-century chartering practice will focus on banks. Banks were the heart of early-nineteenth-century financial markets. They provided the medium of exchange through their note issues, they dominated the money markets and short-term financial markets, and their equity issues—along with government debt and insurance companies—formed the basis of the growing stock market. Richard Sylla (1998) has made a persuasive case that the United States had a world-class financial system by the 1830s. In 1830, the capital of American banks was roughly double the capital of English banks; the markets efficiently priced federal and state bond issues; and banks, insurance companies, and state governments were able to raise large amounts of capital fairly easily.[22] If we want to understand how governments may have augmented financial markets in the early nineteenth century, banks are the place to start.

Sylla (1985) has also shown that government policy toward corporations was largely shaped by the experiences of state governments with banks. There is no doubt that bank charters were the most valuable charters created by state governments, and they were the only charters created by the national government. In 1830, there were 330 state-chartered banks with an average nominal capital of $333,642, not including the Second Bank of the United States, with capital of $35,000,000 (Gilbart [1837] 1967, 47). There were 71 banks with capital of $500,000 or greater. The largest manufacturing companies in 1830 were the textile firms in the northeast; only a few of these firms were capitalized at more than $100,000. It was to banking, not manufacturing, that states would look to promote their fiscal interests. The money simply wasn't in manufacturing, even as late as 1830.

State regulation of the banking system, primarily controls on entry, were critically dependent on the fiscal interest of the state.[23] There was a wide variety of state banking systems throughout the country. The northeastern states were more commercially developed

and had more banks and more bank capital, while banks in the South
and West were fewer in number, although many had large capitalization. The cross-state variation in the number of banks or the amount
of bank capital is dominated by the general level of economic development. In order to compare like with like, I will focus on Massachusetts, New York, and Pennsylvania, all large commercially developed
states having a major financial center (a similar analysis of southern
and western states can be found in Wallis, Sylla, and Legler 1994).
Sylla's estimates of bank capital in Boston, New York, and Philadelphia in 1830 suggest that these three cities alone had the equivalent
of 40 percent of the total bank capital in England. All three markets
were highly developed, but state promotion of banking had produced
significantly different outcomes in each.

Table 3 presents information on each state's share of banks, bank
capital, and population, as a percentage of national totals and of the

TABLE 3. Shares of National and Regional Population, Banks, and Bank Capital (percentages)

| | National | | | Regional | | |
State	Population	Banks	Bank Capital	Population	Banks	Bank Capital
1820						
MA	5.4	9.1	10.3	17.8	28.9	23.8
NY	14.2	10.7	18.6	46.6	34.0	43.0
PA	10.9	11.7	14.4	35.6	37.1	33.2
1830						
MA	4.7	20.0	18.5	15.7	48.5	37.1
NY	14.9	11.2	18.2	49.5	37.2	36.4
PA	10.4	10.0	13.3	34.8	24.3	26.5
1850						
MA	4.3	14.3	16.2	15.5	33.7	35.2
NY	13.4	22.5	21.3	48.4	53.0	46.3
PA	10.0	5.7	8.5	36.1	13.3	18.6
1860						
MA	3.9	11	15.3	15.4	31.2	32.1
NY	12.3	19.2	27.1	48.4	54.3	55.4
PA	9.2	5.1	6.0	36.2	14.5	12.5

Source: Population is taken from U.S. Bureau of the Census 1975. Banks and bank capital for 1820
and 1830 are from Gilbart [1837] 1967, 43–48. Banks and bank capital for 1850 and 1860 are from Sylla
1975, 249–52.

totals for the three states, in 1820, 1830, 1850, and 1860. Massachusetts clearly had the largest banking system relative to its population in each of the four years. New York had shares of banks and bank capital that fell below its population shares in 1820 and 1830, but it had reached parity with its population share by 1850 and 1860. Pennsylvania was always a laggard in the number of banks and the size of its bank capital, despite having the largest city (and the nation's capital from 1790 to 1800).

All three states shared the same banking policies in the 1790s and 1800s. A small number of banks were chartered in each state. These banks were regarded as public utilities, whose purpose was to provide a circulating medium and loans for government and commerce. The states often reserved the right to take a share in the stock of the banks that they chartered, and all three states received regular dividends on their stock. It was not until the first decades of the nineteenth century that their banking policies began to diverge.

Pennsylvania chartered the Bank of North America (BNA) in 1781. In 1784, the bank successfully resisted an attempt to charter a second bank, the Bank of Pennsylvania, largely by promising the state that it would broaden its shareholder base and allow the promoters of the Bank of Pennsylvania to purchase stock in the BNA. After the creation of the national Bank of the United States in 1791, based in Philadelphia, there was an attempt to charter a second Bank of Pennsylvania in 1794. This time the new bank was successful in outbidding the BNA for a new charter. The BNA had offered the state the opportunity to buy BNA stock at a preferential price, but the Bank of Pennsylvania offered the state a better deal in its own shares. The scenario was repeated again in 1803 when the Bank of Philadelphia applied for a charter, again opposed by the existing banks. The state, mindful of its existing investment in the Bank of Pennsylvania, was leery of chartering a new bank and thus reducing the value of its stock and dividends, but the new bank offered substantial inducements. After a long negotiation, a charter was issued to the Bank of Philadelphia. The bank paid the state $135,000 in cash; the state had the right to subscribe to $300,000 in stock by tendering U.S. bonds, which would be returned to the state should the bank fail, plus additional rights to purchase stock in the future; and the bank incurred the obligation to lend the government up to $100,000 at 5 percent for a period not exceeding ten years.[24] Another bank was chartered in 1809, again in the face of opposition by existing banks and in return for a substantial charter fee. Schwartz concludes:

> The offer of monetary inducements for the granting of a charter, which began as a voluntary solicitation of the legislature [by the bank promoters], came to be looked upon as a necessary accomplishment of a petition for incorporation. The committee reported that since the petitioners sought a charter for profit-making purposes, the state had a right to require a payment for the privileges it conferred. (1987, 5)

For the next four decades, Pennsylvania would continue to sell bank charters, collect dividends, and restrict the number of banks in order to protect its fees and dividends. Table 4, taken from Wallis, Sylla, and Legler 1994, reports revenues from bank sources as a share of total state revenues. Pennsylvania received roughly 20 percent of state revenue from bank dividends and charter fees well into the 1840s.

Massachusetts began in much the same way, chartering a relatively small number of banks, owning stock in a number of them, and closely identifying the fiscal interest of the state with the banks. In 1812, however, most of the existing bank charters came up for renewal. The state expanded its holdings in the bank system by chartering the Bank of Massachusetts, with capital of $3 million, of which the state subscribed a third. The state already had substantial bank holdings (the Handlins [1969] report a total of $1.8 million in 1812). In 1812, the state also imposed an annual 1 percent tax on bank capital.[25] Unlike Pennsylvania, where banks paid large charter fees, political competition in Massachusetts had resulted in more liberal chartering at lower fees, over the strenuous opposition of the existing banks. When revenues from the tax on bank capital began flowing into its treasury, the state began to see that its fiscal interest lay in increasing the number of banks. By 1820, the state had liquidated all of its bank stock and was liberally providing charters. In 1829, "a general act was passed prescribing the powers and duties and internal organizations of all banks that might thereafter be incorporated and also of those existing banks whose charters should be extended or capital increased" (Dodd 1936, 211). This was a general regulatory statute. Chartering still required a special act of the legislature, but the structure of charters was now set, and the state essentially incorporated all the banks that applied and met the requirements. As table 4 shows, from the 1830s onward the bank tax was the single most important source of revenue for the state, in most years providing more than half of total state revenues (figures before 1830 are unavailable).

From similar starting points, banking in Pennsylvania and Massachusetts thus diverged sharply. New York followed a middle path. As table 3 shows, New York's share of population in the three-state region was larger than its share of banks or bank capital in 1820 and 1830, a situation reversed in 1850 and 1860. New York is a very interesting case, since it was a state where bank charters were openly and explicitly used for political purposes. Like Pennsylvania and Massachusetts, New York had begun chartering banks in the 1790s, obtained bank stock on which it earned dividends, and gradually expanded the

TABLE 4. Bank Revenues as Share of Total Net Revenues (decade averages)

State	1800	1810	1820	1830	1840	1850	1860
CT	0.00	0.09	0.09	0.27	0.37	0.34	0.45
DE	0.01	0.12	0.44	0.43	0.56	0.52	0.4
MA				0.61	0.45	0.34	0.21
ME	0.00	0.00	0.00	0.00	0.00	0.00	0
NH	0.00	0.00	0.00	0.03	0.01	0.00	0
NJ					0.00	0.00	0.03
NY	0.04	0.06	0.06	0.01	0.01	0.01	0.01
PA	0.42	0.38	0.53	0.23	0.09	0.04	0.06
RI	0.00	0.02	0.02	0.24	0.41	0.46	0.46
VT	0.00	0.00	0.03	0.08	0.10	0.04	0.02
Average	0.06	0.08	0.15	0.21	0.20	0.17	0.16
MD		0.29	0.05	0.09	0.18	0.04	0.03
NC			0.31	0.34	0.44	0.01	0
SC	0.05	0.09	0.13	0.01	0.05	0	0
VA	0.00	0.12	0.02	0.00	0.09	0.13	0.1
Average	0.02	0.16	0.13	0.11	0.19	0.04	0.03
IL				0.03	0.04	0	0
IN				0.03	0.04	0.07	0
MI					0.03	0.01	0.01
MN							0
OH		0	0	0.01	0.04	0.01	0.02
Average				0.02	0.04	0.02	0.01
AK					0.06	0	0.01
MO						0.13	0.06
MS			0	0.04	0.02	0	0
TN					0	0	0.14
Average			0	0.04	0.03	0	0.04

Source: Wallis, Sylla, and Legler 1994.

Note: Blank cells in the table are decades without data. The decades run from the year ending in five to the year ending in four, that is, "1830" is 1825 to 1834. The "Average" rows are the simple average of states in each region.

number of chartered banks in the early decades of the century. Beginning in 1814, under the leadership of Martin Van Buren and the "Albany Regency," the New York Republican Party began systematically using the granting of bank charters for political purposes.

The first step was making the charters more attractive. "Actually, the first step in the political management of the banking business had been taken in 1814 when the state stopped subscribing to shares in newly chartered banks or requiring the promoters of new banks to give a bonus to the state for their charters."[26] The Republicans successfully opposed attempts to impose a tax on bank capital in 1815, 1818, and 1819. In 1821, they succeeded in placing a clause in the new constitution requiring two-thirds of the votes in the legislature to create a new bank charter. By granting charters only to bankers who were Republican and willing to actively support the party, Van Buren and the Regency were able to consolidate their hold on the party and the state government. Limiting charters increased their economic value and in so doing increased their utility as political favors to be distributed by the Republicans.

The excesses of the Regency produced a reaction. In 1838, while the Republicans were out of the majority, the Free Banking Act was passed. The law was a general incorporation act for banks, and the number of banks incorporated now increased. The state already had a tax on capitalization in place, although there had been difficulties in applying it to corporations as diverse as railroads and banks. Ultimately, the tax became similar to the bank capital tax in Massachusetts, and it was imposed on free banks after 1841. By the 1840s, then, New York had acquired the same fiscal interest in promoting the number of banks and their capital as Massachusetts, and the number of banks and their capital increased accordingly.

Rockoff's study of free banking in the 1840s (1974) provides additional evidence on the rates of return to banks in New York, Philadelphia, and Boston, presented in table 5. Entry limitations in Pennsylvania restricted the number of banks and raised profit margins. Free entry (subject to the conditions of the Free Banking Act in New York and the general regulatory act in Massachusetts) produced more competition and lower bank profits in Boston and New York. Capital was certainly mobile enough to take advantage of these differences, but government regulation hindered that mobility.

Fiscal interest clearly mattered in the development of American banking. Although the number of banks and dollars of bank capital are not perfect measures of banking services available to the public, they are systematic measures of the degree of financial development. American states had the capacity to pursue market-augmenting policies by stimulating and allowing financial development to take place. States like Massachusetts found it in their fiscal interest to promote banks, and those states ended up with relatively large banking sectors. While a fiscal interest approach can help explain the differences between Massachusetts and Pennsylvania, once the state's fiscal interest is understood, the theory is no help in explaining why the two states acquired different fiscal interests in the first place. There was little to distinguish the two states with regard to banking in 1811, and one would be hard pressed to predict the development of Massachusetts banking up to the passage of the capital tax. Can the fiscal interest model explain the transition to free banking and general incorporation?

V. The Case for General Incorporation and Free Banking

New York's adoption of free banking had little to do with fiscal interest. Massachusetts did not adopt a free banking act until the 1850s, although it effectively followed a free banking policy for fiscal reasons. Therein lies the rub: there is no clear evidence that states adopted free banking acts for fiscal reasons. States with a fiscal interest in free entry didn't need to adopt free banking laws.[27] States appear to have adopted general incorporation acts for reasons other than fiscal interest. To the extent that fiscal interest helps us to

TABLE 5. Dividends as a Percentage of Par Value of Bank Capital

Year	New York	Boston	Philadelphia
1849	8.79	8.06	9.79
1850	8.70	8.36	10.60
1851	9.38	7.82	10.30
1852	9.03	7.78	10.27
1853	8.85	8.08	11.13
1854	8.87	8.65	11.40
1855	9.08	7.98	11.00
1856	8.61	7.81	10.26
1857	7.73	7.73	7.12
1858	6.91	7.43	8.03
1859	7.56	7.31	8.03

Source: Data from Rockoff 1974, 157, table 3.

understand the transition to general incorporation, it is in the negative: states with close ties to existing corporations, whose fiscal interests were threatened by general incorporation acts, moved to mandatory general acts with more reluctance. In order to demonstrate the forces at work, this section will focus on the timing of constitutional restrictions prohibiting incorporation by special act.

There is a sweeping, general explanation of why general incorporation acts spread throughout the country after 1840. General incorporation was part of the antielitist rhetoric and policies of Jacksonian Democracy. Corporations were attacked as vehicles of special interests, as special grants of privilege to a favored few, unavailable to the general population and therefore incompatible with democratic ideals.[28] General incorporation acts did not remove all of the potential evils of corporations, particularly not of banks, but they did eliminate the stain of special privilege. If corporate status was freely available to all citizens, it could not be the domain of a privileged few. No matter how one viewed the utility or dangers of corporations, it was still possible to agree that the special charter system created special privileges. As Hurst points out, much of the anticorporation sentiment had little or nothing to do with corporations or the merits of different types of corporate forms; it was much more concerned with individual equity and equality (1970, 30–57). Only the most rabid opponents suggested elimination of corporations altogether.

There is a great deal of merit to this explanation. The revolutionary and constitutional settlement had created a republican rather than a democratic form of government in the United States. Suffrage and officeholding were not open even to the general population of free white males in most states: wealth and property restrictions were the rule rather than the exception. The federal Constitution left to the states the question of who could vote and hold office, and the internal organization of state governments and polities was similarly clearly beyond the bounds of federal authority. Representation in state legislatures was often grossly and deliberately disproportional. There was an ongoing debate over whether representation should be based on wealth or population.[29] To modern ears, much of this debate rings false since we are not accustomed to hearing ardent supporters of representative government and a strong voice for the people arguing that only property holders should have the vote. Whereas we might fear that the poor would rise up and demand the redistribution of all property, they feared that men without property would be unable to maintain their independence as voters and that their votes, as a result, would be available to corrupt interests with money to spend.[30] The fear was less that the poor would vote their own interests than that they would become the pawns of corrupt, well-organized factions and parties.

Between 1800 and 1840, some of the most heated political debates were over the extension of the franchise, and by 1840 most states had moved to a system of universal free, white, male suffrage, with much more equal (though still imperfect) representation and with open requirements for officeholders. The mood of the times celebrated the triumph of democratic, antielitist government and government policies as the fulfillment of the true spirit of 1776. The adoption of general incorporation acts is a piece of this ideological shift in government policy, crowned by the triumph of Jacksonian Democracy. There are, however, a few problems with applying this conventional ideological interpretation to the economic policies of the Jacksonian era.

First, there is now a half century of literature in political science and political history that traces its origins back to this very question: what was Jacksonian Democracy really about? In *The Concept of Jacksonian Democracy* (1961), Lee Benson questioned whether economic issues really divided the electorate. That is, in an age when so many questions facing the government were economic in nature, does the economic status of voters in fact predict their voting patterns; were the leaders of the competing parties drawn from different socioeconomic groups; and did Jacksonian policies champion the interests of a particular economic strata? The answer, in a word, is no.[31] The "new political historians" have found that Benson's results for New York are duplicated throughout the early nineteenth century everywhere in the nation. Party affiliation, church affiliation, and ethnic origins are much more powerful predictors of voting patterns than per capita income, wage rate, or industry of employment.[32]

Second, remember Schwartz's description of Pennsylvania banking. The opponents of the proposed Bank of Philadelphia were not antibank zealots; they were the stockholders and managers of the existing Bank of Pennsylvania. Bray Hammond's (1957) exposition of Jackson's war against the Second Bank of the United States (BUS) pits bankers in New York (pro-Jackson, anti-BUS) against bankers in Philadelphia (anti-Jackson, pro-BUS), rather than (as economic interest groups) antibank agrarians against probank urban, commercial elites.[33] Urban commercial elites were pro- and anti-BUS depending on whether their own particular banking interests would be furthered or frustrated by extending the bank's charter. The *Charles River Bridge* case was brought to the Supreme Court not because of antimonopoly sentiments but because another company wanted a charter to build a bridge that would compete with the existing Charles River Bridge. The Age of Jackson was an ideological era, and political ideology and rhetoric were critically important facets of the political process that we seek to understand; nevertheless, the interest groups that battled over corporate policy in the states were those that sought corporation status for themselves, and perhaps sought to deny it to their competitors, not groups that were basically pro- or anticorporation in general.

There was a broad and deep suspicion of corporations in America because corporations (1) represented special privileges not available to everyone, (2) created potential concentrations of wealth and power that could distort the political system, and (3) had adverse economic effects because of monopoly power or because corporations were less dynamic than individual enterprises. The first two points resonated with revolutionary ideals, but these concerns failed to generate a general anticorporation movement. People typically were against specific corporations and in favor of others.

> Although anticharter arguments were frequently stated as if they applied to all corporations without exception, in practice opposition usually settled on some corporations only. Even the Pennsylvania legislators who campaigned against the BNA and the reincorporation of Philadelphia [the city] apparently raised no objections to the charters granted "every day," as one legislator put it in 1786, to "half a dozen or 20 people for some purpose or another." Similarly, in 1792 James Sullivan carefully distinguished the incorporation of a bank from that "to build a bridge, or to cut a canal," which he found unobjectionable. Banks were probably assailed more often than any other kind of corporation. But consider the position of a delegate to the Massachusetts constitutional convention of 1853 who launched a rhetorically powerful attack on corporations "of a business character." Among corporations "for other purposes," which were apparently exempted from his criticisms, he included railroads, insurance companies and banks! (Maier 1972, 73–74)

Americans may have been fearful of corporations in the abstract, but in the concrete they wanted access to the corporate form to carry out their own initiatives and plans.

It is ironic that out of this skeptical environment there emerged a set of general incorporation laws that enabled virtually anyone with adequate means to acquire the benefits of corporate status. To sort this out, we need to revisit Mancur Olson's fundamental concern over the power of special groups to form redistributive coalitions, in view of the importance of corporations to the fiscal interests of state governments. This way of thinking about the adoption of free banking or general incorporation laws suggests that three general interests are involved, in addition to the state's fiscal interest. First is the interest of the existing corporations, which wish to protect their privileges. Second are the interests of the corporations that wish to be formed. Third is the general social predilection against grants of special privilege.

An obvious test is provided by states with no existing corporations. New states have not yet created corporations, and in new states we might expect that the weight of public antagonism toward special privilege, along with the hopes of corporations as yet unformed, would lead these states to adopt general incorporation laws. After 1840, states entered the Union at irregular intervals. Table 6 shows the dates at which states adopted constitutional restrictions requiring that all incorporations be under general laws. The table separates states into two groups: existing states that modified their constitutions to include the restriction and new states that adopted the restriction in their first constitutions. Every new state admitted to the Union after 1846 had a constitutional provision requiring incorporation by general law at the time it became a state.

The four states that did not have constitutional restrictions by 1930 were all in New England: Massachusetts, Rhode Island, Connecticut, and New Hampshire. We have talked at some length about Massachusetts. Three of the four states (New Hampshire was the exception) had a tax on bank capital, had a substantial fiscal interest in banks, and followed a free entry policy even when they did not have free banking laws. As late as 1860, bank revenues accounted for 45 percent of state revenues in Connecticut, 21 percent in Massachusetts, and 46 percent in Rhode Island. The other state that relied heavily on a bank capital tax and allowed free entry into banking was Delaware, where 40 percent of state revenues came from banks in 1860. Delaware did not adopt a constitutional restriction until 1897.

At this point, it is not possible to do a more thorough quantitative analysis of the timing of state adoption of general acts or constitutional restrictions, as not enough information is available. Two examples can be offered instead. One is New Jersey, where a strong and privileged corporation established fiscal ties to the state government, which protected its interests well into the 1870s. The other is New York, where revulsion against special privileges produced free banking as well as one of the first constitutional bans on incorporation by special act.

On February 4, 1830, the state of New Jersey granted charters to both the Delaware and Raritan Canal Company and the Camden and Amboy Railroad and Transportation Company to open a canal and a railroad, respectively, across the state. The charters were far from liberal. The state had the option to purchase one-quarter of the capital of each company, and transit duties were to be levied on freight and passengers on both lines. The transit duties were straight revenue measures, "the object of which is to secure a revenue to the

TABLE 6. Dates of Constitutional Provisions Requiring Incorporation under General Laws

Existing States		New States	
State	Year	State	Year
Louisiana	1845	Iowa	1846
New York	1846	Wisconsin	1848
Illinois	1848	California	1849
Michigan	1850	Minnesota	1858
Maryland	1851	Oregon	1859
Ohio	1851	Kansas	1861
Indiana	1851	West Virginia	1863
Missouri	1865	Nevada	1864
Alabama	1867	Nebraska	1867
North Carolina	1868	Colorado	1876
Arkansas	1868	North Dakota	1889
Tennessee	1870	South Dakota	1839
Pennsylvania	1874	Montana	1889
New Jersey	1875	Washington	1889
Maine	1875	Idaho	1890
Texas	1876	Wyoming	1890
Georgia	1877	Utah	1896
Mississippi	1890	Oklahoma	1907
Kentucky	1891	New Mexico	1912
South Carolina	1895	Arizona	1912
Delaware	1897		
Florida	1900		
Virginia	1902		
Vermont	1913		

Source: Data from Evans 1948, 11, table 5.

Treasury without embarking in any expenditure of capital."[34] The state subsequently realized that it could make more money by selling privileges to the companies. The legislature passed an act in late 1830 making it lawful for the railroad to give the state one thousand shares of fully paid stock in return for a guarantee that the state would not charter another railroad to haul freight or passengers between New York and Philadelphia. The state could void the promise by returning the stock.

After difficulties in getting the canal started, largely because of fears that the railroad would be too competitive, the two companies merged. In 1832, the "Joint Companies were able to secure passage of the infamous 'monopoly bill' under the terms of which the companies presented the state with an additional 1000 full-paid shares on which dividends were to be paid 'as if the state had subscribed for such stock and paid the several installments thereon.'" In return for this gift, the Camden and Amboy received the following privilege.

> That it shall not be lawful, at any time during the said rail road charter, to construct any other rail road or railroads in this state, without the consent of the said companies, which shall be intended or used for the transportation of passengers or merchandise between the cities of New York and Philadelphia, or to compete in business with the rail road authorized by the act to which this supplement is relative. (Cadman 1949, 55–56)

New Jersey would charter other railroads, but all of them fed into the Camden and Amboy.

The state was set financially. Table 7 shows dividends on railroad stock and transit duties as a share of ordinary state expenditures from 1834 to 1850, as calculated by Tuttle.[35] In some years during the 1830s and 1840s, the state was able to forgo collection of the property tax, and in 1848 it was abolished altogether. Revenue was the key. In 1834 and 1835, a rival turnpike company petitioned the state for the right to build a competing railroad. The committee appointed to report on the petition turned it down "to preserve inviolate, sacred, and unimpaired, the *faith,* the *integrity,* and the *revenues* of the state, by a strict adherence to the system of policy which has laid the foundation of our Internal Improvements, *the principle of protection as a means of revenue.*"[36] "The faith, the integrity, and the revenues of the state" was an unbeatable combination. The monopoly companies were a classic redistributional coalition, and they were able to hold their position against all comers until their properties were leased to the Pennsylvania Central in 1871.[37]

Few corporations were as special as the Camden and Amboy, but hundreds, if not thousands, of corporations received special privileges from the state governments that created them, often in direct exchange for payment. There was no hiding these special favors, as corporate charters were public documents. Occasionally there was a public outcry, and always there were questions about the propriety of charters, but underlying it all was the understanding of a quid pro quo, special privileges for revenues. General incorporation acts could blunt some of this criticism by making the corporate form available to all, thus solving one of the equity problems. Prohibiting special corporation acts altogether solved the remaining equity problem, as everybody now would receive the same treatment, and further solved the problem of corrupt influence of corporations in the legislatures (at least in terms of charters). In states like New Jersey, however, abandoning special charters came at the expense of the state's fiscal interest.

Adoption of a free banking or general incorporation act created a potential political benefit by serving groups without charters. In the

TABLE 7. Dividends from Railroad Stock and Transit Duties As a Percentage of Ordinary State Expenditures

Year	Percentage of Expenditures
1834	51
1835	95
1836	69
1837	58
1838	46
1839	61
1840	79
1841	65
1842	54
1843	74
1844	62
1845	62
1846	67
1847	64
1848	105
1849	93

Source: Tuttle 1920, cited in Cadman 1949, 401.

conflict over free banking in New York, these interests were crucial. As explained earlier, the Albany Regency had used the granting of bank charters to control the Republican Party in New York (which would become a branch of the Democratic Republicans under Jackson). The policy not only angered Whigs but left non-Republicans who wished to establish banks without access to charters. The situation in New York was complicated further by the presence of an anti-corporate, antibank splinter party, the Equal Rights Party, known as the Locofocos. "Since the Locofocos preached anticorporation, anti-charter doctrines and particularly opposed any banking system on paper currency, they inevitable broke with the Democratic [Republican] party built by Martin Van Buren."[38] As long as the Albany Regency controlled the state, there was nothing the Whigs or Locofocos could do to realize their goals.

The business depression of 1837 brought the Whigs into power, and in alliance with the Locofocos they passed the Free Banking Act of 1838. The law established minimum capital requirements for banks at $100,000, laid down rules for the operation of banks, limited liability of bank shareholders, and established a state board of bank commissioners with broad supervisory powers and responsibilities. As Benson points out, "it is ironic that American historiography had tended to credit the Locofocos and their Radical Democratic allies with [the Free Banking Act's] passage" (1961, 98). It is true that the Locofocos were antimonopoly, and the free entry provisions of law addressed that. But the Locofocos were against any barriers to entry (the $100,000 minimum capitalization was inconsistent with that), they were adamantly against paper money and banks of issue (the act authorized banks to issue paper money), and they thought that bankers should be fully liable for currency issues (the act created explicit limited liability for shareholders). In short, the Free Banking Act met only one of the goals set out by the Locofocos, free entry. The Locofocos provided very effective political cover for the Whigs but received little in return.

There were no fiscal interests at stake in New York, at least not in the Free Banking Act. The state was already taxing corporations, including banks, through the capitalization tax. The Regency realized the economic benefits of limited charters in the form of political favors, not in higher charter fees, as in Pennsylvania. Expansion of the number of banks and bank capital under the act would bring in more revenue, but there is no evidence that this prospect played a crucial role in passage of the act.

The strong aversion to the granting of special privileges in the United States that grew out of the revolutionary experience, and was sharpened by the ongoing struggle for universal suffrage in the early nineteenth century, was a major force in the adoption of general incorporation acts. This aversion manifested itself in many ways, most of them rhetorical rather than substantive. The establishment of permanent national political parties in the 1830s was, in part, due to the Jacksonians' ability to capitalize on these sentiments, even if the Democrats' policies did not follow their own rhetoric.[39] General anticorporation sentiments shared in the aversion to special privilege, but actual opposition to incorporation nevertheless tended to be specific to individual companies or to limited classes of corporations, such as banks. There was never a general ban on all corporations in any state. The feeling against special privilege was strong enough, by the 1840s, to secure constitutional restrictions against special incorporation in every state that entered the Union after 1845. These were states without large existing corporate interests.

New Jersey, with its strong attachment to the special charter of the Camden and Amboy, adopted a general incorporation act in 1845. It was not until 1875, however, that New Jersey prohibited incorporation by special act altogether. By that time, the special relationship between the state and the railroad had ended (as will be discussed). As long as the railroad's special charter provided the state with revenues, the state kept the option of special charters open. Similarly, Pennsylvania, which continued to glean revenues from the creation and renewal of bank charters, did not prohibit special acts until 1874.

The most effective opponents of special corporate privilege were either other corporations or, in most cases, other groups that wanted to form corporations but were prevented from doing so by the vested power of existing interests. Once established, corporations acted like Olsonian redistributive coalitions. The fiscal interest of the state—in this case the payments that competing new corporations were willing to make to the state to obtain charters—determined whether entry would occur. Only in cases in which states stumbled onto the option of taxing inputs or outputs, rather than selling corporate privileges, did states allow free entry. Indeed, those states encouraged free entry. In states where the early history of corporate-state relations had created a fiscal tie between the interests of specific corporations and state revenues, special incorporation tended to last longer.

VI. Federal Preemption of Bank Chartering

With the notable exception of the First and Second Banks of the United States, the federal government had left corporate chartering and revenues to the states. Except during the exigencies of war, the tariff proved to be equal to the revenue demands of the national government. The Civil War changed all that. The Union government sought funds through taxation, borrowing, and currency issues. In 1863, the national government tapped into the fiscal potential of the state banks by encouraging them to obtain new charters as national banks.

The incentive for state-chartered banks to switch to national charters was a strong one. National banks had the authority to issue national banknotes, which were backed by federal government debt. The National Banking Act allowed national banks to purchase federal bonds, hypothecate (deposit) them with the comptroller of the currency, and issue up to 90 percent of the face value of the bonds in banknotes. In order to induce banks to switch their charters, the act sweetened the offer by imposing a tax on the note issues of nonnational banks, originally at 3 percent of face value and later at 10 percent. The 10 percent tax effectively put the state-chartered banks out of business as note-issuing institutions. The new national banks could invest in Treasury bonds, pocket the interest, and issue notes equal to 90 percent of the value of their original investment. The market for federal debt was strengthened and the interest burden of financing the war substantially reduced. It was a case of pure fiscal interest driving a change in policy. "Congress enacted the legislation primarily to increase the government's borrowing power during the war by requiring all national banks to invest a portion of their capital in government bonds" (Sylla 1969, 659).

Was this change good or bad for the economy? The creation of national banks certainly reduced competition in the banking industry, particularly through the establishment of minimum capital requirements, which reduced entry. On the other hand, the creation of a network of larger banks of issue facilitated the further development of a national capital market, though one that was tilted toward larger banks in the major urban centers.

VII. The Move to Liberal Incorporation Laws

While the move to general incorporation was spread out over time and states, the move to more liberal incorporation laws in the 1880s and 1890s was concentrated in two states, New Jersey and Delaware. In New Jersey, conflicts with the Camden and Amboy (after it was leased to the Pennsylvania Railroad) produced declining revenues from transit duties and dividends in the early 1870s. In 1875, when it adopted a constitutional restriction requiring general incorporation, New Jersey gave up a century of issuing special charters. The state quickly turned to other sources of corporate revenues. Unlike in the early nineteenth century, when manufacturing firms were small relative to banks, by the 1880s they had grown large and were beginning to raise capital through equity sale in stock markets.[40] General incorporation acts for manufacturing firms, with their limits on capitalization, prescriptions on internal company structure, and prohibitions and impediments to interstate operations, had become too restrictive for the new national corporations such as Standard Oil.

New Jersey was the first state to capture the potential fiscal benefits of liberal chartering policies. Through a series of acts, the state steadily liberalized its general incorporation acts to allow companies greater latitude in raising capital, choosing lines of business, operating across state lines, and setting internal governance. After 1896, when all of these changes were collected in the general corporation law revision, franchise taxes and charter fees accounted for at least 40 percent of state revenues until 1915.[41] A wave of business consolidations occurred in manufacturing after 1895, and, as Nelson shows, over 79 percent of the capital involved in consolidations between 1895 and 1904 was merged into corporations domiciled in New Jersey.[42] New Jersey attracted corporations to its borders, not by encouraging them to locate there physically but by enabling them to establish a corporate headquarters in their state that could direct the operations of a company (or holding company) spread throughout the nation.

In 1913, New Jersey abandoned its liberal policies and adopted a relatively strict set of antitrust laws. The new laws dramatically reduced the revenues from franchise taxes and charter fees after 1914. The state reversed its position after World War I, but by that time Delaware had stepped in to take New Jersey's place. Delaware attracted corporations by adopting much the same general incorporation laws as New Jersey. By maintaining its laws over time (unlike New Jersey), Delaware remained the leading domicile state for large corporations well into the twentieth century. In 1956, over a third of the nation's six hundred largest nonfinancial corporations were located in Delaware (Hurst 1970, 150).

Hurst concludes that the liberalization of general corporation laws in New Jersey and Delaware was motivated by nothing more than "their own greed for revenue" (1970, 12).[43] What distinguished the 1880s from the 1830s was New Jersey's decision, in the Holding Company Act of 1888, to allow its corporations to hold the stock of corporations located in other states. Until that change, out-of-state corporations were "foreign" and states could discriminate against foreign corporations on a number of dimensions. After the New Jersey changes, it became extremely difficult for a state to protect its corporations against foreign competition. What followed, almost immediately, was the development of large, modern, national and multinational firms in manufacturing, with easy access to capital through growing equity markets.

VIII. Conclusions

I have assumed that the development of the banking system was a central element in the development of American financial markets, in line with Sylla's contention that the American financial system was, in historical and comparative terms, well developed by the 1830s. Government played a critical role in developing these markets. All but two of the chartered banks operating in the American economy between 1790 and 1860 were creations of state governments. The number of banks grew rapidly, as did the amount of their capital. Millions of dollars were mobilized to finance short-term trade credits, commercial development, and longer term investments in land and manufacturing. And banking was only the entering wedge. State governments incorporated thousands of manufacturing firms, and by the end of the century those firms were on the leading edge of technological change and economic development. New forms of multistate and then multinational business were again promoted by state incorporation policies. This was a clear case of market-augmenting government.

Why did the government do it? Fiscal interest goes a long way toward explaining the pattern of government policies across states. Most states acquired some fiscal interest in corporations, and the form that their interest took was critically important. States that owned corporations outright strictly limited entry, sometimes establishing state monopolies. States that established entry fees, in the form of bonuses for corporate charters, also tended to limit entry in order to increase the value of charters. States that taxed inputs or outputs, on the other hand, tended to allow free entry. In each case, the behavior of the state was consistent with its fiscal interest, taking the form of its fiscal structure as given. The national government's preemption of bank chartering in 1863 was, similarly, clearly motivated by fiscal interests. The adoption of liberal general incorporation acts in New Jersey and Delaware was driven completely by fiscal considerations.

The theory is less successful at predicting which type of taxation will emerge. Fiscal structures and corporate policies are endogenous. We can nonetheless identify conditions in individual states that conditioned their development. (North would call this path dependence; Olson would call these explanations ad hoc.) Systematically accounting for the factors that determine revenue structures is beyond our reach at present. It seems fairly clear, however, based on the discussion of bank chartering, that the concept of "encompassing interest" will not take us very far: all American states had roughly the same encompassing interests in economic development.

North argues that we need a model of ideology, or of mental models, in order to understand how institutions evolve over time. I agree; I have tried here to demonstrate how commonly held beliefs about the legitimacy of incorporation affected government policy. The student of early America is blessed with a rich history of what people thought and believed, and I have tried to draw on that literature here. At the same time, it is difficult to associate changes in ideology with changes in policy. The move to general incorporation acts cannot be explained by fiscal interest. At best, the overriding concern that government not create special privileges, demonstrated in practice by the growing number of states with universal suffrage, created an intellectual and political environment in which special incorporation acts were continuously challenged. Why that social predilection became concretely embedded in general incorporation acts and constitutional prohibitions on special charters after 1840 is not so clear. States with strong fiscal ties to existing, specially chartered corporations may have moved more slowly to prohibit special charters, but there was no obvious fiscal interest served by general incorporation acts.

The American solution to the problem was neither to eliminate corporations nor to prevent special interests from operating. As I have tried to show, an important and positive part of the revolutionary legacy in the United States was the positive emphasis placed upon free association. The determination that government should promote association and organization, not just fail to suppress it, was probably uniquely American in the early nineteenth century. This "ideological" view was just as prevalent as the predilection against special privilege. Positive public support for associations of all types, combined with the fiscal benefits of promoting incorporation, provided Americans with a world-class financial system by the 1830s and the world's leading manufacturing economy by 1900. It was truly a case of market-augmenting government.

Notes

This essay was prepared for the conference Market-Augmenting Government, organized by the Center for Institutional Reform and the Informal Sector (IRIS), held in March 1999. It germinated in a series of discussions I had with Mancur Olson in the weeks before his untimely passing in the winter of 1998. I would like to thank Chas Cadwell and Omar Azfar for giving me the opportunity and the spur to develop these ideas.

The quotation that appears at the beginning of this essay is from Joseph K. Angell and Samuel Ames, *A Treatise on the Law of Private Corporations* (1831).

1. Hurst 1970, 1. "In sum, when we began making important use of the corporation for business in the United States from about 1780, there was little relevant legal experience on which to draw. For 100 years, we proceeded to use the corporate instrument on a scale unmatched in England. In that development we built public policy toward the corporation almost wholly out of our own wants and concerns, shaped primarily by our own institutions. The one definite inheritance was the idea that some positive act of the sovereign was necessary to create corporate status. But we gave our own content to that idea" (8–9). See also Maier 1992, 1993.

2. "Marshall's Court ruled that the [New Hampshire] statute was invalid because it violated the clause in the federal Constitution, which forbids a state to pass any bill impairing the obligation of contract. To rule that a corporation charter enjoyed the protection of a 'contract' under the constitutional provision was a clear-cut act of judicial lawmaking. Indeed, the lawmaking is so clear as to indicate that the Court was pursuing an objective which it rated of high importance. The case did not involve a business corporation. But business corporations were playing a rapidly growing part in the economy, in great measure because their charters gave them operational utilities similar to those which Marshall's opinion noted as making the college an effective, continuing organization. Contemporaries did not emphasize the decision as important for business corporations. But this was, in fact, its prime functional significance" (Hurst 1970, 62–63).

3. The only state-level income estimates for the nineteenth century are completely unsuited for a test of this type. Easterlin's estimates of per capita income vary across states only because of differences in industrial structure

of employment across states. As a result, we can't use Easterlin's numbers to test whether different corporate structures made banking or manufacturing more or less productive across states.

4. Bank charters typically ran a distant third to charters for public utilities (primarily in transportation) and for manufacturing. See Evans 1948, among others, for counts of the types of business that received charters in the nineteenth century. I will return to this issue later in the essay.

5. The CREH must rank among the most successful scholarly efforts of its type of all time. Books commissioned or supported include Hartz on Pennsylvania, Primm on Missouri, Benson on New York, and Goodrich on Canals. The ideas of the committee are described in a memorandum prepared by Herbert Heaton and published as appendix G of *Commonwealth,* along with correspondence between the Handlins and the committee. See Cole's remarks on the committee's work in his review article in the *Journal of Economic History* (1970).

6. On the early history of corporations see Davis 1961, 30–107; on charitable corporation in particular, see 81–85.

7. This literature is now extensive. The major works include Wood 1969, 1992; Bailyn 1967; and Pocock 1975. Also see Banning 1978, Maier 1972, and McCoy 1980.

8. John Brewer's *The Sinews of Power* (1990) is a thorough treatment of the growth of the British military and the corresponding growth in the fiscal power and sophistication of the British state in the eighteenth century.

9. The large number of public utility incorporations is important. These charters were for "special action franchises" to create a corporation to carry out a specific function. This type of charter rarely came under general incorporation acts, even later in the century, since they typically granted special privileges (such as eminent domain) to the corporation. These charters could not be standardized.

10. This might, in part, be because Hurst is citing Dodd's book on Massachusetts at this point, and Dodd clearly gives the impression that special charters rapidly became standardized (1954, 195–271): "These charters of all of them were much like that of the Nantucket Bank, a few contained clauses varying from the norm" (204); "The first of these, that of the Merchants bank, contained a number of new features which thereafter became usual" (207); "most of the banks chartered between 1811 and the enactment of the Banking Act of 1829 incorporated by reference to a large part of the act chartering the State Bank" (209).

11. In this regard, we should note Cadman's caution about interpreting what appear to be standardized charters: "The beneficial effect of standardization clauses in special charters has often been stressed in discussions of the history of incorporation. It is true that in New Jersey many clauses came to be more or less standardized, but the use of stereotyped phraseology did little to correct the abuses suggested above. A standard clause could be al-

tered slightly to change the effect in some important particular or, more important, omitted entirely in certain cases. Again it should be stressed that it was relatively easy to convince a legislature to make certain deviations from a norm in a special case when there was no general statute to set a pattern. Before 1845, the only New Jersey charters that showed almost no important variations were those of turnpike companies" (1949, 18).

12. The first of these was included in the Louisiana constitution of 1845; see Evans 1948, 11, table 5, for a list of adoption dates throughout the country.

13. A list of the acts can be found in Seavoy 1982, app. 2, 283–85. The "roughly" in the text reflects the fact that the state was continually adjusting its laws and regrouping types of business activity under different acts. For a discussion of the 1811 general act for manufacturing, see pages 68–70.

14. See Kessler 1940, 877, 879, and the discussion in Dodd (1936, 417–8). The numbers reported in Evans 1948, 17, suggest that roughly 60 percent of charters for manufacturing firms were issued under the General Act and the remainder as special acts.

15. For a catalog of Massachusetts Acts, see Dodd 1936, 475–79. Dodd includes a similar list on legislative acts for every state in New England as well as a few others.

16. In this regard, the *Rise and Decline of Nations* could have been titled *The Decline of Nations* without doing an injustice to the argument.

17. This simple, but realistic, view of neoclassical theory is laid out in the opening chapters of North 1981.

18. Had per capita output grown at a rate of .1 percent per year, it would have been 2.7 times higher in 1700 than it had been in 700, and 7.4 times higher than it had been in 300 B.C. Somewhere in that hypothetical range the population would have starved or frozen.

19. This discussion is taken from Olson 1993. See the discussion in McGuire's essay in this volume as well as McGuire and Olson 1996.

20. A labor union that employed a third of the workers in an economy would have much greater stake, that is, a more encompassing interest, in the overall level of income than a labor union with 1 percent of the workers in an economy. Ceteris paribus, the larger union would be less likely, at the margin, to pursue redistributive policies that reduce overall income because their members would bear a much larger share of the loss (Olson 1982, 49–50).

21. It may not be in the state's interest to allow unlimited entry if the new entrant actually reduces output, as might be the case in a fishery with overfishing.

22. That American banks had more capital than English banks does not imply that the American banking system was larger or more sophisticated than the English. Many English banks were partnerships, and the partners had an incentive to minimize the amount of their capital formally involved in the business, while most American banks were corporations whose

charters required a substantial amount of paid-in capital in order for the bank to operate.

23. This section is based on Wallis, Sylla, and Legler 1994. In that essay, we analyze the relationship between fiscal interest and bank regulation throughout the country.

24. The discussion of Pennsylvania banking is based on Schwartz 1987, 6–15.

25. Handlin and Handlin 1969, 120. The discussion of Massachusetts is based on Handlin and Handlin 1969, 113–121; and Dodd 1936, 201–18.

26. Seavoy 1982, 91. The discussion of New York is based on pages 81–148.

27. When Massachusetts finally adopted a formal free banking law in 1851, no new banks were created.

28. For an extensive sampling of the anticorporation literature in Massachusetts, see Maier 1993, 58–73.

29. Donald Stabile's book (1998) has a nice explanation of how the rule counting slaves as three-fifths of a person came about in the constitutional compromise over the allocation of representation and taxation. Would slaves be people, wealth, or both?

30. See Green's (1966) history of constitutional reform in the South and Williamson 1960.

31. A neat and compact summary of Benson's findings is contained in Benson 1961, chap. 15, 329–38: "Jacksonian Democracy: Concept or Fiction?"

32. Perhaps the most influential of the new political historians is Silbey (1991), who has written extensively on these questions. I have also found McCormick's essays (1986) to be enormously helpful.

33. Hammond 1957, 369–451.

34. This discussion of New Jersey is taken from Cadman 1949. The quote is from the *Emporium and True American* newspaper, January 23, 1830, as quoted in Cadman 1949, 54.

35. *Annual Reports of the State Treasurer,* in P. M. Tuttle, "History of Railroad Taxation in New Jersey," Ph.D. diss., Harvard University, 1920, 40 (typewritten manuscript held at the New Jersey State Library, cited in Cadman 1949, 401).

36. *Votes and Proceedings of the General Assembly,* 59, sess. 2 sitting (1835), 223, as quoted by Cadman (1949, 58), italics in the original.

37. "The vilification heaped on New Jersey by the press and public of other states, the efforts of other New Jersey railroad groups to break the monopoly, the ardent campaign of the Whig press of the state, and persistent and spirited opposition from such prominent New Jersey residents as the economist Henry C. Carey were unavailing" (Cadman 1949, 59).

38. Benson 1961, 95–96. There is a great deal of confusion in party names during this period. Seavoy refers to Van Buren's party as the Republican Party. Benson refers to it as the Democratic Party. I will try to keep the two

straight. For our purposes here, the two main parties were Whigs and De-mocratic/Republicans.

39. Here is how Benson (1961, 80–81) puts the point: "After Jackson's Bank veto message in 1832, and particularly after 1837, when Martin Van Buren awoke to the political possibility of Locofocoism. . . . Democratic rhetoric was designed to sound something like class war. One Whig response to that rhetoric was to portray the Democrats as 'desperate and revolution-ary enemies of Law and Order' who would impose 'agrarian and destructive legislation' and bring about 'popular demoralization, ruin and revolution. . . .' But class war rhetoric need not reflect reality. In fact, it has frequently been used to conceal rather than to reveal the socioeconomic status and political objectives of those who use it. Moreover, it cannot be automatically assumed that class war rhetoric actually influenced political reality and changed the so-cial structure of political leadership."

40. Manufacturing firms had always used incorporation, but stock was not widely traded in impersonal markets until the 1880s.

41. See Grandy 1989, 682. The discussion of New Jersey is based on Grandy 1989; Nelson 1959; Lamoreaux 1985; and Dodd 1954.

42. See Nelson 1959, 76, table 37, and the discussion on pages 64–70.

43. The bulk of the discussion is based on Hurst 1970, 147–52.

References

Angell, Joseph K., and Samuel Ames. [1832] 1972. *A Treatise of the Law of Private Corporations Aggregate.* New York: Arno.

Bailyn, Bernard. 1967. *The Ideological Origins of the American Revolution.* Cambridge: Harvard University Press.

Banning, Lance. 1978. *The Jeffersonian Persuasion.* Ithaca: Cornell University Press.

Benson, Lee. 1961. *The Concept of Jacksonian Democracy: New York as a Test Case.* Princeton: Princeton University Press.

Brewer, John. 1990. *The Sinews of Power: War, Money, and the English State, 1688–1783.* Cambridge: Harvard University Press.

Cadman, John W. 1949. *The Corporation in New Jersey: Business and Politics, 1791–1875.* Cambridge: Harvard University Press.

Cole, Arthur. 1970. "The Committee on Research in Economic History: An Historical Sketch." *Journal of Economic History* 30 (4): 723–41.

Davis, John P. 1961. *Corporations: A Study of the Origin and Development of Great Business Combinations and of Their Relation to the Authority of the State.* New York: Capricorn.

Dodd, Edwin Merrick. 1936. "Statutory Developments in Business Corpora-tion Law, 1886–1936." *Harvard Law Review* 50:27–59.

———. 1954. *American Business Corporations until 1860, with Special Ref-erence to Massachusetts.* Cambridge: Harvard University Press.

Evans, George Heberton. 1948. *Business Incorporations in the United States, 1800–1943.* Baltimore: Waverly.

Gilbart, James W. [1837] 1967. *The History of American Banking.* New York: Augustus M. Kelley.

Goodrich, Carter. 1960. *Government Promotion of American Canals and Railroads.* New York: Columbia University Press.

Grandy, Christopher. 1989. "New Jersey Corporate Chartermongering, 1875–1929." *Journal of Economic History* 44 (September): 677–92.

Green, Fletcher M. 1966. *Constitutional Development in the South Atlantic States, 1776–1860.* New York: Norton.

Hammond, Bray. 1957. *Banks and Politics in America from the Revolution to the Civil War.* Princeton: Princeton University Press.

Handlin, Oscar, and Mary Flug Handlin. 1969. *Commonwealth: A Study of the Role of Government in the American Economy, Massachusetts, 1774–1861.* Cambridge: Harvard University Press.

Hartz, Louis. 1948. *Economic Policy and Democratic Thought: Pennsylvania, 1776–1860.* Chicago: Quadrangle.

Hurst, James Willard. 1970. *The Legitimacy of the Business Corporation in the Law of the United States, 1780–1970.* Charlottesville: University of Virginia Press.

Kessler, W. C. 1940. "A Statistical Study of the New York General Incorporation Act of 1811." *Journal of Political Economy* 48 (6): 877–82.

Lamoreaux, Naomi R. 1985. *The Great Merger Movement in American Business, 1895–1904.* New York: Cambridge University Press.

McCormick, Richard L. 1986. *The Party Period and Public Policy.* New York: Oxford University Press.

McCoy, Drew R. 1980. *The Elusive Republic: Political Economy in Jeffersonian America.* Chapel Hill: University of North Carolina Press.

McGuire, M. C., and M. L. Olson. 1996. "The Economics of Autocracy and Majority Rule: The Invisible Hand and the Use of Force." *Journal of Economic Literature* 34, no. 1 (March): 79–96.

Maier, Pauline. 1972. *From Resistance to Revolution.* New York: Norton.

———. 1992. "The Debate over Incorporations: Massachusetts in the Early Republic." In *Massachusetts and the New Nation,* edited by Conrad Wright. Boston: Massachusetts Historical Society.

———. 1993. "The Revolutionary Origins of the American Corporation." *William and Mary Quarterly,* 3d ser., 50:51–84.

Nelson, Ralph L. 1959. *Merger Movements in American Industry, 1895–1956.* Princeton: Princeton University Press.

North, Douglass C. 1981. *Structure and Change in Economic History.* New York: Norton.

Olson, Mancur. 1965. *The Logic of Collective Action.* Cambridge: Harvard University Press.

———. 1982. *The Rise and Decline of Nations.* New Haven: Yale University Press.

———. 1993. "Dictatorship, Democracy, and Development." *American Political Science Review* 87:567–76.

Pocock, J. G. A. 1975. *The Machiavellian Moment.* Princeton: Princeton University Press.

Primm, James Neal. 1954. *Economic Policy in the Development of a Western State: Missouri, 1820–1860.* Cambridge: Harvard University Press.

Rockoff, Hugh. 1974. "The Free Banking Era: A Reexamination." *Journal of Money, Credit, and Banking* 6 (2): 141–67.

Schlesinger, Arthur M. 1946. *The Age of Jackson.* Boston: Little, Brown.

Schwartz, Anna. 1987. "The Beginning of Competitive Banking in Philadelphia." In National Bureau of Economic Research, *Money in Historical Perspective.* Chicago: University of Chicago Press.

Seavoy, Ronald E. 1982. *The Origins of the American Business Corporation, 1784–1855: Broadening the Concept of Public Service during Industrialization.* Westport, CT: Greenwood.

Sellers, Charles. 1991. *The Market Revolution: Jacksonian America, 1815–1846.* New York: Oxford University Press.

Silbey, Joel H. 1991. *The American Political Nation.* Stanford: Stanford University Press.

Stabile, Donald. 1998. *The Origins of American Public Finance: Debates over Money, Debt, and Taxes in the Constitutional Era, 1776–1836.* Westport, CT: Greenwood.

Sylla, Richard. 1969. "Federal Policy, Banking Market Structure, and Capital Mobilization in the United States, 1863–1913." *Journal of Economic History* 29 (December): 657–86.

———. 1975. *American Capital Markets, 1846–1914.* New York: Arno.

———. 1985. "Early American Banking: The Significance of the Corporate Form." *Business and Economic History,* 2d ser., 14:105–23.

———. 1998. "U.S. Securities Markets and the Banking System, 1790–1840." *Federal Reserve Bank of St. Louis Review* 80 (May–June): 83–98.

Tuttle, P. M. 1920. "History of Railroad Taxation in New Jersey." Ph.D. diss., Harvard University.

U.S. Bureau of the Census. 1975. *Historical Statistics of the United States: Colonial Times to 1970.* Washington, DC: U.S. Bureau of the Census.

Wallis, John Joseph, Richard Sylla, and John Legler. 1994. "The Interaction of Taxation and Regulation in Nineteenth Century Banking." In *The Regulated Economy: A Historical Approach to Political Economy,* edited by Claudia Goldin and Gary Libecap. Chicago: University of Chicago Press.

Williamson, Chilton. 1960. *American Suffrage: From Property to Democracy, 1760–1860.* Princeton: Princeton University Press.

Wood, Gordon S. 1969. *Creation of the American Republic.* Chapel Hill: University of North Carolina Press.

———. 1992. *Radicalism of the American Revolution.* New York: Knopf.

Comment

Robert S. Summers

Professor Wallis's main conclusion appears in section 8 of his stimulating essay. There he concludes that the U.S. experience with state incorporation policies was a clear case of market-augmenting government. In particular, he stresses that state governments developed and
commissioned the corporate form, incorporation developed banking,
and banking developed financial markets—which in turn further accelerated the development of large manufacturing firms with easy access to capital through growing equity markets.

But Wallis's paper also addresses the reforms of laws on incorporation that took place during the nineteenth century and later. The
reformist movement—from what one might call open-ended incorporation laws (catering to special interests) to incorporation laws cast
in the form of general rules—was itself a salutary development that
augmented markets even more. Developing countries today are concerned with what kind of incorporation law to adopt. It would be interesting to hear Wallis's prescriptions of a model law. What would its
main features be? What would he certainly not allow?

At the end of his essay, Wallis poses the question: why did state
governments adopt the incorporation policies they did? The question
might be targeted more specifically: why did these governments
move to a *reformed* incorporation law expressed in *general rules?*
With the question thus rephrased, would Wallis still stress the form of
the fiscal interest of states as the prime explanatory factor?

Wallis does agree with North that "we need a model of ideology,
or of mental models, in order to understand how institutions [such as
corporations and corporate laws] evolve over time." He points out that
he has tried in his essay "to demonstrate how commonly held beliefs
about the legitimacy of incorporation affected government policy." The
values and principles of the rule of law surely qualify as a "model of
ideology, or of mental models," and this set of values and principles
should probably be credited with a greater role than Wallis seems to
allow in explaining the reformist development of incorporation laws.

266

First of all, can these laws really be called laws at all? Many of the early incorporation "laws" conflicted sharply with major principles and values of the rule of law. Whatever a legislature adopts is not necessarily, in concept, a genuine law. A so-called law on incorporation that allows a legislature or an executive official or agency to do whatever happens to serve its interests, and to do so quite inconsistently from case to case without any binding criteria for decision making whatsoever, certainly strains our fundamental conception of what a law is.

Second, the principles and values of the rule of law presumptively favor framing the law in the form of general rules. Most of the early incorporation laws appear to have failed this criterion. Lawmakers, when required to put their law in the form of rules, are forced to think through the generalized application of any proposed disposition of a case. The defects of a policy can seldom be more starkly seen than when drafted in fully generalized form, whereby beneficial disposition of a special interest is extended to all like cases. The early incorporation laws were not of this nature, and they were administered, apparently, quite arbitrarily.

I am puzzled by the statement that "it is difficult to associate ideology with changes in policy." Admittedly, it is hard to know *how much* of a role principles of the rule of law played in the reform movement, but a role for these principles cannot be dismissed in the overall change from an unlawlike regime to a much more lawlike one.

Several points of relevance emerge for the issue of reform in developing countries. First, it is important to address issues of organization, particularly the organization of economic units such as corporations. Second, it is a mistake to combine the chartering process with the regulation of corporations. Third, developing countries should acquaint themselves not only with the discipline of framing all laws in the form of general rules but with *all* of the principles and values of the rule of law.

Finally, while developing countries need to be aware of the vices of monopolies, crony capitalism, and white collar corruption, they must not at the same time lose all regard for private corporate entities as a group. The exercises of a few will always taint the whole; far from being viewed as a salutary force, such private entities may in some of these countries come to be viewed, in the vivid words of Thomas Hobbes, as " 'mere' worms within the entrails of the body politic."

Global Challenges and the Need for Supranational Infrastructure

Todd Sandler

Dating back to Adam Smith, economists have recognized that a well-functioning market system needs some government-provided activities to provide a just system, laws, national defense, and public goods (e.g., roads, schools, police). Many of these government activities represent the infrastructure, or basic framework, underlying the operation of markets, where traders voluntarily exchange their property rights to goods and services in their pursuit of mutual gains. Laws, police forces, and courts, for example, provide for the protection and enforcement of property rights, without which market transactions would be severely limited (see, e.g., Demsetz 1964 and Pejovich 1990). Why purchase or provide a commodity if the control over its benefits cannot be decided by the purchaser or provider? When property rights are incompletely assured to the provider, the good is often underproduced and suboptimal resource allocation results. Pure public goods, which possess nonexcludable and nonrival benefits,[1] are often underprovided (Bator 1958), insofar as individuals have an incentive either not to pay or to underpay for the goods, thus taking a "free ride" or an easy ride on the amounts contributed by others.

In a provocative essay, "Big Bills Left on the Sidewalk: Why Some Nations Are Rich and Others Poor," Mancur Olson (1996) attributes the poverty of nations to ill-conceived institutions and policies rather than to a lack of resources. These poorly designed institutions and policies yield the wrong incentives to economic agents, whose actions therefore fail to further the well-being of the economy. According to Olson (1996), the improvement of these policies and institutions through better governance can lead to the big bills on the sidewalk being real—the possibility of achieving social welfare gains. Market-augmenting governance is a policy that can improve social welfare by allowing prices and profits to signal correctly the direction of resource allocation (Azfar and Cadwell, this volume). Social infrastructure, along the lines of Adam Smith's roles for government, consists of activities and institutions that increase social welfare by enhancing market transactions. This infrastructure serves as a public input that can enhance the production and trading activities in the public and private sector.[2]

The notion of market-augmenting governance also applies at the supranational level, where nations and/or multilateral agents (e.g., multilateral firms) are participants in exchanges. The world today is besieged by market failures at the transnational level. These failures involve the provision of public goods (e.g., curbing global warming, maintaining world peace, and stemming acid rain), the correction of externalities (e.g., controlling organized crime), and the enforcement of property rights. If the global community is to address these market failures adequately, then some kinds of supranational infrastructure are required to facilitate the appropriate correction. Even when international market exchanges do occur, the underlying conditions that enforce and protect property rights must be in place at the supranational level. The provision of this infrastructure (e.g., an enforcement mechanism for contracts) poses greater obstacles at the supranational than the national level. In the latter, subnational governmental units institutionally accept that they must subjugate their authority on some issues to a central government that attempts to correct market failures. At the supranational level, however, nations vigorously guard their autonomy and are loath to subordinate their revenue collecting, policy-making, or security operations to a higher authority. The world today still consists of nations that try to remain autonomous over most of their exchanges (Kindleberger 1986; Sandler 1997).

The provision of supranational infrastructure and policies faces some serious challenges. Often incentives for voluntarily providing this infrastructure are perverse in terms of free-riding difficulties, in which a nation is better off if it can limit its contributions and rely on those of others (Olson 1965). For some global contingencies, a large number of participants are needed, and this critical mass requirement may inhibit collective action (Dixit and Olson 2000; Hardin 1982; Marwell and Oliver 1993; Olson 1965; Sandler 1992). In still other scenarios, there may exist both winners and losers from the provision of some forms of supranational infrastructure, and these losers will surely oppose provision. The transaction costs associated with achieving agreement on supranational infrastructure are apt to be high, thus further inhibiting successful bargaining regarding provision (Dixit 1996; Dixit and Olson 2000; Sandler 1997). Asymmetries abound in terms of the provision of supranational infrastructure, making it difficult to reach a consensus, as nations differ in terms of their endowments, status, and information. For instance, information asymmetries between principals (e.g., nations) and their agents (e.g., international organizations, which act to correct market failures) can give rise to agency costs.[3] These agency costs, required to motivate risk sharing between the agent and principals, represent transaction costs that can result in third-best, or worse, outcomes.[4]

The primary purpose of this essay is to analyze market-augmenting *and* market-failure-correcting policies in the form of supranational infrastructure. (I include here some infrastructural emendations that are not directly market augmenting, although they may indirectly create favorable conditions for markets to operate—e.g., bringing peace to an unstable region can promote capital inflows.) The essay identifies and clarifies the factors that inhibit this provision at the transnational level and suggests the means for fostering provision of supranational infrastructure. In some areas, such as shipping, telecommunications, postal services, and air travel, the required infrastructure has naturally developed in the form of conventions and allocative mechanisms (Zacher 1996); hence, favorable environmental factors can assist some types of supranational infrastructure.[5]

The essay is intended as a conceptual exercise to highlight the need for supranational infrastructure in an increasingly interconnected world of sovereign states. Regions of the world that are more effective at instituting market- and efficiency-enhancing policies regarding transnational infrastructure fare better than other regions. Olson's (1996) message with respect to the relative difference between nations' growth and prosperity can clearly be applied to regional groupings of nations.

I. Global Challenges: Markets and Market Failures

On Markets and Market-Augmenting Infrastructure

Although there has been a growing disparity between the income levels of the richest countries and poorest countries,[6] a number of less developed countries—particularly in Asia—have greatly improved their well-being (Jones 1997; Azfar 1999). These emerging-market economies have added to the world's growth of markets. The breakup of the Soviet Union and its client states, in their ongoing transition to more market-based economies, have bolstered the trend to a greater reliance on markets worldwide in recent years. The relaxation of some trade restrictions has also reinforced this trend by allowing for freer international exchanges of goods, services, and capital.

Moreover, the end of the Cold War has reduced some security uncertainties, thereby leading to a significant decline in defense spending. For example, North Atlantic Treaty Organization (NATO) allies allocated approximately 5.0 percent of gross domestic product (GDP) to defense in the 1980s, while these same nations spent only 2.7 percent of GDP on defense in 1997 (NATO Office of Information and Press 1995, 359, table 3; NATO 1997). Similar downward trends apply to most parts of the world (Arms Control and Disarmament Agency 1997). Since government distortions (e.g., subsidies to defense research and development) and monopoly elements characterize the defense industry (Sandler and Hartley 1999), the significant declines in defense spending and procurement also support the recent growth of markets.

If this international growth of markets is to achieve its full potential impact on the world's social welfare, infrastructure at the transnational level is needed to facilitate these market transactions. A number of crucial pieces of infrastructure, however, are still missing at the international level, and their absence limits efficiency gains. Better means for enforcing property rights to intellectual goods—an element of market-augmenting infrastructure—are needed if such goods are not to be underproduced. Currently, those countries that are the greatest producers of intellectual goods—computer programs, books, movies, compact discs—are understandably the ones that are pushing the hardest for more uniform enforcement of intellectual property rights worldwide, but these countries' efforts have not always been either effective or coordinated. The protection of these property rights poses a challenging collective action problem because there would be both winners (those who create the intellectual goods) and losers (e.g., those who pirate them).[7] The underprovision of such goods not only hurts the current generation through suboptimal production, but it also harms future generations that may not inherit potential discoveries. In fact, intellectual goods will always be underproduced from an intergenerational perspective insofar as the gains conferred on future generations, particularly distant ones, cannot really be appropriated owing to the sequencing of generations (see, e.g., Bromley 1989 and Doeleman and Sandler 1998). The practice of discounting future benefits means that few actual benefits are assigned to future generations even when their benefits are recognized by a generation in the process of providing an intergenerational public good or input.[8] Altruism offsets this tendency, if the altruistic generation does not apply a discount factor to spillover benefits conferred on future generations from a public asset produced today. Nevertheless, mechanisms and conventions to protect these intellectual goods transnationally can do much to promote efficiency, even though a first best remains unattainable.

At the international level, another market-promoting infrastructure is a set of standards of contracts, founded on accepted principles of contract law. In particular, transitional and emerging-market economies must adopt contractual standards modeled after those in the developed world if they are to protect property rights in a sufficiently unambiguous manner. This is probably a self-correcting problem because it is in these countries' self-interest to abide by accepted standards even when this means sacrificing some autonomy in framing these standards. A related infrastructure concern, which poses potential difficulties in today's environment of multinational actors and multilateral exchanges, involves where a party takes a case to be adjudicated when contract disputes arise. If a party can choose the venue or country where the case is heard, then the party can exercise a strategic advantage (e.g., electing to hold the trial in the country farthest away from the other party or else making its base where laws are favorable to its interests). To get more uniform judgments and limit such strategic behavior, an international network of courts should be instituted, devoted to property rights disputes among non-state agents engaged in multilateral exchanges. The World Court and World Trade Organization settle disputes only between nation-states and are *not* open to firms or private individuals who must resolve contract disputes involving interests and exchanges in two or more countries.

A third required market-augmenting infrastructure involves coordinated efforts to control international networks of organized crime, a growing problem today. Organized crime reduces the importance of property rights and also creates instabilities and uncertainties, which can distort the flow of capital and keep capital returns from equalizing across countries, thereby distorting capital efficiency. Faced with differing standards of enforcement, organized crime (e.g., the Russian "mafia") will locate in those places with the lowest enforcement standard, posing a threat to the interests of both foreigners and citizens of the host country. If an organized crime network targets the property of foreign nationals living in the host country, there is apt to be underdeterrence by the local police, who are more concerned with the lives and property of citizens. If, however, the crime network poses a significant threat to the host country's interests (e.g., tourism or foreign direct investment), there may result an overdeterrence that causes the criminals to move to a neighboring country.[9] Overdeterrence results because the externality imposed on the neighboring country, as the criminals set up shop elsewhere, is not taken into account by the deterrence decision. An international police force to battle such crime networks constitutes a market-augmenting policy that limits market-distorting influences on property rights but one that is very difficult to achieve as nations are reticent to sacrifice their autonomy over any internal security and policing matters to an international authority. Interpol is a feeble effort to coordinate law enforcement internationally, and, except for coordinating information, it has not met with much success.

A fourth market-augmenting infrastructure requirement involves controlling financial market instability that can resonate throughout the world, such that the collapse of a Japanese bank can cause large stock market gyrations half a globe away. The increased integration of financial markets in recent years inevitably means that market instabilities in one location can spill over to markets worldwide (Lanyi and Lee, this volume). To limit these instabilities, economies worldwide must adopt sound and uniform standards of banking, accounting, and investment practices. Many of these practices have been instituted in the industrial countries in response to speculative crashes in the past, and they should be adopted also by the transitional and emerging-market economies. For example, stock markets worldwide may want to institute "safety valves" to halt trading on volatile days, not unlike those imposed by Wall Street after Black Monday in October 1987. The institution of improved financial practices worldwide represents a collective action problem, as nations evaluate the trade-off between the sacrifice of their autonomy and the increased stability and trade associated with instituting sounder and more uniform financial practices. Nevertheless, because it is in the interests of these emerging-market economies to institute these financial practices, and because the consequent loss of autonomy is not great, the prognosis is good that such uniform practices will be adopted. The favorable conditions that have promoted uniform conventions in shipping and aviation (see sec. II) also apply to sound financial practices. Even autocrats have incentives to institute these practices to attract capital and increase economic activities from which they can extract taxes. A more difficult collective action dilemma arises when some international authority must be created to monitor and ensure compliance with these practices because nations worry about enacting sanctions that may later be applied to them. Additionally, the creation of this authority creates purely public benefits that induce free riding (Heckathorn 1989).

Market Failures

In recent years, a host of environmental challenges have involved the stratosphere, the troposphere, the land, the rivers, and the seas (see Heal, this volume). Economic activities in one nation can transcend borders and have adverse consequences on nations not party to the transaction. Thus, the emissions of sulfur and nitrogen oxides from burning fossil fuels and driving vehicles can produce acid rain that may fall in downwind countries. Some emissions disperse so widely as to result in global spillovers—for example, the release of greenhouse gases (GHGs) warms the atmosphere and may have significant climatic consequences. Similarly, the emission of chlorofluorocarbons (CFCs) has thinned the stratospheric ozone layer, thus exposing living things worldwide to heightened levels of ultraviolet radiation. Actions by countries to exploit their natural assets can also affect people globally—for example, tropical deforestation's impact on biodiversity.[10]

Market failures of a public-good or externality character occur in other areas as well. In the health area, the identification and monitoring of new diseases can benefit people everywhere. When a cure to a disease is found, this cure provides benefits to the current and all future generations. Such a cure is surely an intergenerational global public good and, as such, is likely to be underprovided. Preventing the spread of diseases and pests is an instance of a transnational public good, which, without international coordination, is destined to be provided in a suboptimal fashion. Crisis management and other security concerns can also present market failures in terms of externalities at the transnational level and thus require some form of supranational infrastructure to avoid a misallocation of resources. Unstable regions of the world that acquire weapons of mass destruction (WMDs) create externalities in terms of heightened risks and harmful spillovers from biological, chemical, or nuclear releases. The free flow of capital and other resources may then be inhibited by these arms escalations. The Nuclear Nonproliferation Treaty, the Biological Weapons Convention, and the Chemical Weapons Convention represent the international community's response to this WMD threat (Sandler and Hartley 1999, chap. 1); however, the nuclear weapon tests in India and Pakistan of May 1998 underscore the ineffectiveness of these treaties. Yet another security matter concerns the impact of ethnic conflicts on regional and global security and stability. The supranational infrastructure designed to address these security challenges is the United Nations peacekeeping forces; however, the tremendous expansion of UN peacekeeping missions in recent years has stretched UN capabilities to the limit. During the first four decades of the UN there were fourteen missions, while during 1988–97 there were thirty-three new missions (Sandler and Hartley 1999; United Nations Department of Public Information 1996). In Bosnia, the UN had to eventually turn this complex mission over to NATO's superior forces because UN resources were overextended. In March 1999, NATO, not the UN, intervened to end ethnic cleansing in Kosovo and institute a peace agreement.

These examples represent a rich array of market failures plaguing the world today. A common response to such contingencies is for the global community to frame a treaty that recognizes the problem and pledges the ratifiers to take some kind of action—for example, the Montreal protocol on limiting ozone-depleting substances and Helsinki protocol on reducing sulfur emissions in Europe. An important question is whether these treaties and other responses by the international community intended to correct market failures represent an adequate supranational infrastructure.

II. Supranational Infrastructure

Supranational infrastructure consists of institutions, norms, conventions, or activities that facilitate market transactions and/or alleviate market failures at the transnational level. This infrastructure may be local, as between neighboring countries, or regional or even global in scope. Infrastructure supporting market transactions includes standards for writing and enforcing contracts and norms for regulating transportation and communications. Supranational infrastructure intended to address market failures consists of agreements, enforcement mechanisms, institutions for coordinating actions, and means for carrying out policy initiatives.

Considerable progress has been made in providing market-augmenting infrastructure. International trade requires infrastructure in the form of transportation and communication networks[11] Such networks must address a number of collective action issues: interoperability or interconnectedness, accidents and mishaps, jurisdictional rights, and competitive practices (Zacher 1996). In international shipping, the International Maritime Organization oversees international trade and institutes conventions on accidents and accident prevention, innocent passage, pollution, and other concerns. The International Civil Aviation Organization enacts regulations to promote air traffic flows and increase safety in the skies. For telecommunications, the International Telecommunication Union (ITU) establishes practices to curb signal interference and allocates the frequency bands of the electromagnetic spectrum to various specific purposes. In addition, the ITU promotes the adoption of standardized equipment. The Universal Postal Union enacts regulations that facilitate the free flow of mail and limits damage to international mail. In recent years, countries have cooperated in an effort to curb monopoly power in the air travel, telecommunications, and shipping industries.

The successful creation of these infrastructure mechanisms raises two crucial questions. Why has collective action worked for these supranational structures? Can these favorable influences be encouraged in areas where the needed infrastructure has not been forthcoming? A significant factor inducing nations to establish these international institutions and to submit to their regulations involves *mutual self-interest* in achieving the free flow of trade and communication among countries (Zacher 1996). Although nations must sacrifice some autonomy over commerce and communications by satisfying these regulations, the true loss of autonomy is modest, so that the gain from the conventions does not have to be large to still provide each nation with a net gain. Indeed, these conventions have more to do with restricting the actions of *firms and individuals* than with restricting the autonomy of the participating *governments*. By instituting common practices, these international regimes limited the transaction costs in addressing trade and communication impediments and so provided significant gains to participants. Moreover, since most nations already have similar regulations at home (e.g., allocating frequencies among alternative uses and procedures to avoid accidents at sea), the adoption of standardized practices did not mark much of a departure from the status quo.

Another supporting factor is the underlying game structure associated with adopting standardized practices. The adoption of standards represents a *coordination* game structure, which, unlike Prisoner's Dilemma, does *not* have a dominant strategy of defection that provides greater payoffs regardless of the actions of others (see, e.g., Binmore 1992; Farrell 1987; and Sandler 1992). If there are only two players, each is better off by adopting a single standard, even if it is not his or her own (which would give the greatest payoff).[12] When there are *n* players deciding a standard, each player can still gain by adopting a *single* standard regardless of whose it is. This follows because the choice of multiple standards leads to lower payoffs for everyone than those associated with the *n* equilibria where a single standard is chosen.[13] The basic problem that arises is *how to coordinate* so that a single standard may be picked. The role of an international institution is to focus attention on whichever standard appears best in terms of total payoff. If several standards offer an equivalent payoff, then the international institution must arbitrarily focus on one of them in order to facilitate negotiation (see the ensuing discussion on correlated equilibrium).

Collective action has worked in providing the necessary transnational infrastructure for telecommunications and transportation because nations all stood to gain and (in contrast to transnational externalities such as global warming) unilateral defection would not benefit the defector. Perceived payoffs promoted instituting and maintaining cooperation. Furthermore, the necessary coordination was essentially an extension of the kinds of behavior that were already in place at the national level in most countries. This was particularly true of the major industrial countries, which played an important leadership role in instituting these international organizations.[14] Transaction costs were limited and the loss of national autonomy modest. If similar institutions are to be erected to facilitate other aspects of transnational trade and communications among nations, then similar underlying factors must be encouraged, which is not always possible. For example, controlling the arms trade can adversely influence the arms-trading countries, so that, unless they are compensated for their trade losses, they will not participate in directives restricting this trade and will covertly undermine the efforts of others.

Significant collective action challenges characterize the provision of infrastructure to address market failures at the supranational level. For illustration, consider the use of treaties, a common practice for dealing with environmental challenges. Typically, a transnational externality must first be identified. Once its cause is understood and its consequences are judged sufficiently severe, countries will convene a meeting to frame a convention, which recognizes a potential problem and sets in motion efforts to evaluate it. If, as in the case of ozone-depleting substances, the problem is later seen to be real and to merit collective action, then a protocol is framed that pledges the ratifiers to act to alleviate the problem. Subsequent amendments and protocols can follow if further actions are warranted.[15]

These protocols do little to provide for enforcement at the transnational level, requiring instead that countries do their own enforcement. If ratifying countries fail to live up to their commitments, negative world opinion is the typical punishment. Real enforcement would require that countries put in place a mechanism that can be used against them when they fail to achieve a treaty's stipulations. Such a mechanism threatens ratifiers' autonomy and would be costly to institute. Heckathorn (1989) notes that most collective action problems present two possibilities for free riding: at the agreement stage and the enforcement stage. The enforcement stage provides less incentive to potential participants, on average, to overcome the free-rider problem.

Even successful treaties, such as the Montreal protocol, experience enforcement problems that may require some form of supranational infrastructure. At the nation-state level, the overwhelming majority of countries have imposed steep taxes on CFCs and other measures to foster the switchover to more benign substitutes; nevertheless, cheating has occurred at the individual level. The smuggling of CFCs into the United States in recent years may be second only to cocaine (Economist 1997, 48). To eliminate this challenge, the Montreal protocol relies on ratifiers' own customs officials to control smuggling at home; these officials do not, however, have the authority or means to go after the source of supply abroad. Furthermore, these officials may be ill-equipped to address the level of smuggling. Some form of international enforcement is needed, again raising issues about winners (countries hosting smugglers) and losers (all other countries) as well as the infringement of a nation's autonomy.

Treaty formation is a slow process, which, with the help of some infrastructure, could be streamlined. A good deal of time is taken up with, first, recognizing a contingency and, second, studying it, before a protocol stipulates actions to be taken. Global and regional coordination would be a lot quicker if the global community could permanently maintain a body of scientists, social scientists, statisticians, and medical experts to evaluate pending environmental and other concerns. Such a body would be comparatively inexpensive but could save the world community billions or more in facilitating faster and more decisive action when warranted. Such an infrastructure would only provide information for treaty making and would not constrain nations' participation decisions regarding supranational agreements. The Intergovernmental Panel of Climatic Change (IPCC) is serving such a role for global warming, while a proposed Intergovernmental Panel on Biodiversity, modeled after IPCC, would serve a similar role for species preservation. My proposal would go beyond these specific responses by instituting a broad-based permanent body of experts who would continually monitor supranational contingencies. By eliminating the need to create problem-specific panels, it would allow for faster action. Quicker action may mean that nations will have to do less than when a problem has been longer term, and this smaller commitment also favors reaching an agreement.

Another supranational infrastructure requirement involves finding financing for projects supporting the expansion of international markets or the correction of market failures. To date, this financing has taken the form of membership fees and assessments paid to international organizations. Thus, the United Nations charges its members assigned shares of the cost of peacekeeping operations, whereas the International Monetary Fund assigns quotas to its members, creating a pool of resources that can be drawn upon by member countries with balance of payments problems. Funding requirements are currently tied to institutions addressing specific concerns; there is no general fund financing based on income or indirect taxes. When nations impose taxes to control a transboundary externality, the proceeds go to the collecting country and may not necessarily be used to alleviate the problem. The difficulty of generating revenues at the supranational level inhibits the provision of infrastructure.

Correlating Strategies as a Supranational Infrastructure: A Novel Proposal

The provision of public goods, including supranational infrastructure, can involve diverse game structures. In the case of standards, we have seen that a coordination game structure with multiple Nash equilibria applies, while the provision of an enforcement mechanism involves a Prisoner's Dilemma. When multiple Nash equilibria occur, a central authority that can *correlate* the strategic choices of the agents can improve expected payoffs. In so doing, such correlation mechanisms can themselves be viewed as a form of supranational infrastructure for addressing market failures.[16]

To illustrate, consider a public good that abides by a best-shot technology for aggregating contributions (e.g., curing a disease). Suppose that each of two countries (A and B) can contribute either one or no units of the public good and that only the first unit contributed gives a benefit of 6 to both countries, at a cost of 3 to the provider. (The second unit gives a benefit of zero, for the same cost.) In the game matrix of figure 1, A is the row player and B is the column player. If a single country contributes, it receives a net payoff of 3 (when costs of 3 are deducted from the benefits of 6), while the noncontributor gets the free-rider payoff of 6. If neither nation contributes, payoffs are zero; if, however, both contribute, each receives 3 ($= 6 - 3$). There are two pure-strategy Nash equilibria, located at cells b and c, where just one nation contributes. The trick is to find a way to coordinate which country takes the action and which sits back. If a mixed-strategy equilibrium is employed, where nation A (B) contributes p (q) percent of the time and does not contribute $1 - p$ ($1 - q$) percent of the time, then I can solve for the probabilities that make each nation indifferent between its strategies. In particular, I solve for the q and $1 - q$ for nation B that gives nation A the same expected payoffs from its two strategies. Similarly, I find p and $1 - p$ for nation A that gives nation B the same expected payoffs from its two strategies. These probabilities are $p = q = 1/2$ for the game depicted. When this mixed strategy is used, each nation receives an expected payoff of 3.

Suppose that a coordinating apparatus randomizes between the strategy combinations in cells b and c with probabilities of 1/2, so that a probability of zero is attached to cells a and d. The resulting correlated equilibrium gives an expected payoff of 4.5 ($= 3/2 + 6/2$), a marked improvement over the uncorrelated mixed-strategy Nash equilibrium. When multiple Nash equilibria exist, correlated strategies may provide improved expected payoffs. The existence of a mechanism to coordinate actions when the players cannot be sure about the other players' actions can thus be a beneficial infrastructure for addressing some kinds of market failures. The entity doing the correlating can be a supranational institution or a third-party nation serving in a leadership capacity.

In other instances, a coordinating mechanism can institute contractual arrangements that take a game devoid of a dominant strategy, such as an assurance game, and transform it into one with a dominant

A's Strategy \ B's Strategy	Contribute	Don't Contribute	
Contribute	3, 3 $\quad a$	* 3, 6 $\quad b$	p
Don't Contribute	* 6, 3 $\quad c$	0, 0 $\quad d$	$1-p$
	q	$1-q$	

Fig. 1.   Best-shot assurance game

strategy. For an n-person assurance game with a threshold level of effort required before any benefits are received, Tabarrok (1998) has devised such a "dominant assurance contract" by offering compensation to players who contribute even though the minimal level of cooperation is not achieved. This contractual arrangement can promote sufficient contributions so that the compensation does not, in fact, have to be paid. If institutional arrangements are conceptualized as alternative game structures, then efforts to correlate strategies or to introduce action-promoting contracts constitute novel forms of supranational infrastructure. The same applies to actions that foster networking among nations confronting market failures.

III. Factors Inhibiting the Provision of Supranational Infrastructure

To understand how to promote supranational infrastructure, we must recognize factors that inhibit this infrastructure. If these impediments can be removed or circumvented, then progress can be achieved. For many supranational infrastructure scenarios, partial cooperation may be the likely outcome, when contributors are limited to those nations that place the greatest value on the activity. Partial cooperation can be problematic when the reactions of the noncooperators serve to offset the additional provision of the cooperators. Suppose that a set of nations puts forward a mechanism to control the arms trade with unstable, resource-rich regions as a means of reducing uncertainty and risks. If nonparticipants increase their arms production and sales,[17] then the welfare of the cooperators may be less than in the absence of cooperation, as the additional costs of the cooperation outweigh the resulting enhanced-security benefits. In a world of identical nations, crucial factors determining the desirability of partial cooperation would be the number of nonparticipants *and* their marginal reaction to an increase in the provision of infrastructure by the cooperators. The existence of a large number of nonparticipants with a large marginal reaction bodes ill for partial cooperation when actions of the nonparticipants can reduce the efforts of the cooperators (Buchholz, Haslbeck, and Sandler 1998). Of course, some forms of infrastructure provision cannot be reduced by nonparticipants. In the more realistic situation of heterogeneous nations, the *capacity* of the nonparticipants to offset or undo the cooperators' efforts, and not merely their numbers, is an essential consideration determining the success of partial cooperation. Thus, cooperative efforts by a few large nations to provide the required infrastructure may be sufficient, despite a large number of noncooperators.

Another inhibitor of supranational infrastructure concerns its time-profile of payoffs, involving large outlays of costs in the near term with benefits following much later. If the government official making the decision applies a high discount rate, then these longer run benefits must be quite substantial to give the decision maker a perceived net benefit from providing the infrastructure (see note 8). Countries with decision makers who have relatively shorter time horizons in office would be less inclined to support infrastructure projects with deferred benefits, as a high discount rate results from the short time horizon. There is some evidence that specific autocracies have on average shorter lengths of rule than democracies (Bienen and van der Valle 1989), and this consideration, if applicable, limits autocracies' support of some forms of supranational infrastructure. Insofar as this infrastructure may also siphon off tax revenues from an autocrat, who is interested primarily in maximizing these revenues, this diversion may also limit an autocrat's support (see, e.g., McGuire and Olson 1996).

Supranational infrastructure may also be hampered by large transaction costs, especially when large numbers of nations must be brought together. In the provision of a discrete public good, which must be of a certain size, Dixit and Olson (2000) demonstrate that even a small transaction cost may be sufficient to keep a group from bargaining to an optimal provision decision. Supranational infrastructure often comes in a discrete size, and their two-stage analysis, involving an agreement and a provision stage, is frequently applicable.

Moreover, the implication of partial cooperation is that a large number of participants may be needed to ensure that the providers of the infrastructure stand to gain.

Asymmetries may create further obstacles for supranational infrastructure intended to address market failures. An essential asymmetry is the distinction between winners and losers for some kinds of transnational infrastructure. For instance, the institution of transnational crisis management forces, designed to address incidents of unrest that could destabilize neighboring countries, may reduce the welfare of those countries that export revolutions abroad. Similarly, countries that anticipate a gain from an environmental contingency, such as global warming (Caplan, Ellis, and Silva 1998), may oppose efforts to facilitate treaty making that might ameliorate the problem. Asymmetries in countries' endowments and tastes can have both positive and negative consequences for the supply of supranational infrastructure. If one or two large nations reap sufficient benefits from providing some forms of infrastructure, they may single-handedly do so, like the U.S. Centers for Disease Control, or U.S. crisis management efforts on a number of occasions. If these same countries are relied upon too often, however, fatigue may set in, leading them to become unwilling to provide other forms of infrastructure at a later time. Another negative consequence may result if the provider designs the transnational infrastructure to serve its own national agenda. This hegemonic bias applied to the infrastructure can alienate countries from using it, thus limiting its purpose. Such criticisms have been leveled at the International Monetary Fund and the World Bank regarding a U.S. agenda. A strategic asymmetry may exist if one country or set of countries manages to move first in contributing to the infrastructure, thus turning the other countries into followers. This first-mover advantage allows the leader, which will be the large country, to shift more of the contribution burden onto the followers (Sandler 1992). Hence, when a large country does not underwrite the entire investment itself, it may exercise a strategic advantage to get other countries to assume a large share of the burden.

Asymmetric information may also be a factor. Some of the potential contributors to an infrastructure project may be informed about the benefits and costs of the proposed undertaking while others are not, thus leading to a strategic asymmetry. Asymmetric information may also arise with an international institution (e.g., the United Nations) established to provide the infrastructure, creating a common agency problem in which many principals (i.e., countries) must rely on the unobservable efforts of the agent institution. To motivate the agent to act properly, an incentive mechanism (entailing agency costs) must be designed, limiting first-best outcomes and paying the agent positive rents in good states.

IV. Means of Fostering Infrastructure Provision

In promoting the provision of supranational infrastructure, effective policy must recognize that nation-states place a high value on their autonomy. When the desired infrastructure permits the exclusion of nonpayers and provides monitoring of utilization rates, then a club arrangement can be instituted that preserves nations' autonomy and bases charges on benefits received. To illustrate, consider INTELSAT, a satellite communication network in geostationary orbit some 22,300 miles above the equator, carrying the vast majority of transoceanic messages, including television, telephone, and other transmissions.[18] The INTELSAT communication system represents a club good, since access to the network can be restricted by coding and scrambling signals and the network can be simultaneously used by its members. A properly designed toll internalizes the crowding externality (in terms of noise or interference) as an increased volume of signals share the same frequency band. For each unit of utilization (e.g., a minute of transmission), the per-unit toll is equated to the marginal congestion costs and is equal for all members. Members whose demands are greater utilize the network more frequently and pay more in total tolls. Toll proceeds can reimburse capital expenditures and fund upgrades to the system. When transnational infrastructure can be operated as a club, autonomous nations can support such infrastructure without the need of a supranational government. In fact, INTELSAT is a private consortium, with both firms and countries as members. LANDSAT, which is used for remote-sensing surveying, became a private enterprise after the U.S. government sold it to private interests. Thus, transnational infrastructure does not always have to be provided publicly, *especially when exclusion can be practiced.* Club arrangements fail for supranational infrastructure when nonpayers cannot be excluded from benefits, as for peacekeeping and global warming.

To avoid some of the influences of asymmetries, it is essential that supranational institutions not appear to be extensions of the richest nations. This means that fees must not be too concentrated on a few major nations. The political problems arising from perceptions of the capture of multinational institutions by a few rich countries can undermine their ability to provide global public goods. This insight is often ignored for real world institutions (e.g., the United Nations, the World Bank, or the International Monetary Fund). When, however, a few nations shoulder a disproportionate burden, these nations will push a national agenda in order to derive sufficient country-specific gains to justify their participation. In some cases (e.g., the World Bank), this asymmetric support is unavoidable because of the skewed distribution of world GDP. Nevertheless, if other moderate-sized economies could be made to do more, then this disproportionate support and the undesirable consequences that come from it can be curtailed. The asymmetric incentives of winners and losers, in certain kinds of infrastructure provision, can be countered through side payments to the losers. Finally, having an international institution coordinate contributions can at times eliminate first-mover advantages by making all actions by participants simultaneous.

An important procedure for curbing transaction costs is to maintain as much national autonomy as is feasible when designing an institution that provides infrastructure at the transnational level. Nations view losses to their autonomy as significant transaction costs of engaging in international cooperation. Limits on these "interdependency costs" can assist the emergence of an institution (Sandler 1997). As indicated earlier, clubs limit such losses of autonomy through a toll payment designed to increase the total fees of a participant who reveals a greater preference for the shared good through its utilization. Transaction costs are further held in check, and the institution is thus more likely to form, when the institution is kept loose with infrequent meetings, a large consensus decision rule and modest mandated fees. At times, transaction costs can be contained by using an established transnational organization to supply additional infrastructure requirements. This rationale is based on the sharing of common costs among two or more tasks, which, in turn, gives rise to economies of scope or a fall in the average cost per unit of an activity. Of course, eventually these economies of scope can be exhausted as additional infrastructure needs are served by the same organization.

From the study of public finance at the national level, we know that some means of collecting taxes or fees must be engineered to permit a supranational authority to finance a public input or good. For clubs, the revenues are the tolls; for international organizations, the revenues are either membership fees or special assessments. If members do not pay, then privileges can be curtailed or cut off. A treaty to curb pollutants usually relies on the ratifiers' abilities to impose taxes to curb pollutants. Some common funding may be mandated for administration of the treaty (e.g., the Multilateral Fund of the Montreal protocol), but such funding tends to be modest, so that the ratifiers' own taxing abilities are relied upon to meet treaty obligations. In the case of some transitional and emerging-market economies, however, the ability to collect taxes to provide the country's own infrastructure—let alone support supranational infrastructure—is very limited. For example, the Russian economy during the last few years has suffered, in part, from its inability to collect taxes. Other emerging-market economies face similar problems. A public finance system, which can collect revenues to finance public goods and social investment and to correct externalities, is a necessary infrastructure at both the national and transnational levels. As infrastructural needs at the transnational level grow over time, some transnational sources of funding are required. A likely approach might be to tax internationally traded items since countries that trade obtain the greatest advantage from a well-functioning market economy with market failures controlled. Any taxes on these traded goods should be levied against the more inelastic goods to minimize the excess burden.

The issue of partial cooperation also requires attention. A reasonable approach would be to entice the most important contributors on board, provided that their action can dwarf the collective response of noncontributors to undermine the cooperative action. To hold out until everyone joins might be very costly in terms of losses in efficiency and would give leverage to the remaining nonpartcipants to capture a large portion of efficiency gains (Dixit and Olson 2000).

Can redistributive taxes at the transnational level promote the provision of infrastructure with public-good properties? Suppose that this redistribution is from small to large contributor countries (assuming that a public finance mechanism at the transnational level exists that could direct this transfer). The neutrality theorem indicates that such a redistribution could not change the level of the infrastructure if it is purely public (Cornes and Sandler 1994, 1996). Next suppose that the tax is just imposed on the noncontributors, so that they are made to support the efforts of the contributors. In this scenario, purely public infrastructure can be increased in a *Pareto-optimal fashion* if there are a large number of noncontributors, a high marginal value for the infrastructure by the noncontributors, and a limited aggregate free-riding response by contributors to this change in the purely public infrastructure (Cornes and Sandler 1998). Thus, cooperation regarding infrastructure can be enhanced through taxes on noncontributors under some circumstances. When infrastructure is impurely public or possesses joint products, greater latitude for redistribution policies exists, but the welfare implications of these redistributions are unknown.

Since the provision of transnational infrastructure presents a classic collective action problem, Olson's (1965) remedies may also prove efficacious. First, selective incentives to some of the potential contributors can change their underlying pattern of payoffs so as to support contributing. In some instances, the presence of nation-specific payoffs may make supporting an infrastructure project a self-enforcing dominant strategy. Clearly, the promotion of infrastructure in some member states by the European Union (EU) has had significant country-specific payoffs (e.g., highways in Wales and the Republic of Ireland) while also providing some EU-wide benefits. Second, a federal structure may be useful, where the support of the infrastructure is begun at the regional level (where values are more homogeneous) before being extended more widely. These regional pieces of infrastructure can then be linked to provide a transnational orientation, not unlike the operation of national unions with their local chapters or the United Way with its local organizations.

Supranational structure has thus far been analyzed from a static vantage point. In the real world of international transactions, situations are fluid. Technology may create new forms of infrastructure or may influence the costs and benefits from instituting this infrastructure. Countries may break apart and new countries may form. Tastes of countries may change and so may leadership. Axelrod (1984) shows that cooperation may be achieved as an evolutionary process as high-payoff strategies are rewarded, so that the share of cooperators in the population increases. When this is the case, supranational infrastructure will have lower transactions costs and be easier to achieve. It is essential that any supranational infrastructure be reevaluated over time and updated when needed.[19]

V. Concluding Remarks

This essay analyzes the provision of infrastructure for improving market efficiency and correcting market failures at the transnational level. For telecommunications, postal services, and air travel, this infrastructure is primarily provided by international agencies because the required sacrifice in national autonomy is modest and participating nations receive a net gain from the infrastructure provided. When coordination is required, as in the adoption of industry standards, these international agencies can reduce uncertainty by focusing the nations on the action providing the largest payoff to the participants. This can be particularly useful when mixed strategies might be employed and/or multiple equilibria exist. Despite their successes, infrastructure for correcting market failures must clear significant hurdles imposed by high transaction costs (including the perceived loss of autonomy), partially cooperative responses, uncertainties, unfavorable incentive structures, and sundry asymmetries. Means of addressing some of these impediments are indicated. The collection of revenues to finance purely public infrastructure at the international level, with nonexcludable benefits, is, arguably, the greatest challenge that must be faced. Currently, international organizations and treaties rely on nations' internal taxes to provide fees and assessments and to tax activities with negative transnational externalities. At the transnational level, there is a need for some form of public finance that applies to international exchanges to underwrite transnational infrastructure designed to correct market failures.

If the international community gains insights into what has worked in the past when instituting other kinds of infrastructure, institutions can be designed to facilitate cooperation. Such designs must account for nations' reluctance to sacrifice autonomy, transaction costs, the underlying incentive structure, and the time-profile of benefits and costs. By altering incentive structures, institutional arrangements can do much to promote better collective outcomes. Transnational institutions must resist the inclination to become too integrated and, in so doing, to severely limit members' autonomy. If exclusion can be practiced, then clubs represent an institutional arrangement that can finance the infrastructure while preserving national autonomy. Informed policy-making at the transnational level in providing infrastructure can result in picking up the "big bills left on the sidewalk" and enhancing the wealth of the international community.

Notes

While assuming full responsibility for any remaining errors, I have profited from comments by Geoffrey Heal and Anthony Lanyi on an earlier draft.

1. On the definition and properties of public goods, see Cornes and Sandler 1996, 8–12 or Sandler 1992, 3–7.

2. An input is public if it enters two or more agents' production functions and yields production benefits that are nonrival and nonexcludable. Nonrivalry and nonexcludability may be full or partial. Social capital or infrastructure serves as a public input by increasing firms' outputs. On public inputs, see Manning, Markusen, and McMillan 1985 and McMillan 1979.

3. At other times, a country may be an agent for an international organization, as occurs when a country tries to fulfill commitments associated with an International Monetary Fund (IMF) loan.

4. Dixit (1996) characterizes economic policy-making as a common-agency problem, where two or more principals share one or more agents, who may possess information not available to the principals. Common-agency problems suffer from both agency costs and free-riding problems. The latter stem from the principals' incentive to pass the agency costs on to their counterparts.

5. This essay presents an economist's viewpoint of supranational infrastructure while taking account of some related contributions by political scientists. There is a vast literature in political science on international regimes in which the emphasis has been on power, as in the case of hegemonic stability theory (Keohane 1984). Others have examined the formation of these regimes in terms of mutually beneficial bargaining and/or leadership (see, e.g., Keohane 1984; Krasner 1983; and Young 1989). The current essay is interested rather in displaying the underlying game structure of regime building and the means of fostering incentives in such regimes. Additionally, the essay is specifically focused on supranational *infrastructure*, which is not the concern of much of the related political science literature.

6. Between 1960 and 1994, the richest fifth of all nations had their share of world income rise from 70 to 85.8 percent, while the poorest fifth of all nations had their share fall from 2.3 to 1.1 percent (United Nations Development Programme 1992; 1994, 35; 1998).

7. The portion of winners and losers can change over time. As poorer countries develop, there will be a greater number of winners from protecting intellectual property rights. It is important to remember that as the underlying conditions of international participants and the environment alter the incentives behind supranational infrastructure, and hence its design, can change.

8. The issue of the underprovision of these long-lived public goods and the appropriate rate of discounting is complex and unresolved. Even a small discount rate can greatly diminish distant benefits of these intergenerational public goods so that smaller levels of provision will be forthcoming. Some researchers (e.g., Sandler and Smith 1976) have argued for a zero discount rate, while others (e.g., Heal 1997) have made a convincing case for a proportional rather than exponential rate of discounting. Unlike most physical capital, some kinds of intellectual and environmental capital have exceed-

ingly long lifetimes, indicating the need for an alternative discount practice. The proper rate of discount is beyond the scope of this essay.

9. The model in Sandler and Lapan 1988 concerns the choice of targets by terrorists. The same model structure could be applied to study the effects of deterrence on an organized crime network's choice of target and place of operations.

10. On these global and regional environmental challenges, see Barrett 1994, 1998; Carraro and Siniscalco 1998; Heal 1997; Helm 1991; and Sandler 1997, 1998.

11. An excellent treatment of regimes in shipping, air transport, postal services, and telecommunication is provided by Zacher 1996.

12. This can be shown with the following two-player game in normal form.

B:

		Standard A	Standard B
	Standard A	* 2, 1	0, 0
A:			*
	Standard B	0, 0	1, 2

where player A can choose either standard A, most favored by player A, or standard B, most favored by player B. If both players choose standard A, then player A receives 2 and player B receives 1. The payoffs are reversed between the two players when both choose standard B. When two different standards are chosen, each individual gets the lowest payoff of zero, so that coordination is in both players' interest. This game has no dominant strategy and two Nash equilibria in pure strategies—the cells marked with the asterisks. There is also a mixed-strategy equilibrium where each player randomly selects the other player's preferred standard one-third of the time.

13. Generalizing the game in note 12, we see that the adoption of the ith of n standards, one associated with each of n players, would give the ith player 2 and everyone else 1. The adoption of two or more standards would give everyone zero. In this scenario, the pure-strategy Nash equilibria are for exactly one standard to be adopted.

14. On leadership, see Keohane 1984, Kindleberger 1986, and Young 1989. Effective leaders must be countries, which can have a large impact on the problem; hence, Fiji cannot be an effective leader for global warming, but the United States can be an effective leader for peacekeeping.

15. Barrett (1998) identifies five distinct stages to treaty making, which include: (1) prenegotiations or a cheap talk phase, (2) negotiations, (3) ratification, (4) implementation, and (5) renegotiation or periodic restructuring. Participants may differ at different stages.

16. On correlated equilibria, see Arce 1997, Binmore 1992, and Fudenberg and Tirole 1991.

17. These arms sales may be for profit or some legitimate political goal (e.g., defending human rights). Regardless of the reason, increased arms sales by nonparticipants offset efforts by the participants to curb such trade. Arms may find their way into "less legitimate" conflicts, unrelated to where they were sent; for example, U.S. arms sent to Afghan rebels are thought to have been used by terrorists against Western targets.

18. INTELSAT is described in further detail in INTELSAT 1995, Sandler 1997, and Sandler and Schulze 1981.

19. I thank Geoffrey Heal for this insight.

References

Arce, Daniel G. 1997. "Correlated Strategies as Institutions." *Theory and Decision* 42 (3): 271–85.

Arms Control and Disarmament Agency. 1997. *World Military Expenditures and Arms Transfers, 1996/7*. Washington, DC: ACDA.

Axelrod, Robert. 1984. *The Evolution of Cooperation.* New York: Basic Books.

Azfar, Omar. 1999. Sufficient Conditions for Rapid Convergence. Mimeo, IRIS, University of Maryland, College Park.

Barrett, Scott A. 1994. "Self-Enforcing International Environmental Agreements." *Oxford Economic Papers* 46 (4): 878–94.

———. 1998. "On the Theory and Diplomacy of Environmental Treaty-Making." *Environmental and Resource Economics* 11 (3–4): 317–33.

Bator, Francis A. 1958. "The Anatomy of Market Failure." *Quarterly Journal of Economics* 72 (3): 351–79.

Bienen, H., and N. van der Walle. 1989. "Time and Power in Africa." *American Political Science Review* 83 (1): 19–34.

Binmore, Ken. 1992. *Fun and Games.* Lexington, MA: D. C. Heath.

Bromley, Daniel W. 1989. "Entitlements, Missing Markets, and Environmental Uncertainty." *Journal of Environmental Economics and Management* 17 (2): 181–94.

Buchholz, Wolfgang, Christian Haslbeck, and Todd Sandler. 1998. "When Does Partial Cooperation Pay?" *Finanzarchiv* 55 (1): 1–20.

Caplan, Alan J., Christopher J. Ellis, and Emilson C. D. Silva. 1999. "Winners and Losers in a World with Global Warming: Noncooperation, Altruism, and Social Welfare." *Journal of Environmental Economics and Management* 37 (3): 256–71.

Carraro, Carlo, and Dominico Siniscalco. 1998. "International Environmental Agreements: Incentives and Political Economy." *European Economic Review* 42 (3–5): 561–72.

Cornes, Richard, and Todd Sandler. 1994. "The Comparative Static Properties of the Impure Public Good Model." *Journal of Public Economics* 54 (3): 403–21.

———. 1996. *The Theory of Externalities, Public Goods, and Club Goods.* 2d ed. Cambridge: Cambridge University Press.

———. 2000. "Pareto-Improving Redistribution and Pure Public Goods." *German Economic Review* 1 (2): 169–86.

Demsetz, Harold. 1964. "The Exchange and Enforcement of Property Rights." *Journal of Law and Economics* 7 (2): 11–26.

Dixit, Avinash K. 1996. *The Making of Economic Policy: A Transaction-Cost Politics Perspective.* Cambridge: MIT Press.

Dixit, Avinash K., and Mancur Olson. 2000. "Does Voluntary Participation Undermine the Coase Theorem?" *Journal of Public Economics* 76 (3): 309–35.

Doeleman, Jacobus A., and Todd Sandler. 1998. "The Intergenerational Case of Missing Markets and Missing Voters." *Land Economics* 74 (1): 1–15.

Economist. 1997. "Phew, the Ozone Layer May Be Saved." *Economist* 344 (8034): 48.

Farrell, Joseph. 1987. "Cheap Talk, Coordination, and Entry." *Rand Journal of Economics* 18 (1): 34–39.

Fudenberg, Drew, and Jean Tirole. 1991. *Game Theory.* Cambridge: MIT Press.

Hardin, Russell. 1982. *Collective Action.* Baltimore: Johns Hopkins University Press.

Heal, Geoffrey. 1997. "Valuing Our Future: Cost-Benefit Analysis and Sustainability." UN Development Programme Discussion Papers, no. 13, New York, UN Development Programme.

Heckathorn, Douglas D. 1989. "Collective Action and the Second-Order Free-Rider Problem." *Rationality and Society* 1 (1): 78–100.

Helm, Dieter, ed. 1991. *Economic Policy towards the Environment.* Oxford: Blackwell.

INTELSAT. 1995. INTELSAT *in the '90s.* Washington, DC: INTELSAT.

Jones, Charles I. 1997. "On the Evolution of the World Income Distribution." *Journal of Economic Perspectives* 11 (3): 19–36.

Keohane, Robert O. 1984. *After Hegemony: Cooperation and Discord in the World Political Economy.* Princeton: Princeton University Press.

Kindleberger, Charles P. 1986. "International Public Goods without International Government." *American Economic Review* 76 (1): 1–13.

Krasner, Stephen D., ed. 1983. *International Regimes.* Ithaca: Cornell University Press.

Manning, Richard, James R. Markusen, and John McMillan. 1985. "Paying for Public Inputs." *American Economic Review* 75 (1): 235–38.

Marwell, Gerald, and Pamela Oliver. 1993. *The Critical Mass in Collective Action.* Cambridge: Cambridge University Press.

McGuire, Martin C., and Mancur Olson. 1996. "The Economics of Autocracy and Majority Rule: The Invisible Hand and the Use of Force." *Journal of Economic Literature* 34 (1): 72–96.

McMillan, John. 1979. "Individual Incentives in the Supply of Public Inputs." *Journal of Public Economics* 12 (1): 87–98.

NATO. 1997. "Financial and Economic Data Relating to NATO Defence." Press Release M–DPC–2(97)147, December 2, NATO, Brussels.

NATO Office of Information and Press. 1995. *NATO Handbook*. Brussels: NATO.

Olson, Mancur. 1965. *The Logic of Collective Action*. Cambridge: Harvard University Press.

———. 1996. "Big Bills Left on the Sidewalk: Why Some Nations Are Rich, and Others Poor." *Journal of Economic Perspectives* 10 (2): 3–24.

Pejovich, Svetozar. 1990. *The Economics of Property Rights: Towards a Theory of Comparative Systems*. Dordrecht: Kluwer.

Sandler, Todd. 1992. *Collective Action: Theory and Applications*. Ann Arbor: University of Michigan Press.

———. 1997. *Global Challenges: An Approach to Environmental, Political, and Economic Problems*. Cambridge: Cambridge University Press.

———. 1998. "Global and Regional Public Goods: A Prognosis for Collective Action." *Fiscal Studies* 19 (3): 221–47.

Sandler, Todd, and Hartley, Keith. 1999. *The Political Economy of NATO: Past, Present, and into the 21st Century*. Cambridge: Cambridge University Press.

Sandler, Todd, and Harvey E. Lapan. 1988. "The Calculus of Dissent: An Analysis of Terrorists' Choice of Targets." *Synthese* 76 (2): 245–61.

Sandler, Todd, and William D. Schulze. 1981. "The Economics of Outer Space." *Natural Resources Journal* 21 (2): 371–93.

Sandler, Todd, and V. Kerry Smith. 1976. "Intertemporal and Intergenerational Pareto Efficiency." *Journal of Environmental Economics and Management* 2 (3): 151–59.

Tabarrok, Alexander. 1998. "The Private Provision of Public Goods via Dominant Assurance Contracts." *Public Choice* 96 (3–4): 345–62.

United Nations Department of Public Information. 1996. *The Blue Helmets: A Review of United Nations Peace-Keeping*, 3d ed. New York: United Nations.

United Nations Development Programme. 1992. *Human Development Report, 1992*. New York: Oxford University Press.

———. 1994. *Human Development Report, 1994*. New York: Oxford University Press.

———. 1998. *Human Development Report, 1998*. New York: Oxford University Press.

Young, Oran R. 1989. *International Cooperation: Building Regimes for Natural Resources and the Environment*. Ithaca: Cornell University Press.

Zacher, Mark W. 1996. *Governing Global Networks: International Regimes for Transportation and Communications*. Cambridge: Cambridge University Press.

Comment

Geoffrey Heal

The issue addressed in Sandler's essay is a critical one: how can we assure an adequate supply of the international infrastructure that is increasingly necessary for the stable management of a global economic and political system? Clearly, the problems in choosing and financing infrastructures at the global level are significantly more complex than those at the domestic level and—to judge by the results—not yet adequately understood.

Sandler starts with a quote from Olson, who attributes poverty of nations to ill-conceived policies and institutions rather than lack of resources. The point is persuasive, especially in light of the success of various Asian tigers, most of which were resource poor (although rich in skilled labor). But these cases also show that policies and institutions that work in one economic and political environment may not work in others. A classic example is Japan, whose economy was the envy of the world in the 1970s and 1980s and is now the despair of professional economists everywhere. We don't just need to get things right once; we need to keep them right.

Sandler gives some interesting examples of areas in which global infrastructure has evolved spontaneously and effectively: shipping, air travel, telecommunications, and postal services. We can all think of other areas where this has not happened. What makes for the differences? Why do we have infrastructure in place for postal services but not for peacekeeping? Sandler suggests, quite persuasively, that the former is a *coordination game* and the latter is not and that coordination games are more likely than many others to have efficient equilibria. It is also implicit in his remarks that those areas in which infrastructure is well provided are those in which the participants can establish a club—a point worthy of more attention.

This is a very central and important issue, indeed. For example, why can't intellectual property rights issues be managed in the same way as telecommunications? Is it a matter of too many divergences of interest—asymmetries, in Sandler's terminology—such that U.S.

producers have one interest and Chinese another? If so, can we expect this problem to correct itself as developing countries begin to develop their own industries that depend on intellectual property rights?

Sandler talks of the problems of intergenerational underprovision in the context of discounting. This truly complex issue has been thrown into sharp focus by the recent interest in sustainability. What (if anything) can governments do to change—especially, to lower—the rate of discount that the market uses? This question was asked in the 1960s, in the context of development economics, but I am not aware of a convincing answer. Can the technology of contemporary public finance add anything here? We presumably need an approach to innovation and the development of intellectual property that takes a very long view of the benefits, just as in evaluating the conservation of environmental assets we need a long view. Intellectual property and environmental assets last much longer than physical property. Physical property lasts perhaps a decade, and in the high-technology field a three-year write-off is common. In contrast, a watershed may last millennia, Pythagoras is as useful today as in 400 B.C., and Shakespeare is if anything more popular five hundred years after his death than he was while alive. So the time horizons in intellectual and environmental capital are quite different from those in physical capital. The issue of underproviding for the future is a very central one, for which governments should indeed augment the market.

Instability of financial markets is another issue that Sandler addresses and, again, a topical and important issue. He talks of the need for better information, such as accounting practices and banking standards, which is certainly a necessary if not a sufficient condition for the resolution of some of the instabilities of international financial markets. Why has this not happened in banking as it has in the areas of telecommunications, aviation, and shipping? Is finance not amenable to the club or coordination approach? Or do asymmetries of interests get in the way again?

The Optimal Number of Governments for Economic Development

Robert D. Cooter

"Does government correct or create market failures?" For several decades, this question framed debate among economists about the state's role in the economy.[1] The state *corrects* market failures by supplying public goods and suppressing external harms, whereas the state *creates* market failures by restricting competition and protecting monopoly power. Recent history in developing countries, however, points to a further role of the state: supplying the fundamental legal framework required by markets for private goods. A modern economy requires technical specialization and a fine division of labor, which in turn requires exchange among strangers at a distance in time and space. Clear property rights and enforceable agreements facilitate cooperation among strangers who do not share mutual trust. So the legal framework for markets especially entails property and contract law.

In view of this history, Mancur Olson reformulated the economic question of the state as, "How does government augment the economy?" According to Olson's formulation, government augments the economy by supplying both public goods and the legal framework for private goods. Stable governments and incorruptible officials augment markets best. Conversely, government instability and corruption undermine the supply of public goods and the security of property and contracts. This essay is concerned with the connection between instability, corruption, and democracy. Under certain circumstances, replacing broad, deep governments with shallow, narrow governments increases stability and reduces corruption. My general conclusion is that developing nations that are plagued by instability and corruption probably have too few elections and too few democratic governments. Under these circumstances, more extensive democracy augments markets better than less extensive democracy.

I. Hierarchies and Elections

An automobile manufacturer can choose to make tires for its cars in a subsidiary or buy tires from another firm. Making tires involves one firm using hierarchical organization (i.e., vertical integration of the tire-making function), whereas buying tires involves two firms transacting in a market.

According to the standard formulation, firms are hierarchies bounded by markets.[2] Hierarchies work by means of orders, whereas markets work by means of bargains. At the point where an organization touches a market, administration ends and trade begins; vertical integration therefore subtracts markets, and vertical disintegration adds markets. Along the vertical dimension, then, the extent of hierarchy and the number of markets measure the same thing with different signs. Optimizing the extent of hierarchy is consequently the same as optimizing the number of markets.

Turning from the private to the public sector, the ministry of education can administer local schools or, alternatively, the citizens in each locality can elect a school board. The ministry of education is a single organization, and each school board is a small government. In this example, administration involves one hierarchical organization, while politics involves many governments. Just as the private sector consists of hierarchies and markets, so the public sector consists of hierarchies and governments. Orders direct hierarchies, and elections direct democratic governments. At the point where a public organization touches an election, administration ends and politics begins; vertical integration thus subtracts elections, and vertical disintegration adds elections. Along the vertical dimension, the extent of hierarchy and the number of elections measure the same thing with different signs. Optimizing the extent of hierarchy is consequently the same as optimizing the number of elections vertically.

My analogy between the firm and the state has focused on vertical integration or disintegration. Now I turn from vertical to horizontal organization. One firm can manufacture cars and another can grow cucumbers or a single firm can do both. Similarly, an elected town council can control police while a separately elected school board controls schools, or the town council can control both police and schools. In general, the scope of a government's power can encompass many issues or just a few. When one democratic government controls each issue, the citizens vote for many sets of officials. In a democracy, the citizens vote for as many sets of officials as there are governments. Horizontal integration subtracts elections and horizontal disintegration adds elections. Along the horizontal dimension, the scope of government and the number of elections measure the same thing with different signs. Optimizing the scope of government is consequently the same as optimizing the number of elections horizontally.

This essay concerns the optimal number of democratic governments. I search for the optimum along the vertical dimension in which hierarchy trades off with government, and I also search along the horizontal dimension for the optimal breadth of each government. This approach yields some novel conclusions about instability and corruption, which especially (but not uniquely) afflict developing nations. In the private sector, many small firms imply shallow hierarchy and narrow product lines, and in the public sector many small governments imply shallow hierarchy and narrow government. This essay explains under what conditions replacing broad, deep governments with shallow, narrow ones increases stability and reduces corruption.

Organizational Space

Figure 1 depicts organizational space with the vertical dimension representing the depth of hierarchy and the horizontal dimension representing the breadth of each government.[3] A point in the organization space of figure 1 is specified by a given depth of hierarchy and breadth of government or, equivalently, by a given number of elections on the vertical and horizontal dimensions.

Different points in the organization space of figure 1 correspond roughly to countries with different political subdivisions. Deep hierarchy and broad government, as indicated by the origin of the graph, characterize unitary states like Japan or France. Moving vertically from the origin holds the breadth of government constant while hierarchy becomes shallow. This move roughly depicts the change from a unitary state to a federal system like that of Canada or Australia. The provinces of Canada and the states of Australia have broad powers subordinated in some respects to the federal government. Moving horizontally from the origin holds the depth of hierarchy constant while governments narrow. This move depicts the multiplication of special governments with single purposes. To illustrate, in the San Francisco area special district governments with separate elections provide regional parks, public transportation, water, and other local public goods. Finally, moving diagonally from the origin, governments

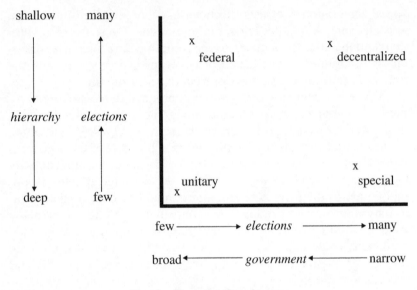

Fig. 1. Organizational space

narrow and hierarchies become relatively shallow. This move depicts the simultaneous decentralization and fragmentation of government.

This essay concerns the optimum in the organizational space represented by figure 1. The optimum occurs at the depth of hierarchy and breadth of government that maximizes the satisfaction of citizens. By inserting utility curves representing the satisfaction of citizens in figure 1, I could depict the optimum, but I will avoid this complication.[4] Instead, I will analyze separately the optimum along the vertical and horizontal dimensions.

This Paper Is Not About . . .

Figure 1 depicts the two dimensions that characterize the problem that I call the "optimal number of governments." I will isolate and examine two variables—the horizontal and vertical number of elections—that affect the performance of government. Explaining variance in the performance of governments in general requires a model with many more dimensions. The omitted dimensions cause confusion between the optimal number of governments and related problems. To avoid confusion, I want to mention some problems that this essay is *not* about.

Locating the optimal boundary between the public and private sector has engaged the best minds in economics, and their findings contributed to global privatization in the 1990s. The boundary between the public and private sector, however, is not my topic. The problem of the optimal size of the state differs from the problem of the optimal number of governments. In effect, my analysis varies the number of governments while holding constant the size of the state.

Convention distinguishes the branches of government into the executive, legislature, and judiciary. Dividing power among the branches of government has engaged the best minds in political theory. Their findings contributed to the spread of stable democracies and the rule of law. The division of powers, however, is not my topic. The problem of the optimal division of powers within a state differs from the problem of the optimal number of governments. In effect, my analysis varies the number of governments while holding constant the division of powers.

Sometimes people can choose among alternative governments by moving or stipulating jurisdiction in a contract. Governments can compete to attract people, either by moving people to governments, as through migration, or by moving government jurisdiction to people, as through choice of laws in a contract. Economists have identified circumstances under which competition can cause a race to the top or a race to the bottom.[5] Ideally, competition among governments can optimize their number just as competition among firms can optimize their number. Competition among governments, however, is not my topic.

An efficient economy provides people with the greatest feasible satisfaction of their preferences for private goods. Similarly, an efficient state provides citizens with the greatest feasible satisfaction of their preferences for public goods and the legal framework for private markets. Just as markets respond to consumers, so elections respond to citizens. Given favorable circumstances, the responsiveness of elections to citizens makes democracy the best form of government for satisfying preferences. Instead of *asking,* this essay *assumes* that democracy is the best form of government. Having assumed that some form of democracy is best, I ask how many elections are optimal.

Just as law constrains abuse by judges, so civil service rules limit corruption in state administration. The civil service is apparently the best form of administration to prevent corruption among officials. Instead of *asking,* this essay assumes that a civil service bureaucracy is better than politicized bureaucracy. Having made this assumption, I determine the optimal depth of bureaucracy.

II. Factor or Splice?

I begin with an analysis of political instability. The conventional analysis of unstable democracy focuses on the relationship between the legislature and the executive. The executive provides coherence through orders. Infighting in the legislature, however, can cause paralysis or chaos. Given these facts, increasing executive power at the expense of the legislature can increase stability. The gain in stability, however, creates a risk to democracy: the executive might suspend elections and rule by decree. In the conventional analysis, the executive provides stability and potentially endangers democracy, whereas the legislature provides democracy and potentially endangers stability.

Instead of the usual analysis, I view stability as depending on the number of governments. Under certain circumstances, single-purpose governments are more stable than comprehensive governments. Under these circumstances, increasing the number of governments and narrowing their scope, or organizing single-issue referenda, increase stability. I will explain the circumstances under which increasing the number of elections increases political stability.

Broad jurisdiction *splices* independent issues together like the strands of a rope. By splicing I mean combining issues and deciding them all at once. For example, the U.S. Congress often enacts omnibus legislation with extensive logrolling. To get spliced indirect democracy, citizens should elect representatives to assemblies with power over many different issues. In contrast, narrow jurisdiction *factors* politics into independent issues, like a mathematician dividing a large number into prime numbers. By factoring I mean separating issues and deciding them one at a time. For example, citizens may elect a town council to control the police and a school board to control schools. To factor *indirect* democracy, citizens should elect separate governments for separate issues. To factor *direct* democracy, citizens should decide each issue in a separate referendum. In figure 1, factoring represents a move to the right along the horizontal axis, whereas splicing represents a move to the left.

Sometimes a constitution factors, as when the town's constitution establishes an elected council and a separately elected school board. Alternatively, a constitution may allow for factoring without requiring it. For example, the state constitutions in the United States prescribe procedures for establishing special governments for such activities as parks, transportation, and water. Citizens can establish or abolish special governments by following the prescribed procedures. Alternatively, the constitution may limit or forbid factoring, as when it prevents a branch from delegating authority or a government from ceding authority.

I have discussed clear-cut cases of factoring, but unclear cases often occur. In the European Union, the selection of ministers forming the Council of Ministers differs for different issues. Thus, the council may consist of the national ministers of agriculture to decide a question about farm subsidies, whereas it may consist of the national ministers of transportation to decide a question about railroads. The national ministers of finance, however, often dictate to other national ministers. Does changing the council's membership according to the issue in question amount to factoring the issues? As I will explain, the answer depends on transaction costs.

Transaction Costs of Bargaining

I will use a simple model of collective choice to analyze factoring and splicing in indirect and direct democracy. In the civil service, officials rank from low to high and administration proceeds by orders. In contrast, members of the town council hold the same rank and government often proceeds by bargains. *In general, superiors give orders and equals bargain.*

Instead of pure hierarchy or pure equality, government typically mixes orders and bargains. To illustrate, in some American cities the members of the town council bargain with each other in the shadow of the mayor. A strong mayor causes the town council to proceed relatively more by orders, whereas a weak mayor causes the town council to proceed relatively more by bargains. Similarly, the oxymoron "first among equals" traditionally describes the relationship between the British prime minister and his cabinet. As suggested by this phrase, British cabinet ministers bargain with each other in the prime minister's shadow.

As explained, reality mixes orders and bargains, but my analysis separates them for clarity's sake. Assume that each government consists of elected officials who bargain with each other. Spliced government lowers the transaction costs of bargaining across issues. To illustrate, the advocates of strong police may want to cut a deal with the advocates of rich schools. If the town council controls police and schools, the council members can bargain and agree to implement strong police and rich schools. Conversely, factored government raises the transaction cost of bargaining across issues. To illustrate, if the town council controls police and the school board controls schools, the advocates of strong police may have difficulty cutting a deal with the advocates of rich schools.

I have explained that factoring raises, and splicing lowers, the transaction costs of bargaining across issues. Now I consider what determines whether citizens benefit more from low or high transaction costs.

Complements

Reasoning by analogy with the private sector, proponents justify horizontal mergers in private firms based on "complementarities" that create "economies of scope." To illustrate, automobiles and cucumbers are unrelated products. Manufacturers of automobiles and growers of cucumbers, however, may face comparable labor regulations. Consequently, merging the manufacturer of automobiles and the grower of cucumbers might save total costs of regulatory compliance.

Similarly, the citizens under the jurisdiction of a government might have complementary tastes in public goods. To illustrate, consider an example with two citizens, A and B, and two public goods, X and Y. If A intensely wants X and feels indifferent about Y, whereas B intensely wants Y and feels indifferent about X, then A and B have complementary tastes for X and Y. A and B can cut a deal to help satisfy their most intense desires. B supports A's efforts to obtain X, and A supports B's efforts to obtain Y.[6]

The scope of complements determines the potential gain from political bargains. When different political factions have complementary tastes for public goods, splicing lowers the transaction costs of political bargains, thus increasing both the probability of a bargain and the size of the resulting surplus.

Conflict

Citizens, however, may have noncomplementary tastes. To illustrate, if A intensely likes X and B intensely dislikes X, then A and B have noncomplementary tastes for X. The differences in preferences of A and B for X provide no basis on which to cut a deal. Given purely noncomplementary preferences, politics becomes a game of pure conflict in which one player's win is another's loss.

Conflict in a democracy can cause instability for reasons clarified by some technical terminology. By definition, the *core* of a game is the set of unblocked distributions. Since every proposal in this case is blocked by an alternative, the game has an empty core. Majority rule games of distribution with symmetrical players generally have an empty core. To see why, assume that three voters, denoted A, B, and C, must distribute $100 among them by majority rule. Initially, someone proposes to divide the money equally: (A,B,C) = ($33,$33,$33). A's counterproposal is to share the surplus equally with B and give nothing to C: (A,B,C) = ($50,$50,$0). A and B can implement A's counterproposal under majority rule, and A's counterproposal makes A and B better off than the initial proposal, so A's counterproposal blocks the initial proposal. It is not hard to see that *any* proposal is blocked by another proposal. Thus A's proposal is blocked by B's counterproposal to distribute the surplus

(A,B,C) = ($0,$75,$25).

When the core is empty, each player can make credible demands whose satisfaction is infeasible.[7] The contest for redistribution by majority rule destabilizes every possible coalition. Generalizing these results, Arrow proved that any democratic constitution can result in cyclical voting.[8] Voting cycles, especially those provoked by a contest for redistribution, destabilize democracies, especially in developing countries.

Median Rule

Instead of cycling, many democracies produce stable government that pursues policies near the center of the political spectrum. Under certain conditions, voting among paired alternatives along a single dimension of choice yields an equilibrium at the point most preferred by the median voter. The median rule explains why the center dominates the politics of many democracies.[9]

A problem of majority rule concerns intensity of sentiment. Democracy gives equal weight to all votes, regardless of how strongly the voter feels about the issues. From an efficiency perspective, however, more weight should be given to intensive preferences. To illustrate, assume that the chairman of a three-person committee asks each one to write his or her vote concerning a certain proposal on a slip of paper. When the slips are collected, the chairman reports, "I have two slips marked 'Yes' and one marked 'No, No, oh please,

please No!'" Majority rule gives equal weight to a bland "Yes" and a passionate "No." The unresponsiveness of majority rule to the intensity of feeling about issues causes its inefficiency.

Being unresponsive to intensities, the median rule is not generally efficient by the cost-benefit standard. Under a very special assumption involving symmetrical preferences, however, the median rule is cost-benefit efficient.[10]

If factoring results in asymmetrical distributions of preferences, then the median rule results in efficient outcomes. Splicing, however, enables the factions to bargain across issues and express their intensity of sentiment by trading votes. Asymmetrical distributions of preferences thus create complementarities and economies of scope that splicing potentially exploits. When the median rule is efficient, the voting equilibrium leaves no scope for bargaining. In the typical case, however, the median rule is inefficient, so successful bargaining creates a surplus.

City Council and School Board

I have explained that splicing lowers the transaction cost of bargaining across issues and successful bargaining across issues can increase the satisfaction of voters with complementary tastes. Splicing also increases the risk of failed bargains and circular votes. When spliced voting causes intransitivity, factored voting may improve the outcome by allowing the median voter to prevail on separate dimensions of choice. Median rule on separate dimensions of choice often satisfies the preferences of voters more efficiently than an unstable contest of distribution. Intransitive preferences in multidimensional choice may factor into single-peaked preferences on each single dimension of choice. In general, single-purpose government is like a safe stock with a modest yield, whereas multipurpose government is like a risky stock that pays a lot or nothing.

To develop these points, I turn to a quantitative example. Assume that expenditures on police and schools are the two majority political issues in a small town. Police and schools especially represent the two ways in which government augments markets. Police are essential to secure property rights and enforceable contracts. Schools are essential to preparing people to participate in a modern, technological economy.

First consider splicing the issues of police and schools. A town council that decides both issues provides a forum for bargaining. If

	school expenditures		police expenditures	
	low	high	low	high
liberal	0	11	1	0
conservative	1	0	0	11
moderate	2	0	3	0
total	3	11	4	11

Fig. 2. Voters' net benefits

bargaining succeeds, council members who care intensely about police may trade votes with council members who care intensely about schools, so that each one gets what he or she wants most. If bargaining fails, the council members may waste resources in an unstable contest of distribution. Second, consider factoring the issues. A town council that controls police and a separately elected school board that controls schools denies a forum for bargaining over the two issues. With bargaining obstructed and assuming single-peaked preferences, the median voter prevails on each dimension of choice.

Figure 2 sharpens the example with numbers. Assume that voters in a town are divided into equal numbers of liberals, conservatives, and moderates. Expenditure can be high or low for schools and police, with the resulting net benefits for each group of voters indicated in figure 2.[11] The liberals intensely prefer high expenditures on schools and mildly prefer the savings in taxes from low expenditures on police. The opposite is true of conservatives, who intensely prefer high expenditures on police and mildly prefer the savings in taxes from low expenditures on schools. The moderates mildly prefer the tax savings from low expenditures on police and schools. The row labeled "total" indicates the sum of net benefits to the three groups.

Assuming majority rule, contrast the consequences of splicing and factoring issues in figure 2. If the issues are factored, then two out of three voters (conservatives and moderates) vote for low expenditures on schools, so factoring results in low expenditures on schools. Furthermore, two out of three voters (liberals and moderates) also vote for low expenditures on police, so factoring results in low expenditures on police. Thus, factoring results in low expenditures on schools and police.

If issues are spliced, the voters must choose among four combinations of public goods depicted in the columns of figure 3. The net

Expenditures on Schools and Police, Respectively

	(1) (high,high)	(2) (low,low)	(3) (high,low)	(4) (low,high)
liberal	11	1	12	0
conservative	11	1	0	12
moderate	0	5	3	2
total	22	7	15	14

Fig. 3. Voter's net benefits from combinations of public goods

benefits to voters depicted in figure 3 are calculated from the numbers in figure 2. For example, (low,high) indicates low expenditures on schools and high expenditures on police, which results in a payoff of zero for liberals, 12 for conservatives, and 2 for moderates.

The numbers in figure 3 can be used to deduce the winner in a vote between any two alternatives. If voters simply vote their preferences in figure 3, without bargaining or trading, then an intransitive cycle results. Specifically, two of three voters (liberal and conservative) prefer (high,high) rather than (low,low). Two of three voters (conservative and moderate) prefer (low,low) rather than (high,low). Two of three voters (liberal and moderate) prefer (high,low) rather than (low,high). And, finally, two of three voters (conservative and moderate) prefer (low,high) rather than (high,high). As explained, column 1 beats column 2, 2 beats 3, 3 beats 4, and 4 beats 1. Thus, voting in figure 3 results in an intransitive cycle.

Figures 2 and 3 illustrate the general principle that splicing dimensions of choice can cause intransitivity where none exists on any single dimension of choice. Instead of simply voting their preferences, however, splicing may cause the voters to bargain with each other and cooperate. Since liberals care more about schools than police, whereas conservatives care more about police than schools, they have complementary tastes and could profitably trade votes. A platform calling for high expenditures on schools and police allows the liberals and conservatives to get what they want on the issue that each one cares the most about, as required for efficiency.[12] Stabilizing such an agreement requires the parties to abandon the majority rule game of distribution, which has no core,[13] and cooperate with each other.

Whether comprehensive government or single-purpose governments satisfy the preferences of political factions better depends on the ability of politicians to cooperate. In general, splicing issues increases the gains from cooperation and factoring issues decreases the losses from conflict. Finding the optimal number of governments requires balancing these considerations. These facts suggest the prescription, "Splice when cooperation is likely and factor when conflict is likely."

Factoring by Referenda, Splicing by Legislation

Most constitutions that permit referenda restrict them to a yes or no vote on a single issue.[14] To illustrate, Californians might be asked to vote yes or no on restricting abortions and yes or no on capital punishment, but the law precludes Californians from being asked to vote yes or no on restricting abortion *and* restricting capital punishment. A practical reason compels restricting each ballot initiative to a single issue. Logrolling, which combines issues in a single vote, requires bargaining. Bargaining among different groups requires representation. Ballot initiatives bypass elected representatives. Thus a multiple-purpose ballot initiative would invite bargaining without any framework for it.

In legislatures, the members often bargain, compromise, and draft a single bill that combines different issues. In contrast, rules restricting ballot initiatives to a single issue prevent logrolling, so different groups have little incentive to bargain or vote strategically. When citizens vote their preferences on a single dimension of choice, the median usually prevails. In general, direct democracy factors the issues, so the median voter should prevail. In contrast, members of legislatures bargain, compromise, and roll logs. In general, indirect democracy splices issues, which should result in bargains or cycles.

The contrast between splicing and factoring predicts some consequences of a shift from indirect to direct democracy. A change from indirect to direct democracy often replaces cycles or bargains among representatives with the preference of the median voter on each dimension of choice.[15] Is this change better or worse? That depends on how well indirect democracy works. Given informed voters and competitive elections, indirect democracy produces effective representation of political interests. If representatives bargain successfully and cooperate with each other, then citizens get their way on their preferred issues. Under these circumstances, indirect democracy satisfies the preferences of voters better than direct democracy does.

Indirect democracy, however, can also create a political cartel whose members conspire to blunt electoral competition. For example, the spectacular disclosure of corruption among leading Italian politicians in the 1990s suggests that citizens had little influence over deals struck by their representatives. An opaque political process and proportional representation made Italian electoral competition relatively ineffective. Under these circumstances, a change to direct democracy can break the political cartel.

In addition, indirect democracy can cause an unstable contest of redistribution among interest groups. Changing to direct democracy can increase stability, which should increase the satisfaction of citizens with politics.

I have explained that direct democracy causes the median voter to prevail on each dimension of choice, which is better than a cycle or a political cartel and worse than perfect bargaining by elected representatives. This proposition summarizes the main difference in theory between direct and indirect democracy. Besides this large difference, some small differences are sometimes important.

First, direct democracy gives more weight to those citizens who actually vote, whereas indirect democracy gives more weight to the number of citizens living in a district. To illustrate, assume that poor people, who vote at relatively low rates, live in poor districts. Indirect democracy apportions representatives by population, so the number of representatives from poor districts reflects the number of poor citizens, including those who do not vote. In contrast, direct democracy responds to the citizens who actually vote. Thus, in the preceding example, in which rich people vote at higher rates than poor people, direct democracy gives more weight to the opinions of rich people. This phenomenon may tilt California ballot initiatives in favor of older, conservative, white citizens.

Second, critics of direct democracy allege that the majority of citizens will vote to redistribute wealth from the few to the many. For example, if most citizens buy auto insurance, they will vote to cap its price. Or, if most citizens rent houses, they will vote for rent control. More generally, critics of direct democracy allege that the majority of citizens will vote to undermine the rights of the minority.

This criticism, however, has a weak foundation in theory. From the viewpoint of theory, direct democracy *favors* voting, which does not necessarily harm minorities more than spliced voting. Spliced voting encourages citizens to coalesce into blocs in order to bargain with each other. While a system of proportional representation can guarantee representation in political bargaining to every minority group, two-party competition contains no such guarantees. When groups coalesce, some minorities may suffer permanent exclusion from the ruling coalition.

In contrast, after factoring the issues, the minority on one dimension of choice is seldom the same group of people as the minority on another dimension of choice. Any single person with complicated political views wins on some dimensions of choice and loses on others. In general, factoring issues can dissolve large blocs of citizens and ensure that everyone wins some of the time. In addition, all the nonmedian voters participate in determining the median voter. Thus everyone's preferences have an effect on voter equilibrium.

Any democratic system of politics, whether direct or indirect, requires protection of minorities, such as ethnic groups and wealthy people. Forms of protection include bicameralism and constitutional rights.[16] Thus, the Bill of Rights in the U.S. Constitution constrains the states, so a federal judge would nullify a California referendum that violates the Bill of Rights. This fact imposes an essential constraint on California's referenda. Furthermore, on may political issues, the bicameral U.S. Congress can preempt states by enacting federal legislation.

Besides the legal obstacles, transaction costs currently limit the frequency of referenda. Specifically, electoral rules usually require the costly gathering of signatures to create a ballot initiative, thus limiting the number of referenda placed on the ballot. In the future, however, technological developments such as collection of signatures over the Internet and electronic voting could dramatically lower the transaction cost of direct democracy. With lower costs, the pace of referenda will accelerate, thus forcing citizens to vote on a barrage of hopeless proposals and to decide close votes over and over again.

Is there a better means of rationing referenda? Bonding offers an attractive alternative. According to this approach, supporters could place a proposition on the ballot by posting a money bond with the electoral commission. If the proposition performs well in the election, the bond will be returned. Conversely, if the proposition performs poorly in the election, the bond will be forfeited to the state. For example, in lieu of 100,000 signatures, supporters of an initiative might post $100,000, which they would forfeit unless the initiative won, say, at least 45 percent of the votes.

Compared to collecting signatures, bonding reduces the transaction costs of direct democracy. Compared to cheap collection of signatures by Internet, bonding discourages frivolous or previously defeated initiatives. By bonding ballot initiatives, constitutional law could reduce the velocity of direct democracy without stopping it or imposing unnecessary costs. Note that some countries, notably New

Zealand and the United Kingdom, already require candidates for Parliament to post a bond that they forfeit for poor performance in elections. Also note that a market for bonds would allow poor groups to mount an initiative for a popular issue.[17]

Optimal Breadth of Government

Citizens need an elected legislature so that their representatives can bargain together; as discussed earlier, increasing the breadth of government creates economies of scope by allowing vote trading among people with complementary tastes. But broad government can also cycle, or engage in redistributive contests. Under these circumstances, citizens would benefit from narrower government, which substitutes the median rule for bargains. Figure 4 shows social value increasing and then decreasing as the breadth of government increases. Unstable democracies are presumably to the left of the optimum, x^*. To increase stability, these democracies should factor political issues. Beyond x^*, however, too many elections cause the loss of too much surplus. At the optimum x^*, the gain from more stability exactly offsets the loss from the foregone surplus as the number of elections increases.

III. Deepen or Devolve?

Now I turn from the problem of stability to the problem of corrupt administration. The usual analysis of corrupt administration focuses on the depth of political appointments in the state bureaucracy. Political appointees escape the rules imposed on civil servants to constrain corruption. As political appointments go deeper, more officials take bribes. Consequently, increasing civil service appointments at the expense of political appointments can reduce corruption in administration.

Instead of the usual analysis, I view corruption as depending on the number of governments. Under certain circumstances, reducing the *height* of the bureaucracy reduces corruption. I will explain the circumstances under which increasing the number of elections along the vertical dimension decreases political corruption.

I begin by summarizing the arguments that I will develop in detail. Centralized government deepens hierarchy by requiring administration to reach down to localities. As the chain of command lengthens, officials can divert more resources away from their intended

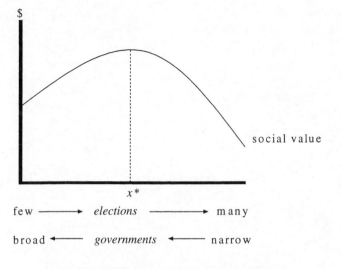

Fig. 4. Optimal breadth of government

purposes. Deep hierarchy, consequently, promotes corruption. To reduce the diversion of resources, officials at the top impose rigid rules
on administrators. Given the fast pace of social and economic change,
however, rigid rules impose heavy costs. To reduce rigidity, a constitution can devolve power and shorten the chain of hierarchy. As power
devolves in a democracy, however, the number of elections increases.
Too many elections can drain the reservoir of civic spirit that animates
voters, causing a decline in the quality of participation. The optimal
number of elections balances the decline in the quality of participation against less diversion and more flexibility obtained by adding
more elections. Now I will demonstrate these facts more formally.

Rule Game

I begin by depicting a simple agency game of administration to show
how deeper hierarchy causes more resource diversion and less flexibility. After delegating responsibility to an agent, should the principal
give the agent discretion or require the agent to follow a rule? Principals impose rules on agents for a variety of reasons, such as reducing
transaction costs, improving coordination, increasing predictability, reducing disparity, and facilitating transparency. Instead of discussing
many reasons, I will reduce the problem of imposing rules to its simplest elements and analyze one fundamental trade-off. Imposing rules

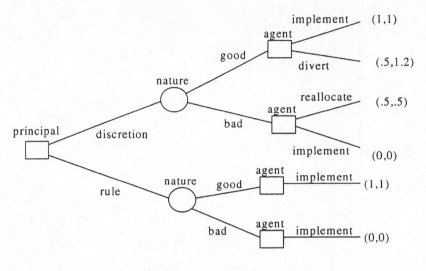

Fig. 5.   Rule game

on agents reduces their opportunities to divert resources, whereas giving discretion to agents allows them to respond flexibly to changing circumstances. Diversion of resources is the cost of flexibility in an organization.

I will formulate the rule game in order to analyze the trade-off between diversion and flexibility. In the rule game, nature chooses a state and then the agent acts. Knowing nature's state, the agent who enjoys discretionary power can respond flexibly to events as they develop. The principal wants the agent to reallocate resources when unexpected events occur, and the principal does not want the agent to divert resources when events occur as expected. Discretion gives the agent control over the decision, whereas a rule requires the agent to implement the principal's plan under all circumstances. The principal must decide whether to give the agent discretion or impose a rule.

Figure 5 depicts the rule game concretely as a tree. First, the principal decides whether to give the agent discretion or impose a rule. Second, nature chooses a good or bad state. Third, if the agent has discretion, the agent decides whether to follow the principal's plan or divert resources. Alternatively, if the principal imposes a rule, the agent must follow the rule regardless of the state of nature.

The payoffs from different paths in the game tree appear in parentheses at the right side of figure 5, with the principal's payoff written first and the agent's written second. Relative payoffs illustrate

		Agent	
		implement	reallocate
Nature	good (lucky)	1.0 (reveal)	.5 (hide)
	bad (unlucky)	0 (reveal)	.5 (hide)

Fig. 6. Principal's payoff from giving discretion to the agent

important facts, whereas absolute payoffs signify nothing. The principal's plan is designed for a good state. If a good state materializes, the payoff to the principal is higher when the agent implements the principal's plan (1) rather than diverting resources to an alternative project (.5). If a bad state materializes, however, the payoff to the principal is higher when the agent reallocates some resources to the alternative project (.5) instead of implementing the principal's plan (0). So a loyal agent with discretion implements the principal's plan in a good state and reallocates resources to an alternative project in a bad state.

The agent's interests do not coincide perfectly with the principal's. In a good state, the agent's payoff is higher when he or she diverts resources to his or her preferred project (1.2) rather than implementing the principal's plan (1). In a bad state, the agent's payoff is also higher when he or she reallocates resources to his or her preferred project (.5) rather than implementing the principal's plan (0). The agent's dominant strategy is to divert resources, which serves the principal in a bad state and disserves the principal in a good state.

Now I turn from what the actors do to what they know. As in the delegation game, the rule game assumes that the principal who delegates a task to the agent knows the entire payoff matrix and observes his or her own payoff but does not observe the state of nature or the agent's act. Figure 6 summarizes what the principal can infer from what he or she observes. When the payoff equals 1, the principal can infer from figure 6 both the state of nature (good) and the agent's act (implement). Similarly, when the payoff equals 0, the principal can infer from figure 6 the state of nature (bad) and the agent's act (implement). When the payoff equals .5, however, the principal cannot infer whether the agent's reallocation was loyal (bad state) or disloyal (good state).

Solution

The rule game's solution is a pair of strategies that maximize each player's expected payoff, given the strategy of the other player. To solve the game recursively, assume that the principal gives discretion to the agent. The last decision in time is the agent's choice between implementing the principal's policy or reallocating resources. As depicted in figure 6, the agent's payoff from reallocating exceeds his or her payoff from implementing, regardless of the state of nature, so the agent has a dominant strategy.[18] Knowing this, the principal computes his or her best strategy by assuming that the agent will use discretion to reallocate resources. The rule in question is designed for good states. As depicted in figure 5, imposing a rule on the agent yields a higher payoff to the principal in a good state, whereas giving discretion to the agent yields a higher payoff to the principal in a bad state. In this example, the rational principal imposes a rule when the probability of a good state, p, exceeds .5, and, otherwise, the rational principal gives the agent discretion.[19] The game's solution can be summarized as follows:

$p \geq .5$ →   principal imposes rule, agent implements,

$p < .5$ →   principal gives agent discretion, agent diverts.

I mention in passing several more special assumptions in my formulation of the rule game. First, my "solution" solves the problem of delegating power for a given contract between the principal and agent. Computing the optimal contract for the principal and agent requires another formulation of the problem.[20] Second, I computed the game's solution when rationally self-interested actors play it once. In reality, the actors may repeat the game, which gives the agent more reason to cooperate. Third, I implicitly assumed that the principal cannot invest in monitoring the agent. In reality, monitoring increases the risk of punishment, which deters diversion by agents. Finally, I assume that agents are self-interested, whereas some agents may remain loyal due to moral commitment.

Graph

Figure 7 graphs the trade-off between diversion and flexibility characterized by the rule game. The horizontal axis in figure 7 represents constraint of the agent by rules, which increases when moving to the right. The rule of law implies that officials follow rules rather than exercising discretion. Consequently, the horizontal axis in figure 7 characterizes more constraint by rules as an increase in "legality." Con-

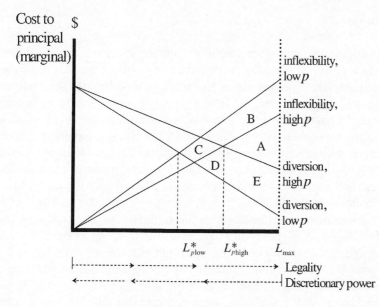

Fig. 7. Flexibility-diversion trade-off

versely, the horizontal axis in figure 7 also represents the agent's discretionary power, which increases when moving to the left. In figure 7 legality and discretionary power are polar opposites.

The vertical axis in figure 7 depicts the principal's marginal costs. Moving from left to right, the principal imposes more rules and allows less discretion to the agent, so diversion costs typically decrease and inflexibility costs typically increase at the margin.[21] The intersection of the marginal cost curves in Figure 7 corresponds to the level of legality that minimizes the principal's total costs.

The costs of inflexibility and diversion depend on the environment's predictability. Good luck reduces the cost of inflexibility, so an increase in the probability of a good state causes the "inflexibility curve" to shift down in figure 7. Conversely, good luck increases the diversion of resources by agents, so an increase in p causes the "diversion" curve to shift up in figure 7. Combining these effects, an increase in the probability of good luck from p_{low} to p_{high} causes the principal's preferred level of legality to shift up from L^*_{plow} to L^*_{phigh} in figure 7.

In general, predictability makes rules more attractive to principals, whereas unpredictability makes discretionary power more necessary.

Examples

To illustrate the rule game, assume that the minister of health constructs a plan to maximize the number of kidney transplants. Implementation of the plan requires the work of an administrator and cooperation from the nurses. If the nurses cooperate, the minister's payoff (1) comes from the administrator implementing the plan. If the nurses resist, however, the minister's highest payoff is higher when, instead of implementing the plan (0), the administrator reallocates some funds to another program (.5). The minister must decide whether to impose rules that enforce the plan or give the administrator discretionary power.

The minister cannot observe the behavior of the nurses or the administrator. A high payoff (1) enables the minister to infer that the administrator implemented the plan and the nurses assisted, and a low payoff (0) enables the minister to infer that the administrator implemented the plan and the nurses resisted. In contrast, with an intermediate payoff (.5) the minister cannot infer whether the administrator reallocated funds in response to the nurses' resistance or diverted funds even though the nurses cooperated. If the nurses are more likely to cooperate than resist, the minister's payoff is higher from imposing the rule. Conversely, if the nurses are more likely to resist than cooperate, the minister's payoff is higher from giving discretion to the administrator.

A second example concerns procurement by the state. In many state universities, a professor who wants to purchase a computer has to follow prescribed procedures that constrain the choice of sellers and the terms of the contract. Procurement rules typically reduce the purchaser's discretion in order to avoid kickbacks or bribes.

A third example concerns challenges to the legality of actions by state agencies. Assume that the court interprets a statute and imposes a rule on a state agency. Individuals harmed by departures from the rule have the right to sue the agency, thus alerting the court concerning the agency's misbehavior. To illustrate concretely, federal courts interpreted the U.S. Constitution as requiring the police to recite a list of procedural rights when charging a person with a crime ("Miranda warnings"). If police obtain evidence about a crime by failing to recite these procedural rights, the courts exclude the illegally obtained evidence from trial. Like all rules, the procedures do not fit every case. Even so, the courts apparently prefer to prescribe the rules for all cases rather than giving discretion to the police.

Significance of the Rule Game

Having developed the model of rules, I next consider its significance. The Constitution or other fundamental law sometimes *requires* officials to make rules and follow them. The rule game predicts some consequences of the constraints of legality. Requiring more legality than the principal prefers imposes costs on him or her. Specifically, the principal loses to the extent that the cost of agent's inflexibility exceeds the reduction in diversion costs. The magnitude of the principal's loss depends on the environment's predictability. The harm is greater when the environment becomes less predictable and bad luck becomes more probable.

Figure 7 illustrates these facts. To be concrete, assume that the probability of good luck equals p_{low}, so the principal prefers L^*_{plow}. Now assume that the principal is forced to increase legality to L_{max}. The resulting loss to the principal equals the amount by which the cost of inflexibility exceeds the marginal cost of diversion in the interval $[L^*_{plow}, L_{max}]$, as indicated by the area A + B + C + D + E in figure 7. If the probability of a good state rises from p_{low} to p_{high} in figure 7, the principal's loss from a requirement of maximum legality L_{max} shrinks from the area ABCDE to the area A.

Politics, Civil Service, and Courts

In many state bureaucracies, politicians occupy the top offices and civil servants occupy the subordinate offices. To illustrate, the U.S. president appoints the head of most agencies, each head chooses a personal staff, and the civil service fills most jobs below the head's personal staff. Alternatively, political appointment can go deep into administration. In a patronage system, the winners in the game of politics distribute state jobs to loyal followers as the spoils of victory. To illustrate, patronage operates deep in administration in the city of Chicago and many developing countries.

Administration by civil servants suffers from inflexibility, whereas administration by political appointees suffers from corruption. The best system apparently provides for political appointment at the top level in the bureaucracy and civil service control below the top. The rule game can explain why patronage produces more efficient government at high levels of administration, and civil service rules produce more efficient government at low levels of administration.

Think of the state as a chain of relationships in which each official is an agent relative to those above him or her. In the typical state bureaucracy, civil servants are agents relative to the political appointees heading the organization, political appointees heading the organization are agents relative to elected officials, and elected officials are agents relative to the citizens who vote. In each of the chain's links, a combination of discretion and legality orders the relationship with the agent. Now I explain why efficiency requires discretion to dominate legality at the top of the chain and efficiency requires legality to dominate discretion at the bottom of the chain.

The closer they are to the top of the chain, the more citizens know about officials. In U.S. foreign affairs, the communications media scrutinize the president, monitor the secretary of state, occasionally notice an ambassador, and mostly ignore civil servants in the State Department. When the principal has more information, the agent has less scope for undetected diversion of resources. In terms of figure 7, more information for the principal causes diversion costs to rise more slowly, as the agent receives more discretion.

While voters have relatively *good information* about top officials, the environment of high politics is also *unpredictable.* In figure 7, low predictability increases the costs of inflexibility. To illustrate, unpredictable diplomatic crises require a flexible response by the secretary of state.

Extensive monitoring and an unpredictable environment tip the balance in favor of giving broad discretion to officials at the top of agencies. Broad discretion requires politics, not the civil service. Rather than imposing rules, voters communicate goals to top officials. So efficient administration in a democracy requires political control over top officials in state agencies.

Conversely, the public cannot scrutinize lower levels of administration. Consequently, the public holds top officials responsible for any diversion of resources detected in the lower levels of administration. To discharge their responsibility, high officials impose rules to reduce diversion by low officials. In terms of figure 7, less information for the principal causes diversion costs to rise more quickly as the agent receives more discretion. Rules constrain such abuses. So efficiency in a democracy requires civil service rules to control employment at less visible levels of administration. (High officials also have other reasons to make rules for a complex bureaucracy.)[22]

The problem of monitoring also arises in a judicial hierarchy. When faced with disputes, courts sometimes can choose between deciding each case on its own merits or developing general rules that apply to all cases. Case by case adjudication retains flexibility for lower courts and permits them to diverge from the preferences of higher courts. In contrast, rules reduce flexibility in lower courts and compel lower courts to conform more to the preferences of higher courts.[23]

My discussion of politics, administration, and courts suggests three vague boundaries that demarcate significant changes in discretionary power. First, officials enjoy *strong* discretion when the law leaves them free to pursue political goals. To illustrate, legislators have strong discretion in proposing legislation, and the executive has strong discretion when selecting a cabinet. Second, officials enjoy *weak* discretion when the law prescribes goals and leaves officials free to choose the means. To illustrate, a civil engineer in the ministry of roads can decide how to build a road required by an executive order, and the ministry of education can design a program to improve literacy as prescribed by legislation. Third, *pure legality* leaves officials without any discretion, which results in mechanical decision making. To illustrate, a table that prescribes an exact punishment for each crime or the exact division of assets on divorce leaves little discretion to judges.

Legislators and the executive typically have political discretion, and civil servants typically have technical discretion. The situation of judges is more complicated. Common law systems give judges discretion to make some kinds of law, whereas civil law systems sometimes aspire to eliminate the discretionary power of judges. Philosophers of law disagree about the ideal mix of politics, technique, and legality in judging.[24] In any case, pure legality, or the mechanical application of law, fails for most decisions. British unions periodically paralyzed the railways by means of a tactic called "work to rule," which means that the workers implemented all rules literally. Like the railroads, courts that apply rules mechanically cannot do justice.

Voting

I have explained that a deeper hierarchy better disguises the diversion of resources, whereas more elections and a more shallow hierarchy lowers the cost of monitoring by citizens. Thus, more elections can reduce corruption and increase flexibility. Now I want to explain how holding too many elections dilutes the civic spirit required for effective elections. Citizens must decide whether to vote and how to vote. First, I will analyze how a rational citizen will vote, and, second, I will analyze whether a rational citizen will vote.

Self-Interest or Public Interest?

I like ice cream better than cabbage because of the taste, he likes San Diego better than Seattle because of the weather, and she likes the Republicans better than the Democrats because she is conservative. Among the many reasons that people have for their preferences, I will contrast two broad types. On the one hand, a citizen can vote based on material self-interest. A narrowly self-interested voter asks, "Which outcome will do more to increase my own wealth and power?" On the other hand, a public-spirited voter asks, "Which outcome will benefit the country more according to my political philosophy?"

To supply efficient quantities of public goods, officials need information about the policy preferences of citizens. By supplying this information, self-interested voting sometimes promotes efficiency in the supply of public goods. All too often, however, citizens use politics to obtain advantages for themselves at the expense of others. Banks want loan guarantees, farmers want price supports, unions want tariffs, artists want subsidies, taxis want fewer licenses for cabs, the elderly want property tax exemptions, and so forth. This kind of self-seeking wastes resources and oppresses the powerless. While people seldom criticize a consumer in the grocery store for following self-interest when filling his or her shopping cart, people often criticize citizens for voting their self-interest.

Do most citizens vote their self-interest or the public interest? The determinants of voting behavior have been studied for many years. Survey research reveals that voters know little about issues or candidates, so they typically rely on guidance from political parties, ideology, and informed friends or associates. In spite of their ignorance, however, citizens tend to vote for candidates who promote the interests of the groups to which they belong. For example, farmers tend to vote for candidates who subsidize agriculture, ethnic groups tend to vote for candidates who benefit minorities, and investment bankers tend to vote for candidates who liberalize finance.[25]

Supporting candidates who advance a group's interests can benefit a person by showing solidarity with its members.[26] To illustrate, dairy farmers in a rural community may be more willing to cooperate with other dairy farmers who endorse milk subsidies. Conversely, an ethnic group may censure members who oppose preferential treatment for minorities.[27] In general, groups develop ideologies that advance a self-serving conception of the public interest, like the automobile executive who believes that "what's good for General Motors is good for America."

Why Vote?

Journalists often deplore the fact that only about half of the eligible citizens vote in major U.S. elections and participation has fallen since the nineteenth century.[28] Voter participation rates are similar in other countries, except where democracy is new; the law compels citizens to vote, as in Australia and Argentina; or the names of nonvoting citizens are posted in public, as in some Italian towns. Unlike journalists, however, economists find voter participation rates mysteriously *high*. Models of self-interest predict much lower voter participation rates than actually occur, and here is why. A self-interested citizen will decide whether or not to vote by comparing the cost of voting and the expected benefit. Given current rates of voter participation, the probability is historically negligible that a single voter in a large election will affect the outcome. So the effort required to vote exceeds the expected benefit for voters in large elections.

Some notation clarifies this point. The value of the time required to vote usually measures its opportunity cost, which I denote C_i for citizen i. For simplicity, assume that the citizen cares about who wins the election, not the margin of victory. Let p_i denote the probability that citizen i's vote decides the election's outcome. Let B_i denote the increase in citizen i's wealth or power obtained by getting his or her preferred outcome in the election.[29] Thus, the expected benefit from voting equals $p_i B_i$. According to the *self-interested theory of voter participation,* a citizen votes when $p_i B_i \geq C_i$, and a citizen does not vote when $p_i B_i < C_i$. The self-interested theory of voting predicts that voter participation rates will fall until $p_i B_i$ approximately equals C_i. The *paradox of voting* refers to the fact that current levels of voter participation far exceed the rate at which $p_i B_i$ equals C_i. If the self-interested theory of voting accurately described the behavior of most citizens, voter participation rates would fall far below current levels.

To illustrate, assume that having your preferred candidate win the election is worth \$1,000 to you. Assume that voting requires one hour of your time, which you value at \$10. Self-interest prompts you to vote if p_i \$1,000 $\geq$ \$10, which implies that $p_i \geq 1/100$. In large elections, the probability of any one vote being decisive is *much* smaller than 1/100.

Computing the subjective probability of being decisive, p (which is called the *power of a vote*) depends on what the voter thinks other voters will do (Palfrey and Rosenthal 1985). According to one calculation,[30] the power of a vote in a typical U.S. general election approximately equals 10^{-8}. Under any reasonable assumptions, the power of a vote is so small in a large election that purely self-interested citizens would not bother to vote at current rates.

If narrow self-interest does not explain why people vote at observed rates, what does? An important tradition in political theory dating from Aristotle holds that political participation appeals to the social nature of people. According to this tradition, people express themselves by performing civic duties and self-expression is intrinsically satisfying.[31] Deliberative theories of democracy stress the satisfaction that people take in exercising the responsibilities of citizenship, such as voting.

By voting rather than not voting, I increase the probability that people who agree with my politics will like the election's results. So people who agree with my politics will say that I ought to vote. Moreover, the fact that citizens often praise voters and criticize nonvoters indicates the existence of a social norm. Besides self-expression, people may do their civic duty to obtain praise or avoid criticism from others.

To represent the influence of civil duty, let v_{1i} denote the value to i of fulfilling i's civic duty, where v_{1i} is large for some people and small for others. According to the civic virtue theory, everyone votes whose value v_{1i} outweighs the net cost $C_{1i} - p_{1i}B_i$. Thus, citizens vote when $v_{1i} \geq C_{1i} - p_{1i}B_i$.[32] This formula encapsulates a *mixed motive theory of voting*, which combines self-interest and civic duty. The mixed motive theory has testable implications.[33]

The mixed motive theory of voting also helps to explain why people inform themselves about how to vote. Just as rationally self-interested people would not bother to vote at observed rates, so rationally self-interested people would not bother to obtain the information needed to decide how to vote. A very low probability of being decisive undermines the incentive to vote and also the incentive to become informed. A combination of self-expression and social obligation, however, might cause voters to obtain information about how to vote. To represent the influence of civil duty, let v_{2i} denote the value to i of fulfilling i's civic duty by learning a little more about the election. Let c_{2i} denote the cost of political information to i, and let

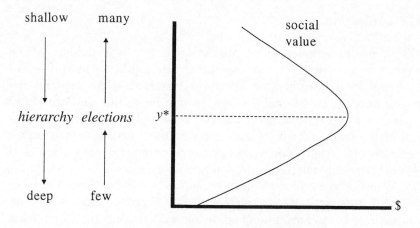

Fig. 8.   Optimal height of administration

b_{2i} denote the increase in the decisive voter's benefit from knowing more about how to vote. According to the civic virtue theory, person i gathers political information until $v_{2i} \geq c_{2i} - p_{2i}b_{2i}$.

Democracy is a great motivator. Perhaps civic virtue v_1 and v_2 increases with the initial growth of democracy. Increasing the number of elections, however, eventually begins to dilute civic virtue. When the total number of elections is large, the value v_1 or v_2 for any particular election decreases with a further increase in the number of elections. By these facts and the preceding formulas, too many elections results in a fall in voter participation and in voter information about each election.

Optimal Height of Administration

Too deep administration dilutes democratic purposes and gives too much discretion to administrators, in which case the constitution should replace *hierarchies* with *elected governments*. Conversely, too many elections can drain the reservoir of civic spirit that animates voters, in which case the Constitution should replace *governments* with *hierarchies*. Figure 8 depicts social value as increasing and then decreasing as the height of hierarchy increases. Corrupt democracies are presumably below the optimum y^*. To reduce corruption, these democracies should devolve power.

IV. Conclusion

Government augments the private economy by providing public goods and the legal framework for private markets. Instability and corruption undermine the ability of government to augment the economy. The usual analysis commends centralizing authority until the threat of dictatorship offsets the gain in stability and efficiency. In other words, the idea is to create a government strong enough to protect property rights and personal safety but so circumscribed that it does not indulge in public predation.

I propose a nonconventional solution to this problem. A democracy plagued with political instability should reduce the scope of unstructured bargaining among politicians and increase the scope of the median rule. To achieve this substitution, political issues should be factored. To factor, replace comprehensive government with single-purpose governments and substitute indirect democracy with direct democracy. Each single-purpose government and referendum requires a separate election, so the number of elections must increase.

Each link in the chain of a deep bureaucracy provides an opportunity to divert resources. Imposing rules on administrators reduces corruption at the cost of less flexibility. In a period of rapid social and economic change, strict rules meant to reduce corruption impose an especially high cost in terms of administrative inflexibility. Instead of more rules, a democracy plagued with corruption should reduce the depth of its bureaucracy. Each additional level of government in a federal system requires a separate election, so the number of elections must increase.

At the beginning of this essay, I explained that I would isolate and examine two variables—the horizontal and vertical number of elections—that affect the performance of government. My analysis omits consideration of many other variables. Under some circumstances, interaction with additional variables could nullify my conclusions. To illustrate, in some postcommunist countries without effective local elections, the devolution of power might increase corruption. Fiscal feudalism is a situation in which small localities insulate themselves from world trade by creating regulatory and tax barriers, often in order to sustain corrupt bureaucrats and hegemonic politicians. Instead of federalism, devolution might produce feudalism. In spite of this qualification, my model identifies real forces at work in political economy that conventional theories neglect. Determining the relative power of these forces requires empirical research combining laboratory experiments, econometric research comparing states, and case studies.

Notes

I would like to thank Martin McGuire (and other participants in the IRIS conference on market-augmenting government) for comments on the first draft of this essay. It draws upon Cooter 2000, pt. 2.

1. For example, contrast Schultze 1977 and Stigler 1975.
2. Coase 1937, 386; Williamson 1975, 1985.
3. While the feasible points are probably discrete (you cannot hold half an election), the space is continuous.
4. This exercise requires a social welfare function. The philosophical questions posed by this controversial idea deflect from this essay's point.
5. For example, see Tiebout 1956 and Romano 1987. I review these theories in chapter 5 of *The Strategic Constitution* (2000).
6. Since Riker 1962, the economic theory of political coalition formation focuses upon the "minimal winning set" or a similar idea. Another possibility is to focus on the most complementary coalition. The most complementary coalition maximizes the gains from trading votes. See chapter 3 of Cooter 2000.
7. Each member of a potential coalition may demand his or her marginal contribution to it as the price of joining. A member's marginal contribution to the coalition may be computed as the fall in the coalition's total value caused by the member quitting. Here I apply the *shapely value* of a coalition member (see Luce and Raiffa 1967, 249). With *increasing returns to scale* (superadditivity), however, cooperation does not create enough value for each member to receive the marginal product of membership, so paying the marginal product of membership to everyone is *unfeasible*. To illustrate concretely, consider a coalition formed by A and B that distributes the surplus equally between them: (A,B,C) = ($50,$50,$0). If either member of the coalition were to leave it, the payoff to the coalition would fall from $100 to zero. By this logic, the marginal product of each of the two members of the coalition equals $100 but the total product of the coalition also equals $100. Consequently, paying $100 to each member of the coalition is unfeasible. Unfeasible demands may be *credible*. A threat by a member of a majority coalition is credible, according to one definition, if another coalition could satisfy the demand without worsening its own position. To illustrate by the preceding example, consider the coalition formed by A and B that distributes the surplus equally between them: (A,B,C) = ($50,$50,$0). If B were to withdraw from the coalition, the coalition's payoff would fall from $100 to zero. Noting this fact, assume that B demands a payoff of $75 to remain in the coalition. The threat is credible because B could leave the coalition and

form a new coalition with C, distributing the surplus (A,B,C) = ($0,$75,$25), which makes B and C better off. A, however, can make the same demand as B. So A and B can each make a credible demand for $75. Both demands cannot be satisfied because there is only $100 to distribute. So each demand is credible and both demands are unfeasible.

8. Arrow [1951] 1963.

9. The crucial condition for this result is that each voter has single-peaked preferences. With single-peaked preferences, a voter's satisfaction always increases when moving toward the voter's most preferred point along the single dimension of choice. With multiple-peaked preferences, a voter's satisfaction increases at some point when moving *away* from the voter's most preferred point. To illustrate, some voters—call them YUPPIES—prefer a high level of expenditure on public schools, in which case they will send their children to public school, but if the level is not high they would prefer it to be low so they can send their children to private school and save on taxes. The worst alternative for the YUPPIES is a moderate level of expenditure on public schools. I review these results in chapter 2 of *The Strategic Constitution* (2000).

10. Majority rule counts voters, whereas cost-benefit analysis adds individual values. Counting voters gives the same result as adding individual values under the assumption of "strong symmetry." Under strong symmetry, each nonmedian voter who gains from a change away from the median can be matched with at least one voter who loses, and the loser loses no less than the winner wins. In notation, let x_m^* denote the point most preferred by the median voter. Consider any alternative x^*. Let J denote the set of individuals that (strongly) prefers x_m^* to x^* and let K denote the set of individuals that (weakly) prefers x^* to x_m^*. By strong symmetry, for each k in K there exists a j in J such that $u_j(x_m^*) - u_j(x^*) \geq u_k(x^*) - u_k(x_m^*)$. This fact implies

$$\sum_{i \in J \cup K} u_i(x_m^*) \geq \sum_{i \in J \cup K} u_i(x^*)$$

11. I implicitly assume additively separable utility functions for each group, so any group's total utility equals the sum of its utility on each of the two issues.

12. Cost-benefit efficiency requires choosing the level of expenditures that maximizes the sum of net benefits, which occurs with high expenditures on schools and high expenditures on police.

13. Since the voters' preferences form an intransitive cycle, any coalition formed simply by trading votes in figure 3 is dominated by another coalition (empty core). For example, a liberal-conservative coalition to obtain (high, high) is dominated by a liberal-moderate coalition to obtain (high,low), a liberal-moderate coalition to obtain (high,low) is dominated by a conservative-moderate coalition to obtain (low,low), and so on. Thus, the liberal-conservative coalition might not prove to be stable. To guarantee its stability, the

parties would need the ability to make sidepayments. With sidepayments, the liberal-conservative coalition dominates other possible coalitions and no possible coalition dominates the liberal-conservative coalition.

14. See California Constitution, Art. II, sec. 8(d).

15. The median rules can, however, fail when voting on a single dimension of choice when preferences are not single peaked. Furthermore, with factoring and single-peaked preferences, nonseparable utility functions in multidimensional space can destabilize the median rule on each separate dimension of choice.

16. Levmore 1992.

17. Also note that people accused of crimes in the United States must post bail to avoid jail while awaiting trial. The person who appears for trial recovers the bail, whereas the person who fails to appear for trial forfeits the bail. In reality, most people borrow money for bail from a professional bail bondsman, who charges a rate based on his or her assessment of the risk. Similarly, with ballot initiatives a market should develop allowing supporters to borrow the bond. Lenders would charge low rates for promising ballot initiatives that carry low risk, and lenders would charge high rates for unpromising initiatives that carry high risk.

18. The following summarizes the agent's payoffs.

Agent's Payoffs Assuming the Principle "Give Discretion to Agent"

Agent's Act

		implement	reallocating
State of Nature	good	1	1.2
	bad	0	.5

19. If p denotes the probability that the state of nature is good, imposing a rule and giving discretion to the agent yield the same expected payoff to the principal when p solves equation

$$\underset{\text{rule}}{1p + 0(1 - p)} = \underset{\text{discretion}}{.5p + .5(1 - p)}.$$

Solving this equation yields $p = .5$, which is the tipping point.

20. In a general game of contracting, the parties could adjust the payoffs by making sidepayments, which could improve their incentives. To illustrate, if $p < .5$, instead of retaining the contract resulting in the payoffs in figure 5, the principal and agent both prefer a contract in which the principal promises to pay the agent a bonus of .3 conditional on the agent receiving a payoff of 1. This contract, like any optimal contract, induces the agent to maximize the joint payoffs.

21. *Marginal* diversion costs typically decrease (and marginal inflexibility

costs typically increase) because the principal typically imposes rules first on those activities for which diversions cost most and inflexibility costs least.

22. As the state bureaucracy grows, regulatory agencies pose obstacles to citizens, who turn to elected officials for help. Providing help requires knowledge that increases by interacting with the state bureaucracy over many years (see Fiorina 1977). In doing such "casework" for constituents, the incumbent in the legislature has the advantage of experience over a challenger. Following the principle "The best guide to a maze is its architect," legislators have an incentive to create a bureaucratic maze so that voters reject challengers and rely on incumbents as guides. Thus, incumbent politicians sometimes seek an electoral advantage by increasing the complexity of administration faced by citizens and retaining control over it.

23. In common law systems, trial courts decide facts and appeals courts decide law. In these systems, case by case adjudication allows lower courts to control more outcomes by making them turn on facts. Consequently, general rules allow higher courts to control more outcomes by making them turn on law.

24. Ronald Dworkin has argued, for example, that each legal dispute has one right answer, thus suggesting that judges have little discretion (1977). These views evolved somewhat in Dworkin's *Law's Empire* (1986). Empirical studies often conclude that judges on high courts implement their own political philosophies (Brenner 1982).

25. Campbell et al. 1960.

26. In *Law and Social Norms* (2000), Eric A. Posner emphasizes this mechanism for creating social norms.

27. For the dynamics of "ethnification," see Kuran 1998.

28. A bumper sticker observed on a pickup truck in Berkeley read "If God had intended us to vote, He would have given us candidates."

29. To illustrate, in a vote between a Republican and Democratic candidate the benefit B_i of a Republican voter i equals $u^i(x_r) - u^i(x_d)$.

30. See the discussion in Hasen 1996. Using a different method of calculation, Romer (1996, 200) concludes that the probability of a tie in a U.S. presidential election in which 50 million people vote is approximately 10^{-4}.

31. Expressive voting theory is explored in Brennan and Lomasky 1993.

32. Let $f(v,b)$ denote the density function representing the distribution of social value v and material benefit b among citizens. The total number of voters in an election, according to this theory, equals the sum of all the voters for whom v exceeds $C - pB$, or

$$\text{voter participation} = \int_{C-pB} f dv.$$

33. As with the self-interested theory, the mixed motive theory predicts that voter participation should increase when: the power of a vote p increases, the private material benefit B_i from winning the election increases,

or the opportunity cost of voting C_i decreases. In addition, the mixed motive theory predicts that voter participation increases when the value of conforming to the social norm v_i increases. Increases in v_i might occur because more people internalize civic virtue, the social advantage from political participation increases, or the social cost of not voting decreases.

References

Arrow, Kenneth J. [1951] 1963. *Social Choice and Individual Values.* 2d ed. New York: Wiley.

Brennan, Geoffrey, and Loren Lomasky. 1993. *The Pure Theory of Electoral Preference.* Cambridge: Cambridge University Press.

Brenner, Saul. 1982. "Ideological Voting on the U.S. Supreme Court: A Comparison of the Original Vote on the Merits with the Final Vote." *Jurimetrics Journal* 22:287–93.

Campbell, Angus, Philip E. Converse, Warren E. Miller, and Donald E. Stokes. 1960. *The American Voter.* New York: Wiley.

Coase, Ronald. 1937. "The Nature of the Firm." *Economica* 4:386.

Cooter, Robert. 2000. *The Strategic Constitution.* Princeton: Princeton University Press.

Dworkin, Ronald. 1977. *Taking Rights Seriously.* London: Duckworth.

———. 1986. *Law's Empire.* London: Fontana.

Fiorina, Morris P. 1977. *Congress: Keystone of the Washington Establishment.* New Haven: Yale University Press.

Hasen, Richard L. 1996. "Voting without Law?" *University of Pennsylvania Law Review* 144:2135–79.

Kuran, Timur. 1998. "Ethnic Norms and Their Transformation through Reputational Cascades." *Journal of Legal Studies* 27:623–59.

Levmore, Saul. 1992. "Bicameralism: When Are Two Decisions Better Than One?" *International Review of Law and Economics* 12:145–62.

Luce, Duncan, and Howard Raiffa. 1967. *Games and Decisions: Introduction and Critical Survey.* New York: Wiley.

Posner, Eric A. 2000. *Law and Social Norms.* Cambridge: Harvard University Press.

Riker, William. 1962. *The Theory of Political Coalitions.* Westport, CT: Greenwood.

Romano, Roberta. 1987. "The State Competition Debate in Corporate Law." *Cardozo Law Review* 8 (4): 709–57.

Romer, Paul. 1996. "Preferences, Promises, and the Politics of Entitlement." In *Individual and Social Responsibility: Child Care Education, Medical Care, and Long-Term Care in America,* edited by Victor Fuchs, 195–200. Chicago: University of Chicago Press.

Schultze, Charles L. 1977. *The Public Use of Private Interest.* Washington, DC: Brookings Institution.

Stigler, George. 1975. *The Citizen and the State.* Chicago: University of Chicago Press.

Tiebout, Charles. 1956. "A Pure Theory of Local Expenditures." *Journal of Political Economy* 64 (5): 416–24.

Williamson, Oliver E. 1975. *Markets and Hierarchies, Analysis and Antitrust Implications: A Study in the Economics of Internal Organization.* New York: Free Press.

———. 1985. *The Economic Institutions of Capitalism: Firms, Markets, Relational Contracting.* New York: Free Press.

Comment

Martin C. McGuire

Regarding Robert Cooter's essay and its special relevance in honoring the work of Mancur Olson, two events of the year 1956 are worthy of report. The first is a conversation I had with Mancur Olson[1] concerning the distinctions between Joan Robinson's *Economics of Imperfect Competition* and Edward Chamberlain's *Theory of Monopolistic Competition.* Well do I remember Mancur's earnest and passionate preoccupation with that debate; this was possibly the first I knew of his interest in the question of how the size of a group influences its effectiveness in providing itself with a collective good.[2] The second event worth reporting is the publication of Charles Tiebout's "A Pure Theory of Local Expenditures" (1956), which launched the gargantuan and flourishing literature on the theory of local public goods, local government jurisdictions, and clubs.[3]

Both Tiebout jurisdictions and Buchanan clubs are based on three basic principles of government organization.

1. Each government jurisdiction should be sized so that average cost per person is minimized. This requires that $MC_N = TC/N$, where N is the number of people in a jurisdiction, TC is the total cost of provision, and MC_N is the marginal cost of adding another person.
2. The population of each jurisdiction should be as homogeneous as possible with respect to tastes (demand prices, really) for the public good.
3. The amount, X, of public good supplied in each jurisdiction should satisfy the Samuelson efficiency condition $MC_x = MRS_J$, where MC_x represents the incremental cost of an incremental increase in X and MRS_J represents the jth person's marginal valuation of X relative to money.

Central to the Tiebout-Buchanan prescription for government organization is the conclusion that jurisdictions should be as homogeneous as possible because each person by assumption can locate in only one jurisdiction. The crucial idea for normative design of a government or jurisdictional structure then becomes the trade-off between decreasing the number of jurisdictions and thus increasing size (so as to gain from economies of scale) and the increase in diversity that accompanies larger size and requires costly compromises among citizens in the provision of local public goods.

Into this picture, then, place Mancur Olson. Writing a decade later in "The Principle of Fiscal Equivalence" (1969), he called our attention to the existence, at that time, of over 75,000 jurisdictions and suggested that each should incorporate as citizen-voters (who collectively make local tax and expenditure decisions) only those individuals who are affected by the decisions. The political or constitutional extent of a jurisdiction, in other words, should be congruent with the population affected by its decisions. Olson recognized, of course, that this might well lead to a significant proliferation of jurisdictions. How can this be reconciled with the economies of scale addressed by Tiebout and Buchanan? Olson's answer was simple: by allowing individuals to be included in more than one jurisdiction.

Using a concrete example drawn from Robert Cooter's essay, table 1 indicates this difference between the Tiebout-Buchanan and Olson approaches. The table shows a society with four types of people: those with high demand for both schools and police, those with low demands for both, those with high demands for schools and low demands for police, and those with just the opposite tastes. Tiebout suggests as an ideal four jurisdictions—one for each police-school combination—with jurisdictions homogeneous and populated by one person each (one individual here stands for an efficient-sized group of identical individuals. I am ignoring the so called "integer problem").[4] Olson, on the other hand, implicitly recommends four jurisdictions, each populated by two individuals with each individual located in two different jurisdictions.

TABLE 1.   The Structure of Preferences for Schools and Police

	Preferences for Police	
Preferences for Schools	high 2	low 2
high 2	1	1
low 2	1	1

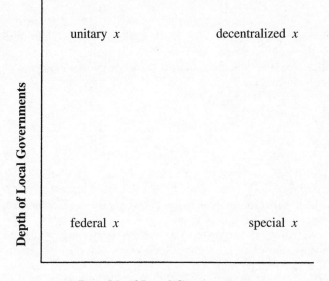

Breadth of Local Governments

Fig. 1.   Optimal number of governments

Which of these two camps does Cooter endorse? His essay can in fact be used most effectively to consolidate the two approaches. Consider his figure 1 (reproduced here in slightly modified form). The vertical dimension is Tiebout's. Implicitly, at least, governments are multipurpose, providing an entire package of local public goods. Tiebout is concerned with movements up and down the y axis, assuming that each government is "unitary" in Cooter's terms. As fewer and fewer governments are allowed, cities/counties/states/regions become larger and larger. More people are included because of cost savings from scale economies, but greater compromise is required because, as more people are included, the dispersion of preferences increases.

The horizontal dimension is Olson's. Moving to the right, each person belongs to an increasing number of special jurisdictions. The lower right corner is the limiting case of one jurisdiction for each person for each good. The upper left is one monolithic, all-providing government, for which the term *local* is meaningless.

Notes

1. This took place in our University College, Oxford, Junior Common Room, in the spring term of that year.

2. In this case, the collective good is the price everyone gets to charge to the market consumers.

3. Together with Buchanan 1965.

4. See McGuire 1974.

References

Buchanan, James. 1965. "An Economic Theory of Clubs." *Economica* 32:1–14.

Chamberlain, Edward. 1950. *Theory of Monopolistic Competition.* Cambridge: Havard University Press.

McGuire, Martin C. 1974. "Group Size, Group Homogeneity, and the Aggregate Provision of a Pure Public Good under Cournot Behavior." *Public Choice* 18 (summer): 107–26.

Olson, Mancur. 1969. "The Principle of Fiscal Equivalence." *American Economic Review Papers and Proceedings* 59:479–87.

Robinson, Joan. 1933. *Economics of Imperfect Competition.* London: Macmillan.

Tiebout, Charles. 1956. "Pure Theory of Local Expenditures." *Journal of Political Economy* 64:416–24.

A "New Institutional Economics" Perspective on Market-Augmenting Government

Roger R. Betancourt

Just as many of the contributors to this volume, I initially encountered the notion of market-augmenting government in the work of Mancur Olson. An early version of his essay (written with Clague, Keefer and Knack) on contract-intensive money[1] presented several insightful ways to look at the world. First, the essay argues that there are two types of markets: those in which transactions are or tend to be self-enforcing, illustrated by spot markets; and those in which they are not, illustrated by future-oriented markets. Second, the essay suggests that the role of government in each type of market is different. In the former, governments provide law and order services as well as a reliable medium of exchange in the form of money. In the latter, they must provide, in addition, contract-enforcement services. Third, the essay stresses that most markets in modern economies are future oriented and that a failure to provide contract-enforcement services hinders economic development. Finally, it goes on to propose contract-intensive money (CIM), or the ratio of demand and time deposits to the broad money supply (M2), as a measure of the effectiveness of governments in providing contract-enforcement services and tests its explanatory power in various ways. In that context, the essay also provides a narrow and essentially descriptive view of what we are presently calling market-augmenting government services.

Earlier work by North (1990) provided a useful classification of markets as traditional and modern and emphasized the need for an impartial judiciary in the latter type. The distinction between spot and future-oriented markets and the emphasis on contract-enforcement services (and their measurement) considerably enhances this classification. It also leads easily to the question "what happens when governments fail to provide market-augmenting services?" Markets may then fail to exist, they may operate at a very low level of transactions, or alternative institutions may arise to provide substitute market-augmenting services. For our purposes, it is useful to focus on the last alternative. With respect to the first two types of services provided by governments, which support all types of markets and especially spot markets, both historical and current examples of alternative institutions are easy to find. For example, Russian mafia activities are, among other things, an institutional device that substitutes for the inability of the Russian government to provide the market-augmenting services of law and order.

With respect to the provision of contract-enforcement services, the array of alternative institutions that may arise to perform this function is quite broad. In evaluating Cuba's limited reforms in markets in which transactions are not self-enforcing, I found several contract-enforcement devices in relation to foreign investment (Betancourt 1998): the use of a Paris court to settle disputes with foreign investors, exemptions from the country's labor code, and corruption in Bardhan's sense (1997) of use of public office for private gain. More generally, in regimes in which the legal system can be easily manipulated by the government, the role of the government in the provision of contract-enforcement services, if it exists at all, exists at a very rudimentary level and/or is provided through mechanisms other than an independent impartial judiciary system. Is it possible in this setting for institutions to arise that are an alternative to an impartial judiciary and can allow these economies to perform well and future-oriented markets to develop? In Cuba, the answer is no; in China, however, the answer is a definite yes, over the last twenty years.

In the case of China, at least two major institutional reforms are associated with its recent economic performance. The development of the household responsibility system in 1979 eliminated a major element in the repression of spot markets by securing the property rights of agricultural households with respect to the fruits of part of their efforts. The development of town and village enterprises in the early 1980s eliminated an important element in the suppression of some future-oriented markets by allowing these enterprises to become the residual claimants of the fruits of their efforts. Why have these two institutions flourished in the absence of an independent judiciary? What alternative contract-enforcement mechanisms arise in the Chinese system? One can argue that the agricultural markets relevant for the success of the household responsibility system are precisely those in which transactions are largely self-enforcing; hence, all that was necessary was to stop suppressing them. This argument is not convincing for the more industrial markets relevant for the town and village enterprises. One possible explanation for their economic success is the combination of their becoming residual claimants and facing interjurisdictional competition (Qian and Weingast 1996).

Understanding the role of market-augmenting government services is fundamental to answering this type of question about growth. But this will require in turn an understanding of the existence of alternative institutions that may perform market-augmenting services or of how different governmental structures may perform these functions. Keeping this functional perspective in mind is helpful in assessing the contributions of the essays and perhaps more importantly in pointing out major gaps in our current understanding.

Do different types of governments provide different levels of market-augmenting government services? An earlier work by McGuire and Olson (1996) considers two extreme types of government, utopian democracies and pure autocracies, and shows that a utopian democracy has an incentive to take into account the excess burden of taxation and thus to provide an optimal[2] level of a public good that improves economic performance in the private sector. A pure autocracy has no incentive to take into account this excess burden of taxation and thus provides a different level of the public good, chosen independently of the level of taxation in this case. Actual governments can be modeled as a linear combination of these two extremes. McGuire here interprets the public good as a market-augmenting government service and extends the model by showing how governments fail to provide optimal levels of market-augmenting services due to their pursuit of redistribution, discrimination in segmented markets, and corruption on the tax and expenditure side.

While this analysis is insightful, the specification of the public good in the model in fact seems more compatible with public goods such as infrastructure than with market-augmenting services such as law and order, a medium of exchange, or contract-enforcement services. The former increase market output *directly* by using additional quantities of resources and may therefore be subject to diminishing returns. While the latter can indeed be viewed as public goods, they increase market output *indirectly* by increasing the gains from exchange through a reduction of uncertainty and a lowering of transaction costs and may thus be subject to threshold effects and increasing returns. This suggests that governments augment markets by providing two very different types of services or public goods: those that increase market output directly, which we think of primarily in terms of quantity, and those that increase market output indirectly, which we think of primarily in terms of quality. Revisiting McGuire's arguments with this distinction in mind may be a fruitful area for future research.

Two different dimensions are also at the heart of the essay by Cooter on the optimal number of governments for economic development. He takes the type of government as given, namely, democracies, and asks how many levels of government we should have along the vertical dimension (the number of layers in a federalist system) and the horizontal dimension (according to functions to be performed, which he calls factoring). He shows that in situations in which conflicts are likely to prevail disaggregating the number of functions of governments (or factoring) avoids intransitive election cycles, whereas in situations where cooperation is likely to prevail, these intransitive cycles would not arise, and combining the functions of governments allows voters to enjoy the benefits of cooperation through bargaining. Similarly, along the vertical dimension if uncertainty is large, you want flexibility in the relations between the principals (politicians) and the agents (bureaucrats), but this increases the possibilities for corruption to prevail in the bureaucracy. Such possibilities are mitigated by increasing the number of elections through devolution. Choosing the optimal level of government along both dimensions improves the performance of democratic governments by diminishing political instability and corruption. In our context, it improves the capacity of democratic government to provide market-augmenting services of whatever kind.

Not surprisingly, four of the other six essays deal with aspects of financial markets. It is precisely in these future-oriented markets, with their intertemporal separation of the gains from exchange to at least one of the two parties to an exchange, that the provision of contract-enforcement services plays its most critical role. These contract-enforcement services—that is, provision of secure property rights across time, space, and even states of nature—are at the heart of financial exchanges.

Lanyi and Lee's essay looks at the East African financial crisis from three perspectives. First, they attribute a role in the crisis to the autocratic nature of East Asian governments while discussing some of the factors leading to the evolution and dissolution of stable autocracies (sometimes paralleling Olson's arguments about democracies in the *Rise and Decline of Nations*). In particular, the persistence of faulty macroeconomic policy is singled out as more likely in an autocracy, which raises, however, the uncomfortable issue of democratic Japan's similar macropolicies and economic decline since 1988. Second, they analyze the role of corporate and financial governance in determining the allocation of credit in general and in the East Asian countries. They make a very convincing case for the existence of major problems with respect to governance by creditors and owners due to lack of enforcement, poor regulation of the financial sector, and limited competition in the domestic goods market. They note that these deficiencies may have asymmetric effects in good and bad times. This section of the essay provides an instructive discussion of the variety of market-augmenting services governments must provide for the efficient functioning of financial markets. Third, they address the relationship between international financial arrangements and domestic governance. While interesting in its own right, this section is quite speculative in many respects and sheds little light on market-augmenting government.

A relevant issue that is not addressed in the essay is the debt/equity ratio of nonfinancial firms in the crisis-stricken Asian economies. Their debt/equity ratios were around 3:1, in contrast to typical ones of less than unity in the Americas and Western Europe.[3] The market-augmenting services that need to be provided by governments may be very different in the two circumstances unless one assumes that this ratio itself is evidence of financial mismanagement or underprovision of market-augmenting services in this area. In either case, we want to know what alternative institutional arrangements allowed these economies to grow so fast for so long under these circumstances. Is it that "corruption" was an effective substitute for market-augmenting services in the financial sector, by lowering uncertainty and encouraging financial transactions for many agents during the expansionary period, but it became an ineffective one in the later phases, perhaps due to the opening of the capital accounts?

Summers provides us with an account of good contract law, especially for loans secured by personal property. He identifies eight characteristics that these laws must have for augmenting the market for such loans, and he also points out typical shortcomings in this area. An important feature of his argument is that these laws must have a sound underpinning in the basic institutions of society, and in a general respect for the rule of law by the members of society, if these characteristics are to be achieved. In other words, the provision of market-augmenting services in terms of good contract law in this area requires other, more general market-augmenting services for enforcement to be feasible. He recognizes, just as North (1990) did, that we don't have an answer to the fundamental question of how to produce the market-augmenting service that we label "respect for the rule of law" in a society.

Wallis takes a historical perspective to analyze the granting of charters to corporations in the United States by American states during the nineteenth century. He concentrates on bank charters in the early period (1790 to 1840) because of their monetary importance to the states and because the United States had a well-developed financial system by 1830, at least by the standards of the time. During this early period, these charters were special charters that had to be granted by the state legislatures. They vary quite a bit in terms of the monopoly privileges granted—some of them would have done Soeharto proud—and how the states' fiscal interest was pursued. Nonetheless, during this period they tended to emphasize one-time payments and the receipt of dividends from the chartered corporations. Subsequently, there is a transition to general incorporation acts, frequently a different one for each type of business, for which taxes on capital become a more attractive revenue-raising mechanism for the states. Finally, in the 1880s New Jersey adopts a quite liberal single-type general incorporation act, lifting most restrictions.

The period prior to the 1840s provides an example of an institutional arrangement whereby government is providing market-augmenting services in a less than optimal manner, by modern standards, yet both the financial sector and, more generally, the American economy were doing well during this period. One possibility is that competition among states limited the worst consequences of this system. It is also possible that this institutional arrangement was suitable at that stage of development given the population size and levels of economic activity in these states but lost its virtues as size increased. In any event, Wallis concludes that the transition to the "superior" general incorporation system, in banking as well as in other areas, was driven far more by ideological revulsion against the notion of privilege associated with the special charters than by revulsion against inefficiencies introduced by the special charter system. Given the variety of conditions among the states, more detailed research is needed to disentangle the role of ideology from other considerations in adopting the more attractive form of market-augmenting government with respect to banks.

Levine's essay focuses on another financial market: stock markets. Two market-augmenting services provided by governments in these markets are (1) securing the property rights of minority shareholders and (2) regulating the disclosure of information by firms in these markets. Levine develops two empirical indicators of these services: *shareholder's rights,* which is an aggregate of five dummy variables indicating voting rights of minority shareholders; and *account,* which is an index of accounting standards based on an assessment by the Center for International Financial Analysis and Research. A well-developed stock market is one in which it is relatively easy to trade ownership of companies, and (it is argued) this helps a country grow faster. Levine measures this ease of trade by Value Traded, or the value of shares traded relative to gross domestic product (GDP). Account provides a powerful explanation of Value Traded while Shareholder's Rights does not, although both play an important role in explaining other features of stock market development. Finally, Levine shows, using a cross-country time-series data set, that value traded and two other stock market indicators have a positive and statistically significant effect on growth while controlling for a variety of other variables.

Tests of overidentifying restrictions are used to establish that the legal and regulatory environment, as measured by Levine, do not have an independent effect on growth. An interesting result in the essay is that banking sector development, measured as credit to the private sector divided by GDP, has an effect on growth that is complementary to stock market development (in the sense of having the same sign and being statistically significant) but the *interaction* of the two has no effect on growth. Levine's analysis is extremely useful because it generates specific results with respect to features of market-augmenting government services that are in general difficult to measure. Nonetheless, it could be highly misleading to go farther, deriving numerical estimates of the effects on growth of reforms based on this methodology. For instance, the resources and the amount of time required to change the index Account from forty-five to fifty could differ dramatically from those required to go from fifty-five to sixty, and the implicit assumption in this type of calculation is that they are the same.

In the remaining two essays, we move from the financial realm to other future-oriented markets. Heal points out the subtle role of market-augmenting government in the environmental area by characterizing and differentiating two types of innovations that have emerged in the last twenty years: the creation of markets for *tradable permits* in pollution rights and the creation of markets for the services of nature's assets or capital through *privatizing and securitizing.* Given that the public good (or bad) is privately produced, which is the case, for example, with sulfur dioxide emissions, the government creates a market in pollution rights by providing two specific market-augmenting services: setting the level to be produced in any given year and generating secure property rights through the issuance of tradable permits.[4] These services increase the gains to society from its necessary interactions with the environment by internalizing externalities in the consumption of the public good.

The second type of innovation is more recent and specialized. In the case of ecosystems that generate services with commercial value, Heal argues that a well-developed property rights infrastructure can allow the markets to generate the desired conservation outcome if producers can appropriate the benefits of providing these services to consumers. Ecotourism in South Africa is perhaps the best example. Well-defined property rights in land together with contract-enforcement mechanisms have allowed a private corporation to restore farmland by contracting with the owners to do so while retaining management of the ecotourism reserves to which these restored lands are added. This is an example of how divided ownership of an asset (in the terminology of Barzel 1989) increases the gains from exchange. This divided ownership is made possible by means of the provision of market-augmenting services by governments in the form of secure property rights over the land and contract enforcement services that allow the corporation to use the land and restrict what the owner-farmers can do.

One of the issues that arises in the environmental area is the need to define the market for permits in terms that go beyond national boundaries in some cases. While Heal points out that distributional considerations between countries make it more difficult to create markets for pollution permits in these cases, Sandler's essay makes it clear that this is only the tip of the iceberg in terms of the difficulties of providing market-augmenting services across national boundaries. He also discusses a number of reasons why countries should in fact be interested in doing so. Two points stand out in Sandler's essay. First, he shows that if the structure of incentives over an issue can be characterized in terms of an assurance game (multiple Nash equilibria) rather than a Prisoner's Dilemma game (a single Nash equilibrium), a central authority that can correlate the strategic choices of agents can improve expected payoffs. Second, the former is more likely in the provision of standards (for example) than in the provision of peacekeeping forces to eliminate ethnic cleansing. Indeed, authorities that provide transnational market-augmenting services independently of governments have arisen through private sector efforts, despite collective action problems. Sandler points out that INTELSAT's communications system is an example that exists precisely because it has the features of a club good, namely, nonpayers can be excluded and the network can be used simultaneously by all members. As long as the sacrifice in national autonomy is small, the creation of international agencies to provide market-augmenting services takes place when the net gains from exchange for every nation are large. Substantial net gains generated by adding the benefits to *each agent* in a nation is one reason why these international agencies have arisen in telecommunications, postal services, and air travel.

Both of these essays identify certain conditions, in different economic spheres, where the provision of market-augmenting services by government or other institutions is most effective, namely, where these services have the characteristics of club goods.

By the way of conclusion, I will try to identify some significant gaps in our knowledge of market-augmenting government. Some of the gaps arise because it is difficult to measure market-augmenting services. Perhaps the best aggregate measure of market-augmenting services, the International Country Risk Guide (ICRG) index of institutional performance, has serious shortcomings. The ICRG index includes five components representing five different market-augmenting services, provided completely or mainly by governments. While each component is given equal weight in the construction of the index, Summers's essay implies that the component "rule of law" is somehow more fundamental, for example, than the components "repudiation of contracts" or "expropriation risk," although the index does not capture this distinction. Similarly, although "corruption" and the "quality of the bureaucracy" are treated as additive components of the index, Cooter's analysis implies that these two components in fact interact with the federalist structure of a democracy in determining the actual levels of market-augmenting services provided. Moreover, no measure of regime type is considered explicitly in this index; yet McGuire's arguments imply that the provision of levels of market-augmenting government services vary by regime type.

In economics, one frequently finds a conflict between the diagnostic messages generated by aggregate (or macro) indicators and the ones generated by individual (or micro) indicators. A similar conflict arises with respect to market-augmenting services. For instance, South Korea as well as some Latin American countries (Mexico, Colombia, Ecuador, Chile, and Brazil) score well in the ICRG index. In 1982, these countries scored 26 and above in an index that ranges from zero to 50 and in which the median value was 25.6. Yet South Korea is one of Lanyi and Lee's group of countries most seriously affected by the Asian financial crisis. They point out that South Korea earns a mere 2 (on a direct scale of 1 to 5) on the degree of protection of shareholders' rights, an individual or microindicator of market-augmenting services. And Levine reports that Latin American countries perform poorly with respect to his two indicators of market-augmenting services needed for stock market development, namely, Shareholders' Rights (despite the same name, the indicators used by Levine and Lanyi and Lee are not identical) and Account. Is it that some of the more detailed aspects of the provision of market-augmenting government services in the financial area cannot be captured in aggregate indexes such as ICRG?

Other gaps arise because it is difficult to understand institutional change. Wallis illustrates the nature of institutional change, including the role of ideology, through the shift from special banking charters to general incorporation laws in the nineteenth-century United States. Chile's reform of its banking system in the early 1980s provides an alternative illustration. In order to remedy some of the perceived causes of the crisis of 1982, a regime ideologically committed to laissez-faire introduced strict regulation and supervision of the banking system (Edwards and Edwards 1987). This is an example of a government providing essential market-augmenting services in the banking sector as a result of a crisis. This type of phenomenon, which is certainly relevant to the design of effective policy reform, points to the need for individual country analyses of episodes classified as successes and failures in the provision of market-augmenting services by governments.

More generally, Sandler's INTELSAT example illustrates that governments are not the only institutions in a society providing market-augmenting services—a topic that has not been systematically explored here or elsewhere. Incidentally, some of the institutional examples provided by Heal, in which a market generates the conservation outcome, suggest that the provision of a given level of market-augmenting services may be the joint outcome of public and private efforts. Institutions arise to satisfy some individual or collective need and thus perform functions that have economic consequences. Governments, through various institutional forms of corruption, can provide substitutes for the market-augmenting services of, for example, an impartial judiciary or the rule of law. Given any broad type of regime classification, such as autocracy or democracy, some of the possible institutional alternatives to reliance on an impartial judiciary or the rule of law may be far more efficient or inefficient than others; this topic may provide a fruitful integration of analyses of corruption and market-augmenting government.

Notes

The discussion in this essay evolved out of my role as rapporteur for the conference and is based on the papers presented there, not on their revised versions.

1. Interestingly, the final version of the paper (Clague et al. 1999), is much less focused on the first two issues noted subsequently.
2. It is optimal in the sense of maximizing national income subject to a budget constraint.
3. See Wade and Veneroso 1998.
4. Heal shows how the introduction of a market in permits allows for an efficient allocation as a result of introducing an extra set of prices that leads to personalized prices for the public good, which restore the independence of equity and efficiency in this allocation that equal consumption of the public good had voided.

References

Bardhan, P. 1997. "Corruption and Development: A Review of the Issues." *Journal of Economic Literature* 35:1320–46.

Barzel, Y. 1989. *The Economic Analysis of Property Rights.* London: Cambridge University Press.

Betancourt, R. 1998. "A New Institutional Economics Perspective on Cuba's Reforms." In *Perspectives on Cuban Economic Reforms,* edited by J. Perez-Lopez and M. Travieso-Diaz. Tempe: Arizona State University Press.

Clague, Christopher, Philip Keefer, Stephen Knack, and Mancur Olson. 1999. "Contract-Intensive Money: Contract Enforcement, Property Rights, and Economic Performance." *Journal of Economic Growth* 4 (June): 185–211.

Edwards, S., and A. C. Edwards. 1987. *Monetarism and Liberalization: The Chilean Experiment.* Cambridge, MA: Ballinger.

McGuire, M., and M. Olson. 1996. "The Economics of Autocracy and Majority Rule: The Invisible Hand and the Use of Force." *Journal of Economic Literature* 34:72–96.

North, D. 1990. *Institutions, Institutional Change, and Economic Performance.* London: Cambridge University Press.

Olson, M. 1982. *The Rise and Decline of Nations.* New Haven: Yale University Press.

Qian, Y., and B. Weingast. 1996. "China's Transition to Markets: Market-Preserving Federalism, Chinese Style." *Journal of Policy Reform* 1: 149–85.

Wade, R., and F. Veneroso. 1998. "The Asian Crisis: The High Debt Model vs. the Wall Street–IMF Complex." Mimeo, Russell Sage Foundation.

Contributors

Omar Azfar is Research Associate at the IRIS Center of the University of Maryland, College Park.

Roger R. Betancourt is Professor of Economics at the University of Maryland, College Park.

Charles A. Cadwell is Director of the IRIS Center of the University of Maryland, College Park.

Robert D. Cooter holds the Herman F. Selvin Chair of the School of Law, University of California, Berkeley.

Geoffrey Heal is Paul Garrett Professor of Public Policy and Business Responsibility at the Columbia Business School.

Paul Holden is Director of the Enterprise Research Institute, Washington, DC.

Anthony Lanyi is Director of Economic Policy at the IRIS Center of the University of Maryland, College Park.

Young Lee is Assistant Professor of Economics at Hanyang University, Seoul, Korea.

Ross Levine holds the Carlson Chair in Finance at the University of Minnesota.

Martin C. McGuire is Clifford S. Heinz Professor of Economics at the University of California, Irvine.

Todd Sandler is Robert R. and Katheryn A. Dockson Professor of International Relations and Economics, School of International Relations, University of Southern California.

Jennifer Sobotka is an economist at the Enterprise Research Institute, Washington, DC. She is currently on leave.

Robert S. Summers is the William G. McRoberts Professor of Research in the Administration of the Law at the Cornell Law School.

John Joseph Wallis is Professor of Economics at the University of Maryland, College Park.

Author Index

Subject Index

DATE DUE